OBSESSED

OBSESSED

The Cultural Critic's Life in the Kitchen

ELISABETH BRONFEN

RUTGERS UNIVERSITY PRESS

New Brunswick, Camden, and Newark, New Jersey, and London

Library of Congress Cataloging-in-Publication Data

Names: Bronfen, Elisabeth, author.
Title: Obsessed : the cultural critic's life in the kitchen / Elisabeth Bronfen.
Description: New Brunswick : Rutgers University Press, [2019] |
Includes bibliographical references and index
Identifiers: LCCN 2018039599 | ISBN 9781978803633 (hardcover)
Subjects: LCSH: Cooking. | Bronfen, Elisabeth. | Critics—
United States—Biography. | LCGFT: Cookbooks.
Classification: LCC TX714 .B774 2019 | DDC 641.5—dc23 LC record
available at https://catalog.loc.gov/vwebv/search?searchCode=LCC
N&searchArg=2018039599&searchType=1&permalink=y

A British Cataloging-in-Publication record for this book is available from the British library.

Copyright © 2016 by Echtzeit Verlag GmbH, Basel
English edition copyright © 2019 by Rutgers, The State University of New Jersey
First published in Switzerland in 2016 by Echtzeit Verlag as *Besessen. Meine Kochmemoiren*

Photographs by Mara Truog pages 22, 26, 28, 65, 71, 85, 103, 127,
133, 139, 165, 181, 250, 257, 295, 320, 239, and 332
© Mara Truog

Photographs from the private archive of Elisabeth Bronfen pages 2, 8, 13, 14, 15, and 16
© Elisabeth Bronfen

∞ The paper used in this publication meets the requirements of the
American National Standard for Information Sciences—Permanence
of Paper for Printed Library Materials, ANSI Z39.48-1992.

www.rutgersuniversitypress.org

Manufactured in the United States of America

CONTENTS

OBSESSED

INTRODUCTION

Several years ago, I confessed to a journalist during an interview for a Swiss women's magazine that, for me, a day without cooking is a sad day. While at the time this epiphany came spontaneously, it continues to hold true today. Food—thinking about food, reading cookbooks, and exploring gourmet food stores or farmers' markets at home as well as abroad—is an essential part of my life. The room I am most fond of in my home is without a doubt my kitchen. It is here where I think almost constantly about what I might cook, where I read other people's recipes for inspiration, where I deliberate with myself about the preparation of a particularly tricky dish. Each time I decide what to make, I embark on a new adventure. If the dish turns out the way I imagined it, then I am content. If the dish is something unexpected, I am actually a bit proud. If, however, I produce something that is merely straightforward or has actually failed, I remain calm and composed knowing I can always cook something else. After all, I alone am in charge of making decisions here. The kitchen is, of course, also the place where I share this passion with my guests.

On my kitchen table next to the fruit bowl is an array of antique silver and glass dishes. Some are filled with spices, dried fruits, or nuts; others are still empty, in anticipation of their future delectable use. For me, they stand for the countless culinary possibilities that exist in the kitchen. The things I might still come up with to put into them seem boundless. This still life that I have composed for my own daily use, however, also sets the tone for the role time plays in my cooking, melding together the present, the past, and the future. While a successful dinner party consists of the shared enjoyment of a meal meant to satisfy the hunger of all those sitting at the table, this transient affair must be well prepared in advance. Even before any invitation has been made, I often find myself mulling over a variety of possible combinations of dishes and mentally rehearsing the various steps required to produce them. Sometimes I even involve some of my guests in a discussion about the sequence I have come up with. While both concocting what I hope will be a perfect menu and preparing the actual meal, my gaze invariably falls on the

Rosa, my curious cat

silver and glass dishes on my kitchen table. Not only do they remind me that my guests will soon be gathered there, but later, while cleaning up, they also conjure up the various moments that came together to produce this meal. As relics of an earlier time, these still sturdy and sparkly dishes are, however, also a fitting backdrop for the tranquility that surrounds me when I cook for myself.

Because of my sustained passion for thinking about how to prepare food and experimenting with ever new ideas, I have long harbored the wish—as an author and a teacher—to lure people back into their own kitchens. I am convinced that everyone has time to cook. A heavy workload is no excuse not to cook, and it may actually be the perfect reason for spending quality time in the kitchen. It is simply a question of personal attitude. Cooking has to become a priority in your daily routine; something that you consciously reserve a certain amount of time for each day, which for certain meals may even mean a lot of time. Because I have to remain completely focused on the task at hand, I actually consider cooking to be a privilege that allows me to take time out. If you don't give the work you do in the kitchen your undivided attention, it is easy to cut yourself while slicing vegetables, burn the piece of meat sizzling in your pan, or break a favorite glass because you didn't handle it properly.

But it is also the slow emergence of order from chaos that appeals to me. At first, all the ingredients that I have bought land haphazardly on my kitchen table. As I begin to prepare each of them—peel the vegetables, place the meat or fish into a marinade, stir together a sauce, and chop the herbs—the clutter slowly begins to clear. Once I have my *mise en place* ready—that is, once I have filled my kitchen bowls with the freshly chopped ingredients, sauces, and spices and then arranged them in the sequence in which I will be using them—I can walk through the recipe once more in my mind before actually embarking on the cooking process. The sizzling, hissing, and bubbling accompanying the transformation taking place in the pan or pot serves to punctuate the intense concentration my work at the stove requires, and the fragrance that slowly begins to permeate throughout my kitchen even makes me a bit giddy. Cooking, I find, has such a potent relaxing effect because it allows me to completely block out everything that has preoccupied or distracted me during the day.

A good reason for preparing meals in your own kitchen is, of course, that you can pay attention to the quality of the ingredients you use. Here you are in control of what goes into the food you eat. That is why nutritionists have, for some time now, recommended cooking with fresh, local produce. Far more decisive for me, however, is the conviviality that accompanies home cooking—the spirited exchange of recipes among friends, the inspired competition between cooks (tacitly acknowledged during any dinner invitation), the demonstration of affection that sharing food affords, and the praise one garners with a particularly successful dish. If I am looking to give someone a special treat, I will invite that person into my kitchen or I will give that person something that I have prepared myself as a gift.

It is true that cooking in someone else's home can, in turn, prove to be a culinary experience in its own right. In a kitchen far more spartan than my own, my friend Philip once pointed out to me that to prepare a perfect beef tartar, you really don't need the meat grinder, which, in fact, he didn't own. Flaunting his favorite chef's knife, he demonstrated that it was far more preferable to fastidiously chop the meat by hand before proceeding to the other ingredients. Actually, none of his knives were particularly sharp, so when I was called upon to give him a hand, this newly discovered ritual required not only extreme dexterity on my part but also quite a bit of time. This, however, allowed us to continue our discussion about postmodern art, which had been the subject of the seminar we had just finished teaching together. The full-bodied white wine Philip always serves while getting his *mise en place* ready made this manual effort all the more entertaining.

Taking time to cook regularly at home is, above all, a gift to yourself. It helps, of course, to have a well-organized kitchen, set up in such a way that you have ready access to both the ingredients and the appliances you will want to use without being compelled to rearrange the shelves of your pantry or embark on an extensive search through your cupboards because you forgot where you put your blender. Equally important, however, is embracing a certain degree of obsession. Cooking needs to be on your mind even when you are not actually working in the kitchen. It was my sister, Susan, who taught me that it is both wise and expedient to decide on Sunday what you intend to cook during the course of the week, so as to organize your shopping accordingly. You can, of course, vary the schedule and instead use the farmers' market on a different day as the stimulus for planning your meals for the next couple of days. If something unforeseen happens—an invitation to dine out or at a friend's house—you can always deviate from your original plan. In a similar vein, you will also want to think in advance (maybe even weeks) about what you intend to cook for a special occasion. It may be necessary to tend to a particular dish over the course of several days. For example, the meat or poultry for an aromatically dense stew may need not only to marinate an entire day in the refrigerator but also to subsequently be braised for several hours on the stovetop. And yet, even when the preparation of a dish isn't necessarily all that time-consuming, I find it inexcusable to treat ingredients carelessly. If you have chosen to prepare them, they deserve proper attention. Throwing something together hastily undermines the whole point of cooking.

Indeed, for me, nothing is random or thoughtless when it comes to cooking. Even the dishes that I prepare spontaneously, guided by what I found by chance at the market, thrive on pleasurable recollections of similar dishes I have either thought about or already tried out. It is then that I profit in retrospect from my obsession. I can fall back on the combination of ingredients that I know to be foolproof. And because I have internalized basic cooking gestures, like chopping, mincing, coating, or basting, my preparation takes place effortlessly, as though guided by the spirit of the process. Indeed, my culinary passion has perhaps less to do with the fact that I am almost always prepared to eat something. Instead, I almost always want to think about what

I might prepare to satisfy some desire. Opening my refrigerator—whether for breakfast in the morning, during a break from writing when I am working at home, or at the end of an intense workday in the evening—always poses a challenge in the best sense of the word. Gazing at the delicacies that I have amassed there immediately triggers the anticipation of satisfaction: the tacit keynote to all my cooking.

Alas, my tendency to stockpile is limited to neither the panoply of ingredients, ranging from common to exotic, that crowd the shelves of my pantry, nor the exquisite cooking utensils tucked away in my cupboards. Reading cookbooks also plays a considerable part in my culinary passion. The ones I am currently perusing are always stacked on one of the chairs next to my kitchen table. I also own several hundred cookbooks. Some of them I have voraciously leafed through in search of a particular recipe or the instructions for a particular cooking technique, or I have used them as the source of inspiration for my own experiments. Others, however, are cookbooks by authors whose work I have studied in great detail, most notably Julia Child, whose distinctive style has accompanied me in my own kitchen for several decades. With her classic book *Mastering the Art of French Cooking*, not only did she radically change American cuisine in the 1960s, but she also provided witty advice to generations of new cooks. With unwavering conviction, she declared cooking to be an art form that anyone could master, as long as there was sufficient dedication to the cause. When *The French Cook* (aired for the first time in 1962) finally became available on DVD, I spent an entire summer working my way through this famous television show, sometimes even showing an episode or two that I was particularly fond of to my unsuspecting guests at the end of a dinner party. While Julia Child was the first author with whom I came to cultivate my own intense conversation about cooking, other food celebrities have become imaginary friends as well—M. K. Fisher, Elizabeth David, Claudia Roden, Nigel Slater, or Alice Waters, to name just a few. While reading their books, I have identified with them, empathized with the cooking scenes they describe, made their experiences my own, adopted their advice, and, if only in my mind, re-created many of the dishes they write about.

In fact, I think of recipes in terms of a musical score with which I become engrossed before actually preparing a dish. Just before I start to cook, whichever cookbook I am working with is placed upright into a small, folding music stand I got from my mother, who had herself already repurposed it for this use. The book is then strategically positioned close to the stovetop so that my gaze can move seamlessly from page to pot while I continue to converse with my role models as I follow their directions. Sometimes I catch myself asking out loud, What does Julia want me to do now? Why does Alice suggest doing this? At times, I even argue with these imaginary friends and decide to deviate from their instructions, but they never take offense. And because they have stood by me so reliably in my kitchen, I hear their voices, guiding and admonishing me, even when I am cooking without a book on my music stand.

❧

Inspired by these voices, I have been meaning to write a cookbook of my own for quite some time. My very first attempt was still driven by a clear didactic ambition: I wanted to show the students I was teaching at the University of Zürich in the early 1990s how inspiring and cool working together in a kitchen could be. Jamie Oliver, Nigella Lawson, and Yotam Ottolenghi had yet to become global food celebrities. The book was to be titled *Studentenfutter* (or *Student Feed*), the German word for the nuts and raisins snack privileged by college students. Now many decades later, my concern has shifted: cooking has since become a question of recollection and commemoration. I am now more interested in the way certain foods, like Proust's madeleine, evoke scenes from the past—the places or people I associate with them, the situation in which I either succeeded brilliantly, or failed miserably, to prepare them.

The cookbook I finally came to write is conceived in the spirit of memory work. In it, I want not only to pass on my own words of advice and to share what others have taught me along with what I have learned through experience but also to share memories. The recipes I have gathered together in this volume often call forth reminiscences of their own. Sometimes they are variations of dishes that I read about in one of my cookbooks; sometimes they recall a dish eaten in a restaurant that I found delicious enough to try to re-create on my own. Memory, however, is also pertinent to those recipes that friends were either willing to pass on to me or asked me to include in this cookbook because they had so enjoyed eating them at my place. In each case, my recollection of the moment we shared a particular dish features in the way I have come to describe it. Having had numerous discussions with people about my culinary passion over the years, I have come to realize that a love for cooking has much to do with talking about cooking. One of the easiest ways to strike up a conversation with someone is to bring up the issue of what is satisfying about eating good food. Indeed, there is hardly anything people are more willing to give their opinions on, or argue about, than their favorite recipe, even something as quotidian as a tomato sauce. Bartering is part of these exchanges. After all, you are willing to impart that decisive detail on which, according to yourself, the special charm of a particular dish depends. These conversations are particularly enjoyable, however, because, in addition to the recipe itself, what comes to be exchanged is the satisfaction you anticipate your preparation of this dish will bring. You are sharing your own past enjoyment.

Most importantly, however, the art of cooking I recollect and celebrate in these pages is emphatically conceived as home cooking, even if some of the dishes might require patience or a certain degree of skill. What is essential is the use of good, fresh produce, which means that the ingredients may not always be cheap (or always readily available). While I am equally intrigued with adding new and unexpected aromatic touches to what I remember from my youth and student days as humdrum everyday food, I have never aspired to emulate the intricate culinary arts practiced by renowned chefs in their restaurant kitchens. Instead, I am convinced that simple dishes perfectly prepared and harmoniously seasoned can be equally spectacular. Given that, to me, cooking is a seminal aspect of the art of everyday living, I not only value the ingredients I prepare but also offer them a proper ambience. Although some people find this to be a quaint habit, I always set my kitchen table with the china and the silver cutlery given to me by my mother (including napkin ring and knife rest) even when I am eating by myself. That said, I see no reason not to seat my guests at my kitchen table as well. This way they can be part of the cooking process and I don't miss out on the conversation that takes place while I prepare the next course.

I must admit that my passion for food takes on yet another form of obsession. When it comes to procuring good grocery products, I feel one should always be on the alert. When I am in a foreign city, the places I frequent most, apart from museums and bookshops, are markets of all kinds. Indeed, before I even embark on a journey, I research the gourmet shops in advance, and I would never leave home without a list of my favorites. On the very top of this list is Kalustyan's in Manhattan, a specialty shop for culinary products from around the world. Even today, I wait until I get there to buy my Iranian saffron, only to carry it back with me across the Atlantic in my handbag for

Postwar holidays in Italy—my mother

fear of my luggage getting lost. For many years, befitting its precious content, a glass jar containing these long, dark-red threads has been sitting in a prominent place on the spice shelf, shielded from light but not from my view. When I sit at my kitchen table, this little jar never fails to trigger an imagined dish that makes me smile.

If, for the home cook, it is helpful to know your way around your own kitchen so that looking for a particular spice or the appropriate pan doesn't turn into a major enterprise, it is equally advantageous to be well versed in the basic rules and principles of cooking. For this reason, I have conceived these cooking memoirs as a mixture of master recipes and their variations, the latter rehearsing a range of possibilities that a particular dish offers. Recipes, I suggest, function similar to myths. Like myths, they are narrative units, arranged according to certain rules, which, in turn, allow for a wide range of leeway and idiosyncratic free play. As the French anthropologist and father of structuralism Claude Lévi-Strauss has noted, myths should be conceived as relationships that can be compared; they are variations of each other, organized by a fundamental, overarching structure. Applying his definition of myth to my work in the kitchen, I offer the following reformulation: each individual dish serves as a particular expression of the basic, all-embracing system regarding the preparation of raw and cooked ingredients. While the rules of this system remain constant, each individual, singular dish can be modified endlessly.

For this reason, this cookbook isn't divided up to reflect individual courses, ranging from appetizer to dessert, nor is it organized around particular ingredients or food types. Instead, I have conceived it structurally, according to the way one wants to prepare food. The first chapter is concerned with dishes that showcase raw, marinated, or precooked, refrigerated ingredients. I find there to be something straightforward and immediate about placing one's trust primarily in the pure taste of a particular ingredient, such as exquisitely fresh tuna in a tartare or new potatoes in a salad. With the next chapter, I turn to dishes that can be prepared quickly by frying or sautéing ingredients. Here, my attention is given to what happens in the pan in a very short space of time, usually over high heat, during which one can do little to correct the taste of the dish as it emerges. Diametrically opposed to swift pan-frying is cooking in a pot, not least of all because this requires several steps and far more time. Now, you must wait patiently while the individual ingredients slowly transform and, married with each other, develop their complex flavor. And finally, conceived as a synthesis of the two preceding ways of cooking, I deal with baking and roasting in the oven. Here, too, there is little leeway to correct the texture or taste of the ingredients once the cooking process has begun. Instead, you must simply trust that the heat of the oven will yield success.

In each of these chapters, I explore the basic structure underlying these four ways of cooking while identifying the concept behind specific types of dishes that are typical for each, such as soup, risotto, or stew for the pot; quiche or casserole for the oven. Once you have internalized these principles and can thus trust yourself to know when you must adhere strictly to certain rules and when you can allow yourself to deviate from them in good conscience, it becomes far easier to experiment in your own kitchen. It is, of course, true that a mishap on the stove or in the oven can sometimes lead to an exciting discovery. If the dish does not turn out the way you wanted it to, you are now compelled to look for a creative way to salvage the unfortunate result. And yet, as in music, improvisation in the kitchen requires a self-reliance most readily gained by having mastered the fundamentals of cooking. Only this knowledge affords the freedom to alter ingredients or combine them in fresh ways to fully savor the whole gamut of flavors and aromas. Unconventional combinations tend to succeed only once you know which spices fit together and which enhance (rather than stifle) the taste of the ingredients to be embellished. For this reason, my recipes are meant both as a guide and a challenge. Once you have grasped the idea behind them, you can develop them further, elaborate and refine or modify them.

If, then, all courage to improvise in the kitchen, all passion for invention, is based on observing certain rules with utmost discipline, you are looking for a balance between knowledge and creativity, between assiduous preparation and spontaneity. While any haphazard course of action in the kitchen rarely augurs well, an excessive endeavor more often than not engenders what I call nervous dishes. This is when pure enjoyment is marred because you can't help but feel the cook was trying too hard. Finding a happy balance between skill and enthusiasm is, once again, primarily a question of attitude. Ever steadfast and resilient, Julia Child famously proclaimed, "No matter what happens in the kitchen, you should never apologize." You alone know how the dish you have produced should have tasted. Gaining such self-confidence has, in part, to do with overcoming certain anxieties by facing them head-on. For this reason, I once bought a bag full of artichokes and spent hours meticulously snipping away at them until I had finally fully understood the structure of this edible flower head. Now I can make my way effortlessly to the heart of my favorite vegetable. Similarly, I once spent an entire afternoon pouring oil, drop by drop, into different bowls containing an egg yolk seasoned with mustard and lemon juice until I was finally able to produce the perfect mayonnaise—which, homemade, is incomparably better than store bought. The trick, I discovered, is to start with olive oil.

Achieving self-reliance, however, also entails knowing how ingredients you can't find may be substituted with similar ones and, above all, how you can cut corners while cooking. As gorgeous as homemade chicken broth may be, in the heat and haste of weekday cooking, I have no compunction about using broth cubes. Likewise, I am willing to exchange the heady bourbon vanilla bean with bottled vanilla extract (or vanilla paste) or to resort to dried herbs when no fresh ones are at hand. Making allowances for serendipity also encourages self-confidence in the kitchen. For example, I once ended up with a particularly good pistachio dip because I had not bought enough feta and was thus compelled to add an old Gruyère that was still sitting in my refrigerator. Similarly, after many years of making orange-glazed sweet potatoes the way my mother had taught me, miscalculating my preparation time led me to discover that they could just as easily be roasted in the oven without being boiled first. Because contingencies invariably compel some kind of adjustment, I have always found it wiser to understand the idea behind a particular dish than to rely blindly on the measurements and times recommended by the recipe. It has happened more than once that I have given someone a recipe only to be surprised at how different his or her version of the dish looked and tasted. Something happens in translation. But then again, measurements given in a recipe should be treated as negotiable guidelines. After all, not every garlic clove or shallot is the same size, not every dried bean is equally flavorful. Sometimes it takes longer to transform tomatoes into a thick sauce, sometimes a syrup reduces more quickly, and sometimes the meat in a stew requires more time than usual before it is really tender.

Precisely because there is always an element of chance involved in home cooking (even when you can rely on what you have learned and tested), what ultimately counts is how you present the food you have prepared. I was deeply taken with the dramatic pride of my friend Michael, who produced from his tiny Parisian kitchen a bowl of pasta tossed primarily in finely chopped raw foie gras. There was one detail to which Michael immediately drew the attention of his guests. He had topped this simple pasta with a multitude of black truffle slices. He proceeded to tell us about the woman who had bought the truffle for him at an auction in the south of France and had sent it vacuum-packed by post. This story made his pasta dish all the more luxurious. During that Sunday lunch in Paris, I realized something important: the food that you cook for others—regardless of how simple or complex—deserves to be served with panache. If you convey that you are fully convinced by what you have prepared, others will also be impressed.

Indeed, cooking has as much to do with imagination as with practice. Before I actually start to cook, I conjure up in my mind the taste, the smell, the colors, and the textures of the dishes I want to make. Sometimes the mental image emerges gradually while my gaze wanders along the shelves of my pantry or my refrigerator. Taking stock of what I have is an invitation to concoct different dishes I could make with these ingredients. If, in turn, I am planning a dinner party, I first try to picture the overall atmosphere I want to create. The decision what to make is then contingent on which color or spice I want to use to connect the different courses with each other, on the balance between flavors and textures that makes sense for this particular occasion. Self-confidence alone is not enough for me to indulge my passion for experimentation in my kitchen. Success depends on my having already thought through which ingredients and which aromas I want to combine, how these will affect each other, and how they will change once heat is applied to them. Armed with my imagined scene, I can then embrace the contingencies of improvisation with impunity.

⚜

I have spent more than three years writing these cooking memoirs. In the process, I consulted my cookbooks over and over again. I went through the recipe files and the notebooks that I had been compiling over the years. I invited countless friends over to try dishes out on them. But equally important, I also embarked on a voyage into the past, to the many cooking scenes that have shaped my life. Only in doing so did I discover how intricately interwoven my passion for cooking is with my family history, especially with my parents' stories about their relationship to food. One of the favorite anecdotes my father, the son of Jewish immigrants from Eastern Europe, liked to tell about the humble household he grew up in Brooklyn revolves around the big kosher salami that hung from a thick brown cord attached to the kitchen wall. Nostalgically he would recall that the first slices were still soft and moist, but in the course of the weeks, the salami would slowly dry out. It was never eaten up in one go. To be allowed to cut off a slice was considered an honor. This small detail is meaningful to me because it encapsulates the deep longing he always harbored throughout his adult life—not necessarily for a lost world but rather for a satisfying meal as the measure of a good life. When he married my mother at the end of the Second World War, he was a dashing skinny officer in the American Office of Military Government in Bavaria, but the gradual prosperity of his postwar business came to manifest itself in the steady growth of his stomach. He never mourned after his former lean self. Instead, whenever asked about this transformation, he would proudly declare that it had taken a lot of work (accompanied, of course, with infinite enjoyment) for him to eat himself into his new shape. His protruding stomach was the corporeal sign of his success. It showed that he could now afford any opulent meal he desired.

The immense pleasure he took in sharing meals with others was also his way of showing affection. When, in the early 1950s, he moved to Munich with my mother to set himself up as an American lawyer, he abandoned all orthodox Jewish dietary laws. Only now and then on a Saturday, recalling the cooking of his religious mother, would he decide to take us to the restaurant next to the synagogue. My siblings and I, suddenly transported into a different world and time, were then able to share with him those dishes

Three generations of women around my birthday table

from his childhood that he still had a quiet hunger for—gefilte fish, cholent, chicken soup with matzo balls. Far more often, however, he would take us out to ethnic restaurants where, as a regular customer, he had befriended the owner, who would serve dishes especially prepared for us. Sometimes we were even allowed to go into the kitchen and choose what we wanted from the steaming pots on the stove. Following him on his restaurant tours was not only the beginning of my own culinary expeditions; the joy on his face when he saw my own excitement at being introduced into this new culinary world—watching me, for example, while I devoured with the utmost relish my first *Salzburger Nockerl* (a fluffy, pyramid-shaped dessert made from eggs and sugar)—led me to understand another basic principle of cooking: the complete satisfaction derived from a particularly successful dish has to do

Postwar holidays in Italy—my father

with what the French psychoanalyst Jacques Lacan has called a desire for the desire of the other. Like the food itself, enjoyment is a shared passion.

The restrained joy my mother exhibited while eating her favorite dishes was almost diametrically opposed to the culinary effusiveness of my father. My mother had transformed the terrible deprivations of the war years into her own personal melodrama of frugality. With her 1950s cocktail apron tied around her tiny waist, she would not only always insist on elegance in her kitchen but also, given her skill and endless patience, prepare dishes to absolute perfection. Her response to my voracious appetite was quiet curtailment. She wanted to remain slim at all costs, and she felt I should do the same (a fantasy my body refused to share). Part of her enjoyment of those exquisite dishes that she could now afford consisted of showing self-control. Under the guise of "being economical," she indulged in a strict regulation of all dishes that, for her, fell into the category of luxury. And so, the kosher salami of my father resurfaced in a different shape in my own youth. There was a bakery close to our home that made a particularly intricate strawberry cake, consisting of several different types of pastry and a luscious cream filling. But because my siblings and I were only allowed to have this treat for very special occasions, our desire for it was nourished as much by the scarcity value attached to it as by its exquisite taste.

As opposed as their attitudes toward good food were, my parents always agreed on one thing: they were unconditionally generous hosts. We were always allowed to bring friends home for a meal. The refrigerator, as well as our home bar, was always open to everyone. During family meals, especially on weekends, the food we shared served to negotiate the sophisticated circumstances that, as Tolstoy once wisely put it, make every unhappy family unhappy in its own way. Each one of us would fight for the best pieces of the roast, pounce on the side dishes, and reach greedily for the sauce. Sometimes a dumpling would even fly across the table because someone had too vociferously proclaimed his or her impatience. My mother would often tarry in the kitchen far longer than necessary so as to be the last one to sit down at the table. This allowed her to reproach us for not having waited for her before serving ourselves. Rivalry for food, of which there was always more than enough, set the stage for a spirited war of words between parents and children, which was really a thinly veiled struggle for mutual recognition. The presence of guests, privy to this curious ritual, made sure that the

My mother and I in our living room

Picnic on the lawn with my siblings

Home in a suburb of Munich

spirit of irony was never fully absent from these often raucous meals. The intensity of the conflict only served to demonstrate that sharing good food with each other was the one language we had in common. The dishes my mother prepared for us in her kitchen were what united us as a family, the mark of the familiar between us, of our trust in each other, over and beyond all differences.

If the story of my parents is part of the global diaspora so characteristic of the twentieth and early twenty-first century, it is also the story of a sustained conviviality that goes along with dislocation and exile. Precisely because many people no longer live where they were born, meals shared with friends have come to represent a moveable home, something to be remembered but also something to be relived, adapted to each new living situation. Over the recollection of shared meals, a piece of the past—a lost world, a different time—can once more be resuscitated even while, by reproducing them, a new community can be forged. Indeed, nothing has influenced my own cooking as much as the unfettered hospitality I experienced in my parents. Even if, today, I prepare very different dishes and plan my own dinner invitations under very different circumstances, the keynote of generosity remains the same. And thus, in my kitchen, the three time periods that, according to Sigmund Freud, make up the work of fantasy often come to be merged together. While preparing a meal, I will have recourse to memories. The iridescent touch of a prior event hovers over the dishes I serve my guests. At the same time, this dinner, ephemeral as it is, gestures toward a future moment when it might be repeated. If the aim of successful cooking is tangible gratification, at issue is far more—sustaining a hunger even while it is being satisfied.

COLD DISHES

Raw or Chilled

Bruschetta Feast | Pâtés and Vegetable Dips | Cold Soups | Carpaccio and Tartare | Tataki | Raw Vegetables and Salads | Raw Pasta Sauces | Fruit

Cold dishes are really what I like to eat best. Maybe that has to do with my curiosity in general when it comes to food. At the vegetable stall, I will brazenly ask the vendor whether I might not first try a cherry, a strawberry, or a tangerine before buying something. Invariably, I am met with an understanding gaze. After all, we both know about the seduction of a perfectly ripe piece of fruit. While touching and smelling is also an important indication of how fresh something is, nothing is quite as convincing as testing an ingredient with the tongue. Of course, you can't taste everything first because tasting raw meat, like raw fish, is far more tricky than vegetables or fruit. It thus pays off to develop a relationship of trust with the vendors you buy from on a regular basis—be it at the farmers' market or the supermarket. They are your best source for recommendations and advice, and they are usually happy to get feedback. A well-informed butcher or fishmonger can give you the best suggestions for how to prepare a particular piece of meat or fish, but you also have to be able to trust him or her implicitly when it comes to the freshness and quality of their goods. This doesn't, of course, prevent me from cutting off a piece of a tuna steak or a beef fillet once I have brought it home and try it immediately before putting it into the refrigerator. In its raw state, an ingredient comes closest to its purest taste, its unrefined smell. For an instant, I have a sense of a primordial predator waking up inside me.

Enjoying cold dishes does not, however, mean privileging the natural ingredient over cooked or fried food, nor does it imply the absence of all preparation. It is certainly possible to imagine that when eating raw foods, precisely those culinary rites of our prehistoric ancestors flicker up, whose aftereffects Sigmund Freud suggests continue to inhabit our unconscious wishes (which is why he liked to call the unbridled instincts of the child barbaric). If I, however, am to look to my childhood in order to explain my love for cold dishes, what I immediately invoke is a pleasurable preparation ritual. My sister, Susan, and I would often spend the weekend at our grandmother's home in Schwabing, close to the university. At the time it was not yet common in Munich to go out for brunch, which is why my grandmother developed her own distinct way of celebrating breakfast on Sunday. My sister and I would wait patiently until our Omi would finally wake up and then follow her hungrily into the kitchen. There, dressed in her elegant morning robe, she would begin slicing yesterday's bread rolls, roasting these, and then making open sandwiches with delicious things: Camembert slices, self-made egg salad, truffle liverwurst. The garnish consisted of chopped cornichon, capers, or parsley. I can't recall everything that she would put on these toasted slices of bread, but what I remember distinctly is the precision with which she would cut smoked ham into tiny cubes, only to press these ever so closely to each other onto the butter.

Regardless of how late it was or how hungry we declared we were, she would remain unflappable. Only when everything had been arranged exactly as she wanted it did each of us get her own breakfast plate, covered with these delicacies so that we could go and eat them in the dining room. As I remember this scene again, I come to realize the magic of this ritual, which Susan and I looked forward to each time anew, consisted in the time our Omi's meticulous preparation required. The expectation downright enhanced our enjoyment of the small sandwiches she created, tailored to the individual preferences of each one of us. No one ever got the same set of sandwiches. And everything was directed toward the moment when we were finally allowed to consume them. My memory of this morning ritual is, thus, primarily of the anticipation, not the actual eating. Many years later I discovered a far more elaborately prepared smorgasbord in Copenhagen in a cellar restaurant. In the glass vitrine of the long counter, each small, edible jewel was placed on a plate of its own. Once I had made my choice and taken these to my table, I would first allow my gaze to glide around each one of them reverently before destroying these culinary masterpieces with my first bite. Closer to the simplicity of my grandmother's sandwiches, in turn, were the Venetian *tramezzini* that I discovered in a small trattoria next to the Accademia. The charm of these triangular sandwiches, each with its innards bulging, is irresistible. The crust of the white *pancarré* bread is cut off so that the filling—where tuna meets with olives and capers, asparagus with egg and tomatoes, or ever so finely cut prosciutto with marinated mushrooms—can blend perfectly with the soft bread.

With a whiff of the barbaric invariably connected to the notion of raw food, I can invoke another scene from my childhood to explain where I derive my own atavistic pleasure in raw dishes. We often spent our summer holidays on the Mediterranean, where, to the great astonishment of the local waiters, I soon developed a passion for eating oysters. Devoid of all loathing that overcomes not only children at the thought of eating these fruits of the sea, I would impatiently await the arrival of the opened shells at our table. Soon, my mother and I had developed the shared rhythm of a silent dialogue. Each one of us would take one oyster into her own hand and then cast a favorable glance at it before plunging our forks into the living, white flesh, plucking it out of its shell and consuming it with utmost relish. My stylish mother always insisted that the shells be placed facedown on the platter on which they had arrived. The mounting heap served to indicate our progress, whereby the last oyster was also always the best.

Freud astutely calls the value of transience a scarcity value in time. And, indeed, the fact that our enjoyment was always confined to a dozen oysters increased their value. At the same time, our ritual constituted of an homage to the ocean my mother loved so much; we had literally imbibed a bit of life that came from it. Since then, the countless sushi platters, which by now have become part of our everyday fast food, have helped sustain my enthusiasm for raw fish in a far more multifarious manner, even though—as with oysters—the taste depends on the freshness and thus the place where one lives. Not living close to a coast may mean satisfying your desire for something raw differently—for example, by cutting the beef fillet for a tartare with a sharp knife and, so as to determine when the tiny cubes have the right size, tasting a morsel now and then in the process.

♣

While no puristic culinary approach privileging raw dishes for health reasons is at issue in this chapter, aesthetic and time considerations do play a role. What will be showcased are dishes that are prepared with both raw and precooked ingredients, whereby it is important never to forget that, for sanitary reasons, raw fish and raw meat must be treated with far greater care than raw vegetables or fruit. Cold dishes are colorful, crisp, and in a vital way textured. Sometimes they can be prepared quickly with ingredients that you happen to

A rack of knives by the stovetop

have at hand. Usually, however, they are more likely to be skillfully assembled with things already prepared, and indeed, I like to serve a combination of them to my guests. Dips and pâtés fit well with salads that have been enriched with fruit, cheese, or nuts. But they can also accompany a *tataki*—the Japanese way of preparing a piece of meat or fish by searing it very briefly in a hot pan and then plunging it into ice-cold water, thus stopping the cooking process immediately so that it remains raw inside. In fact, cold dishes need not be relegated to the role of prelude to further courses. They can themselves provide a sequence of dishes that make up an entire meal. This can, at times, be more luxurious; at other times, more sparse. In either case, cold dishes always appear to be light.

For this reason, in summer, when the temperature is high, you might try raw ingredients, even if a pasta dish is what you crave. The minute the hot pasta is tossed with cold vegetables or strips of raw fish, it begins to heat them up. Within seconds a transformation takes place that, while preserving a touch of the rawness of the other ingredients, also adapts them to the cooked pasta they are partnered with. A metamorphosis of sorts also occurs when, so as to prepare a ceviche or carpaccio, meat, fish, or vegetables are left to soak in a marinade. In the refrigerator, they cook by themselves while you dedicate yourself to preparing other dishes. The liquids and spices of the marinade increase the taste of the raw main ingredient even while giving it a distinctive additional aroma. However, what is important to bear in mind regarding most of the recipes presented in this chapter is that the dips are better when left to rest for a while in the refrigerator. The fish or meat must be dressed with a marinade in advance, much as the ingredients for the soups and the salads must, in part, be precooked. Like any pickled roast, these recipes require precise planning not only when it comes to buying ingredients but also concerning their preliminary handling—more often than not, several hours in advance. If you forget to marinate the fish or steam the vegetables, many of the dishes cannot be prepared spontaneously, even if the spices and herbs, as well as the dressings, can be replaced by others.

Cold dishes, in other words, aren't necessarily always something that you can quickly prepare with raw ingredients. Rather, they are dishes for which you need to have already put together key elements, now waiting in the refrigerator for you to fall back on. Carefully thought-out preliminary work, in turn, makes it possible to enjoy dishes that you already concocted, perhaps in a quiet moment a day or two earlier. The joy resides in the anticipation of a meal still to come, the time saved in the swift final assemblage. As is so often the case in successful cooking, spontaneity relies on being well prepared.

One ground rule applies above all else: freshness is key. When it comes to cold dishes, you must direct your attention to the excellent quality of the ingredients you use, to their color and their texture. As the chapter on cooking in a pot will demonstrate, in a stew, the cheaper piece of meat can come into its own, as is also true for less than perfectly ripe vegetables. Cold dishes, furthermore, are particularly suitable for local, seasonal produce. The ingredients you choose should never look tired, limp, or dull. The motto should be "Less is more"! Once you have brought it home, fresh fish needs to be washed immediately, dried thoroughly with paper towels, and wrapped in plastic wrap, stored away in the fridge. If you intend to eat it raw, you should do so the same day you bought it (or within the next day). Fresh vegetables and fruit can also not be kept very long, even if they are left in a cool, dark place in your kitchen. If you missed the moment of perfect ripeness, you can always—in contrast to fish—roast, poach, or stew it. Stored in your fridge, these prepared ingredients can, in turn, be used to embellish any cold dish—for example, a vegetable salad or, as the topping, a bruschetta.

BRUSCHETTA FEAST

Bruschetta with Fresh Ricotta | Bruschetta with Mushrooms | Bruschetta with White Beans and Truffle Oil

The charm of bruschetta consists of its simplicity. This rustic toast with a savory topping originated in the cuisine of Italian farmers, where yesterday's bread would not be thrown away. Instead, roasted over a fire, rubbed with garlic, and sprinkled with olive oil, it would be eaten the next day. These days, of course, to serve bruschetta is no longer a sign of frugality but rather a stylish and yet uncomplicated prelude to a meal with friends. But these snacks, combined with a soup or a salad, can also make up a light meal on their own.

Whatever the occasion, you need a longish, crusty bread. After cutting this into one and a half centimeters (about one-half inch) slices, you place these next to each other on a baking sheet and roast them under the grill in the oven. You will need to stay close by, not only to flip them around once they have taken on a golden color but also to make sure that they don't burn. Now you can place them on a cutting board and continue with the preparation. Although rubbing them with garlic is not obligatory, this step, for me, constitutes the particular charm in making these small sandwiches. As you move the peeled garlic clove back and forth across the crispy surface, it will slowly melt into the toasted bread. While a thin coating begins to evolve on the surface, a seductive smell begins to emanate from it as well. You can decide for yourself whether you want to apply only a touch of garlic or whether, by rubbing the clove into the bread more intensely, you want to produce a more pungent taste. Making sure that the garlicky side is turned upward, you can now proceed to drizzle olive oil generously onto each of the bruschetta slices, endowing them with a spicy moisture that will accentuate the flavor of whatever you choose to put on them.

The topping is, of course, the decisive element. In the most modest case, you simply scatter Italian herbs—any mixture of fresh thyme, oregano, and red chili flakes—onto the moistened side. If, in turn, you are looking for an exotic touch, you can use *za'atar* instead, an herb mixture common in Middle Eastern cuisine, which includes sesame seeds, cilantro, and garlic along with thyme and oregano. Then again, a particularly easy way out is to use a vegetable pesto, either homemade or store bought—my favorite being pistachio pesto—and simply spread it generously onto each slice, decorating it in the end with a bit of arugula, cut into narrow strips. You could also, however, first cover the bruschetta with a layer of soft goat cheese or Taleggio and then spread the vegetable pesto on top. Best known, of course, is the version with ripe tomatoes, cut into small pieces, tossed in a bowl with a handful of basil and olive oil, and seasoned simply with salt and pepper. This topping, however, requires really ripe, tasty tomatoes, so if the season isn't right, you may want to take this dish in a different direction. You can just as well drape a piece of prosciutto or fennel salami onto the toasted, oil-infused bread and garnish it with fig slices. Always add a pinch of salt and freshly ground pepper at the end and, if what you have fabricated appears dry, a whiff of olive oil. Possible combinations are, of course, endless. The following are, however, three versions my guests have repeatedly praised. One must never underestimate the happiness derived from these little crisp delicacies, even if—or perhaps precisely because—they have become so familiar to us.

BRUSCHETTA WITH FRESH RICOTTA FOR 4

1 baguette, cut into slices at an angle
250 g (1 cup) fresh ricotta
lavender salt (see "Close at Hand")
200 g (1¼ cup) fresh fava beans

2 tbsp. olive oil
1 lemon
10 mint leaves, chopped

Shelling fava beans

This fairly straightforward bruschetta simply requires that you first rub the toasted bread slices with garlic and drizzle them with oil before generously covering each with the fresh ricotta. The cheese topping should be as thick as the bread slice itself. If in any way possible, you should buy your ricotta from a cheesemonger or at an Italian food store. The mild sweetness of fresh ricotta is far more intense than the packaged one you find in supermarkets. As a final touch, simply sprinkle each bread slice with pepper and lavender salt. Black salt, with its egg flavor, is also a good choice.

To make this bruschetta more complex, I would add fresh green fava beans (or broad beans), especially in spring, when they are in season. Admittedly, these green pearls are precious in more sense than one because you really need to peel them twice. As with fresh peas, you first open the long, leathery pod and pluck out each individual bean. After cooking them for no more than three minutes in boiling water, rinse them in cold water. You can now gently make an incision on the upper end of each bean with your fingernail. As you press on the bottom end, the smaller bean contained inside will readily slip through this opening. However, this not only makes the preparation time-consuming; compared to the amount of beans bought, the actual yield is also much less. It is possible, of course, to skip the second step, but the satin-like tenderness of the inner bean eaten without its tougher casing is well worth the effort. Regardless in which form you are using them, you ultimately toss the fava beans in a bowl with olive oil, the zest and juice of one lemon, and chopped mint. Finally, dust the ricotta, piled high on each of the toasted bread slices, with lavender salt and pepper before draping the beans on top.

BRUSCHETTA WITH MUSHROOMS FOR 4

1 baguette, cut into slices at an angle	½ tbsp. thyme
250 g (2½ cups) fresh button mushrooms, finely sliced	lavender salt (see "Close at Hand") and pepper
1 shallot	6 tbsp. olive oil
2 tsp. lemon juice	3 tbsp. lemon oil
1 garlic clove, peeled and chopped	

You need to clean the mushrooms first, discard the lower part of the stem, and cut them into very thin slices. To sauté them, choose a pot into which they will fit comfortably when barely covered with water. Immediately add the chopped shallot, the lemon juice, the chopped (or pressed) garlic clove, and the thyme. If you happen to have fresh thyme, you can also simply use a couple of sprigs. Season the mushrooms with lavender salt and pepper and allow them to simmer for about five minutes or just long enough for them to become soft. So that the aroma can penetrate them more intensively, you should let the mushrooms first cool in the spiced fluid before draining them in a colander and blending them in a food proces-sor. To do so you proceed in the same way as when making a mayonnaise. While the motor is running, you pour the olive oil in a thin, steady stream into the mushroom mix until you have produced a smooth, dense paste. If you do not have a food processor, you can, of course, just as easily use an immersion blender. To give a fruity note to the taste of the mushrooms, add a bit of lemon oil (or olive oil and lemon juice) at the end. Season once more with salt and pepper before draping the mushrooms onto the toasted bread slices.

Cutting mushrooms

BRUSCHETTA WITH WHITE BEANS AND TRUFFLE OIL FOR 4

1 baguette, cut into slices at an angle	1 bay leaf
1 L (4 cups) vegetable broth	3 tbsp. olive oil
250 g (1 cup) white beans, soaked	salt and pepper
overnight in cold water	1 bunch parsley
5 garlic cloves	truffle oil to drizzle

If I want a particularly festive bruschetta, I add a few drops of truffle oil to the classic white bean puree. Since this condiment should essentially only be used as a crowning aromatic touch, it is worth investing in really good truffle oil. But this particular bruschetta topping is also costly when it comes to time, because the beans must simmer for more than an hour in the vegetable broth. In this case, it is not a good idea to use precooked canned beans (as I would for other vegetable purees). Instead, you will need to soak the beans in cold water overnight. This means you must not only plan for this dish in advance but also take your time with it. You can, however, cut corners when it comes to preparing the vegetable broth. Indeed, I belong to those cooks who openly admit that they rarely make their own vegetable or chicken broth. I will, without hesitation, use bouillon cubes, bouillon paste, or canned broth, as long as the brand is of excellent quality.

Together with the peeled garlic clove and the bay leaf, the soaked beans should simmer in the vegetable broth on medium heat for about an hour. The actual time depends on how fresh the beans are. If you have been storing them in your pantry for a while already, they will require a longer cooking time. For this reason, before removing the pot from the stove, you want to check whether the beans have really become soft by gently mashing one with a fork. So that they can soak up more intensively the aroma of the spiced broth, let the beans cool in this fluid. Only then drain them in a colander, but make sure to do so over a bowl so that you can collect the broth as well. You may need to use it to correct the texture of the puree at a later stage. Remove the bay leaf but keep the garlic clove. Pour the beans into a second bowl, and, using a fork, mash them and the garlic into a coarse puree. Then using a wooden cooking spoon, fold the olive oil into the cooked beans. You want to preserve a coarse consistency rather than produce a uniform bean puree. If, however, the mixture has become too dense, use some of the broth to dilute it. Add the chopped parsley, and season with salt and pepper before draping the toasted bread slices with this topping. If you don't want too much garlic aroma, you can initially use only three of the cooked garlic cloves and only add the other two after tasting the bean puree. Or you can choose not to rub garlic onto the toasted bread slices. In all cases, however, the final step should be celebrated. I recommend drizzling the precious truffle oil over the bruschetta in the presence of your guests and emphatically drawing their attention to the splendid odor that gently emerges from the opened bottle.

NOTE: Toppings for bruschetta can also be used quite well as dips for raw vegetables. It thus makes sense to prepare more than necessary so as to have something ready in the fridge for the next day or even the day after.

PÂTÉS AND VEGETABLE DIPS

Oriental Avocado Dip | Dessert Avocado Dip | Spicy Tofu Dip | Sweet Tofu Dessert | Red Beet Dip | Chopped Liver | Trout Pâté | American Tuna Salad | White Beans and Tuna Dip

In our home, we always had chopped liver, tuna salad, or egg salad in the refrigerator, allowing us to make our own sandwiches whenever we wanted to. Still today, pâtés and vegetable purees belong to the fixed staples of my daily cooking. Once prepared, they can be stored for several days in the refrigerator—the perfect dish to fall back on when having waited too long before thinking about cooking, when your hunger needs immediate satisfaction, when you find yourself coming home too late to cook, or when unexpected guests suddenly arrive. Pâtés and purees can be served with vegetables, cut into bite-size slices or thin strips. Carrots, celery sticks, Belgian endives, and bell peppers all make for a particularly good fit. Good bread with a neutral taste—like baguette, brioche, or pita bread—nicely complement these pâtés and vegetable purees as well. And like the bruschetta, while they serve as appetizers beautifully, combined with a salad or a soup, they also make a meal on their own. I have come to serve them in bowls from which everyone can serve themselves, secretly hoping that some leftovers will remain. My reward, more often than not, however, is the quiet pride I take in watching how often my guests reach for one or the other dish over and over again until everything is gone.

ORIENTAL AVOCADO DIP FOR 4

2 ripe avocados	½ tsp. ground cinnamon
juice and zest of 1 lemon	½ tsp. cumin
5 tbsp. tahini paste	3 garlic cloves, chopped
3 tbsp. olive oil	1 bunch cilantro leaves, chopped
½ tsp. sumac (or grated lemon zest mixed with salt and black pepper)	

No vegetable dip is as popular as the South American guacamole. Of course, it only really works with luscious ripe avocados, which you blend with the juice and zest of limes, finely chopped chili peppers, spring onions, and olive oil until you have a creamy, dense sauce and then finish by seasoning with a shot of Tabasco sauce. For this less well-known Middle Eastern variation, you also need avocados that are really ripe. If you are out of luck and can only find ones at the market that are still too firm, not all is lost. You can put them into a bowl next to an apple, whose proximity will help them achieve the necessary ripeness. Or put them into a brown paper bag with the apple. In either case, this means you will need to wait a few days before using the avocado. Once more, this proves my point that it is worth planning and shopping in advance.

To prepare this dip, begin by quartering each avocado. This will make it easier to remove the pit. Then gently pull off the outer shell from each quartered avocado and cut it into coarse cubes. It is best to begin by pureeing these with only the juice and zest of the lemon in your food processor. This way you already have a smooth mixture before adding the dense tahini paste and the olive oil. Then add the herbs and the chopped garlic clove and continue blending the avocado mixture until you have achieved a creamy consistency. You shouldn't, however, blend the chopped cilantro but instead use it to garnish the dip at the end. In contrast to a classic guacamole, which you can simply mash with a fork, leaving some of the avocado chunks intact, it is better to use a food processor (or immersion blender) for this version, because the dense tahini paste will otherwise not fully merge with the other ingredients and the taste of sesame will be too overpowering.

DESSERT AVOCADO DIP FOR 4

2 ripe avocados
250 g (1¼ cup) cream
1 lemon

3 tbsp. vanilla extract
3 tbsp. vanilla sugar

If I don't tell my guests that the main ingredient in this dessert is an avocado, even the light green color will not make it easy for them to guess what it is. They usually come up with kiwi. Not only does one not expect to encounter the avocado fruit in a dessert; the delicate freshness, achieved by the combination of cream and lemon juice, harnesses the rich taste one normally associates with avocados. In this recipe, as well, it is crucial that you use very ripe avocados, because if they are still too firm, you will not be able to blend the ingredients into the smooth cream you want to create.

First quarter the avocado and remove the pit. Then pull off the outer shell and chop the avocado into coarse cubes. As with other dips, use a food processor (or immersion blender) to puree them, in this case adding cream, vanilla extract, and vanilla sugar to the juice and zest of the lemon. In between, you should stop and taste the mixture so as to add more sugar or lemon juice if necessary, until you have reached the correct balance between sweetness and acidity. Then fill the avocado cream into an opaque bowl, cover it tightly with tin foil. Let it rest in the refrigerator for at least six hours. This last step is important not only because the cold will intensify the taste of the blended ingredients but also because when exposed to light, the flesh of the avocado fruit readily turns brown. Before serving—if you want some crunch—garnish the cream with finely chopped mint leaves, chopped unsalted pistachios, or grated chocolate. If, however, you are a purist, it is best to omit all further decoration.

SPICY TOFU DIP FOR 4

1 piece silken tofu (250 g or 9 ounces)
1 tbsp. Japanese rice vinegar (or apple vinegar)
1 tbsp. yuzu lemon or lime juice
2 tbsp. olive oil

2 tbsp. wild garlic (or a mixture of garlic and chives), chopped
3 kaffir lime leaves, very finely chopped
2 tsp. pomegranate molasses

Given that tofu is primarily a flavor carrier, it makes a brilliant foundation for both savory dips as well as light desserts. Vital are the other ingredients, which primarily determine the flavor to be achieved, and so it is worth experimenting when it comes to the desired relation between acidity, pungency, umami, and sweetness. The two following suggestions are meant particularly for all those who don't usually work with tofu in their kitchen. My mission is to open your eyes to the unexpected culinary possibilities this healthy ingredient offers.

For the savory dip, which you can serve with bread or bite-size pieces of raw vegetables, cut the silken tofu into cubes and blend it with the vinegar, lemon juice, olive oil, and the chopped wild garlic in a food processor. Then season the dip with pomegranate molasses. Japanese yuzu lemon can readily be replaced with lime and the Japanese rice vinegar with apple vinegar. For the distinct sweet acidity of pomegranate molasses, in turn, there is no real substitute. Therefore, it is worth tracking down this syrup in a store that specializes in Middle Eastern foods to have it on hand in your pantry.

SWEET TOFU DESSERT FOR 4

1 piece silken tofu (250 g or 9 ounces)
2 tbsp. vanilla extract
5 tbsp. orange juice
3 tbsp. maple syrup

1½ tbsp. unsalted pistachios, chopped
honey to drizzle
1 small carton blueberries

As in the recipe for the savory dip, cut the tofu into cubes and blend it with the other ingredients—the vanilla extract, the orange juice, and the maple syrup—in a food processor. You can replace the maple syrup with honey or agave nectar. The pistachios should be unsalted, but they can be replaced with almond slivers. You will want to test the cream while blending it so that, if necessary, you can add more sweetness or more fruit aroma in the process. Drizzle with honey just before serving. This dessert fits particularly well with blueberries but can be served with any fresh or stewed fruit. A crispy-sweet biscotti can also offer the perfect contrast to the tart cream.

RED BEET DIP FOR 4

4 medium-size red beets	1 tbsp. pomegranate molasses
olive oil	1 tbsp. fresh horseradish, grated
250 g (1 cup) Greek yogurt	1 bunch fresh dill

For this dip you could, of course, always use the packaged, precooked red beets readily available in supermarkets. On principle, however, these vibrantly colored taproots taste significantly better if you roast them yourself. This isn't a complicated procedure. You simply need to remember to do this in advance, because they will need their time in the oven. First thoroughly scrub the red beets under warm water so that no more earth clings to their skin but don't peel or trim them. Instead, place the beets in a baking dish that holds them comfortably, sprinkle them with olive oil, and season generously with salt and pepper. Then cover the dish tightly with tin foil and roast the beets at 200°C (400°F) in the oven for about one and a half hours. The roasting time depends not just on the size of the beets but also (as with all pulses) on their age. I recommend checking them after about an hour to see whether, when you cut into one of the beets, your knife runs smoothly through its flesh or whether it needs a bit more roasting time. Allow the beets to cool off before you peel them and cut them into slices or small cubes. Because they will stain not only your hands but whatever else their juice comes into contact with, it is wise to work close to your kitchen sink.

In order to prepare this dip, cut the roasted beets into cubes and blend them with the yogurt, the pomegranate molasses, the plucked dill, and the freshly grated horseradish in a food processor (or with an immersion blender). If you have no fresh dill on hand, you can readily replace it with a tablespoon of dry dill. It is, in turn, with far greater restraint that I would use horseradish from the tube. It simply isn't as sharply pungent and fresh. Also, because you want to retain a certain coarseness rather than produce a finely pureed dip, you should be careful not to blend the mixture too long. Season at the end with salt and pepper.

NOTE: Mediterranean cuisine tends to use a thicker yogurt, known as Greek yogurt or labne. I confess that I far prefer its solid, dense consistency for my dips than the liquid runniness of regular yogurt. For this reason, I was very pleased to discover in one of my cookbooks how easy it is to achieve this texture at home. You simply pour regular yogurt into a sieve that fits on top of a small kitchen bowl and allow it to drain uncovered for several hours in the refrigerator. You can pour away the excess water, transfer the set yogurt into a bowl, and cover it tightly with a lid (or plastic wrap). It will keep for a week in the refrigerator. You can jazz up set yogurt with any pesto or any mixture of chopped fresh herbs. But you can also combine this dip with raw or oven-roasted vegetables, such as the roasted beets in the previous recipe. Or you can mix set yogurt with vanilla extract, lemon juice, and honey and serve it with fruit (or fruit salad) as a light dessert.

CHOPPED LIVER FOR 4–6

3 tbsp. schmaltz (chicken or goose fat)

2 medium onions, chopped

500 g (1 pound) chicken livers

1 bay leaf

a few thyme sprigs

2 hard-boiled eggs, peeled and chopped

2 tbsp. sweet red port wine

salt and pepper

Along with chicken soup, chopped liver is the heart and soul of Eastern European Jewish cuisine. Because the taste of liver can be unpleasantly pungent, some of my friends confess to me that they came to hate this dish in their childhood. For the uninitiated, the idea of eating a mousse prepared from chopped liver can also initially be a disturbing thought. While gazing at the delicate pâtés one can find in any Parisian traiteur, I came up with a secret ingredient that would turn this rustic Jewish comfort food into an exquisitely rich spread. These days, my guests vie with each other over the last morsels in the dish.

It is of course possible to prepare chopped liver with olive oil, but this means losing the distinct flavor of the schmaltz. Over medium heat, let the schmaltz melt in a pan in which the chicken livers fit comfortably. Then add the chopped onions and, keeping the heat fairly low, allow them to caramelize, around twenty minutes. You want them to become soft, taking on a light-brown color and a sweet flavor without turning crispy. Now add the chicken livers along with the bay leaf and the thyme sprigs to the pan and sauté them for roughly ten minutes. They are done when, cutting into them, they no longer bleed. You need to make sure, however, that the livers don't dry out in the pan and retain a certain juiciness. Before continuing with the preparation, remove the bay leaf and the thyme sprigs and allow the liver to cool off. Only at this point should you season the livers with salt and pepper. Then while blending them in a food processor (or immersion blender), add the secret ingredient—the port wine—which transforms this ordinary dish into a marvelous delicacy. It is up to you to decide whether, by pulsing rather than blending the chicken livers, you achieve a coarser consistency (as would be more traditional) or if, as I learned from my mother, you create a delicately smooth pâté. If you want your chopped liver to be especially coarse, you could also simply chop it with a sharp chef's knife by hand. Only once you have finished processing the liver do you add the chopped hard-boiled eggs. Season the dish once more with salt and pepper. Chopped liver will not only keep for three days in the refrigerator; it actually tastes better the next day, because, as is the case with many of the recipes in this chapter, the spices have a conducive aftereffect; they intensify the flavor while the cold yields a more compact consistency.

TROUT PÂTÉ FOR 2

2 smoked trout fillet	1 tbsp. pomegranate molasses
100 g (1 cup) Philadelphia cream cheese	1 small bunch fresh dill (or 2 tbsp. dried dill)
1 tsp. lemon or lime juice	salt and pepper

Not only is the preparation of this pâté very simple; my friends are also invariably enchanted by its fruity, creamy consistency. Begin by breaking up the smoked trout with a fork, then add the cream cheese and the lemon juice and continue to mix everything, still using the fork. Next add the pomegranate molasses and the dill, having first plucked the soft, delicate leaves from the stem. They don't need to be chopped even if they are long. If you have no fresh dill on hand, you can use two tablespoons dried dill instead. In the course of mixing the ingredients together, you want to produce a smooth cream. Season with salt and pepper, but taste the pâté again to see if it might not need more lemon juice or molasses so as to bring forward the acidity meant to balance the sumptuous flavor of the cream. Allow the trout pâté to rest for a few hours in the refrigerator, where it will develop in flavor, before consuming it. It will also keep in the refrigerator for several more days.

AMERICAN TUNA SALAD FOR 2

125 g (5 ounces) canned tuna
2 tbsp. olive oil
½ tbsp. white balsamic vinegar
1 celery stalk, peeled and chopped
2 tbsp. cornichon, chopped
1 garlic clove, chopped

2 tbsp. parsley, chopped
8 tbsp. mayonnaise (preferably
    homemade)
¼ tsp. Dijon mustard
salt and pepper

As quotidian as tuna salad, created at the beginning of the twentieth century, may be, it continues to be a staple in New York delis. If you happen to have bought really good tuna belly in the can, which these days you can find in Italian specialty stores, you should probably serve it with nothing more than a sprinkle of lemon juice and some freshly ground pepper. Adding other ingredients would overpower and thus destroy its delicate flavor. For the classic tuna salad, which I remember from my childhood, however, you do not need the best quality tuna, although you should pay attention to sustainability even when it comes to preserved fish in a can or jar. Mayonnaise is always better when homemade, but you can replace it with crème fraîche if—unable or willing to undertake this chore—you are unhappy with the brand you find in your supermarket. In that case, you should increase the dosage of mustard as well as of the white balsamic vinegar in order to achieve a similar flavor to homemade mayonnaise.

Carefully drain the tuna over a sieve and put it into a kitchen bowl. Using your fingers, pull it apart until you no longer have any lumpy bits. This way you can also feel when you have reached the consistency you are looking for. Peel the celery stalk and chop it into small cubes; do the same with the cornichon and the peeled garlic clove. Chop the parsley and add all these ingredients to the tuna. In another small kitchen bowl, whisk together the olive oil, lemon juice, white balsamic vinegar, and salt and pepper until you have a creamy vinaigrette. Pour it over the salad, and mix everything together. You want to make sure that all the ingredients are uniformly moistened with this liquid. Then fold the mayonnaise and mustard into the tuna mixture and again make sure that this is blended evenly with the other ingredients. Like all my other pâtés, tuna salad is better when prepared in advance and allowed to rest in the refrigerator, where it will also keep for several days.

WHITE BEANS AND TUNA DIP FOR 4

400 g (14 ounces) canned cannellini
    beans

3 tbsp. olive oil
1 tbsp. lemon juice

95 g (3 ounces) canned tuna   1 bunch parsley, chopped
1 tbsp. pomegranate molasses   8 pitted black olives, chopped

For this dip, you can fall back on any canned beans without compunction, although my preference is brown cannellini beans. You will first have to wash them in a colander, taking care that they don't fall apart and that parts of the beans don't remain stuck in the holes. Once you have drained them, drop them into a food processor. The canned tuna you will add must also be drained over a sieve first. Blend the beans and the tuna with the olive oil only as long as it takes to produce a coarse mixture. Season with pomegranate molasses, add the chopped parsley and the chopped olives, and pulse everything for only a few seconds more. The ingredients should mingle with each other without losing their distinct consistency. This dip also improves if left in the refrigerator for a few hours, where it, too, will keep for several days.

COLD SOUPS

Cucumber and Potato Soup | Minted Pea Soup

The advantage to cold soups is that they keep well in the refrigerator and can, with very little effort, be embellished before serving them. Because they are so refreshing to boot, they are a permanent fixture in my summer cooking. Because soup (another one of my favorite dishes) will be discussed in great detail in chapter 4, I feature only two recipes here. These, however, demonstrate the two principles behind preparing cold soups: In the first case, you blend raw (or precooked) vegetables with any combination of oil, vinegar, and herbs you desire in a food processor (or immersion blender). What you are really doing is creating a fluid salad. The most famous example of this is, of course, the Spanish gazpacho, which I always associate with the films by Almodóvar. For his fast-talking heroines, preparing this dish is so natural that they can do so effortlessly, even while involved in heated debates with each other. They, of course, have no time or inclination to blanch the garlic. They simply toss it into the food processor, along with the tomatoes, the red and green peppers, the cucumber, and the white bread; add water, olive oil, and sherry vinegar; and blend everything into a light-red creamy soup. The second principle regarding cold soups is that you can also cook the vegetables in broth as you would for a warm soup and, once they have cooled, blend the soup before chilling it further in the refrigerator rather than reheating it.

Once you have grasped these two methods of preparation and you have figured out your preferred proportion between vegetables and fluidity, the combinations open to you are endless. For the gazpacho version, you can add celery, spinach, and fresh herbs to the cucumber, garlic, and peppers, leaving out the tomatoes completely but not the bread. As for the chilled vegetable soup, adding yogurt will not only give acidity; it also lends itself particularly well to cold soups, while, when exposed to heat, it will readily curdle. When it comes to variations on this basic theme, it is worth bearing in mind that a soup made of carrots, cauliflower, red beets, and green beans or spinach with potatoes makes a delicious dish regardless of whether they are eaten cold or warm. If served cold, a shot of coconut milk or sour cream will lend a velvety richness to any ordinary vegetable soup. So as to illustrate both ways to prepare a cold soup, I offer one recipe for each. As is so often the case with good home cooking, both are enchanting by virtue of their simplicity.

CUCUMBER AND POTATO SOUP FOR 4

1 green bell pepper
4 celery stalks and their leaves
1 small salad cucumber
150 g (5 ounces) cold boiled potatoes
400 g (1⅓ cup) Greek yogurt
250 ml (1 cup) vegetable broth
200 ml (¾ cup) olive oil
3 garlic cloves, chopped

1 bunch parsley, chopped
1 bunch fresh dill, plucked
a handful watercress
2 tbsp. lemon or lime juice
lemon or lime zest
1 tbsp. white balsamic vinegar
salt and pepper

Like the classic vichyssoise, this soup has a refreshing effect on hot summer days. In this case, however, three different green vegetables join the potatoes, taking the place of the leeks and onions. The cream, in turn, is replaced by Greek yogurt. Although, in contrast to a vichyssoise, only the potatoes need to be precooked. This cold soup definitely becomes better if you allow all the ingredients (except for the juice and zest of the lemon) to rest overnight in the refrigerator. Yotam Ottolenghi, from whom I have adapted this recipe, does admit that you will end up with a perfectly satisfying result if you make it on the spot, as long as you make sure to chill the soup before serving.

Begin by deseeding the green peppers, removing the little white bits inside with a small kitchen knife as well and then chopping them coarsely. Peel not only the cucumber and the precooked potatoes but also the celery stalks and cut everything into cubes. Keep the leaves. Then in a bowl for which you have enough room in your refrigerator, mix the three vegetables with the vegetable broth (for which I readily fall back on bouillon cubes or paste), the olive oil, the yogurt, as well as the garlic and the chopped herbs, including the celery leaves. It is best to use your own hands at this stage because only then can you be certain that each ingredient is evenly coated with the marinade. After the vegetables have been immersed overnight in this spiced liquid, blend them in a food processor (or with an immersion blender). If you want more pungency, add a handful of watercress to the ingredients before blending. Add the juice and zest of a lemon and season with salt and pepper only at the end. The ingredients are calculated for four portions not only because it hardly seems worthwhile to make less but also because this soup can be stored in the refrigerator for several days.

MINTED PEA SOUP FOR 4

1¼ L (5 cups) vegetable broth	2 tbsp. olive oil
1 bunch fresh mint leaves, chopped	3 scallions, chopped finely
1 tbsp. dried mint	300 g (11 ounces) raw ham (or
500 g (3½ cups) frozen peas	prosciutto)
1 pinch red pepper flakes	

I have taken the idea for this soup from a book by Nigella Lawson, whose particular blend of British wit and sense for pragmatism has accompanied my own cooking for many years. She quickly convinced me that, rather than insisting on the time-consuming preparation of a vegetable or chicken broth, you could just as well have recourse to bouillon cubes as the foundation for soups, sauces, or a risotto—as long as you choose good quality. I fully understand that making a broth, by allowing chicken bones or vegetables to simmer for many hours on the stovetop, can be a deeply satisfying activity. Not only is this a prudent way to make use of leftovers, but also as importantly, a wonderful aroma fills your kitchen as the chicken soup simmers on the stove. For the flavor I want to achieve with this soup, however, this elaborate preparation isn't necessary. What does take a bit of time, however, is steeping the herbs sufficiently long in the broth to give it the required minty taste. In the sense of a payoff, it is worth making a larger amount of this soup in advance, because it will keep for several days in the refrigerator if stored in an airtight bottle.

Begin by first heating up the vegetable broth in a pot over medium heat and then adding only the stems—not the leaves of the fresh mint—along with the dry mint. Lay aside the mint leaves for the time being; they will be added to the soup later with a few chopped leaves as garnish. The stems and the dried mint must be left to steep for at least thirty minutes in the broth. While you are waiting, use your time wisely and sauté the spring onions in olive oil over medium-low heat in a second pot, making sure to choose one big enough to hold the peas and the broth later on. It will take about ten minutes for the scallions to caramelize. They should neither turn brown nor become crispy, as this would mar the creamy consistency you want to achieve with this soup. Add the frozen peas (they don't need to be thawed) to the onions, sprinkle with a pinch of red pepper flakes, and sauté them until they have become soft. With a bit of dexterity, proceed to fish the mint stems out of the broth before pouring it over the peas, add most of the mint leaves, and simmer for about twenty minutes longer. As is the case when cooking beans, depending on their freshness, the toughness of the peas can cause the cooking time to vary. For this reason, it is always wise to try one first before turning off the heat. As with the classic vichyssoise, let the peas cool before blending the soup in a food processor (or with an immersion blender) until it has transformed into a delicate creamy texture. Finally, season with salt and pepper. In this state, the soup can be stored for several days in the refrigerator. I don't add the sour cream until I am about to serve it, and as a final touch, add some chopped mint leaves and cubed prosciutto: the mint for fresh crispness, the ham for umami spiciness.

CARPACCIO AND TARTARE

Beef Carpaccio with an Oriental Touch | *Scallop Carpaccio* |
Sea Bass Carpaccio | *Salmon Carpaccio* | *Steak Tartare* | *Tuna Tartare*

What is vital in the following dishes is that you allow the meat or fish to soak in the marinade, sometimes for only a few minutes, sometimes for several hours, but never too long, however, because a touch of rawness should be preserved. Equally imperative is freshness and quality not only because eating raw fish can otherwise be precarious; rather, the point of these recipes consists of the minute balance between the taste, which the raw ingredient has to offer on its own, and the spicy marinade coupled with it. The joy of experimentation should never be curtailed when it comes to combining ingredients for such a marinade, but as a rule of thumb, you will want to use twice as much oil as the acidity you choose—be it a fruit balsamic vinegar or the juice of a citrus fruit. When it comes to choosing which type of oil, you simply want to bear in mind that—as with the spices and herbs—the oil should not be in competition with but instead support the taste of the raw ingredient, which, after all, is the star of the dish. For this reason I often prefer a heavier nut oil, like pistachio oil or the very noble argan oil. More courageous cooks than I would serve any type of meat or fish as a carpaccio (with the exception of pork or chicken, exempted for sanitary reasons), even lamb or buffalo. Thinking along more conservative lines, beef fillet can readily be replaced by venison or veal. With fish, you might also want to experiment with different varieties, but before buying anything, you should always ask your fishmonger whether it is really safe to eat it raw. My great enthusiasm for these dishes often entices me to serve generous portions, but in principle, you should calculate 100 grams (3.5 ounces) per person. The following recipes are, thus, conceived for two persons. Served with a salad, they compose a main meal, but they will also serve three persons as a starter.

NOTE: In my kitchen, I always have two milk foamers, even though I never use them to froth up hot milk for a cappuccino. Instead, I use this gadget for my aromatic vinaigrettes, marinades, and salad dressings. I have found that neither whisking a dressing vigorously with a fork nor shaking it in a glass jar offers quite the same wonderfully creamy consistency. Along with the zester, with which I tend to grate the skin off some citrus fruit almost daily, the foamer belongs to those gadgets that I wouldn't want to do without in my kitchen and that, if I am not cooking at home, I am most prone to bring with me, which is also why there are always two foamers in the drawer that holds all my kitchen utensils, just in case, for some unforeseeable reason, one of them doesn't work.

BEEF CARPACCIO WITH AN ORIENTAL TOUCH FOR 2

200 g (7 ounces) beef fillet
2 tbsp. argan oil
1 tbsp. fruit balsamic vinegar (such as apple vinegar or fig vinegar)
1 tbsp. preserved lemon, finely chopped (see "Prepared and Stored in the Refrigerator")
1 tbsp. cilantro, finely chopped
shaved Parmesan
pepper

As is common knowledge by now, you dress a traditional Italian beef carpaccio with olive oil, lemon juice, and freshly ground pepper. To enhance the spice, you sprinkle it with shaved Parmesan and just a handful of basil or arugula leaves. In the following, I have modified this classic dish by giving a Middle Eastern touch to the marinade. To begin, wrap the beef fillet in plastic wrap and put it into the freezer for an hour, but not longer. Slightly frozen, it is easy to cut it into delicate slices, but you will still need a very sharp knife. If your slices aren't thin enough, place them into a refrigerator bag and press them flat with a rolling pin, a wide chef's knife, or a meat mallet (the tool used by butchers for precisely this task). Then divide the beef slices between two plates. To produce a smooth dressing, whisk together the oil with the fruit balsamic vinegar—argan oil fits particularly well with apple or fig—and drizzle it over the beef slices. Covered with plastic wrap, you can leave the plates in the refrigerator, where the meat can absorb the marinade. Or you can consume the carpaccio right away. In either case, just before serving, sprinkle the beef fillet with the preserved lemon bits, the chopped cilantro, and the shaved Parmesan. You can decide for yourself whether you prefer fewer garnishes to foreground the raw taste of the beef or whether you want to showcase its marriage with the textures and flavors of the preserved lemon and cilantro. As a final touch, never forget the freshly ground pepper.

SCALLOP CARPACCIO FOR 2

8 scallops (without their orange roe) Parmesan, shaved
2 tbsp. truffle oil fleur de sel and pepper
pistachios, chopped

You must first wash the scallops and thoroughly pat them dry with a paper towel. In contrast to beef fillet, you do not have to put them into the freezer before cutting them into three to four slices. It is simply important that your chef knife is really sharp. And since you want to taste the creamy sweetness of these saltwater clams, you don't need to cut them paper-thin. If you need time to prepare other dishes, you can, at this stage, divide the sliced scallops on two plates, cover both with plastic wrap, and store them in the refrigerator. Just before serving, drizzle them generously with the sumptuous truffle oil—without, however, drowning them—add a layer of shaved Parmesan, and toss a few pistachios, finely chopped in a mortar, on top. Your eye is the best judge for how much garnish you want. In this case, less is more so that the distinctive flavor of the scallops can really come into their own. The final touch must be a pinch of a coarse salt, such as fleur de sel, and a few turns of your black pepper mill.

SEA BASS CARPACCIO FOR 2

200 g (7 ounces) sea bass fillet
1 medium fennel
1 green chili pepper, seeded and finely
    sliced
juice and zest of 1 lime

2 tbsp. olive oil
1 tbsp. white balsamic vinegar
fleur de sel and pepper
cilantro leaves, chopped

Because you want only a subtle taste of fennel in this dish, you have to assiduously prepare this ingredient in advance. First cut off the bottom as well as the upper stems of the fennel (but keep the feathery green fronds as garnish) and peel the entire surface of the outer leaves so that there are no more dry or withered spots left. Then halve the fennel and, preferably using a small, curved knife, remove the remaining stem inside the leaves, at the bottom. Now you can shred the fennel, beginning with the stem, using either a grater or a very sharp chef's knife (and the equally dexterous hand that goes with it). You shouldn't try to cut corners at this stage, because if your fennel pieces are too thick and the skin still fibrous, it will destroy the delicate flavor of the marinated sea bass. Divide the paper-thin fennel slices among the two plates so that you create an even carpet. Make the vinaigrette next by whisking together the olive oil with the lime juice and the white balsamic vinegar and seasoning it with fleur de sel and pepper. Now slice the fish with the very sharp chef's knife into thin slices and drape these onto the fennel. You want to produce a second, even layer on top of the fennel. Season the fish with fleur de sel and pepper, scatter the thinly sliced chili pepper on top of the carpaccio, along with the fennel fond and the lime zest. Finally, distribute the vinaigrette evenly so that a thin layer covers the entire creation. So that the fish can absorb the marinade and imbue its flavor, cover both plates with plastic wrap and store them in the refrigerator for at least four hours. The sea bass should no longer be transparent and instead turned white to indicate that the meat is now tender. Before serving, dust both plates with a bit of chopped cilantro.

SALMON CARPACCIO FOR 2

300 g (11 ounces) salmon fillet
3 tbsp. pistachio oil
1½ tbsp. calamansi vinegar

1½ tbsp. shiso (or a mixture of mint
    and basil leaves)
fleur de sel and pepper

If no dish comes to mind or I have very little time, I happily fall back on this salmon carpaccio. All you need to do is procure the best sushi-quality salmon you can find, because eating any other salmon raw can be precarious. Wash the salmon briefly under cold water and pat it dry carefully with paper towels. Then cut it into fairly thin strips (but not paper-thin as in the recipe for sea bass carpaccio) and place these into the bowl in which they will subsequently rest in the refrigerator. The key to this otherwise simple dish is the amalgam of pistachio oil and a calamansi balsamic vinegar (made from what is also known as the Calamondin orange). Whisk together the oil and vinegar in a relation of two to one, season with pepper and fleur de sel, pour it over the salmon strips, and carefully fold them into the liquid. After several seconds, the marinade will transform the texture of the raw fish. It should rest in the refrigerator, covered with plastic wrap, for about ten minutes (but not much longer than half an hour, because otherwise you will have produced cured salmon). Just before serving, drape a chiffonade of shiso leaves over the carpaccio. If you can't find this Japanese herb, replace it with basil.

NOTE: The tart sweetness of calamansi balsamic vinegar corresponds perfectly to the rich darkness of the pistachio oil and, in this combination, makes for a versatile condiment: as a dressing for avocado with crabmeat or shrimp, as a sauce for poached chicken breasts, or as the topping for a scoop of vanilla ice cream. For this reason, I always have a small bottle of calamansi balsamic vinegar in my pantry. If you really can't track it down, you can experiment with a mixture of lime juice, orange juice, and cane sugar.

STEAK TARTARE FOR 2

300 g (11 ounces) beef fillet	1 tbsp. olive oil
4 kaffir lime leaves	2 tbsp. ketchup
1 tbsp. capers	1 tsp. Worcestershire sauce
4 cornichons from the jar	1 egg
1 tbsp. parsley, finely chopped	1 tbsp. cognac
1 anchovy, finely chopped	toast
1 garlic clove, finely chopped	salt and pepper

In this dish, the *mise en place* is vital. You want to have everything ready before seasoning the beef fillet with the different aromatics. The thrill of anticipation that accompanies the preparation time increases the indulgence at the end. As boring as chopping each individual morsel of the beef (and the ingredients accompanying it) may be, it helps you appreciate the finished product all the more. For this dish you should, furthermore, pay attention to the quality of the beef you buy and then store it in the refrigerator so that the meat is cold (though not frozen) when you begin chopping it. You could, of course, always have your butcher grind the meat for you, but it is far more appealing to chop it yourself, using a very sharp chef's knife. This way you can control the shape and size. To do this, first cut the entire piece of fillet into thin slices, then place three on top of each other and cut these first into very fine strips, and then (by turning these strips upward by about ninety degrees) cut them into very fine cubes. If they are still too coarse for your taste, bunch the cubes together as though for a chiffonade and once more cut them into fine strips. The charm of this mode of preparation is that you not only feel the texture of the raw meat but also inhale its smell.

Next, chop all the other ingredients. So as to get a particularly delicate result, fold the kaffir lime leaves in half and first remove the hard, inner stem. The soft green leaves you are left with should be chopped so finely that you have an almost powdery texture. The parsley, the capers, the cornichon, the garlic clove, and the anchovies, in turn, should simply be finely chopped. After much experimentation, I have discovered that it is best not to add the fluid aromatics—the olive oil, ketchup, and Worcestershire sauce—individually to the tartare. Instead, whisk them together and add this dressing to the beef fillet so that now moistened, it can absorb the other aromatics better. To make sure that each fillet cube is evenly coated, it is best to use your own hand at this stage. Then resorting back to your fork, if you wish, add all the other ingredients, bit by bit, folding each into the tartare. Use your own eyes to decide the quantity you want of each. One egg yolk, however, is sufficient for two people. Add this, together with the cognac, as the last aromatic before seasoning your tartare with salt and pepper and, if you find it necessary, adjusting the tartness, sweetness, and spiciness. The tartare does not need to rest and can, instead, be served immediately with toast or, if you want a more sumptuous meal, with the classic guilty pleasure—shoestring potatoes.

TUNA TARTARE FOR 2

300 g (11 ounces) tuna, sushi quality	2 tsp. sesame oil
2 tbsp. cilantro leaves (or shiso leaves)	2 tsp. soy sauce
2 tbsp. basil	2 tsp. balsamic vinegar
4 tbsp. argan oil	1 tsp. capers, finely chopped
2 tbsp. lime juice	

¼ preserved lemon, finely chopped   pepper
  (see "Prepared and Stored in the
  Refrigerator")

You should never use anything other than sushi-quality tuna for a tartare and, if necessary, save on the quantity instead. Cut the basil into a chiffonade, and chop the cilantro finely. If you have no access to shiso, you can replace it with a mixture of basil and mint to prepare your chiffonade. The vinaigrette consists primarily of argan oil and lime juice. As you whisk these together in a bowl, take care, as in the other recipes, to use twice as much oil as citrus juice. To deepen the flavor, add the sesame oil, the balsamic vinegar, and the soy sauce, and finish by seasoning with pepper. Because the soy sauce is saline, don't season with more salt. With a very sharp chef's knife, dice the tuna coarsely, add it to the bowl, and dress it with the marinade. After you have made sure that each tuna bit is evenly covered with the dressing, put the tartare in the refrigerator. Just before serving, garnish it with the finely chopped capers and preserved lemons.

TATAKI

Beef Fillet Tataki with Arugula | Tuna Tataki |
Tuna Tataki with a European Touch | Salmon Tataki with Sesame Sauce

In Japanese cuisine, tataki refers to a piece of meat or fish that is briefly seared in a pan and then immediately chilled in ice-cold water. This stops the cooking process immediately, and the steak remains raw inside. Much like sashimi, the tataki is then sliced, not too thin, and served with a sauce. If you want to intensify the flavor, allow the meat or fish to steep in a marinade first. For searing, use an oil that stands up well to heat, such as rapeseed oil. I ate my first tuna tataki many years ago in a small Japanese restaurant in Manhattan's East Village and immediately fell in love with the contrast between the thin outer crust and the raw inner kernel. In the same restaurant, I also encountered shiso leaves for the first time, an Asian blend between mint and basil. These fit perfectly as a garnish for a tataki or for the rice you may want to serve with it. Because the taste of shiso is so unique and so enticing, I recommend having a shiso plant on your balcony or in your garden. Not only is the shiso plant a perennial that requires little attention, but like chives, it also survives all changes in weather.

BEEF FILLET TATAKI WITH ARUGULA FOR 2

250 g (9 ounces) beef fillet (or beef steak)

rapeseed oil (or canola oil)

40 g (¾ cup) kale

40 g (¾ cup) lamb's lettuce

Parmesan

half a lemon

½ tbsp. white balsamic vinegar

2 tbsp. olive oil

This beef tataki is a variation on the appealingly simple Italian dish called *tagliata*, in which a beef steak, still rare, sits on top of arugula dressed with olive oil and lemon juice. When you cut into the meat, the juices flow down into the salad leaves, endowing them with spice and moisture. In this recipe, the kale combined with lamb's lettuce offers a crisp, bitter flavor and the shaved (not grated) Parmesan a creamy sweetness so that, together with the quickly seared beef fillet, three different textures come to be joined together.

To make the vinaigrette, whisk the olive oil with the lemon juice and the white balsamic vinegar and season with fleur de sel and pepper. I dress the salad before preparing the beef. Because in this recipe it will serve not as the bed but rather as the blanket for the tataki, it can absorb the vinaigrette while I proceed to sear the beef fillet in hot rapeseed oil (which stands up particularly well to heat), roughly two minutes on each side. Only after it has been seared, season the meat with salt and pepper. The exact time, of course, depends on the thickness of the meat, which should have formed a brown crust on the outside but remain raw inside. After removing the beef from the pan, cut it into bite-size slices, divide these between the two plates, and cover them with the dressed salad and the thinly shaved Parmesan. The proportion of beef, salad, and cheese is up to you.

TUNA TATAKI FOR 2

200 g (7 ounces) raw tuna, sushi quality

rapeseed oil (or canola oil)

1 tbsp. soy sauce

1 tbsp. broth (vegetable or beef)

1 tbsp. rice wine vinegar (or apple balsamic vinegar)

1 lime

2 tsp. palm sugar

1 tbsp. sesame oil

Because I immediately fell in love with the Japanese way of preparing a tuna tataki, I have been experimenting with this dish over the years and discovered that, once you have grasped the principle, it is good for many variations. The first decision to make is whether you want to marinate the tuna before searing or not. The second concerns the sauce you want to serve with it, which should enhance the flavor of the fish without overpowering it. Furthermore, it is imperative that you buy sushi-quality fish, and because the inside of the tuna should really remain raw, you want to buy a piece that is thick and wide rather than one that is long and thin.

Sear the tuna in a very hot pan in rapeseed oil on both sides as well as along the edges, roughly thirty seconds per side. In order to stop the cooking immediately, plunge it into ice-cold water and pat it dry thoroughly with a paper towel. Then cut it into bite-size slices, not too thin. For the sauce, whisk together the broth, rice wine vinegar (or apple balsamic vinegar), soy sauce, sesame oil, palm sugar, and lime juice. Serve the tuna tataki with rice, garnished with a chiffonade of shiso leaves (or a combination of mint and basil).

TUNA TATAKI WITH A EUROPEAN TOUCH FOR 2

200 g (7 ounces) raw tuna, sushi quality
2 tbsp. soy sauce
2 tbsp. lemon or lime juice
rapeseed oil (or canola oil)
2 beets, roasted
½ tbsp. balsamic vinegar
2 tbsp. argan oil
½ tbsp. lime juice
2 tbsp. cilantro leaves, chopped
fleur de sel and pepper

To give more spiciness to the tuna fillet, you can marinate it in advance in a dressing for which you whisk together soy sauce and lemon juice. Cover the tuna with plastic wrap and allow it to rest in the refrigerator for about two hours. For this recipe, it is again imperative that you choose a piece of sushi-quality tuna that is thick and wide rather than long and thin. You want to sear it in very hot rapeseed oil, about thirty seconds on each side so that you get a crispy crust while it remains raw inside. As in the previous recipe, plunge the seared tuna into ice-cold water and pat it dry thoroughly with a paper towel. Then cut it into bite-size slices, not too thin. Slices of roasted beets perfectly match this tataki, to which a sprinkle of chopped cilantro gives the final touch. You could, of course, always fall back on precooked beets, readily available in supermarkets. However, as the recipe for red beet dip (also in this chapter) illustrates, it is supremely easy to roast beets yourself. In the oven, they not only absorb the flavor of the seasoned oil but also assume a smooth, creamy texture. To dress both the tuna tataki as well as the beets, whisk together the argan oil, lime juice, and balsamic vinegar and season with fleur de sel and pepper.

SALMON TATAKI WITH SESAME SAUCE FOR 2

200 g (7 ounces) raw salmon, sushi
    quality
1 tbsp. olive oil
2 tbsp. fish sauce
3 tbsp. white sesame seeds
1 tbsp. ginger, grated
1 garlic clove, pressed

1 tbsp. sesame paste (or tahini)
1 tbsp. mayonnaise (preferably
    homemade)
2 tbsp. soy sauce
1 tbsp. rice wine vinegar
1 tsp. sesame oil

For this recipe it is important to bear in mind that the salmon fillet must be marinated twice so that the preparation is a bit more time-consuming. As with any raw fish, wash the salmon and thoroughly pat it dry with a paper towel before dividing it into two portions on your cutting board. If you find fish bones, pluck them with tweezers or your fingers. Also carefully remove the dark-gray strip that runs along the center of the back of the salmon. Place the two salmon pieces into a flat dish in which they fit snugly. For the marinade, whisk together the olive oil with the fish sauce and pour it over the salmon. Then cover the dish with plastic wrap, and allow it to rest for at least two hours in the refrigerator. In the meantime, you can toast the white sesame seeds in a small pan for about two minutes. You should keep shaking the pan to make sure that while toasting, the seeds don't burn, then set them aside. Once the two hours are up, take the salmon out of the refrigerator, drain off the marinade, and fry it in hot rapeseed oil, about thirty seconds on each side. You should get a thin crust on the outside, while the inside remains raw. Coat the salmon in the toasted sesame seeds and then wrap it tightly in plastic wrap again. Before you can cut the tataki into bite-size slices, it must return to the refrigerator and rest at least another three hours so that the texture can firm up. To prepare the sauce, whisk together the sesame paste (or tahini), mayonnaise, soy sauce, rice wine vinegar (or apple balsamic vinegar), and sesame oil, and season with fleur de sel and pepper.

RAW VEGETABLES AND SALADS

Fennel with Apple and Parmesan | *Fennel with Orange and Roasted Cumin* | *Green Beans with Spinach and Pear* | *Green Beans with Tarragon* | *Bavarian Potato Salad with Bacon* | *Potato Salad with Wasabi Mayonnaise* | *New Potatoes with Cream* | *Le Puy Lentil Salad with Gorgonzola* | *Black Beluga Lentil Salad with Tomato Flakes and Chèvre* |

Curry Lentils | Button Mushrooms with Kaffir Lime Leaves | Avocado with Shrimp | Salade Niçoise with Seared Tuna | Chermoula Prawns with Oranges

For some time now, salad has no longer been treated as an appetizer or as the side dish that, in classic French cuisine, follows upon a sumptuous main course. My motto, these days, is that a salad is whatever I want it to be. I will often assemble a variety of raw and cooked vegetables and serve these as a main meal. During the summer vacations I used to spend as a child on the Italian Riviera, I was first introduced to the pairing of prosciutto and melon. I have since come to try out different combinations of fruit and cold cuts. Peaches fit incredibly well with prosciutto and burrata, figs with speck and mozzarella. Basil or arugula will offer additional sharpness, while honey or pomegranate molasses will round off the dish with sweetness. Or I will fall back on the old familiar melon but couple it with a salami and pear balsamic vinegar.

Of course, buying fresh salad greens at the farmers' market, washing these copiously, and then dressing them with olive oil, lemon juice, and a whiff of garlic before seasoning with salt and pepper belongs to the most basic culinary gratifications. You need to assiduously extract the "bad" wilted leaves while washing the salad and put only the "good" crisp ones into the salad spinner before drying these thoroughly. If water still clings to the leaves, it will dilute the flavor of the vinaigrette. And even tossing the salad satisfies a very primordial desire. In order to make sure that the leaves are evenly coated with dressing, it is best to use your own hands. At the same time, salad greens can conveniently be washed in advance. After drying them in the salad spinner, you can spread them on a kitchen towel (or paper towels) and roll them up gently. They can be stored for several days in the refrigerator. This way you will always have some salad greens to fall back on.

But if truth be told, a simple green salad, as perfect a dish as this may be, actually bores me, which is why I prefer a combination of salad greens with raw or precooked vegetables and fruit. Chopped, or cut into delicate strips, they inspire me to create an idiosyncratic variety of what French cuisine calls a *salade composée*. Almost anything can be deployed: preserved or seared tuna, smoked trout, steamed shrimp, and of course, a wide array of cold cuts. Delicately sliced carrots, fennel, and zucchini but also grated cauliflower or broccoli endow any salad with an energizing bite. To vary the texture, I like adding cheese or nuts, and to improvise on the lamb's lettuce salad—which in Switzerland comes garnished with hard-boiled eggs—I will add chunks of Roquefort cheese, pear slices, fried bacon slivers, and a handful of sunflower seeds. I am particularly fond, however, of adding a poached or soft-boiled egg to salad greens. With the egg yolk still soft, disappearing into the vinaigrette, it leaves behind a creamy trace, while only the bits of cooked egg white reveal its presence.

When it comes to my experimenting with combinations of salad greens, this may well include spinach, chard, kale, and herbs left intact. The portals to discovery are wide open. Especially in winter, when fresh tomatoes hardly yield any distinct flavor, it is worth falling back on sun-dried tomatoes, preserved in oil. In general, I find it useful to have steamed (or roasted) vegetables, a bit on the undercooked side, on hand in the refrigerator to use as parts of a composed salad as well. Particularly suitable are broccoli, cauliflower, asparagus, beets, carrots, green beans, zucchini, and fennel. You simply need to decide whether you want to dress the vegetables with a sauce based on oil and acidity or one based on yogurt. For my part, I am particularly fond of coupling cauliflower and broccoli with a vinaigrette consisting of lime juice, olive oil, and chopped basil. I will dress cooked asparagus, in turn, with a vinaigrette, for which I whisk together the yolk of a hard-boiled egg with oil, vinegar, and mustard. I use the chopped egg white to sprinkle over the asparagus once it is evenly coated with the dressing. Precooked or oven-roasted red beets, in turn, pair well with a mixture of argan oil and lime juice, tossed with chopped cilantro and walnuts. For precooked carrots, I like to embellish the classic blend of vinegar, oil, and mustard with some orange juice and grated ginger and garnish these with chopped cilantro and pistachio nuts. At the same time, when it comes to salads with steamed carrots, green beans, broccoli, or cauliflower, I am also a great fan of sauces that make use of a mixture of yogurt (one tablespoon) and mayonnaise (one teaspoon), seasoned with lemon juice instead of deploying an oil-based dressing. You could still work with mustard to produce tartness and spiciness. But inspired by Middle Eastern cooking, I prefer a tart sweetness in this case and use pomegranate molasses instead, seasoned with curry powder or tahini. Here, too, chopped herbs such as basil, cilantro, or tarragon offer the final, aromatic touch. The only thing to bear in mind, as you indulge in the joy of experimentation, is which flavors, which consistencies match. Too many different ingredients will destroy the harmonious unity you are looking for in any composed salad.

FENNEL WITH APPLE AND PARMESAN FOR 2

1 big fennel	1 tbsp. lemon juice
1 tart apple (such as Granny Smith)	1 tbsp. parsley
2 tbsp. Parmesan, grated	1 tbsp. roasted pine nuts
½ tbsp. lemon zest	salt and pepper
2–3 tbsp. olive oil	

Cut off the stalks at the top of the fennel, pluck the feathery green fronds, and place them to one side because you will be using them later to garnish the salad. Then peel the entire surface of the outer leaves before cutting the bulb in half. Now using a small, curved knife, cut out the triangular stem on the bottom of the bulb. Then slice the fennel from the bottom up on a microplane grater as thin as possible. You can do this by hand if you have a secure grip and a very sharp knife. The slices must be paper-thin; otherwise, the consistency of the salad will be too coarse. Wash the apple but don't peel it. Cut it in half, deseed it, and grate (or cut) it into paper-thin slices as well. Place it together with the fennel into a bowl, add the lemon zest, olive oil, lemon juice, chopped parsley, and grated Parmesan and mix everything together. Because the fennel is meant to absorb the vinaigrette, allow the salad to rest for at least a half an hour and use the time to prepare your other dishes. Before serving, toss the salad once more; season with olive oil, salt, and pepper; and sprinkle with roasted pine nuts as well as the feathery fennel fronds.

FENNEL WITH ORANGE AND ROASTED CUMIN FOR 2

1 fennel	1 tsp. roasted cumin
2 juicy oranges	½ tsp. chili salt
10 black olives	1 bunch cilantro leaves
2–3 tbsp. lime juice and zest of 1 lime	

Clean the fennel in the same manner as described in the previous recipe, cut (or grate) it into paper-thin slices, and place these on the plate where you will also serve the oranges. Peel these diligently, taking care to cut away not only the hard outer skin but also the bits and pieces of white directly beneath it. To do so, cut off a layer of the upper and lower part of the orange, then place it upright on a cutting board and begin gliding a sharp kitchen knife around the outer skin of the fruit, moving in a circle around the fruit from top to bottom. Cut the orange into as thin slices as you can, and together with any juices, place these on top of the fennel. Deseed the olives, cut them into slices, and sprinkle them over the oranges. Finally, whisk together the olive oil, lime juice, chili salt, and cumin and use this to dress the fennel-orange salad. Its flavor also becomes more intense when the fennel has time to absorb the vinaigrette; therefore, let the salad rest in a cool spot in the kitchen. Garnish only at the very end with a handful of chopped cilantro leaves.

GREEN BEANS WITH SPINACH AND PEAR FOR 2

2 ripe pears	250 g (2¼ cups) haricots verts
2 tbsp. Riesling (or other white wine)	2 big handfuls spinach
1 tbsp. lemon juice	100 g (1 cup) Roquefort
½ tsp. Dijon mustard	100 g (1 cup) toasted walnuts
2 tbsp. olive oil	(or cashew nuts)

Though you could use any green string beans for this salad, the best are the delicate haricots verts. Don't forget that in this salad, the fruit will play a double role, so you want to keep a pear to one side while you use the other one for the dressing. To do so, cut it in half, peel it, and remove the core, then cut it into coarse pieces. Blend these together with the Riesling, the lemon juice, and the mustard in a food processor (or with an immersion blender). While the machine is running, add the olive oil, bit by bit, to create a creamy sauce. Now trim the haricots verts on both ends, wash them, and cut them into bite-size pieces before cooking them in a pot of boiling salt water. Because you want them to stay crisp, immediately plunge them into ice-cold water once they are done, but do so gingerly. You don't want them to fall apart. Drain them and allow them to dry on a kitchen towel while you wash the spinach and dry it in a salad spinner. Now comes the time to turn to the second pear. Peel it, cut it into quarters, remove the core, and slice it before placing it together with the haricots verts and the spinach into a bowl. First dress the salad with the Riesling vinaigrette before topping it with small cubes of Roquefort (or another blue cheese) and the nuts.

GREEN BEANS WITH TARRAGON FOR 2

250 g (2¼ cups) haricots verts	1 tbsp. lemon juice
2 tbsp. tarragon	1 tbsp. pomegranate molasses
2 tbsp. crème fraîche	fleur de sel and pepper

For this salad you could also use any green string beans, but I find that the delicate haricots verts and the sophisticated flavor of tarragon make for a perfect match. After washing the green beans, trim them on both ends and cook them in boiling salt water until they are firm to the bite, then plunge them in cold water, drain them, and dry them on a kitchen towel. Wash and dry the tarragon as well and cut it—I find this works best with kitchen scissors—into thin snippets. Whisk together the crème fraîche with lemon juice, pomegranate molasses, salt, and pepper and dress the haricots verts with it before sprinkling the salad with tarragon. Before serving, season with fleur de sel and pepper, and if necessary, correct the tartness by adding a bit more lemon juice.

BAVARIAN POTATO SALAD WITH BACON FOR 6–8

1 kg (2.2 pounds) waxy potatoes	1 pinch cayenne pepper
1 tsp. caraway seeds	300 g (11 ounces) bacon (or lardon),
300 ml (1¼ cups) beef broth	cut into cubes or sliced
3 tbsp. apple vinegar	1 medium cucumber, very finely
1 tsp. mustard	sliced
1 pinch sugar	salt and pepper

The best choice for a potato salad is waxy potatoes like red thumb, French fingerling, or the old Swiss LaRatte. What is special about this particular mode of preparation is that the potatoes are meant to be dressed with a broth-based sauce while they are still hot. Absorbing the hot fluid prevents them from drying out. For this reason, it is best to prepare the sauce while the potatoes are cooking. Place the unpeeled potatoes in a pot of cold water and season with plenty of salt and caraway seeds. Once the water has begun to boil, turn down the heat; don't cover the pot completely and allow the potatoes to simmer until they are done. In the meantime, in a small pot, mix together the broth, apple vinegar, and mustard, season the fluid with a pinch of sugar and a pinch of cayenne pepper, and let it simmer over low heat. You simply want it to remain warm while you wait for the potatoes to get done. Now on a third plate on your stovetop, fry the lardon (cubed or sliced) in a pan until it has become crisp, and put them into a dish. You could also fry slices of bacon in your pan and, once they have become crisp, break them into pieces. In either case, keep the bacon fat in the pan, because you will be using it again later. Finely slice the cucumber, and put it together with the bacon pieces into a bowl.

As soon as the potatoes are done, peel them while they are still hot and cut them into thin slices (some Germans would insist on paper-thin slices). To assemble the potato salad, choose a bowl or dish with a flat bottom so that, using half of the slices, you produce a first layer of potatoes. Season these with salt and pepper before sprinkling them with the bacon and cucumber mixture, and then cover them with the second layer of potato slices, which you then also season before adding the rest of the bacon and cucumber mixture. Now reheat the bacon fat and drizzle it over the potato salad, then pour the seasoned broth over it as well, enough to coat the slices without drowning them. Toss the potatoes, but do so with caution because you don't want to break the slices too much, nor do you want to mash them in any way. As any potato salad, it will keep in the refrigerator for several days.

POTATO SALAD WITH WASABI MAYONNAISE FOR 6–8

1 kg (2.2 pounds) waxy potatoes
1 L (4 cups) beef broth
6 tbsp. yogurt
6 tbsp. mayonnaise (preferably homemade)
2–3 tsp. wasabi (or horseradish, grated)
1 tbsp. apple vinegar (or white wine vinegar)
2 tbsp. capers, very finely chopped
1 tbsp. chives, chopped
1 tbsp. parsley, chopped
salt and pepper

It is also crucial in the preparation of this salad that the potatoes are allowed to absorb the broth while they are still hot before dressing them with a yogurt-mayonnaise sauce. Put the potatoes in a pot of salt water, allow it to boil, then turn down the heat, and with the lid not completely covering the pot, allow them to simmer until they are done. In a second pot, make the broth and keep it warm over very low heat. Once the potatoes are done, peel them and cut them into thin slices, place them in a bowl with a flat bottom, and pour the broth over them. They should steep for at least one hour in the broth before you pour it off. You can keep it in the fridge as the base for a soup. Mix together the yogurt, mayonnaise, wasabi, vinegar, and the finely chopped capers and dress the potato slices with this sauce. Season with salt and pepper and add the chopped herbs as a final touch. This potato salad will also keep for several days in the refrigerator.

NEW POTATOES WITH CREAM FOR 6–8

750 g (26 ounces) new potatoes
2 shallots
200 g (½ cup) cream
salt and white pepper
150 g (1¼ cup) crème fraîche
2 tbsp. lemon juice
1 garlic clove, grated
1 shot white balsamic vinegar
black pepper

The idea of tossing potatoes in a warm cream sauce comes from Alice Waters—founder of the famous Chez Panisse Restaurant in Berkeley and dedicated representative of the slow-food movement—in one of her lovely Chez Panisse cookbooks. Because you do not need to peel the potatoes for this salad, make sure you wash them thoroughly before cooking them. If you can't find any new potatoes, use small, waxy ones. As in the other recipes, begin by placing the potatoes in a pot of cold salt water, allow it to boil, then turn down the heat and simmer them until they are done. While they are cooking, prepare the sauce. To do so, put the finely chopped shallots along with the cream into a small pot, season with salt and pepper, and warm over very low heat. The shallots should become soft, but the cream should not evaporate. Take the sauce off the heat; add the lemon juice, the grated garlic, and the crème fraîche; and stir until you have a consistent, creamy sauce. Once the potatoes are done, either quarter them or cut them into slices, and fold the cream sauce into them. Season the potatoes with a shot of white balsamic vinegar and freshly ground black pepper. This salad will also keep in the refrigerator for several days.

NOTE: From my friend Pia, I learned another way to cook potatoes for a salad. She suggests putting the unpeeled potatoes in a pot of cold salt water, allowing it to boil. Then cover the pot and turn off the heat. You need to do this in the morning, however, because the pot must remain covered for several hours at least. As the water slowly cools, the potatoes are cooked, assuming a perfectly balanced, creamy texture.

LE PUY LENTIL SALAD WITH GORGONZOLA FOR 2–3

125 g (1¼ cup) Le Puy lentils
2 bay leaves
½ cucumber, finely chopped
2 medium-size carrots
4–6 sun-dried tomatoes, very finely chopped
3 shallots, finely chopped

3 tbsp. olive oil
2 tsp. maple syrup (or marmalade)
40 g (¼ cup) dried cherries (or goji berries), soaked
80 ml (⅓ cup) white balsamic vinegar
120 g (1¼ cup) mild Gorgonzola (or Taleggio)

Wash the lentils in cold water, drain them, and together with the bay leaf, put them in a pot, cover them generously with water, and allow them to simmer twenty to thirty minutes over medium heat. They should be firm to the bite, not mushy. Do not add salt at this stage because this will cause the lentils to become hard. In the meantime, peel the carrots and cut them into very, very fine cubes; peel the cucumber, scoop out the seeds with a spoon, and cut it into fine cubes. Cut the sun-dried tomatoes into very fine cubes as well, and soak the dried cherries (or goji berries) in hot water. You can then put the carrots, cucumbers, and tomatoes into the bowl in which you will ultimately dress the salad. For the sauce, sauté the finely chopped shallots in olive oil in a small pot until they have become soft and caramelized, about ten minutes. Drain the cherries (or goji berries) and add these, along with the maple syrup and the white balsamic vinegar, to the caramelized onions, and sauté these for another ten minutes. Because your aim is to produce a thick sauce, you want to reduce it using low heat and give it as much time as it needs. Once you have achieved a sticky consistency, take the pot off the heat, and season with salt and pepper. When the lentils are done, wash them in cold water over a sieve, allow them to drain thoroughly, and add them to the bowl with the carrot, cucumber, and tomato cubes. Pour the warm sauce over the salad and add Gorgonzola (it can be replaced by Taleggio, feta, or another type of soft goat cheese), broken into coarse chunks. The cheese should melt into the warm lentils before you season them once more for saltiness and tanginess. The salad will keep several days in the refrigerator.

BLACK BELUGA LENTIL SALAD WITH TOMATO FLAKES AND CHÈVRE FOR 4

200 g (1 cup) black beluga lentils (or Le Puy lentils)

2 bay leaves

2 tbsp. olive oil

1 big carrot, finely chopped

2 celery stalks, peeled and finely chopped

2 garlic cloves, peeled and finely chopped

5 sprigs of thyme

tomato flakes (or tomato paste)

1 shot of white wine (or Noilly Prat)

5 tbsp. olive oil

2 tbsp. balsamic vinegar

1 tbsp. Dijon mustard

salt and black pepper

150 g (¾ cup) soft chèvre

1 bunch basil, cut into fine strips

First wash the lentils in cold water, drain them, and place them in a pot generously covered with cold water. Add the bay leaves, but at this point, do not add salt (otherwise they will become hard), and allow them to simmer twenty to thirty minutes. It is best to stir them now and then; if they are absorbing the water too quickly, add some more. You want them to become soft but still firm to the bite. Then wash the lentils in cold water and drain them over a sieve. While the lentils are cooking, you have plenty of time to prepare the *soffritto*, which will serve as the aromatic base for the sauce. To do so, heat the olive oil in a pot big enough to hold the lentils and sauté the carrots, celery, and garlic together with the thyme until they have become soft and begun to caramelize, about ten minutes. Then sprinkle tomato flakes into the *soffritto* (or stir in tomato paste), season with salt and pepper, and mix together thoroughly before adding the drained lentils. Deglaze with a shot of white wine (or Noilly Prat) and turn off the heat. For the vinaigrette, whisk together the remaining five tablespoons of olive oil, balsamic vinegar, and mustard, and season with salt and pepper. Pour the dressing over the lentils, and mix well before folding small bits of the soft chèvre into the salad, allowing it to melt into the seasoned pulses, before sprinkling everything with strips of basil. The lentil salad can keep for several days in the refrigerator.

CURRY LENTILS FOR 4

250 g (1¼ cup) lentils
2 bay leaves
salt and pepper
2 tbsp. coconut oil (or rapeseed oil)
1 onion, finely chopped
1 medium carrot, finely chopped
2 garlic cloves, finely chopped
1 thumb-size piece of ginger, peeled
    and finely chopped

2 lemongrass stalks, outer leaves
    removed and chopped finely
3 kaffir lime leaves, finely chopped
2 tbsp. curry powder
100 ml (½ cup) cream
salt and pepper
1 shot lime juice (or lemon juice)

For this salad, it is also necessary to first wash the lentils and drain them before putting them into a pot, covering them generously with cold water and allowing them to simmer for twenty to thirty minutes, until they are firm to the bite but not mushy. I advise stirring the pot now and then to check if they haven't absorbed too much liquid; if that is the case, add more. Once they are done, wash the lentils in cold water and drain them in a sieve before putting them into the bowl in which you want to ultimately dress them. In the meantime, prepare the sauce, whose flavoring distinguishes it from the classic European *soffritto*. Heat the coconut oil in a medium-size pan, add the finely chopped onions and carrots, and sauté these over medium heat for about seven minutes before adding the chopped garlic, ginger, lemongrass, and kaffir lime leaves as well. After about five minutes, season the *soffritto* with curry powder, and allow the sauce to simmer until all the aromas have blended together nicely. Deglaze the pan with the cream, and pour the sauce over the lentils, mix well, and season with salt and pepper. If you want more tartness, you can add a bit of lime juice.

NOTE: A lentil salad will keep for several days in the refrigerator. It not only complements cold cuts but can serve as the bed for a poached egg, smoked salmon, and smoked trout. The most perfect match of all, however, is lentils with seared scallops. And of course, any green salad will become richer in texture and taste if lentils are added.

BUTTON MUSHROOMS WITH
KAFFIR LIME LEAVES FOR 2–3

500 g (5 cups) brown button mushrooms	zest of 1 lime
2 tbsp. olive oil	1 garlic clove
1 tbsp. lime juice	1 tsp. kaffir lime leaves, finely chopped
2 tbsp. white balsamic vinegar	fleur de sel and pepper

Prepared in a variety of ways, mushrooms will ennoble any salad, making it something more than ordinary. You can cut shitake into thick slices; toss them with olive oil, salt, and pepper; and roast them in the oven (for ten minutes at 180°C/350°F). You can sauté chanterelle in a pan with onions and lemon juice and then use the excess juice that has formed to make a vinaigrette with olive oil and vinegar. A salad, using raw mushrooms cut into delicate slices, in turn is a staple of classic French bistro cooking. The vinaigrette usually consists of olive oil, garlic, and lemon juice with a sprinkle of chopped parsley, basil, tarragon, and perhaps some Parmesan shavings. The critical step is to let the mushrooms absorb the dressing to the extent that it actually cooks them, endowing them with a chewy, moist texture. My fondness for Asian herbs, along with the fact that I once found a bunch of kaffir lime leaves in my refrigerator that needed to be used up, inspired the following variation.

First clean the mushrooms assiduously with a moistened paper towel (or a mushroom brush, if you own such a gadget), dry them thoroughly with more paper towels, cut off the stem, and then cut them into delicate slices. Whisk together the olive oil, the balsamic vinegar, the juice and zest of a lime, the chopped (or pressed) garlic, and the kaffir lime leaves. To chop these, first fold each leaf in half and cut away the hard inner stem before chopping them with a broad kitchen knife until they take on a powdery texture. While mixing the mushrooms with the vinaigrette, make sure that they are all evenly coated. Then let them rest for at least one hour (and up to three hours). You will soon be privy to a marvelous transformation. The mushrooms that initially were light, dry, and firm slowly soak up the dressing, becoming ever darker and softer in the process and imbued with aroma.

AVOCADO WITH SHRIMP FOR 2–3

2 avocado

200 g (7 ounces) small shrimp, peeled

2 tbsp. crème fraîche

1 tsp. lemon juice

1 tbsp. mayonnaise (preferably homemade)

1 tbsp. white balsamic vinegar (or pomegranate molasses)

1 tbsp. chives, chopped

celery salt and pepper

An avocado, cut in half and filled with a vinaigrette, also belongs to the classic French bistro cooking, the first cuisine I tried to emulate. In the case of this dish, what I was particularly impressed with was the dexterity required to eat it. After all, you not only have to cradle each avocado half gently in one hand; rather, using the spoon in the other, you have to make sure to catch just the right dose of the vinaigrette (prepared with olive oil, lemon juice, and mustard) while scooping out some of the light-green flesh of the fruit to have enough for the final bite. You could of course vary the vinaigrette and use the marvelous combination of calamansi vinegar and pistachio oil, which I describe in the recipe for salmon carpaccio (also in this chapter) to fill your avocado halves and—why not—dust them with roasted sesame seeds and chopped cilantro.

But if you don't want to spoon out your avocado, you can also quarter it, remove the pit, peel it and cut it into slices or dice it. For the dressing, I suggest mixing together crème fraîche with lemon juice, white balsamic vinegar, and chives (which I usually simply cut with my kitchen scissors) and seasoning with celery salt and pepper. I then gently fold the avocado into the sauce, making sure not to crush or mash it. Only in the end do I add a handful of cooked small shrimp (or crayfish), in turn carefully folding these into the avocado slices, before seasoning with more salt and pepper and, if necessary, using lemon juice to adjust the tartness. I sometimes even use surimi (the Japanese surrogate for crab made of minced fish, familiar to us as the centerpiece of any California sushi roll) and cut this into delicate strips before folding them into the avocado.

SALADE NIÇOISE WITH SEARED TUNA FOR 2

150 g (5 ounces) raw tuna

2 hard-boiled eggs

200 g (2 cups) haricots verts (or other
   green beans)

8 pitted black olives

2 artichoke hearts preserved in oil

1 tbsp. capers

100 g (1 cup) cherry tomatoes (or
   sun-dried tomatoes preserved in oil)

2–3 handfuls mixed salad leaves

10 basil leaves

3 tbsp. olive oil

1 tbsp. white balsamic vinegar
   (or apple vinegar)

½ tsp. mustard

chili salt and pepper

The first association I have with the combination of fish and salad is invariably the one from Nice. The traditional salade Niçoise, however, uses canned tuna, mixed together with potatoes, haricots verts, tomatoes, hard-boiled eggs, and salad greens. Given that you have probably found this dish only too often prepared in a slapdash manner, packaged in a plastic container at many a fast food counter, it is easy to think you have reached a point of saturation. But the idea that you could also prepare this salad with a tuna tataki gives new life to what has become all too quotidian.

As with the beef tartare, at stake is a somewhat elaborate *mise en place* in advance, while the ingredients don't come to be assembled until the very end. In my recipe, the eggs should be soft-boiled so that the egg yolk can blend more smoothly with the salad dressing. After plunging them into cold water, peel and quarter them and put them aside. Wash the haricots verts, trim them at the bottom and the top, cut them into bite-size pieces, and cook them in boiling salt water, about ten minutes. Plunge them into cold water and then drain them in a sieve. While they cook, you can deseed the olives and cut them into delicate slices; wash the capers and chop them. Also wash the cherry tomatoes and quarter them, or if you are using preserved sun-dried tomatoes, drain them and cut them into slices. The preserved artichokes also need to be drained before you can quarter them. Pluck the basil leaves from their stems and wash them, together with the other salad leaves, before drying them in a salad spinner. Finally, for the dressing, whisk together the olive oil, white balsamic vinegar, and mustard, and season with chili salt and pepper. Now you can assemble all the ingredients in one bowl, pour the vinaigrette over the salad, and toss it gently. The different flavors are allowed to fuse with each other while you prepare the tataki. Wash the tuna, pat it dry with paper towels, and then sear it in a hot pan in rapeseed oil, about one minute on each side. It is meant to form a thin crust on the outside while staying raw inside. Only then can you take it out of the pan, season with salt and pepper, cut it into mouth-size slices, and place it on top of the rest of the salad—its glorious final resting place.

CHERMOULA PRAWNS WITH ORANGES FOR 2

8 prawns, peeled

2 blood oranges

8 sun-dried tomatoes

1 thumb-size piece of ginger, peeled
and chopped

2 big shallots, chopped

1 garlic clove, chopped

5 tbsp. olive oil

1 tsp. ground cumin

1 tsp. mild paprika

3 tbsp. cilantro leaves, chopped

From Marcella Hazan, queen of Italian cookbooks, I have learned how easy it is to transform a salad, composed of delicately grated raw vegetables, into a festive dish by simply adding shrimp. In her recipes, these crustaceans are usually cooked in their shell, then peeled and, still warm, marinated in olive oil and lemon juice for an hour. Unfortunately, the shrimp I am compelled to buy, living in a landlocked city, are usually frozen, and so it was by serendipity that I discovered another way to prepare them. I had forgotten to defrost my shrimp and, impatient to begin cooking, grabbed my water kettle. Placing the shrimp in a bowl first, I covered them with boiling water and allowed them to steep in it for several minutes. To my great delight, they quickly turned pink, and although they were no longer raw inside, the shrimp meet had remained crisp.

For this Moroccan-inspired dish, place the prawns in a bowl and pour boiling water over them. Wait a few minutes until the water has become lukewarm and the prawns have turned pink before taking them out and peeling them. If they were frozen, they may take a bit longer. Pour boiling water over the sun-dried tomatoes as well and allow them to steep for thirty minutes. In the meantime, prepare the oranges. Peel them and then, with a sharp kitchen knife, remove the skin from each segment so that you only have the flesh of the fruit. I admit, to fillet an orange is an arduous task, best performed over a bowl to catch the juice, but it is definitely worth the labor. If, however, you don't have the patience for it, simply divide the orange into its individual segments, but remove the thick skin beneath the outer peel. To prepare the chermoula paste, peel and chop the shallots, the ginger, and the garlic before blending them together with the tomatoes, the spices, and the olive oil in a food processor (or with an immersion blender) until you have a smooth consistency. Then cover the prawns and the oranges with the chermoula paste. It is best to use your hands, because only then can you be certain that all the pieces are evenly coated. Garnish the salad with chopped cilantro.

NOTE: As a basic principle, what you are looking for in a salad dressing is a balance between oil, tart acidity, and pungency. Seasoning with salt and pepper serves to bring out and enhance these flavors. I must admit, I have a tendency to buy bottles of nut oil all the time, simply because I like a particular smell or the fact that it is as yet unfamiliar to me makes it particularly appealing. If you have too many different oils in your pantry, however, they may go rancid more quickly than you can finish them, and only too often I find myself tossing away a bottle before it has actually been used up. For this reason I have tried to discipline myself and now concentrate primarily on those types of oil that I really use often. Those oils that I won't be using every day—such as pistachio oil, argan oil, or truffle oil—I try, in turn, to buy in only small amounts. Because I almost always find the sour taste of vinegar too acerbic, I prefer dark and white Italian balsamic vinegar as well as fruit balsamic vinegar, which in the last few years has begun to appear in gourmet shops in ever bolder varieties. The fact that I am known among my friends for my salad dressing doesn't, however, only have to do with the fact that I would never economize when it comes to the quality of the oils and balsamic vinegars I use, much as I wouldn't regarding the wine I pour into a stew. It also has to do with the fact that I discovered early on in my cooking years that the mustard, which is obligatory in the classic French vinaigrette, can be replaced beautifully with olive paste or with an herb or nut pesto. Finding the perfect balance between acidity and saltiness requires a very delicate touch, and so I find that, as I whisk together the different components for my vinaigrette, I have to repeatedly stop and taste. And given that adding the salad ingredients will once more change the flavor, you always want to correct your spicing once you have dressed it.

RAW PASTA SAUCES

Mild Pasta Salad | *Spicy Pasta Salad* | *Pasta with Raw Tuna*

Pasta is one of my favorite dishes, so I am always looking for new ways to prepare it. The sauce, however, doesn't always have to be cooked but can also consist of succulent ripe tomatoes, prepared as for a salad. For this dish don't choose a fresh, smooth egg noodle, because it isn't firm enough to absorb the raw ingredients, and the egg, moreover, doesn't supplement the raw vegetables very well. Instead, use a tubular type of pasta like penne or rigatoni, because the raw vegetable sauce can penetrate into its round interior rather than sliding off its side. The artisanal pasta (*lavorazione artigianale*) made popular through the Italian slow-food movement, which seeks to prevent the disappearance of local food traditions, may be a bit more expensive, but it is significantly better when it comes to both taste and bite. You can play around with the ingredients of a raw sauce for a pasta salad and decide to showcase a variety of herbs—basil, arugula, mint, or even tarragon. Or you can increase the vegetable factor by adding a mixture of chopped peppers (which I would always peel first), fennel, or preserved artichoke hearts to the cubed tomatoes. Although one would expect Parmesan to top off any pasta salad, you can omit the cheese and instead fold into your salad a ripe avocado, cut into small bites and seasoned with lemon juice and salt. There are no limits to the marriage between hot pasta; fresh, fruity olive oil; salad vegetables; and melting cheese. In the following, I offer two of my favorite variations.

MILD PASTA SALAD FOR 4

800 g (2 pounds) ripe tomatoes
1 fennel, finely chopped
1 garlic clove, finely chopped
1 bunch basil, sliced into fine strips
2 tbsp. mint leaves, chopped
8 tbsp. fruity olive oil

juice and zest of 1 lemon
1 piece of mozzarella, chopped into
    small cubes
500 g (1 pound) penne
salt and pepper

Hardly a dish can be prepared so simply and yet charm so consistently as a *pasta al insalata*. The ingredients, transformed by the heat the warm pasta releases, come together to produce a dish of wonderful textual consistency. Success lies in the details, or rather in the precision with which the few ingredients are carefully prepared. Cut the washed tomatoes into coarse cubes. If you choose cherry tomatoes or datterini tomatoes, you can halve or quarter them. The following rule of thumb applies: the riper the tomatoes are, the more flavorful your sauce will become. As regards the fennel, cut off the hard base and the upper stalks (but keep the fennel frond to one side). Then peel the outer skin to remove all brown bits as well as any tough fibers. After cutting it in half, use a small, curved kitchen knife to cut out the rest of the

Vintage silverware

triangular stem from the bottom of each part. Then chop the fennel into fairly delicate cubes, because otherwise it will overpower the taste of the tomatoes. Mix together the salad vegetables with the finely chopped (or mashed) garlic, the herbs, the olive oil, and the juice and zest of a lemon in a bowl, making sure that everything is evenly coated before seasoning with salt and pepper.

I find it advisable to prepare the salad first so that the tomatoes and the other vegetables can absorb the flavor of the vinaigrette while the pasta is cooked al dente in boiling salt water. After draining the hot pasta, I immediately pour it into the bowl with the tomato salad, then add the chopped mozzarella and mix everything thoroughly before once more seasoning with salt and pepper. It pays off to let the pasta rest for a few minutes so that the flavors can develop and the mozzarella can melt completely. If you want a stronger cheese effect, by all means, grate a bit of Parmesan over the pasta salad before serving.

SPICY PASTA SALAD FOR 4

800 g (2 pounds) ripe tomatoes
10 pitted black olives, cut into fine
  slices
25 g (1 ounce) anchovies, finely
  chopped

10 tbsp. fruity olive oil
3 tbsp. white balsamic vinegar
2 tbsp. tomato flakes (or tomato
  paste)
1 tsp. chili oil

1 bunch basil
1 piece of buffalo mozzarella,
   chopped into cubes

500 g (1 pound) penne
Parmesan, grated
salt and pepper

For this spicier variation, cut the tomatoes into bite-size pieces. The olives must be seeded and cut into fine strips, the anchovies finely chopped. Put the raw ingredients into a bowl large enough to hold the pasta as well. In another bowl, whisk together the olive oil with the balsamic vinegar, the tomato flakes (or tomato paste), and the chili oil until you have a creamy dressing. Pour the dressing over the tomatoes before adding the basil, cut into delicate strips, as well as the burrata (or mozzarella), cut into cubes. Make sure all the ingredients are evenly coated with the dressing. As suggested in the first recipe, it is advisable to prepare the salad first so that the flavor can intensify while the penne (or another tubular pasta) are being cooked al dente in boiling salt water. After draining the pasta, fold it immediately into the tomatoes, and allow it to rest for a few moments so that the flavor can intensify and the cheese can melt. Finally, season the pasta salad with salt and pepper, and if you want to enhance the taste of cheese, grate Parmesan over the finished dish.

PASTA WITH RAW TUNA FOR 2

200 g (7 ounces) ultrathin spaghettini
300 g (11 ounces) raw tuna, sushi
   quality
2 tbsp. sesame oil

2 tbsp. olive oil
1 tsp. chili-garlic sauce (*tobanjan*)
2 tbsp. soy sauce
chives

A very different approach to a raw pasta salad lies at the heart of this Japanese-inspired recipe. Its charm consists of the velvety consistency, which the raw tuna assumes the minute it comes in touch with the hot pasta. For this reason, if you are serving it at a dinner party, this dish can be combined nicely with a fish tartare or carpaccio. It would be up to you to decide which is the starter and which the entrée.

In contrast to the Italian pasta salad, you want to use ultrathin spaghettini or *capelli d'angelo*. Cook the pasta al dente in boiling salt water before draining it in a colander and then putting it in a bowl in which it can be tossed comfortably. Then carefully fold the raw tuna, cut into long strips, into the pasta; the heat from the pasta will immediately begin to cook the fish. At this point, add the sesame oil and olive oil, mix it into the pasta, taking care, however, not to smash the tuna. To increase the spiciness of this dish, add the soy sauce and chili-garlic sauce (*tobanjan*), and one last time gently toss the pasta. If you can't find this Japanese sauce, you can use another Asian condiment containing chili and garlic. If the pasta isn't salty enough, I add a shot of soy sauce before cutting the chives directly over the dish with my kitchen scissors.

FRUIT

Orange Salad

There should always be a bowl filled with seasonal fruit on your kitchen table. This way you can not only enjoy the change in seasons; you also have a healthy answer to the dangerous temptation to nosh on something in between meals. On my own kitchen table, standing directly next to my fruit bowl, is also always a jar with unsalted nuts and dried fruit, because chips of all kinds have been banned. The oily spice of chips only encourages munchies without ever really satisfying this ravenous appetite.

Fresh fruit, moreover, often helps me solve the question of what to serve for dessert. As Alice Waters emphatically propagates in her cookbooks, nothing is as satisfying at the end of a meal as a perfect piece of fruit, which, according to her, you should restrain yourself from doing too much with. It is, of course, much easier to invoke impeccable fruit if one is living in California or France than anywhere else. Nevertheless, spontaneously throwing together different pieces of fruit can bear astonishing results. You should probably try to combine a variety of colors and textures, peel the fruit where necessary, and cut away the bruised or overripe bits, and then dice everything into bite-size pieces. If you toss it with a dressing—and for this you can use marmalade, diluted with water, or fruit syrup seasoned with lemon juice—you will have a refreshing salad.

If, in turn, the fresh fruit requires more processing because it is everything but immaculate, you can boost the flavor, perhaps even amplify it, by adding further ingredients. Combining apples, bananas, mandarins, pears, and dried dates, all cut into bite-size pieces, and dressing these with crème fraîche, vanilla extract, honey, lemon, and a shot of cognac leaves you with a vibrant dessert. Nuts, raisins soaked in grappa, and cherries preserved in a fruit schnapps all help transform a simple fruit salad into something a bit more special. Adding a fruit balsamic vinegar can also yield a combination of flavors, which will allow the fruit to reach the very perfection in taste it can't achieve on its own. While it has, sadly, become common to add sugar to strawberries these days because only then will they taste the way we expect sweet strawberries to taste, balsamic vinegar (or another heavy fruit balsamic vinegar) has the same effect. There is, however, a trick that will encourage the happy conversation between fruit and vinegar even further. Place the rinsed strawberries, cut in half or quartered, into a bowl and drizzle them with the balsamic vinegar, but under no circumstance should you use a spoon to stir them. Instead, place a cutting board, large enough to cover the entire bowl, on top of it, tap the strawberries against it so that, as they bounce up and down inside the covered bowl, they can they mingle with the vinegar. For a bit of pungent crunch, garnish the strawberries with some chopped mint leaves.

ORANGE SALAD FOR 2

2 oranges	1½ tbsp. lavender honey
2 tbsp. olive oil	1 pinch chili salt

By way of concluding this chapter, here is one recipe for a fruit salad whose utter simplicity is perfection. While this salad should rest about an hour before serving, it will also keep in the refrigerator overnight and can, therefore, be prepared in advance. It is best to prepare the dressing first by whisking the olive oil, honey, and chili salt in the bowl, in which you will later want to prepare the oranges. Then carefully peel the fruit. Because you want to make sure that you are removing not only the outer peel but also the thin white skin beneath it, first cut a layer off the top and bottom of each orange. Then peel it like you would an apple, by carefully gliding around the fruit with a sharp knife, from top to bottom. Each time you begin a new orbit, you want to make sure to insert the knife directly under the white skin to cut off the thin membrane separating the white bits and pieces from the fruit's flesh as well. It is best to work over the bowl in which you will later toss the salad to catch the juice as you peel the oranges. Cut these into slices before adding the dressing, then cover the bowl with plastic wrap and allow the orange salad to rest in a cool spot.

While it is, of course, possible to use any honey, consider that this is the flavor that will decisively influence the aromatic combination of the oranges, olive oil, and salt. You can try out whether you want to take the taste into a darker or a sweeter direction much as it is also worth experimenting with the salt you use. My sister, Susan, who, once I gave her this recipe, claims that she makes orange salad almost daily during the winter, however, insists that the best combination is lavender honey and chili salt.

♣ 2 ♣

THE PAN

Dishes Made Quickly

Pasta | Pot Stickers | Sautéed Vegetables |
Sliced Meat and Vegetables in the Pan | Sautéed in One Piece | Chopped |
From the Frying Pan into the Oven

When cooking in a pan on the stovetop, the first thing you need to be aware of is heat: everything depends on it. And so you also need courage to allow the cooking fat you are using to become really hot before adding your ingredients. In some cases, this may even mean that it actually begins to smoke. What makes frying in a pan such a sensuous experience is that this mode of cooking requires all the senses to come into play. With an eager—indeed, perhaps even a slightly anxious—gaze, you must intently follow the transformation taking place in the pan. The moment the ingredients come in contact with the hot fat in the pan, they begin to transform. At the same time, you must listen alertly to the sizzle and hissing accompanying this culinary emergence. Your sense of smell is deployed as well, because the sweetness or pungency of the odor emanating from the pan is key in helping you recognize whether the correct cooking time has been reached. Finally, you may want to use your fingers as well—gently touching a piece of meat or fish, for example—to check whether the texture is right before removing it from the pan.

However, precisely because the simplicity of pan searing or sautéing is predicated on everything happening very quickly, small details can have significant ramifications. Before setting in motion what is to take place in the pan, all the required ingredients should be ready at hand. With good reason, the classic art of cooking insists on a strict *mise en place*. I own numerous small bowls for the chopped herbs, pressed garlic, grated ginger, or the zest of a citrus fruit—along with all other shredded, sliced, or marinated ingredients—which I assiduously prepare before beginning to cook on the stovetop. Only if you pay precise attention to details when preparing, giving yourself enough time for meticulous peeling and chopping everything that you will be using later, can the event in the pan be successful. Fortunately, I learned to have my ingredients prepared in advance early during my student days.

As a student, pan-frying was my primary mode of cooking. During the last two years of my studies at Radcliffe College and Harvard University, I lived on the top floor of a professor's house. In the living room, one of the windowsills had been converted into a countertop, equipped with two small electric hot plates. In this cooking niche, there was, however, room for only one pot, one pan, and a medium-size chopping board. The tub in the bathroom had to serve as my kitchen sink. Because this meant carrying all dishes that needed to be washed across the hall, the utensils used for preparing dishes were best kept at a minimum. When, after finishing my master's degree, I returned to Munich to continue with my PhD, I finally got a kitchen of my own, but I still lacked sophisticated cooking equipment. Throughout my years as a graduate student, my cooking was limited to a few pots and pans, as I spent the money I earned as an assistant at the English Department on books instead.

Since then, I have accrued a veritable arsenal of gadgets, appliances, and cookware in my kitchen along with an array of precious silver overlay glass dishes, a sundry of glass refrigerator jars, and stacks of Pyrex bowls from the 1950s—the spoils from countless trips to flea markets. On the walls of my kitchen hang two magnetic racks with more than twenty knives. These have sometimes impressed but more often than not intimidated many a visitor. Indeed, my kitchen is the first room I tend to show to guests who have never visited my apartment before. While doing so, I like to recall the scene in Hitchcock's psychothriller *Rebecca*, in which the housekeeper, Mrs. Danvers, leads the second wife of Maxim de Winter (played by Joan Fontaine) into the suite of her predecessor. Evoking the mood of a shared clandestine intimacy, she proceeds to open all the closets to reveal the splendid wardrobe of the deceased woman. With a similar panache, I also demonstrate the elegant pull-out shelves of my pantry and proudly point out the tagine and the couscoussière sitting prominently on one of my shelves before drawing attention to the battery of electric kitchen appliances to one side of my stove and the rich assortment of pots and pans stored away in my kitchen cupboards. I elicit the most astonishment, however, when I pull out the drawer in which I keep all the useful (and unnecessary) kitchen gadgets that I have painstakingly accumulated from around the world over many years. This palette of instruments stands at the ready for my kitchen operations.

Ingredients scattered on the kitchen table

A memory of the austerity of my student years resurfaces whenever I spend time abroad as a visiting scholar, although in a slightly eccentric inflection. Convinced that I could never live longer than a few days in any residence without my two favorite knives, my zester, the mixer I need to make salad dressings, and above all a small frying pan, I now carry these utensils with me wherever I go abroad. Culinary dandy that I am, cooking is what allows me to conjure up a sense of familiarity, regardless of where I am located. The fact that even today I am unwilling to forego inviting guests to my kitchen table, despite a busy workday, also goes back to my early years at the University of Munich as well. At that time, in my own kitchen as well as in the kitchens of my fellow graduate students, I learned to relish intense conversations that require the intimacy of a small, private space to evolve. Dishes quickly prepared on the stovetop were particularly popular among us students because they allowed us to concentrate more intensely on our avid discussions.

Yet during my early years as an academic, it was also essential for me to prepare dishes quickly because of my cat, Rosa, who had an indomitable desire for raw chicken, although, for dietary reasons, this was absolutely forbidden. As the self-declared mistress of the apartment, she would jump onto the kitchen table whenever her nose told her I was preparing this prohibited food, and she never grew tired in her effort to steal the chicken I had just meticulously cut into slices. My relentless scolding only served to increase her ravenous desire for transgression. Eventually, she managed to scratch the rubber on the door of my refrigerator with her claws to such a degree that she was able to open it on her own. One night, she decided to steal a raw chicken breast and drag it clear across the apartment, only to place it gently onto my pillow. I couldn't even scold her when I woke up the next morning with this strange gift next to my face. After all, a part of me was reflected in this gesture. Affection undoubtedly expresses itself in a willingness to share with someone else the food you are particularly fond of.

Although I have, since then, been able to match my cooking ingredients with the increase in my financial means, certain preferences have lingered on from these early austere years. Owing to my budget at the time, soggy fish fingers with their sad coating, stored in my deep freeze, were a vital staple in my everyday cooking. The anticipation of consuming them, crisply fried, with an herb-flavored yogurt dip, always elicited joy during the arduous task of writing my dissertation. Since then, this ordinary fish has been replaced by the precious Dover sole, served in a butter and white wine sauce, garnished with chopped parsley. Or it has made way for equally luxurious scallops, pan-seared ever so briefly in a delicate flour coating. From my student years, I also retain a sentimental hankering for pan-fried chicken. In those days I often found myself removing the unsavory tendons from countless chicken breasts before slicing them and sautéing them in a pan. Sometimes they would crown a salad. Other times, accompanied by mushrooms and gherkins and deglazed with cream, they were my poor woman's version of the fancier beef stroganoff, a dish that I always associated with the elegant restaurants in European grand hotels but that I could only afford on very festive occasions. Although it is grown out of fashion, this beef stroganoff has never lost its delectable charm. The patina of another time when it was something truly precious adheres to it.

Above all, however, cooking in the pan is associated with the dish that like no other produces a sense of comfort—pasta. The guilt inherent in knowing that one is eating "something forbidden" is part of the indulgence. Nutritionists, of course, have argued that pasta in and of itself is not the problem for those who must watch their weight but rather the sauce with which it is served. Indeed, the classic combination of butter, cream, and Parmesan, which will ennoble any ravioli, is to be staunchly avoided—as is, of course, the equally classic carbonara sauce, which calls for crisp bacon bits to steep in cream at a low temperature, infusing the sauce with a smoky, salty flavor before Parmesan and egg yolk are added. And yet, from the very beginning, nothing has spurred my culinary creativity quite as consistently as thinking about how to vary a standard pasta sauce by adding different vegetables to the *soffritto* base consisting of chopped onions, garlic, and bacon. The seasons invariably dictate the combinations: fresh peas with asparagus in spring, tomatoes and zucchini with thyme in the summer, chanterelles with parsley in the fall. And to this day, a penchant for guilty pleasures is always most pronounced when, in the decisive moment, my culinary desire is able to outwit my superego and I add, as a final touch, a serious shot of cream to my pasta sauce.

When I moved to Switzerland, where, along with diverse types of butter, I could find the infamous *double crème de Gruyère* (with 45 percent fat content) in any supermarket, it opened up entirely new perspectives on my extravagant pleasure principle. I quickly became convinced that, enriched with cream, nothing fried in a pan can really fail. The smooth sweetness and supple consistency of butter or cream added to sautéed ingredients are what make these dishes so thoroughly comforting. Alessandra, a colleague from the University of Bergamo, gave me the fitting label for the enjoyment that the combination of fat and carbohydrates, so typical of Northern Italian food, affords. She calls it "evil food," and she begins to beam with pleasure each time she recalls the cheese-and-ham *tosti* that her mother used to make for her whenever her father was away on business trips. Indeed, one might surmise that it is precisely because the fat deployed at the beginning and end of any dish made in a pan belongs to the realm of evil that these dishes are so satisfying. By openly admitting that the enjoyment is transgressive, their value is actually enhanced. At times, I admit, reason prevails, and I experiment with pan recipes that require neither butter nor cream. However, as fat has recently had a comeback in nutrition science, I have blithely returned to the first principle of French cuisine: only butter, generously deployed, can give the proper taste to a dish. Any guilty feelings that may lurk in the background serve to sweeten the pleasure afforded.

While growing up in Munich, I did, however, also discover the delights of a less "evil" type of pan cooking—the Asian stir-fry. My parents were good friends with a couple that, upon emigrating from Hong Kong, had opened up one of the first Chinese restaurants in Schwabing, a borough in the northern part of the city. My family would often gather there for Sunday lunch. As a result of the food envy that tended to overcome my siblings on such occasions, we would pounce on each dish that the waiter brought to the table, as if afraid the others would take more than their share. Just as a fear of not getting my full share spurred my own greed at the time, a ravenous appetite still flickers up today when I prepare these dishes. Only during my trips to Southeast Asia, however, did I fully grasp the art of the stir-fry. This mode of food preparation corresponds to the landscape as well as the simplicity of the living conditions there. Along many roadsides as well as canopied squares, one finds rows of small stands where, at any hour of the day, a dish will emerge within seconds in front of the eyes of the eager guests. Often, all it takes is for the ingredients to come into contact briefly with the hot oil, a vigorous swirling of the wok, and the addition of some condiments. The steam that rises up from the smoking cooking vessel matches the hazy light of the scenery.

As exotic as this technique appeared to me during my own first attempts at cooking with a wok, it soon reminded me of my old cast-iron pan, which has accompanied me for so many years. My fondness for fusion cooking, for which this chapter contains several examples, thus corresponds to my sustained search for new variations on familiar pan dishes. Indeed, an encounter between Asian aromas and the continental European *double crème de Gruyère* can consistently lead to an unexpected sense of pleasure.

☙

More than is the case with other modes of food preparation, a binary logic presides over the possibilities that cooking in a pan offers. This mode of cooking reminds me of the structuralist analysis of narrative texts with which my own studies in literature began. Every story, after all, begins with a character faced with making a choice that, once the decision has been made, will, in turn, open up several new possible actions. Once the character has decided which of the available paths to take, this particular sequence finds closure, and yet so as to allow the narrative to continue, the next situation requiring a new decision to be made soon emerges. Applying this structuralist description of narrative bifurcation to cooking in the pan, one might say that the basic decision on which all else depends must address the size of the main ingredient. Do you want to fry it as a whole, or do you want to reduce its size instead by slicing it into strips, cutting it into cubes, or chopping it?

While the point in frying in the pan is the wonderful contrast between the crispy crust and the juicy interior, this immediately calls for new decisions to be made—namely, the amount of movement you want in the pan. If you are frying an ingredient in one piece, you usually want to turn it over only once. Because, in the course of browning, you want your ingredient to take on an even, crispy surface, you must wait patiently for this to happen. The right moment to flip over the piece of meat, poultry, or fish is when it has already begun to detach from the base of the pan. If your ingredient has absorbed the fat too quickly and it looks as if it might burn, you can readily add more fat, deftly regulating the temperature, however, so that the pan does not lose its heat.

Sautéing, in turn, is a technique in which, by briskly tossing or stirring sliced or chopped ingredients, they are kept in motion. As the French word *sauter* implies, the pieces are meant "to jump" in the pan. This, however, entails further decisions to be made regarding the exact amount of movement required for a particular dish. To sauté implies a balance between stillness and movement, especially if you initially brown a sliced ingredient first one and then the other side before flipping them over frequently until they are done. The movement in the latter stage prevents the ingredients from forming an all-too-thick crust and ensures that the individual pieces are cooked evenly. You can, however, also keep the ingredients in constant motion from the beginning, as in the Asian stir-fry. In this case, the sliced or chopped ingredients, upon coming in contact with the extremely hot oil, immediately form a crust while remaining juicy inside.

The desired texture of the crust prompts further decisions. Are you going to fry an ingredient that, like bacon, is robust enough to stand very hot oil on its own? Or have you chosen a more fragile ingredient that requires you to dust it with seasoned flour—or perhaps an even thicker coating of bread crumbs and egg—to protect it from the hot pan? In each case, you must bear in mind that moisture prevents proper browning. Thus if you want to fry rather than braise your ingredients, they must be thoroughly dry. Dusting with flour preempts a moist surface. Adding salt too early may, in turn, produce liquid that will hinder the development of surface crispiness.

The charm of any coating consists, of course, primarily of the scrumptious crispy skin that forms as it absorbs the savory fat in the process of frying. If, in turn, you decide against this "evil" envelopment, you face yet another decision. Are you going to fry your ingredients on their own? Or do you, in order to achieve a softer consistency, want to add some liquid in which your ingredients can sweat? The decision you make depends, of course, on whether the ingredient itself will release liquid after coming in contact with the hot oil, such as mushrooms, but in any case, the liquid that will form in the pan needs to be reduced. Or do your ingredients, such as carrots, require some additional fluid in which to simmer in order to become soft? The best choice may be a hybrid mode of preparation. For example, you may decide to first steam or poach an ingredient and then glaze it in the pan with oil, herbs, and spices. Or you may decide to first sear your ingredient in the pan and then allow it to finish cooking in the oven at a low, even temperature.

As browning meat, fish, or vegetables affords flavor, you should never forget to deglaze the tasty brown bits that form on the inner surface of your frying pan. In the course of browning, these have taken on an intense flavor that will allow you to make a sauce within seconds. But you may also decide to add another step, and with your fried ingredients resting on a preheated plate, you may want to sauté finely chopped garlic, onions, ginger, or celery in the fat remaining in the pan before adding some liquid to enhance the flavor they carry even further. Yet another decision is necessary as there is a choice between using broth, balsamic vinegar, wine, or a spirit. To do this, you should use a wooden spoon to meticulously stir the brown bits sticking on the bottom of the pan and reduce the sauce until it has assumed a consistent density. Then there is still one final decision to make. If you want to enhance the sweetness and make your sauce creamier, beat in some cold butter. However, to prevent the sauce from curdling, you should remove the pan from the flame (or burner). The residual heat of the pan is sufficient for this crowning step.

One more basic element must be added to the four elements—heat, fat, precise *mise en place*, and deft timing—discussed so far. When pan-frying, the correct pan is essential. Quality counts. If you use pans that do not evenly conduct the heat when frying, browning, and searing, your dish will easily burn or your ingredients will hopelessly stick to the inner surface. If, in the proverbial translocation to a desert island, I had to reduce my arsenal to the few pans without which I could not manage to cook, I would take with me my Le Creuset cast-iron pan (twenty-four centimeters or nine and a half inches) in which to fry a steak, a hamburger, or an egg. To this I would add two nonstick, stainless-steel frying pans (twenty-one centimeters and twenty-seven centimeters, or eight and a half and ten and a half inches). Because they have flared but relatively low sides, I would add a classic sauté pan (twenty-one centimeters or eight and a half inches) whose rounded side is eight centimeters (three and one-fourth inches), with a lid that fits snugly so that I can produce steam when necessary.

If pressed, I could further reduce my pans to just a wok, in which, strictly speaking, I can do far more than simply stir-fry. In a pinch, a wok can even serve to boil water for pasta. But I love my pans, if only because they offer me such a wide palate of choices when it comes to how and what I will fry on my stovetop. Gazing at my treasure trove of pans before I even begin with the preparation of a dish allows me to pause and play through in my mind the cooking process I am about to embark on. If I want my shrimp or sliced meat to jump in hot oil, I will choose a pan with a higher side. This way, my ingredients won't leap out of the pan when I toss them rapidly. If, in turn, I want to braise vegetables in liquid after having browned them, I need not only a pan with a higher side but also one with a lid that fits properly so that the liquid won't splash all over my stovetop. If, in turn, at issue is searing an ingredient on both sides, a pan with a broader, flat bottom is more suitable. This affords the piece of meat or fish enough space to quickly develop an evenly crispy surface.

Decisive for the choice of the right pan is, thus, above all the size of the pan bottom. If you want to fry your ingredients rather than braise them, the pan must never be crowded. If the ingredients lie too close to each other, you will get moist steam that will prevent them from becoming crisp. You also need a spacious pan so that all ingredients are in direct contact with the hot inner surface. If you overcrowd your pan, not only will the overlapping ingredients not brown evenly, but because they won't absorb the proper amount of oil as you begin to sauté, they will also most probably stick to the pan bottom. For this reason, if you are frying a larger number of ingredients, it might be necessary to work in batches. The gain in taste and consistency always makes up for the extra time this may take. If, in turn, your pan is too big, you run the risk of the oil not only burning in the places left empty but also contaminating the taste of the other ingredients.

At a crucial moment in his monologue about whether it is preferable to be or not to be, Shakespeare's Hamlet calls out, "Readiness is all." In pan cooking, too, readiness for action is key, in the sense that success depends on whether you are fully prepared to devote your entire attention to what is happening on the stovetop. Part and parcel of this is perfect timing. I confess that I have often been impatient—and I continue to be so even today. But in these few minutes, you must reign in your own eagerness. Every ingredient you put into a cold pan with cold oil runs the risk of sticking to the bottom. As a rule of thumb, always heat your pan while it is still empty and only add the oil (or other fat) after a brief minute, unless the recipe explicitly instructs you to do otherwise. Furthermore, only use as much fat as you need to produce a thin film on the bottom of the pan while turning it gently back and forth over the heat. Allow the fat to heat until it begins to glisten and ripple like a wave so that, as you continue to rotate your pan, the fat or oil glides smoothly across the bottom. If ocular proof is not enough for you, use a drop of water to check whether the pan has reached the required temperature. If you hear a sizzle when the drop comes in contact with the hot fat, your pan is ready.

PASTA

Spaghetti with Barba Di Frate |
Tagliatelle with Figs, Chili, and Cream | *Linguine with Ricotta and Saffron* |
Penne with Tomatoes, Vodka, and Cream

The charm in preparing a ragù Bolognese stems, in part, from the way that all the ingredients are allowed to simmer in the pot for several hours while the different flavors come to be fully amalgamated. The beauty in preparing a pasta sauce in a pan, in turn, consists in the *soffritto*. It serves as the foundation for countless combinations of vegetables, meat, or poultry, which added one after the other, produce several layers of flavor. For a *soffritto*, you can begin either by simply sautéing chopped onions in butter or by using finely chopped garlic and a pinch of chili flakes, combined with chopped onions. If you find garlic to be too intense in flavor, you can replace it with ginger or finely chopped celery. In any case, it is essential that you sauté the *soffritto* over low heat for several minutes (and not over high heat for only a few seconds). The result is a more pronounced infusion of the olive oil or butter. To the *soffritto*, you then first add, in rapid succession, further aromatic ingredients, allowing these to melt into the oil. Only then do you add the main ingredient, which rather than blending completely with the other ingredients, should visually stand out. To round off the dish with a final layer of flavor, sprinkle it with chopped herbs.

For a more savory sauce, I like to use bacon or prosciutto slivers in my *soffritto* as my additional aromatic ingredient, allowing these to become crisp before adding the sliced or cubed vegetables (mushrooms, peas, zucchini, or tomatoes). After these have simmered in the pan for about ten minutes, I will add, as my fourth flavor element, chopped herbs (cilantro, basil, or parsley), allowing these to infuse the sauce only very briefly before I mix it with the cooked pasta. I may, however, decide instead to use a mixture of anchovies, capers, and olives as my second layer of flavor before adding parboiled cauliflower, sun-dried tomatoes, or porcini mushrooms as my main element, allowing these vegetables to simmer in a bit of broth before chopped herbs come into play as the final aromatic touch. If, in turn, I decide to go for a more "drunken" sauce, I will begin with a *soffritto* consisting of olive oil and bacon (or pancetta), then add strips of radicchio (or another leaf vegetable) and sauté until they are soft before deglazing them with red wine, reducing the sauce, and as the creaming third element, adding mascarpone. Chopped parsley, along with grated Parmesan (obligatory in so many pasta recipes), serves to round off the dish. Of course, when looking for ingredients to accompany pasta, I do not limit myself to sautéed vegetables, meat, or seafood. The Asian stir-fry can also be thought of as a pasta dish and—fully in line with the spirit of fusion cooking—be reinterpreted.

If you fastidiously abide by a few basic rules, cooking pasta can never go wrong. The first thing you want to remember is that pasta needs a lot of water so that it can move about freely while cooking. Only if you use abundant water will long spaghetti cook evenly. Otherwise, some will be cooked, others not. When cooking ultrathin tagliatelle, in turn, abundant water prevents them from morphing into a gooey lump. For a pound of pasta, count four and a half liters (eighteen cups) of water and one and a half tablespoons of salt. Even when you are cooking smaller amounts of pasta, never use less than three liters (twelve cups) of water. From years and years of usage, the pot in which I always cook my pasta has formed a mark on the inner side so that I now no longer need to measure how much water is required. Another thing to remember is that you should salt the water only after it has begun to boil and that the water must be brought to a boil again before adding the pasta. Afterward, cover the pot briefly to make sure that the water quickly comes to a boil once more, but then take the lid off. It is crucial not only that you stir the pasta with a long wooden spoon so as to make sure that all the noodles are fully submerged in the boiling salt water but also that you stir the pasta at regular intervals to prevent the individual noodles from sticking to each other. It is not advisable to add olive oil to the water as this merely produces a pool of fat on the water surface. A further word of warning: the cooking time given on the package should be treated merely as an approximate value. Because you can only determine when pasta has been cooked to perfection by intermittently tasting a piece, you must remain close to the stovetop. In the following recipes, the pasta is meant to steep in the hot sauce, so it should always be cooked al dente. Unless you have opted for the Japanese way of preparing noodles, drain pasta in a kitchen strainer but never rinse pasta with cold water. Pasta should still be hot when added to the sauce. It is usually advisable, however, to use pasta tongs so that, having transferred the pasta to the strainer, you can retain some of the salt water. This may come in handy if you want to give a creamy finish to your sauce.

SPAGHETTI WITH *BARBA DI FRATE* FOR 2

1 bunch *barba di frate* (Italian agretti), around 250 g (½ pound) (or very thin asparagus and chervil)

2 tbsp. olive oil

2 anchovy fillets

1 garlic clove, chopped

1 tbsp. capers, chopped

¼ tbsp. chili flakes

250 g (½ pound) spaghetti

1 tbsp. lemon juice or verjus

salt and pepper

butter

parsley

For the longest time, I didn't quite know what to do with the bundles of *barba di frate* that show up on our farmers' markets at the very end of the winter and remain available throughout spring. The long green blades reminded me of thick chives, and so I thought they were only good to garnish a soup or a sauce. Then my friend Daniela told me about an enchantingly simple mode of preparation, which she assures me is equally suitable for other green vegetables such as broccoli, asparagus, or chard.

While waiting for the pasta water to come to a boil, use your time to thoroughly clean the *barba di frate*. This may seem a bit tedious, because in order to remove the soil and the roots, you have to not only generously cut off the bottom of the green blades but also meticulously wash each of them separately before draining them in a sieve. And yet there is something sensual about this preliminary work because as you clean the "monk's beard," it begins to unfold its dark, enticing odor. If the blades are fairly long, you can cut them in half. In a pan large enough to hold both the vegetable and the spaghetti, first warm the olive oil over medium heat, allow the anchovies to melt into it, and then stir in a splash of lemon juice, but don't add the chopped garlic until the anchovies have blended completely with the oil. Once the garlic has taken on a golden color, add the chopped capers as well as the chili flakes and, with a wooden spoon, stir everything together until you have an even consistency. As soon as the water begins to boil, season it generously with salt and begin to cook the spaghetti. Five minutes before they are done, add the *barba di frate*. This allows the spaghetti to already imbibe some of the tart flavor of the vegetables as both finish cooking. Make sure that while draining the pasta, you keep some of the salt water in a separate bowl. After tossing the spaghetti along with the *barba di frate* into the pan with the *soffritto*, add just enough of the cooking water until you have a smooth sauce. To finish off the dish, season with lemon juice, salt, and pepper, and to enhance the sweetness, fold a bit of butter into the pasta before sprinkling some chopped parsley on top.

TAGLIATELLE WITH FIGS, CHILI, AND CREAM FOR 2

300 g (11 ounces) tagliatelle	zest of 2 lemons
2 tbsp. olive oil	100 ml (½ cup) double cream
8 fresh figs	50 g (1½ ounces) Parmesan, grated
2 small, dried chili peppers	salt and pepper

The combination of rich cream, hot chili flakes, and sweet figs is both so simple and so elegant that I have made many guests happy with this sophisticated pasta dish. One friend who insisted on getting this recipe from me even confessed that she had raved about it to her husband that night in bed. He made her promise to cook it for him as soon as possible.

To begin, zest the two lemons and then, with a chef's knife, chop the strips into smaller pieces. Mix the juice of one of the lemons with the cream and season with salt and pepper. The cream can be prepared hours in advance and kept in the refrigerator. This allows it to more fully absorb the flavor of the lemon juice. Use the time it takes to cook the tagliatelle to wash the figs, trim them at the top and the bottom with a chef's knife, and then quarter them. Now you can heat a pan that is large enough to hold all the figs without crowding them. Add the olive oil and wait until it is fairly hot before adding the figs. Vigilance is called for at this point because, in order for the figs to caramelize evenly on all sides, you need to start tossing them gently. To prevent them from burning as you keep turning them, you may need to adjust the heat. Once the figs are properly browned, take the pan from the heat, crush the dried chili peppers with your fingers (you could also use a scant tablespoon of chili flakes), and mix these with the caramelized fruit. Let the figs rest a few minutes so that they can better absorb the chili flavor. Once the tagliatelle are done, add them to the figs and pour the lemon cream over them. After mixing everything together thoroughly, cover the pan and allow the pasta to steep in the sauce for about two minutes, without, however, reheating the pan. Before serving, sprinkle the tagliatelle with grated Parmesan.

LINGUINE WITH RICOTTA AND SAFFRON FOR 4

500 g (1 pound) linguine

250 g (1 cup) ricotta

1 big handful Parmesan, grated

1 generous pinch saffron threads

nutmeg, grated

salt and pepper

I have purposely kept directions for how much cheese to use in this dish a bit vague to underscore that what counts is the combination of ingredients, not the exact amount. According to my friend Francesca, who showed me how to make this pasta dish, the preparation is supposed to be casual—as though it were merely the accompaniment to an exciting conversation taking place around a kitchen table. Strictly speaking, of course, you don't really need a pan for this recipe either; simply a big bowl will do. However, given the binary logic around which this chapter is organized, I have included it as the exception to the rule, which, by virtue of contrast, allows me to define more precisely the basic principles for making pasta sauces in a pan. I have also included it because these linguine, prepared with hardly any effort at all, make such a stunningly satisfying meal.

While you wait for the linguine to cook, mix the ricotta with the grated Parmesan in a big kitchen bowl. Add the saffron threads at the very beginning so that they can merge with the ricotta and endow it with a delicate orange color. Don't use more than a pinch, however, because otherwise the taste of saffron will overpower all the other ingredients. Then while the linguine are cooking, keep adding a tablespoon of the boiling salted water to the ricotta until you have a perfectly creamy sauce without any lumps. Take care, however, not to add too much at once, because the sauce is supposed to be richly dense rather than watery. The amount of grated Parmesan can vary. Its main role is to give a spicy note to the sauce. As the final touch, season with salt, pepper, and a pinch of nutmeg. Once the linguine are done, toss them into the bowl and vigorously mix everything together with a wooden spoon, coating the pasta evenly with the creamy ricotta sauce. Sprinkle with a bit more of the grated Parmesan and salt to taste before serving.

PENNE WITH TOMATOES, VODKA, AND CREAM FOR 4

4 tbsp. olive oil

4 garlic cloves, chopped

½ tsp. dried chili flakes (or crushed red pepper)

800 g (28 ounces) canned tomatoes

500 g (1 pound) penne

250 ml (1 cup) La Gruyère double cream (or other heavy cream)

4 tbsp. vodka

1 bunch cilantro

Patricia Wells, for many years the famous Paris-based restaurant critic of the now defunct *International Herald Tribune*, describes in her book *Trattoria* how her husband would always beam when she told him she had made his favorite vodka pasta. I, too, have guests who, when asked what they would like me to cook for them, spontaneously wish for this dish. Ironically, the vodka itself isn't what makes up the charm of this sauce. Indeed, you don't necessarily notice at first that it is one of the ingredients. Instead, in combination with the chili flakes and the chopped cilantro, it offers an enigmatic addition to the overall flavor of the dish, leaving the uninitiated guest to ask why this creamy tomato sauce is so addictive.

Heat the oil together with the chopped garlic, the dried chili flakes, and a pinch of salt in a pan with tall sides and big enough to hold the penne. Sauté the garlic over medium heat for about three minutes, allowing it to take on a golden color but not to turn completely brown. Then add the tomatoes and allow them to simmer for about thirty minutes. From time to time, you should stir them with a wooden spoon, crushing them to produce a coarse, dense sauce. The tomato sauce can be prepared hours in advance and reheated over low temperature while the penne are cooking in the salt water. When they are finished, add them to the sauce, reduce the heat, pour the vodka over the penne, and mix thoroughly. Then pour the cream over the penne and once more mix thoroughly. Finally, cover the pan and, over very low heat, allow the penne to soak up the sauce, about five minutes. Before serving the dish, garnish with chopped cilantro.

POT STICKERS

Pot Stickers with Ground Pork and Bok Choy | Pot Stickers with Ricotta and Vegetables | Pot Stickers with Ricotta and Pears

Pot stickers, the Chinese ravioli filled with meat, seafood, or vegetables, are one of my great passions. Although they are fried twice—both before and then again after being steamed—they are meant not to stick to the pan but to form a tantalizing crispy bottom instead. For the longest time, they were so hard to find in European restaurants that every visit to New York City brought with it a thrill of anticipation. Finally, I would again be able to enjoy these delectable dumplings in Chinatown. I have probably tested thousands of different pot stickers, admittedly of varying quality, in an effort to perfect the consistency and flavor of my own filling. I have even made the wrappers from scratch, mixing water and flour into a gooey dough that invariably sticks to my fingers, but as one of my Chinese cookbooks puts it, this will take the better part of an afternoon. In New York City's Chinatown, dumpling skins were always readily available, with varying thickness and even different flavors. For many years, I would wait until the last day before flying home to buy as many packages as I could fit in my suitcase. They cost less than a dollar, but the long way they needed to travel before landing in my kitchen makes them precious. Since Asian dim sum has become fashionable in Zürich as well, I can now find dumpling wrappers (or gyoza skins) readily in the deep-freeze section of our own local Asian food markets. I no longer need to stock up. Defrosted, they will keep one week in the refrigerator.

POT STICKERS WITH GROUND PORK AND BOK CHOY FOR 30 PIECES

150 g (1¼ cups) bok choy (or napa cabbage), chopped very finely
50 g (2 ounces) dried porcini mushrooms, soaked in hot water
450 g (16 ounces) ground pork
1 tbsp. soy sauce
1 tbsp. fish sauce (*nam pla*)
1 tbsp. mirin (Japanese rice wine)
2 tbsp. shallots, very finely chopped
3 cm (½ inch) ginger, peeled and grated

1 tbsp. white sesame seeds
1 tbsp. cilantro, chopped
½ tsp. brown sugar (or palm sugar)
1 egg, beaten
1 red chili pepper, deseeded and chopped very finely (or ¼ tsp. dried chili flakes)
panko bread crumbs
2 tbsp. rapeseed oil (or canola oil)
1 package pot sticker or gyoza wrappers

FOR THE SAUCE

200 ml (1 cup) soy sauce
1 tbsp. sesame oil
100 ml (½ cup) apple balsamic vinegar (or Japanese rice vinegar)

1 tbsp. ketchup
1 tbsp. balsamic vinegar
1 tbsp. toasted white sesame seeds
chives, chopped

After much experimentation, I have developed a filling for my pot stickers that my friend Mic, who is as addicted to them as I am, has decided to call "pockets of delight." The key to success is that you chop all the ingredients for the filling as finely as you possibly can. This does, of course, mean longer and somewhat more cumbersome advance preparation, but only then will you get an even texture with a balanced flavor. After all, you want all the ingredients

Dishes on my kitchen table

to be blended together into a compact filling without any coarse bits protruding from it. The individual elements of the filling, in turn, can vary. Rather than ground pork, you could also use ground beef, lamb, or chicken. Smoked bamboo can be replaced with dried porcini or shitake mushrooms, soaked in hot water. If you can't find bok choy, you could use chard or savoy cabbage. The filling simply needs some leafy greens as a basis to give it the required bite.

Because, in the end, all the ingredients will be mixed together in a kitchen bowl, the sequence in which you chop them doesn't really matter. I tend to begin with the cabbage and the soaked porcini mushrooms, reducing both to ever so tiny morsels and add them to the ground meat first. Because I usually get a bit bored during the meticulous chopping of the cabbage, I tend to move to the fluid ingredients next, pouring these into the bowl before once more turning to the remaining vegetables. Then I proceed to diligently chop the shallots, ginger, and cilantro as finely as possible before placing them into the bowl as well. After whisking the egg, I add it to the filling, along with the sesame seeds and the sugar. If you have no fresh chili peppers, you can just as easily use dried chili flakes. As my final touch, I add a handful of panko bread crumbs to bind the filling, making sure, however, that it doesn't become too dry. I usually prepare the filling in advance, not only because it is so time-consuming but also because, left in the refrigerator, the flavor tends to intensify.

Filling the dumpling wrappers may, initially, seem to be a bit tricky, but with practice, you will quickly get the hang of it. You will need a small bowl of water, a coffee spoon, a kitchen towel, and a cutting board where you can set aside the pot stickers. Take the gyoza wrapper in the hand you are less dexterous with, heap a spoonful of filling into the center, and then, using the index finger of your free hand, sprinkle water all around the edge of the wrapper before gently folding it over the filling. With the help of the water, it is easy to press the inner sides of the wrapper together along the edges, giving you a semicircle-shaped dumpling. Make sure, however, that you don't overfill the wrapper; otherwise, excess filling will break through this seam and the dumpling won't seal properly. Place the filled wrappers next to each other, gently pressing each one down on the chopping board. This creates the flat bottom on which they will stand in the pan and ultimately become crisp. To prevent the pot stickers from drying out, I cover them with a slightly moistened kitchen towel. This way, they can be prepared at least an hour in advance.

While frying pot stickers, everything depends on the attentive concentration so decisive for all pan dishes. First heat the pan, then add the oil. Allow it to get very, very hot before placing the individual pot stickers next to each other such that they stand upright on the bottom of the pan. Do not, under any circumstance, give in to the temptation of trying to fry too many at the same time, as they will steal the heat required for proper browning from each other and remain soggy. Or they may cling together and rip when you try to separate them. I use small tongs to test whether they have begun to develop a brown crust, and if they aren't frying evenly, I move the individual pot stickers around in the pan. When they are ready, I pour a cup of water over the dumplings and cover the pan so that they can finish cooking in the steam now trapped there. However, you will need to take the lid off every now and then to make sure that the water hasn't evaporated too quickly. Add more if this is the case. Only when the dough has become translucent are the dumplings ready. In the final stage of preparation, the pot stickers are meant to fry, uncovered, over medium heat until the water has completely disappeared and they have once more developed a crust on the bottom. Here, too, alertness is called for. You need to catch the precise moment when all sogginess has turned into crispness but before the bottom of pot stickers scorch.

The dipping sauce that I serve with my pot stickers consists of a mixture of sweet, sour, and saltiness typical of Asian cuisine. Blend the sesame oil, apple balsamic vinegar, and soy sauce with the ketchup. If you want more bite, add sesame seeds and chopped chives. The sauce will keep for a week in the refrigerator and can be used as a salad dressing as well.

POT STICKERS WITH RICOTTA AND
VEGETABLES FOR 30 PIECES

2 tbsp. olive oil

1 medium-size onion, finely chopped

100 g (¾ cup) carrots, very finely chopped

150 g (1½ cups) zucchini, very finely chopped

100 g (1¼ cups) mushrooms, very finely chopped

½ tbsp. thyme

250–500 ml (1–2 cups) porcini or vegetable broth

250 g (1 cup) ricotta

1 generous handful Parmesan, grated

2 tbsp. rapeseed oil (canola oil)

orange olive oil

white pepper and salt

1 package pot sticker or gyoza wrappers

My friend Linda, who because of her Italian-American background always serves ravioli before the main course, encouraged me to come up with a fusion version of the Asian pot sticker. The meat filling in the classic pot sticker makes her suspicious of what it actually contains. So I decided to try using the ricotta-based filling of the traditional Italian pasta dish while keeping the combination of chewiness and crispness typical of the pan-fried dumpling wrapper.

Begin by caramelizing very finely chopped onions in olive oil over low heat, about ten minutes. In the meantime, peel the carrots, wash the zucchini, clean the mushrooms, and cut all the vegetables into fine cubes. Add these to the onions; season with thyme, salt, and pepper; and sauté them over medium heat until the vegetables have begun to soften. Then add enough broth to cover the vegetable cubes, and having covered the pan with a lid, allow them to braise until they have become soft enough that you can mash them with a fork. If you find that the broth has evaporated too quickly, you can always add more. Once the vegetables are done, take them off the heat and allow them to cool before mixing them with the ricotta. You want a smooth, slightly chunky filling. To balance the flavor and to produce a denser consistency, season with grated Parmesan.

These dumplings are assembled in exactly the same way as the Asian pot stickers. Place a heaping teaspoon of the vegetable-ricotta filling into the center of each wrapper, use your index finger to sprinkle water around the inside edge of the wrapper, and then press them together into a semicircle shape. As you place these filled wrappers next to each other on a chopping board, gently press each one down to create a flat bottom so that they can stand in the pan rather than lie on one side. As in the previous recipe, heat the pan and cover the bottom with a thin film of rapeseed oil, but don't put the individual dumplings into the pan until the oil is really hot. They should fry until the bottom has turned brown and crisp (but not scorched). Then add water, cover the pan, and steam them. If the water evaporates before the dough has turned translucent, add a bit more. Once the dumplings are ready, take the lid off the pan and allow them to continue frying until they have, once again, developed a crispy bottom. Before serving, drizzle with orange olive oil, season with freshly ground pepper, and top with some more grated Parmesan.

POT STICKERS WITH RICOTTA AND PEARS FOR 30 PIECES

3 pears	1 lemon
1 tbsp. butter	1 tbsp. pear balsamic vinegar
1½ tbsp. maple syrup	1 package gyoza or pot sticker
1½ tbsp. vanilla extract	wrappers
1 tbsp. fresh lavender, chopped	pistachio nuts
250 g (1 cup) ricotta	

My pleasure experimenting led me to develop a dessert version of the ricotta-filled pot sticker, which again you first fry, then steam, and then fry a second time. Once again, fusion signifies a happy marriage of taste and texture. The crispy bottom and the chewy sides of the dumpling make for an enticing contrast to the sweet, fruity cheese filling. As in the previous recipe, the ricotta serves as the base, while for your fruit, you can choose between apricots, peaches, apples, or cherries. My favorite, however, are pears. Peel and core them, and cut them into fine cubes before sautéing them in butter over medium heat. Don't add the syrup (or honey) until the pears have begun to caramelize, and keep stirring them as they continue to sauté until they have become soft but retained a bit of bite. To enhance the aroma of the filling, season the pears with vanilla (using either vanilla extract or vanilla paste) as well as very finely chopped lavender. Mix everything thoroughly, then take the pan off the heat and allow the fruit to cool. In the meantime, in a kitchen bowl, blend the ricotta with the lemon juice and the pear balsamic vinegar until you have an even, creamy texture before folding in the sautéed pears. The filling will keep for several hours in the refrigerator.

As in the previous recipes, heap a teaspoon of the ricotta-pear mixture into the center of each wrapper, and seal it along the dampened edges to form a semicircle shape. Place the individual pot stickers next to each other on a cutting board, gently pressing them down to create a flat bottom. Fry them first in hot oil, then cover the pan and steam them. When the skins have become translucent, remove the lid and finish frying them until the bottom of each pot sticker has again become crisp. Before serving, I drizzle them with the same fruit balsamic vinegar that I used in the ricotta filling. If you want more bite, top them with slivers of unsalted pistachio.

NOTE: All three variations can easily be prepared in advance because pot stickers (like any ravioli) are easy to freeze. All you need to remember is that, as they thaw, they will exude moisture. For this reason, I place the dumplings while they are still frozen next to each other on a cutting board covered with paper towels. To make sure that they don't stick together, I also turn them around now and then. This way the paper towels absorb the moisture evenly.

SAUTÉED VEGETABLES

❧ SAUTÉED
Green Asparagus with Shaved Parmesan | White Asparagus Sautéed | Porcini Mushrooms with Parsley | Belgian Endives with Cilantro

❧ FRIED AND BRAISED
Grated Zucchini | Grated Red Beets | Curried Chestnuts

❧ PRECOOKED AND SAUTÉED
Spinach with Butter and Parmesan | Spinach with Sesame and Soy Sauce

Whether you sauté vegetables, meat, poultry, or fish, the ingredients must be in motion in the pan. Only then will your meat remain juicy and your vegetables remain crunchy and fresh. Because the heat is meant to achieve its effect quickly, the ingredients should be cut into fine slices or cubes. This way, they can form a crust instantly while remaining juicy inside and not drying out. In fact, you can also shorten the cooking time of soups and stews, which will be discussed in chapter 4, by cutting all the solid ingredients that you are using into small pieces.

When frying in hot oil, you are once more confronted with choices. Usually I brown my ingredients in olive oil and only use butter to cream the sauce at the very end. If I want an extremely hot pan—as is the case with the Asian stir-fry—I prefer to use rapeseed oil. However, should you decide to use butter from the very beginning, it is best to mix it with olive oil. This keeps it from turning brown too quickly (or scorching) when you raise the heat. If you don't hear a sizzle immediately when you add your ingredient to the pan, it isn't hot enough yet, and you would do well to remove your ingredient again. For this reason, it is always advisable to test the heat of your pan with a drop of water first. If, in turn, an ingredient absorbs the oil too quickly and it looks as though it may stick to the bottom, you can add more oil, but do so from the edge of the pan. This way it can gather heat as it glides along the inner surface of your pan. Nevertheless, you should restrain yourself regarding the fat you are using. Only a thin film of oil or butter should cover the bottom of the pan. The ingredients are meant to dance in the pan, not swim in fat (unless you are deep-frying them). For this reason, it is also advisable to know how your vegetables behave and await with patience the transformation that is about to unfold in the pan. Sliced eggplant, for example, will absorb almost all the oil in the pan immediately. If you follow your impulse to promptly add more oil, they will ultimately become mushy and fatty.

The question of when it is best to add salt and pepper to an ingredient also opens up choices. I usually season meat and fish lightly before I begin pan searing or sautéing, unless they have already been soaking in a marinade. I also season the flour for the coating I use for a chicken cutlet or for sliced meat, sometimes with salt and pepper, sometimes with grated Parmesan. By contrast, when sautéing vegetables, I season with salt and pepper only once they have begun to brown. When it comes to eggplant and zucchini, however, I salt them generously and let them sit in a sieve for at least ten minutes before sautéing. This extracts some of the water they would otherwise release in the pan, making them soggy. I usually only add herbs, in turn, in the end so that, still firm to the bite, they serve as a contrast to the other ingredients in texture and flavor.

In order to illustrate the principle of decision-making at the heart of pan-frying, the following recipes have been divided up into various ways of cooking. Like meat and fish, certain sliced vegetables can be seared in the pan; others require additional liquid to cook. Still others are best blanched first and then finished in the pan. The ingredients suggested are interchangeable, the recipes an invitation to further experimentation.

SAUTÉED

GREEN ASPARAGUS WITH SHAVED PARMESAN FOR 2

1 pound green asparagus	½ tbsp. white balsamic vinegar
3 tbsp. olive oil	lavender salt and pepper
1 tbsp. lemon juice	Parmesan

Green asparagus does not need to be peeled. Simply cut off the lower part of the stalks, wash them, and dry them with paper towels. In a bowl, preferably with a flat bottom, dress the asparagus with one tablespoon of olive oil and salt, using your hands to make sure that each stalk is covered with the marinade. While the grill pan is heating on the stovetop, blend the remaining olive oil with the lemon juice and the white balsamic vinegar, and season with lavender salt and freshly ground black pepper. Once the pan has begun to smoke (simulating an outdoor grill), place the marinated asparagus stalks obliquely across the parallel ridges and sear them until they have begun to wilt. Using tongs, turn over each of the stalks so that they sear on all sides and are marked by the ridges. By continuing to turn them, you prevent them from burning as they become soft. When they are done, dress them with the vinaigrette and sprinkle them with ultrathin slices of Parmesan.

WHITE ASPARAGUS SAUTÉED FOR 2

10 fresh white asparagus	Parmesan
1½ tbsp. butter (or clarified butter)	vanilla salt and white pepper

When improperly cooked, white asparagus, a vaunted delicacy on the European continent, can often be boring, tasting watery or bitter. Heston Blumenthal, doyen of sous-vide cooking, however, has come up with a perfect way to retain the flavor of this vegetable: sautéing the stalks in butter.

In contrast to its green sibling, with white asparagus, not only must you trim the bottom, but you must also generously peel the stalks. You can tell whether you have removed enough of the bitter skin by cutting each stalk at an oblique angle into larger pieces, about four centimeters (one and a half inches) each. Wherever fibers still cling to the stalk, you need to peel some more. For frying, I prefer to use clarified butter because of its high smoking point, but you could also use regular, unsalted butter. Because I want the asparagus pieces to retain their bite, I first sear them at high temperature, shaking the pan to make sure that they brown evenly. After turning down the heat, I cover the pan, sauté the asparagus pieces another five minutes, take off the lid, and season them with vanilla salt and freshly ground white pepper. I then cover the pan once more and allow them to sauté another five minutes. So as to enhance the sweetness of the asparagus that the butter has unleashed, I sprinkle them with grated Parmesan before serving. Slices of prosciutto or boiled ham are the perfect accompaniment for this dish.

PORCINI MUSHROOMS WITH PARSLEY FOR 2

400 g (14 ounces) fresh porcini mushrooms	1 garlic clove, finely chopped
	1 tbsp. lemon juice
2 tbsp. goose schmaltz (or duck fat)	1 tbsp. parsley, finely chopped
2 tbsp. shallots, finely chopped	salt and pepper

When the first fresh porcini mushrooms appear at my farmers' market, I can never keep myself from splurging on them, so I have tried out all kinds of ways to prepare them—from raw salads to stews. I like them best, I discovered, when sautéed because the crispy crust offers such a seductive contrast to the sweet, juicy meat of these particular mushrooms. This does, however, require working patiently in batches and never crowding the pan with mushroom slices. Otherwise, you will get a mushroom ragout.

Using a small kitchen knife, begin by removing any earth still clinging to the porcini. Because you want them to have as little contact with water as possible, clean them afterward with a moistened brush (or moist paper towels). So that they won't release too much liquid while searing, dry them thoroughly with paper towels before cutting them into coarse slices. Once the goose schmaltz has become quite hot, add the first batch of mushrooms to the pan and sauté them—first on one side, then on the other—until they have browned and developed a crispy surface. Set this batch aside on a warm plate, heat the remaining schmaltz, and sauté the second batch. Your eye is the best judge whether you may need more fat. The mushroom slices shouldn't be too oily, but they should also not stick to the pan or scorch. Once the second batch is done, place these porcini slices aside as well. Using the same pan, caramelize the finely chopped shallots and the equally finely chopped garlic over low heat, about ten minutes, then deglaze the pan with lemon juice. Now you can return the porcini slices to the pan, lower the heat, and allow them to warm up again without cooking them any further, then sprinkle them with chopped parsley and season with salt and pepper. The contrast between the crisp outer crust and the sweet meaty mushrooms is best enjoyed immediately.

BELGIAN ENDIVES WITH CILANTRO FOR 2

1 tbsp. butter	1 tsp. brown sugar (or palm sugar)
1 tbsp. olive oil	1 tbsp. cilantro leaves, chopped
2 big Belgian endives	balsamic vinegar
½ tsp. salt	

For this version of the classic French bistro dish, warm the butter and the oil over medium heat in a nonstick frying pan. In the meantime, wash the Belgian endives, cut them in half, and without drying them, add them to the pan. You want them to be slightly moist. Season with salt, and more generously, sprinkle them with sugar. Over fairly low heat, fry them first on one side, then on the other. The combination of sugar and fat helps caramelize the outer leaves. Cover the pan and allow the endives to simmer for about five minutes. When they are soft inside, you can remove the lid and raise the heat to reduce the liquid they have emitted. Before serving, garnish the endives with chopped cilantro and a few drops of balsamic vinegar.

FRIED AND BRAISED

GRATED ZUCCHINI FOR 2

1 pound zucchini	zest of 1 lemon
1½ tsp. salt	1 tbsp. lemon-infused olive oil
1 tbsp. onions, chopped	salt and pepper
1 tbsp. olive oil	

Along with chopping, slicing, or shredding, grating vegetables helps reduce the cooking time. In particular, zucchini, which can quickly become soggy when fried in slices, takes on a pleasant, fresh texture when cut into snippets. Wash the zucchini, cut off the top and the bottom of each one, and then proceed to shred them using a coarse vegetable grater. Place them in a kitchen strainer, toss them with one and a half teaspoons of salt, and leave them to draw for at least ten minutes. Squeeze out as much of the water they have released as you can, and dry the snippets thoroughly on paper towels. Due to the preliminary salting, the zucchini will not only cook more quickly in the pan but also absorb the spices more rapidly. You can use the time in between to caramelize the chopped onions over low heat, since this should take about ten minutes as well. Add the grated zucchini to the pan, along with the finely chopped zest of a lemon, and sauté—but not too long, as you want the grated zucchini to retain some bite. To enhance the lemon flavor, add a shot of lemon olive oil, mix thoroughly, and season with salt and pepper.

GRATED RED BEETS FOR 2

250 g (9 ounces) red beets, coarsely grated
1 tbsp. butter
¼ tsp. white balsamic vinegar

¼ tsp. white wine vinegar
salt and pepper
1 tbsp. butter

Although I am particularly fond of oven-roasted beets, they can also be grated and panfried to produce a quick side dish. Before shredding them on a coarse vegetable grater, however, you need to wash and peel them. All this is best done over the kitchen sink because they will invariably give off splashes of red juice in the process. Once the butter has warmed in the pan, add the beet snippets, and sauté them for about four minutes. Then barely cover them with water, and simmer them over medium heat for another five minutes. After adding the balsamic vinegar and the wine, season with salt and pepper. Cover the pan with a lid, and allow the grated beets to simmer over medium heat for at least ten minutes, but keep checking to see if they need a bit more water (though never add too much at a time). While the balsamic vinegar will help them caramelize, you want them to retain their bite rather than produce a beet purée. To achieve a creamy sweetness, finish the dish by adding some butter to the grated beets, mix thoroughly, and season once more with salt and pepper.

CURRIED CHESTNUTS FOR 2

2 shallots, very finely sliced
2 tbsp. olive oil
250 g (9 ounces) cooked chestnuts
10 tbsp. water
5 tbsp. vegetable broth

3 tsp. brown sugar
50 ml (5 tbsp.) sherry vinegar
salt and pepper
1 tbsp. curry powder

For the longest time, I was puzzled by how to cook the fresh chestnuts that appear at our farmers' market each autumn. Then it dawned on me that, cut into slices like carrots, they could be panfried and then allowed to simmer in a spicy broth. The preparation time for this dish can be shortened tremendously if you are able to procure chestnuts that have already been peeled and precooked.

As with so many other pan dishes, first sauté the finely chopped shallots in olive oil over low temperature. In the meantime, cut the chestnuts into thick slices or quarter them. As soon as the shallots have become golden brown, add the chestnuts to the pan and keep turning them to brown them on all sides. Then add the water, brown sugar (which can be replaced by marmalade), and vinegar, stirring everything together thoroughly. Season with salt, pepper, and curry powder; stir again thoroughly; put the lid on the pan; and let the chestnuts simmer, about ten minutes, until the liquid has thickened. If they need more time to become soft, you can add water, but never too much at a time. You want them to be glazed by the curry spice and retain their bite. These chestnuts go well with cheese, a vegetable couscous, charcuterie, and dark meat.

NOTE: Dried chestnuts need to soak overnight in cold water. Bear in mind that they will double their weight, so the amount you use will need to be adjusted. For pan-frying you can also use vacuum-packed chestnuts, sold in bags or glass jars.

PRECOOKED AND SAUTÉED

SPINACH WITH BUTTER AND PARMESAN FOR 2

1 pound fresh spinach (or 2 pounds frozen spinach)	1 tbsp. vegetable stock powder (or 1 vegetable stock cube)
½ leek	1 bay leaf
2 tbsp. olive oil	butter
	Parmesan, grated

Marcella Hazan, my uncontested guide when it comes to classic Italian food, gives instructions in her books over and over again on how to first blanch spinach, chard, or carrots before glazing them in a pan. As is the case with pasta sauces, the basis for pan-frying vegetables is also a *soffritto*, usually consisting of garlic and onions along with chili flakes and anchovies, to which the vegetables are added as the second element. The following two recipes offer variations on this theme.

The first one comes from Richard, the husband of a colleague of mine at the University of Bergamo, who first introduced me to the "evil" deliciousness of this dish. Richard assures me it is just as easy (and far less cumbersome) to use frozen rather than fresh spinach, since there is so little difference in the outcome. Since he is a professor of analytic philosophy, I trust him when he claims that only a purist would go to the trouble of washing them, steaming them, squeezing all the water out of their fresh leaves, and chopping them before the cooking operation can actually begin. He also replaces the onion and garlic *soffritto* with half of a slender leek, which he suggests cutting finely into slices and sautéing over very low heat in olive oil. The leek should become transparent but not brown. If it browns, the heat was too high, and you should start again with the other half of the leek. Once the leek is ready, add the frozen spinach along with the vegetable stock powder (or cube) to the pan and stir thoroughly. Add the bay leaf as well and then cover the pan with a lid. As the spinach begins to melt, it will produce water. This can be topped up, but never too much at a time—just enough to prevent any scorching. Although the pan should remain covered throughout the process, this should not stop you from occasionally poking the spinach with a spoon to see how it is progressing. Only when the spinach has dried and contracted should you turn off the heat. Then add the butter—the crowning element of this dish—and plenty of it. Make sure that you carefully fold it (rather than mash it) into the spinach leaves. Finish with a sprinkling of finely grated Parmesan, which should just begin to melt as you serve the dish.

SPINACH WITH SESAME AND SOY SAUCE FOR 2

1 pound fresh spinach (or 2 pounds frozen spinach)	1 tsp. sugar
	2 tsp. soy sauce
4 tbsp. white sesame seeds	3 tbsp. vegetable broth

The second variation of this spinach dish is a Japanese version. For this version, it is also just as easy to use frozen rather than fresh spinach. The abundant use of sesame seeds makes up in richness for the lack of butter. It is best to make the sauce in a *suribachi* bowl (the Japanese version of a mortar) because of the rough grooved pattern on the unglazed inside, against which you crush the sesame seeds with the wooden pestle. But you can also use an ordinary mortar or a blender. Because it isn't always easy to find dashi broth, I have replaced it with vegetable broth.

Prepare the dressing for the spinach by first roasting the sesame seeds in a dry pan. They should brown and give off a toasty but not scorched smell. Pound them in the mortar (or blend them), and then add first the sugar, mixing thoroughly, before pouring in the soy sauce and the broth. Stir everything together to form a smooth paste. Add more sugar or soy sauce until you have reached the desired balance between sweet and saltiness. If you have decided to use fresh spinach, wash and blanch it before squeezing out all the water. If you are using frozen spinach, simply squeeze out the water that is produced as it thaws. In either case, cut the spinach into four-centimeter-long (one-and-a-half-inch-long) pieces, place it in a kitchen bowl, and fold the dressing into the green leaves.

SLICED MEAT AND VEGETABLES IN THE PAN

Vegetable Sundry with Sliced Chicken | Salmon Strips with Snow Peas and Sun-Dried Tomatoes | "Beef Stroganoff" for My Mother

⁂ ASIAN STIR-FRY
Beef with Oyster Sauce | Chicken with Shitake Mushrooms and Asparagus | Kung Pao Prawn

Nothing is more straightforward and less time-consuming than to sauté sliced, diced, or shredded ingredients in a pan. It does, however, require investing a bit of time in advance preparation. You don't want to take the pan off the stovetop and risk losing both heat and the momentum just because you forgot to chop some of the vegetables. The foundation for a dish of sliced ingredients is almost always a kind of *soffritto*, for which you sauté chopped onions in butter or olive oil over fairly low heat, about ten minutes, until they have begun to caramelize. If you want a milder flavor, you can replace onions with peeled and finely chopped celery. To enhance the aroma of your *soffritto*, you can add garlic, ginger, or chili flakes to the onion, or—as with a classic curry—you can add paprika, turmeric, cumin, or nutmeg from the beginning to enrich the flavor of the onions while they are caramelizing. Although the sequence for sautéing the sliced ingredients in the *soffritto* depends on the recipe, in each case the individual pieces—of meat, poultry, fish, or seafood—should be juicy inside while developing a thin crust on the outside. Even heat is as crucial as a balance between browning and turning your ingredients. And in the end, you should always deglaze the savory brown bits that have formed at the bottom of the pan with lemon juice, sherry, or cream. This is what gives the final aromatic touch to any pan dish.

The Asian stir-fry also consists of frying various sliced ingredients consecutively and finishing off the dish by stirring in a sauce. What makes it trickier is that the ingredients often have to be tossed into the wok in quick succession and then kept in constant movement. For this reason, not only do you need to have everything ready at hand, but you also need to make sure that the oil in the wok is so hot that it begins smoking. The point of the high rounded sides of this Asian pan is that, as you keep turning the ingredients, they glide not only across the hot bottom but also along the hot sides of the wok, cooking more rapidly. But because the ingredients are meant to come in contact with the extremely hot wok only very briefly, it is necessary to either slice, shred, and cube them very finely or blanch them in advance. Meat, poultry, and seafood are, furthermore, often marinated in advance so that the thin coating enveloping each piece can immediately form a protective crust. It is, of course, always possible to replace a wok with a sauté pan as long as it has high, rounded sides.

Like any other pan dish, cooking a stir-fry also consists of layering various elements. Any combination of chopped garlic, chili, and ginger, enhancing the flavor of the main ingredient, can be thought of as an Asian *soffritto*. The sequencing in a stir-fry is, however, slightly different. Once you have seared the main ingredient, you remove it from the wok. Having wiped the wok with paper towels, you allow it to regain intense heat before frying the spices and the vegetables. The liquid that serves as the sauce is heated up last, before you return the main ingredient back to the wok. I prefer using rapeseed oil not only because of the high smoking point but also because of its nutritional value. Regarding the amount of oil to use, there are two options. In the first, somewhat more costly method, you initially use two hundred and fifty millimeters (one cup) of oil in which to poach the meat, poultry, seafood, or tofu. Having poured this away, you then use another two tablespoons of oil for frying the other ingredients. In the more common method, you fry the main ingredient in one to two tablespoons of oil and then add another tablespoon for the vegetables and the spices. Don't be too stingy with the oil or you will risk scorching your ingredients.

My fondness for fusion cooking has led me to replace Asian vegetables in my stir-fries. Rather than bamboo slivers or soybean sprouts, I prefer corn, green beans, chard, peppers, cauliflower, or Brussels sprouts. I also like replacing the common peanut with pistachio or cashew nuts. If you opt for nuts that are already salted or spicy, this will, of course, further enhance the flavor of your dish, although this breaks with the tradition of classic Chinese cuisine. As the main ingredient, poultry, beef, pork, shrimp, and tofu are interchangeable. Of course, every visit to an Asian supermarket brings with it the temptation to try out new sauces and pastes. Experience, however, has shown that because I can never use them up quickly enough, they simply take up space in my refrigerator and slowly but surely go bad. My purchases are now limited to soy sauce, sesame oil, fish sauce, oyster sauce, hoisin sauce, and the one or the other chili sauce.

VEGETABLE SUNDRY WITH SLICED CHICKEN FOR 2

2 chicken breasts	3 tomatoes
flour for dusting the chicken breasts	2 tbsp. tomato flakes (or tomato
1 tbsp. olive oil	paste)
1 shallot	4 tbsp. Noilly Prat (or white wine)
1 garlic clove	2 tbsp. heavy cream
2 slices of ham	2 tbsp. parsley
1 medium-size zucchini, grated	2 tsp. thyme
250 g (9 ounces) mushrooms	salt and pepper

I call this a dish of sundries because it consists of a mixture of vegetables and meat, for which instead of chicken, you could also use turkey breast or pork tenderloin and combine this with any bite-size vegetables. The garlic in the *soffritto* can be replaced with ginger, and—as in a pasta sauce—you can also add finely chopped anchovies and capers. If you are using corn, you can season the cream with mustard. For a mixture of zucchini and peppers, add lemon juice and lemon thyme to the cream. Or you can leave out the cream completely and opt for an Asian note by sautéing shredded white or green cabbage in a *soffritto* consisting of ginger and onions until it has become soft. Remove it from the pan, and in a second step, brown your slices of pork tenderloin (or tofu) before returning the cabbage to the pan and seasoning everything with oyster sauce, chili-garlic sauce, or a tonkatsu sauce (the Japanese version of ketchup). I also call this recipe a dish of sundries because, during my years as a student and young assistant at the University of Munich, I always fell back on this meal whenever I simply needed to use up the vegetables that had accumulated in my refrigerator before they went bad.

Begin by preparing the sundry vegetables and meats. Slice the tomatoes, grate the zucchini, salt them, and let them rest in a sieve before using them. Clean and slice the mushrooms; chop the shallot, the garlic, and the parsley; and pluck the thyme leaves off their stems. Cut the ham into fine slices. Remove the tendon from the chicken breasts and cut them into bite-size strips. For their coating, put some flour on a plate and season with salt and pepper. Once your *mise en place* is ready, heat the pan and sauté the finely chopped shallots over medium heat in olive oil until they have become translucent, then add the garlic and continue sautéing for another thirty seconds, because you don't want it to brown. Then add the ham slices to the pan. Now it is time to coat the chicken pieces in the seasoned flour, shaking off any excess. As soon as the onions have caramelized and the ham has become nicely crisp, add the chicken to the pan and keep turning the pieces until they too have developed a nicely browned skin. Add the tomatoes, the grated zucchini, and the sliced mushrooms, and sauté these vegetables in the pan as well. If you can find tomato flakes, use them to make the sauce more velvety and intensify the flavor. If you can't find them in a spice shop, replace them with tomato paste. Blend the cream with the Noilly Prat to deglaze the pan before seasoning with salt and pepper and showering your dish of sundries with the chopped herbs. You can serve it with buttered noodles, rice, or bread, but I usually eat it plain, just as it is.

SALMON STRIPS WITH SNOW PEAS AND SUN-DRIED TOMATOES FOR 2

2 tbsp. olive oil	250 ml (1 cup) cream
250 g (9 ounces) salmon fillet	125 ml (½ cup) Noilly Prat
125 g (1 cup) pine nuts	5 tbsp. soy sauce
6 sun-dried tomatoes	125 g (4½ ounces) Parmesan, grated
200 g (2 cups) snow peas	1 handful each of basil leaves and
6 baby corn	thyme
2 garlic cloves	250 g (9 ounces) linguine
1 shallot	salt and pepper

My enthusiasm for fusion cooking, which came up in the late 1990s, soon led me to discover the unusual but utterly enticing combination of cream and soy sauce. To me, it offers a particularly happy marriage between Asian seasoning and European pan-frying, with each complementing the other. As in any Asian stir-fry, all the ingredients should be prepared in advance.

This also means that you could get almost everything ready in the morning and store the sliced and chopped ingredients in their respective bowls in the refrigerator. The actual pan-frying will not require more time than it takes to cook the linguine, which I like to serve with this dish.

As with any other fish, wash the salmon, and dry it thoroughly with paper towels. If the skin is still on, remove it, cutting away the gray strip of fat, which though healthy looks unappetizing. Also remove any fish bones with tweezers before slicing the salmon into bite-size strips. Soak the sun-dried tomatoes in a small bowl with hot water for twenty minutes. Once they have become soft, pour away the water, and cut them into very fine strips. In the meantime, roast the pine nuts in a dry pan, tossing them to make sure that they brown evenly without scorching. Blanch the baby corn briefly in boiling water before cutting it into bite-size pieces as well. Wash the snow peas, and cut them diagonally into bite-size strips. Finely chop the shallots and the garlic, and put them aside in the same bowl. Blend the cream with the Noilly Prat (which you can replace with Vermouth). The herbs should not be chopped until you are about to begin cooking; otherwise, they will lose flavor. Wash the basil and cut it into a chiffonade. Pluck the thyme leaves off their stems.

Once your *mise en place* is ready, begin by cooking the pasta. Heat the pan, add the olive oil, and when it is hot, sauté first the shallots for about five minutes and then add the garlic. The latter will begin to sizzle after about fifteen seconds, which is an indication that it is time to add the soaked sun-dried tomatoes, the corn, and the snow peas to the pan. Sauté the vegetables for about a minute, then pour the soy-cream over them and allow it to come to a boil. Once the vegetables have blended with the cream sauce, lower the heat, and then add the salmon strips. You want to sauté these for only a minute. They should be browned on the outside but still pink on the inside. Add the chopped herbs at this point, but be careful that you fold them into the other ingredients rather than stir them. You don't want the salmon to flake and fall apart. When the pasta is ready, drain it in a colander, add it to the pan, and together with the pine nuts, toss everything one last time. You can sprinkle with grated Parmesan if you like before serving.

"BEEF STROGANOFF" FOR MY MOTHER FOR 2

300 g (11 ounces) beef fillet
2 tbsp. clarified butter
1 shallot, finely chopped

150 g (1¾ cups) mushrooms, finely sliced
2 tbsp. cornichons (or other pickled cucumbers), chopped

5 tbsp. soy sauce
250 ml (1 cup) cream
1 tsp. cayenne pepper

verjus (or sherry vinegar)
1 tsp. cilantro leaves, chopped
salt and pepper

Beef stroganoff was one of Marlene Dietrich's favorite dishes, and because my mother was a passionate fan of the Hollywood diva, she also loved this dish. Because she never quite forgot the austerity of the war and postwar years, she was a very economic housekeeper and, replacing the costly fillet with ground beef, simply called her thriftier version "Russisches" (meaning generically a Russian dish). Her delight at culinary inventions has inspired me to a further version in which, in turn, I bring into play the delectable combination of cream and soy sauce.

Cut the beef fillet into strips (about one centimeter or about a quarter inch in width), and season these with salt and pepper. Then heat one tablespoon of butter in the pan, and add the beef when it has gotten quite hot. The fillet strips are meant to be seared while remaining slightly pink inside. You don't want them dry and tough. Remove the meat from the pan, and set it aside in a bowl. Lower the heat, and add the second tablespoon of butter to the pan, using it to loosen the brown, savory bits that have formed on the bottom, then add the finely chopped onions, and caramelize these for around ten minutes. In the meantime, blend together the cream and the soy sauce in a small bowl. Once the onions have become soft and slightly brown, add the finely sliced mushrooms to the pan, and sauté these as well. Season with cayenne pepper, and deglaze the mushrooms and onions with the soy-cream mixture. The sauce is meant to boil down to a thick, velvety consistency before you add the verjus (or if you want more acidity, lime juice). Season with pepper to taste. Return the seared beef fillet strips to the pan, along with the finely chopped cornichon. As you mix everything together, the beef will heat up again, but do not let the sauce come to a boil. Garnish with finely chopped cilantro. This fusion version of beef stroganoff is best accompanied by tagliatelle, tossed in butter.

ASIAN STIR-FRY

BEEF WITH OYSTER SAUCE FOR 2

225 g (8 ounces) lean beef steak (or
    beef fillet)
1 tbsp. soy sauce

2 tsp. sesame oil
1 tbsp. Shaoxing rice wine
2 tsp. cornstarch

Antique carafes

6 big, fresh shitake mushrooms	1½ tbsp. spring onions, finely
3 tbsp. rapeseed oil (canola oil)	chopped
3 tbsp. oyster sauce	

This may be the simplest example of a stir-fry because you only need oyster sauce to season the dish. What you must, however, bear in mind is that the meat needs to rest in the marinade for at least twenty minutes. Begin by slicing the beef steak into fairly narrow strips; around five centimeters (two inches) long and one centimeter (a quarter inch) wide. For the marinade, first blend together the soy sauce, sesame oil, rice wine (or dry sherry), and cornstarch in a small bowl, then add the beef and mix thoroughly, making sure that each strip is fully coated with the marinade. Now you can clean the shitake mushrooms, cut them into coarse slices, cut the spring onions into thin slices, and turn on your rice cooker. Once all the ingredients are ready, heat the wok, add the oil, and allow it to get extremely hot. Now add the beef strips to the pan and sear them on all sides, stirring constantly. By keeping the strips in motion, you can use the entire surface of the wok, including the sides, to fry them. When they look done, remove them from the pan and drain them in a colander; if you want your beef to remain pink inside, this may take only a minute or two. Pour away the oil, wipe the wok with paper towels, and heat it again before adding more oil. Once again, it should be really hot before you add the mushrooms and quickly stir-fry these as well. When they are done, set them aside with the meat. Pour away the excess oil, wipe the wok with paper towels, and then return it to the stovetop. Reheat the wok and add the oyster sauce once the pan has become hot again. The sauce is meant to simmer briefly before you add the beef strips and the mushrooms once more to the wok and mix everything thoroughly. Garnish with the spring onions and serve with rice.

CHICKEN WITH SHITAKE MUSHROOMS
AND ASPARAGUS FOR 2

2 chicken breasts

2 tsp. cornstarch

1 tsp. sesame oil

2 tbsp. oyster sauce

1 tbsp. soy sauce

1 tsp. brown sugar

150 ml (⅔ cup) chicken broth

250 ml (1 cup) rapeseed oil (canola oil)

3 big shitake mushrooms

3 small chili peppers, cut into strips

2 tsp. ginger, chopped

2 tsp. garlic, chopped

½ pound green asparagus

2 tsp. cornstarch mixed with 2 tbsp. water

The *mise en place* for this typical stir-fry is far more elaborate because, along with slicing the vegetables, you must make not only a marinade for the chicken but also a separate sauce for seasoning the dish in the end. Moreover, you will be using quite a bit of oil in which to poach the chicken for several seconds rather than briefly searing it, as in the previous recipe. The sesame cornstarch mixture serves as a protective coating, so each individual chicken piece will become crisp outside while remaining juicy inside. In a second step, the vegetables, finely chopped or blanched, will then be stir-fried in far less fat. You can replace the chicken with pork, shrimp, or tofu (in which case you won't need a marinade). As a substitute for asparagus, you can use corn, green beans, broccoli, or snow peas. Just bear in mind that you want vegetables whose texture offers a contrast to the soft fleshiness of the shitake mushrooms.

Begin by meticulously removing the tendon in each of the chicken breasts with a sharp kitchen knife, then cut them into bite-size strips. In a bowl, dissolve the cornstarch in the sesame oil, stirring vigorously to get rid of all lumps. Then toss the chicken in the mixture. It is best to use your fingers to make sure that each piece is evenly coated. Let the chicken rest while you deal with the other ingredients. In a second bowl, blend together the oyster sauce, soy sauce, sugar, and broth, and put these aside as well. Wash the asparagus, trim off the wooden bits at the bottom, and then cut them into smaller bite-size pieces. After blanching the asparagus in boiling water, drain them in a colander over cold water. Because this will immediately stop any further cooking, the asparagus will remain crisp and retain its bright-green color. Clean the mushrooms, and after cutting them into fine strips, place them in another bowl. Finally, in your last bowl, mix together your three aromatic ingredients—the chili, ginger, and garlic—and place these aside as well.

Because in this stir-fry all the ingredients will have to be added to the wok in quick succession, you should keep your sundry bowls close at hand. Start by heating the wok, then the oil, and wait until it has gotten quite hot before adding the sliced chicken. Immediately begin to stir so that while the chicken pieces are being poached in the hot oil, they are also constantly in motion. Once they are browned on both sides, remove them with a slotted spoon and drain them in a sieve. Pour the oil into a bowl, and keep it to one side. Now wipe the wok with paper towels, allow it to get very hot again, and reheat three tablespoons of the previously used oil. Add the chili-ginger-garlic *soffritto* to the wok, and fry it for fifteen seconds (but no longer; otherwise, it might scorch), then add the mushrooms, tossing and turning them constantly as they brown. Next to follow are the asparagus pieces, then after mixing them thoroughly with the other ingredients, pour in the broth mixture and allow it to come to a boil. When you think the asparagus is almost done, return the chicken slices to the pan, toss them with the other ingredients, and turning down the heat, allow them to simmer while you dissolve two more tablespoons of cornstarch in water. Pour this into the wok and stir vigorously to thicken the sauce. Drizzle a bit of sesame oil over the dish and serve with rice.

KUNG PAO PRAWN FOR 2–3

rapeseed oil (canola oil)	1 tbsp. rice wine vinegar
400 g (14 ounces) prawns	1–2 dried chili peppers (or ½ tsp.
80 g (½ cup) roasted peanuts	dried chili flakes)
200 g (2 cups) snow peas	2 garlic cloves, finely chopped
2 scallions, finely sliced	2 tbsp. ginger, finely chopped
1 tbsp. soy sauce	2 tbsp. Shaoxing rice wine (or Noilly
2 tsp. chili paste	Prat)
1 tbsp. hoisin sauce	2 handfuls cilantro leaves
1 tsp. brown sugar	

In her book *Land of Plenty*, Fuchsia Dunlop explains that this classic Chinese dish was considered politically incorrect during Mao Tse-tung's cultural revolution. It derived its name, "Gong Bao," from the fact that it had been invented for a governor who ruled in the Szechuan province in the late nineteenth century. So as not to recall this bureaucrat of the Chinese empire, it was renamed "quickly fried chicken cubes" (*hu la ji ding*) and only rehabilitated officially in the 1980s. In the restaurants of Chinese émigrés like the friends of my parents, it was, of course, assigned a prominent place on the menu for precisely this reason. So as to demonstrate the play on varieties that stir-frying makes possible, the version I offer uses shrimp instead of chicken cubes.

In preparation for the kung pao sauce, blend the rice wine vinegar with the soy sauce, chili paste, hoisin sauce, and the brown sugar in a bowl and set aside. While you can substitute apple balsamic vinegar for the rice wine vinegar, the fiery chili paste and the hoisin sauce cannot be replaced, even if this means a trip to your local Asian market. Peel the shrimp, and using the tip of a small kitchen knife, remove the fine white intestine running along the lower rounded side before cutting them in half lengthwise. Cut the snow peas in half, blanch them in boiling water, drain them, and place them aside in a bowl. In another bowl, have the peanuts ready (and although this breaks with the tradition of Chinese cuisine, it is worth using spiced peanuts if you want more flavor). Depending on how pungent you want the dish to be, you can either use only one or several dried chilies, which you crumble with your fingers and set aside in a separate dish. Then finely chop the garlic and ginger and mix these together in their own little bowl. Finally, cut the spring onions into fine slivers, chop the cilantro, and place them into separate bowls.

Once the *mise en place* is done, heat the wok, add two to three tablespoons of oil, and wait until it has become very hot. Sear the shrimp, keeping them in motion constantly until they have taken on a pink color. Remove them from the wok and drain them in a sieve. Now add the peanuts to the pan and fry them, stirring constantly, for about ten seconds, until they have taken on a light-golden color. Remove them from the wok with a slotted spoon and drain them on paper towels. Next quickly stir-fry the snow peas, then remove them and set them aside. Now it is time to wipe the wok with paper towels, reheat it, and add two to three more tablespoons of oil. Once the oil is very hot, fry the crumbled chili for several seconds, then add the spring onions and allow these to fry for five seconds before adding the ginger-garlic mixture.

Stirring constantly, fry it for about fifteen seconds. Now you can add the kung pao sauce and let it come to a boil before returning the shrimp and the snow peas to the wok as well. Mix everything thoroughly, and then season with rice wine before removing the wok from the heat. Garnish the dish with the fried peanuts and the chopped cilantro, and serve it with rice.

SAUTÉED IN ONE PIECE

❦ WITHOUT COATING

Salmon Steak with Lemon | Lamb Fillet with Eggplant |
Citrus-Flavored John Dory | Red Snapper with Sun-Dried
Tomato Pesto and Preserved Lemon | Tofu Steak with Tomatoes |
Tofu Steak with Citrus Sauce | Tofu Steak with Marinade

❦ WITH COATING

Chicken Breasts with Capers, Preserved Lemon, and Cilantro | Chicken Breasts
with Almond Coating and Pistachio Pesto | Italian Veal Escalopes with
Lemon and Parsley | Fusion Veal Escalopes with Morels |
Scallops with White Wine | Stuffed Zucchini Blossoms

If you decide to fry poultry or fish in one piece, these will not be kept in motion constantly, as is the case when your primary ingredient is sliced, diced, or shredded. Instead, you usually only turn them once, after they have formed a crust on one side. For this reason, choose as your main ingredient pieces that are not too thick—chicken breasts, veal or pork cutlet, fillet of fish, or a steak. In order for them not to become dry, they should take the same time to cook inside as to brown on the outside. So as to stay true to the principle of binary choices, the following recipes have been divided up based on whether the main ingredient is to be exposed to the hot fat directly or not. Ask yourself the following key questions: Is my steak robust enough to be fried in a pan without coating? Or does my fillet need a mantle of flour, finely grated almonds, or bread crumbs, in part to protect it but also because this alone will produce a thin, crispy outer layer.

Regardless of whether you decide against or in favor of a coating, once more attentiveness and dexterity is called for. You should only turn your main ingredient once it comes loose easily from the bottom of the pan. If it doesn't, it isn't ready yet. To prevent it from sticking to the pan in certain places, don't—as you would if sautéing—allow the main ingredient to jump in the pan. Instead, shake the pan itself now and then, allowing the main ingredient to glide along the bottom. Success when flipping it over depends on two things: Add the main ingredient to the pan only once the fat has gotten properly hot. Whether fillet, steak, cutlet, or escalope, it must constantly be in touch with the oil; otherwise, the meat or poultry may rip or the fish may fall apart. If a browned ingredient threatens to stick to the pan, don't scrape it off and instead allow it to cook a bit longer over lower heat. The resistance is a sign that the ingredient is still busy forming a protective crust. Furthermore, choose a pan in which the fillets, steaks, or escalopes have enough room when placed side by side. If they are too close to each other, or even worse, on top of each other, their outer surface will not come into contact with the hot fat immediately, and thus they will not brown evenly. Instead, they will release too much juice, and you will not achieve the combination of crispy outside and succulent inside, so fundamental to frying in the pan.

WITHOUT COATING

SALMON STEAK WITH LEMON FOR 2

2 salmon fillet, each 170 g (6 ounces)
½ tbsp. olive oil
½ tbsp. butter
1 tbsp. lemon juice and the zest of
    half a lemon
salt and pepper

1 generous pinch Italian herbs (or
    another dried herb mixture)
½ tbsp. parsley
Noilly Prat
butter

As simple as frying salmon in the pan may be, it can just as easily miscarry. Exposed to the heat too long, the salmon will become dry and tough. To make sure that you will produce a juicy fillet, you must not only wash the salmon first but also dry it thoroughly with paper towels, because an excess of moisture will prevent it from browning crisply.

Begin by seasoning the salmon steak on both sides with salt, but hold the pepper. Then heat the pan and add the olive oil along with the butter and the lemon juice. Once the butter has melted, place the salmon steak into the pan, and reduce the heat to medium. Since you want the salmon steak to be crispy on the outside but remain rare on the inside, flip it over after a minute or so, but not before it has formed enough of a crust to come loose readily. In no case should you give in to the temptation to press down on the salmon steak with your spatula, hoping to accelerate the cooking process. This will only cause the salmon to release some of its juices. Once you have flipped it over, season the browned side with pepper, and sprinkle it with the lemon zest and the herb mixture. After about two minutes, take the salmon from the pan, flip it over onto a plate, and season the other side with pepper. Then deglaze the pan with Noilly Prat and butter, making sure to stir around the brown bits that have formed while frying. Pour the sauce over the salmon and serve with a salad or steamed vegetables.

LAMB FILLET WITH EGGPLANT FOR 2

3 eggplants	2 tbsp. rapeseed oil (canola oil)
3 tbsp. soy sauce	½ tsp. sesame oil
1½ tsp. ginger, grated	2 lamb fillet, each 200 g (7 ounces)
2 garlic cloves, finely chopped	cayenne pepper
100 ml (½ cup) vegetable broth	shiso leaves, cut into thin strips
1 pinch sugar	sesame seeds

Begin by coating the entire surface of each of the eggplants with oil, and make small incisions with a kitchen knife in various places before roasting them under the broiler. You will need to keep turning them with tongs so that the skin turns black and wrinkled all over while the flesh of the fruit itself becomes soft. After about twelve minutes, you can take the eggplants out of the oven and drain them in cold water over a sieve. They have to cool before you can pull off the singed skin. Cut the eggplants into four-centimeter-(one-and-a-half-inch-) broad pieces and put them aside in a bowl.

While the eggplants are roasting in the oven, make the dressing. Finely chop the ginger and garlic, and then blend these with soy sauce, vegetable broth, and sugar in a small kitchen bowl until the sugar has completely dissolved. Pour this dressing over the eggplants, and mix everything well, using your hands to make sure that each piece is evenly coated. To fry the two fillets of lamb, you will need a pan in which they both fit snugly without overlapping. First heat the rapeseed and the sesame oil. Season the meat with salt, pepper, and a pinch of cayenne pepper. As soon as the oil is hot, sear the meat on each side, about three minutes if you like it rare; otherwise, a bit longer. Remove the pan from the heat, but before cutting the meat into bite-size slices, allow the lamb to rest on a chopping board for at least five minutes. To serve, place the lamb and the eggplant on individual plates, drizzle with the remaining dressing, and garnish with shiso leaves and sesame seeds. The Japanese shiso can be replaced with a blend of mint and basil.

CITRUS-FLAVORED JOHN DORY FOR 2

1 handful fresh herbs (mint, dill, basil, sage)
olive oil
2 John Dory fillets
1 garlic clove, finely sliced

2 tbsp. orange zest, chopped
salt and pepper
50 ml (¼ cup) fish broth
70 ml (⅓ cup) lemon juice
70 ml (⅓ cup) orange juice

What is unusual about this recipe is that you add the fish, along with the olive oil, to a cold pan, allowing the heat to envelop the fish before adding the fluid. Because this dish involves a combination of frying and steaming, you need a pan with a lid that fits properly.

Begin by slicing the garlic and chopping the fresh herbs. Put them aside in a small bowl. Blend the fish broth with the lemon and orange juice, and set the marinade aside as well. Wash the John Dory, and dry it thoroughly with paper towels. When your *mise en place* is ready, add a generous shot of olive oil to your pan, enough to cover the bottom with a thin film. Place the fish into the pan, skin side down (i.e., if you were able to find a John Dory with the skin still on). Sprinkle both fillets with garlic slices and chopped herbs and season with salt and pepper. Now you can heat the pan over medium temperature, and when you begin to hear a sizzle, pour the marinade over the fish and cover the pan. Allow the fish to cook another four minutes; it should not fall apart. Once you have removed it from the pan, raise the heat, allow the sauce to come to a boil, then over medium heat, reduce it, and finish by creaming with butter. Season with salt and pepper before dressing the John Dory with the sauce.

NOTE: Although classic European cuisine stipulates that fish should be served with rice, I prefer very thin pasta, tossed in butter or truffle oil. The pasta ever so elegantly soaks up the sauce that goes along with pan-frying.

RED SNAPPER WITH SUN-DRIED TOMATO PESTO AND PRESERVED LEMON FOR 2

200 g (1⅓ cups) sun-dried tomatoes
1 preserved lemon along with 1 tbsp. of its juice (see "Prepared and Stored in the Refrigerator")

1 garlic clove
130 g (1 cup) almond slivers
1½ tsp. chili salt (or 1¼ tsp. salt, ¼ tsp. chili flakes)

1 tbsp. capers	2 red snapper fillets
1 bunch cilantro	1 tbsp. rapeseed oil
5 tbsp. olive oil	salt and pepper
240 ml (1 cup) hot water	

For this dish, you will need to make the pesto first. Cut the sun-dried tomatoes, the preserved lemon, and the garlic clove into coarse strips, and pluck the cilantro from the stems, leaving a few leaves aside for garnishing later. Using your blender (or emersion blender), mix the almonds, chili salt, olive oil, and hot water with the tomatoes, lemon, and cilantro until you have a coarse paste. You can make the pesto in advance if you keep it in the fridge in an airtight jar.

While your nonstick frying pan is heating up on the stovetop, wash the fish, dry it thoroughly with paper towels, and season on both sides with salt. You can replace the red snapper with John Dory or sea bass; you simply want to choose a fish that is not too delicate. Add the rapeseed oil to the hot pan, and let it heat up before frying the fish fillet in the pan, skin side down, for three minutes. Turn the fish over, fry it another two minutes on the other side, and season with pepper. To serve, spoon the sun-dried tomato pesto onto each dish, place the fish fillet on top, and garnish with the remaining cilantro leaves.

TOFU STEAK WITH TOMATOES FOR 2

300 g (11 ounces) firm tofu	fresh cilantro
4 large tomatoes	1 orange
1 tbsp. rapeseed oil (canola oil)	2 tsp. furikake rice seasoning
4 tbsp. Japanese noodle sauce	

While it is perfectly fine to serve silken tofu with salad dressing and some oven-roasted cherry tomatoes as though it were a piece of mozzarella, it is best to treat firm tofu as you would a steak. The following three recipes offer different ways in which this can be done. In the first recipe, the spicy tomato sauce is the distinguishing ingredient, while the tofu merely serves as a flavor carrier. Indeed, you might think of it as a replacement for pasta.

Dry the tofu thoroughly with paper towels, making sure to remove as much liquid as possible. Cut it in half lengthwise, and season both sides with salt and pepper. Heat the pan, add the rapeseed oil, wait for it to get hot as well, and then fry the two pieces of tofu until they have taken on a golden-brown color, about three minutes. After turning both pieces over to fry on the other side, cut the tomatoes into small cubes, and place them next to the tofu steaks to fry as well. After three minutes, pour the noodle sauce over the tomatoes, and continue frying them over medium heat until they have begun to caramelize. In the meantime, zest the orange, chop the cilantro, and sprinkle both, along with the furikake rice seasoning, over the tofu steaks once these are ready.

TOFU STEAK WITH CITRUS SAUCE FOR 2

300 g (11 ounces) firm tofu	1 tbsp. rapeseed oil (canola oil)
1 lemon	1 egg
1 orange	3 tbsp. panko
1 tbsp. honey	chives
1 tbsp. soy sauce	

For this second pan-fried tofu recipe, you will prepare a separate sauce for the tofu steaks by bringing the juice and zest of both citrus fruit along with the honey and the soy sauce to a boil in a small pot. Allow the sauce to simmer over low heat while you begin preparing the tofu by thoroughly drying it with paper towels, removing as much liquid as possible. Then cut it in half lengthwise, and season each side with salt and pepper. To coat the tofu, beat the egg in a small bowl, spoon it over the upper side of each piece of tofu, and then cover these with panko. You may want to press the panko lightly into the egg to make sure that the coating will cling to the tofu steaks. Heat the rapeseed oil in the pan before adding these, with the egg-panko coating side down, and fry them until they have become golden brown, around five minutes. Turn the tofu steaks over, and fry the other side, another two minutes, before taking them off the heat. At this point the citrus sauce should be ready, reduced to a thickish consistency. Pour it onto each plate first, then place the tofu with the coated side on top, and garnish the steaks with chives, cut into fine slivers.

TOFU STEAK WITH MARINADE FOR 2

300 g (11 ounces) firm tofu	1 tbsp. apple balsamic vinegar
1 tbsp. sesame oil	(or Japanese rice wine vinegar)
5 tbsp. soy sauce	1 tbsp. ginger, chopped
2 tbsp. mirin	1 tsp. brown sugar

A third way to prepare a tofu steak is to marinade it before frying. For this version, blend the sesame oil, the soy sauce, the mirin, and the apple balsamic vinegar along with the ginger and the sugar in a bowl. As in the previous recipes, thoroughly dry the tofu with paper towels, and cut it in half lengthwise. Pour the marinade over the two pieces of tofu, and allow them to soak up the sauce for at least an hour. Heat the rapeseed oil in a pan, and sauté the tofu steaks, about four minutes on each side. Before serving, dress them with the remaining marinade.

WITH COATING

CHICKEN BREASTS WITH CAPERS, PRESERVED LEMON, AND CILANTRO FOR 2

2 chicken breasts
flour (or ground pistachios) to coat
1 tbsp. olive oil
1 shallot
¼ tsp. chili flakes
1 tbsp. capers

¼ preserved lemon (see "Prepared
    and Stored in the Refrigerator")
250 ml (1 cup) broth
1 tbsp. cilantro, chopped
salt and pepper

During my early years as a cook, I would often fry whole chicken breast along with the sundry vegetables that happened to be in my refrigerator. They usually became nice and crisp on the outside but were often disappointingly dry inside. In one of Julia Child's books, I then discovered that if you pound chicken breasts until they are evenly thick, about one and a half centimeters (half an inch), they not only remain juicy inside but also fry much more quickly.

Rub a bit of oil onto each side, place the chicken breast inside a refrigerator bag, and then pound the thicker, upper part until you have a more or less even surface, but be careful not to produce any holes in the meat. Season the chicken breasts on both sides with salt and pepper, and then toss them in the flour (which you can substitute with ground pistachios), making sure they are evenly coated. Shake off any excess flour, and allow them to rest on a plate, covered with plastic wrap, for about five minutes. Even if this prolongs the cooking time, you should not omit this step. The pounded chicken must feel comfortable in its coating before it is exposed to the hot fat.

Use the time to chop the shallot, capers, and cilantro for the sauce. Cut the preserved lemon into thin strips as well, and set aside all these ingredients, which you will be using for the sauce, in separate bowls. Then heat the pan, and allow it to get hot before adding the oil. Once the oil is hot as well, begin frying the pounded, coated chicken breasts. After four minutes you can turn them and fry them another four minutes on the other side. If you aren't sure whether they are done, you can take them out of the pan and make an incision in each of them. The chicken may be slightly pink inside. To prepare the sauce, remove the chicken breasts from the pan, and put them aside. Using the same pan, sauté the chopped shallot over medium heat, about five minutes; stir the chili flakes into the shallots; and then add the capers and the lemon strips as well. Deglaze the pan with the broth, and reduce the liquid until you have a sauce thick enough to coat a spoon. Allow the chicken breast to steep in the sauce briefly to heat them up again before sprinkling some chopped cilantro on top.

CHICKEN BREASTS WITH ALMOND COATING
AND PISTACHIO PESTO FOR 2

2 chicken breasts

3 tbsp. almond flour

100 g (4 ounces) unsalted, peeled
   pistachio

1 bunch parsley

1 bunch cilantro

2 garlic cloves

150 ml (⅔ cup) olive oil

100 g (4 ounces) Parmesan, coarsely
   grated

3 tbsp. hot water

salt and pepper

verjus (or sherry vinegar)

Given the panoply of choices that cooking in the pan offers, you can also use almond flour to coat the pounded chicken breast. This, in turn, opens up a new set of choices. Do you simply want to serve the chicken with a sauce produced by deglazing the pan, or do you want to serve it with a pesto more befitting the crunchy almond flour crust? And because any pesto will keep for up to a week in the refrigerator, you can readily make it in advance and have less to think about when frying your chicken.

For the pesto, mince the pistachios along with the parsley, the cilantro, and the garlic in a blender (or a mortar); season with salt; drizzle in the olive oil; and then add the coarsely grated Parmesan. To finish the pesto, add enough hot water to produce a smooth, creamy consistency.

Begin, as in the previous recipe, by rubbing both sides of the chicken breasts with a bit of oil, then place them inside a ziplock plastic bag and pound them until they are evenly thick, about one and a half centimeters (half an inch).

Season with salt and pepper, and drag them through the almond flour, making sure that both sides are evenly coated. Place them, covered with plastic wrap, aside on a dish where they should rest for several minutes. Heat the oil in a hot pan and fry the chicken breasts, about four minutes on each side. Remove the chicken from the pan, and warm as much of the pistachio pesto as you want to use, adding a bit of verjus (or lemon juice) to thin down the sauce.

ITALIAN VEAL ESCALOPES WITH
LEMON AND PARSLEY FOR 2

1 tbsp. olive oil	flour
2 tbsp. butter	salt and pepper
300 g (11 ounces) veal escalope, very	2 tbsp. lemon juice
thinly sliced (2 per person)	2 tbsp. parsley, chopped

Tender veal escalopes also require a flour coating to protect them so that they will remain juicy while exposed to the hot oil in a pan. In contrast to the chicken breasts, however, they should not rest in this coating; otherwise, you will not get the delicate crust that makes for the charm of this classic Italian dish. For this reason, first heat the oil and one tablespoon of butter over medium heat. Once the butter has begun to foam, drag the veal escalopes through the flour, shake off any excess, and place them in the pan. You do not want to crowd your pan, so if necessary, work in batches. Only if the escalopes have enough room in the pan will they obtain the desired juicy consistency. At this point, dexterity is called for because the thinly sliced meat should only brown on each side for about half a minute. The golden-brown crust will tell you when they are done. Season with salt and pepper after removing them from the pan. Turn down the temperature, and add the lemon juice to the pan, using your wooden spoon to stir in all the brown savory bits that have formed on the bottom. Cream the sauce with one tablespoon of butter, then return the escalopes to the pan to warm them up again. Before serving, sprinkle with the chopped parsley.

FUSION VEAL ESCALOPES WITH MORELS FOR 2

150 g (5 ounces) dried morels (and	1 tbsp. sesame oil
milk for soaking)	⅛ tsp. chili flakes
150 ml (⅔ cup) cream	1 tbsp. ginger, chopped
5 tbsp. dry sherry (or Noilly Prat)	1 lime
1 tbsp. soy sauce	1 tbsp. olive oil

1 tbsp. butter

300 g (11 ounces) veal escalope (2 per person)

flour for coating

1 scallion

1 bunch cilantro

As a riff on another classic Italian dish—veal escalope in a marsala cream sauce—I have come up with an Asian-inspired variation. For the sauce, mix the cream, sherry, soy sauce, and sesame oil with the chopped ginger, lime zest, and chili flakes and put aside in a bowl. Although you could use fresh morels, these mushrooms are almost better when dried, in which case you want to soak them in lukewarm milk for at least an hour. Drain them, and then cut them in half or, if they are very small, keep them whole. Cut off the bottom of the scallions, remove the outer skin, and cut them into paper-thin slices. Chop the cilantro. Once your *mise en place* is ready, heat the oil and the butter in the pan, and as in the previous recipe, wait for the butter to begin to foam before dragging the meat through the flour, shaking off any excess. Sauté the escalopes for thirty seconds on each side, place them on a plate, and season with salt and pepper. Work in batches if you have more escalopes than fit into the pan without overlapping. If you have any excess fat in the pan after frying all the meat, pour this away, then add the morels along with the sauce to the pan, allow it to come to a boil, and continue simmering it over medium heat until it has become a light brown and smoothly dense, about four minutes. Return the escalopes to the pan, turn them in the sauce to reheat them, season to taste with lime juice, and before serving, sprinkle with the chopped cilantro and the scallion slivers.

SCALLOPS WITH WHITE WINE FOR 2

6 scallops

1½ tsp. olive oil

flour

salt and pepper

1 shallot, chopped

150 ml (⅔ cup) white wine
   (or Noilly Prat)

2 tbsp. lemon juice and 1 tbsp. lemon zest

1 tbsp. capers, chopped

3 tbsp. butter

salt and pepper

parsley, chopped

Along with Dover sole, the scallops belong to my favorite seafood, and I prepare both in the same way. The combination of lemon and capers boosts the sweetness of the scallop meat particularly well. To begin, wash the scallops and dry them thoroughly with paper towels. In contrast to the veal escalope,

I season them with salt and pepper before coating them with flour. The pan also needs to be quite hot before adding enough oil to cover the bottom. Then add the scallops to the pan and sear them for one and a half minutes on each side. They should have a golden-brown crust but remain juicy. Take the pan off the heat, cover it, and allow the scallops to finish cooking in the trapped warmth without becoming too dry inside. I must admit, more than once my scallops did not become crisp because I couldn't buy them fresh, still in their shell, as they can only be found in large fish markets. Because scallops must be processed before being transported, they will often release liquid while being seared. This means you may have to give up on the idea of a crisp outer surface. In no case, however, should you fry them longer than necessary, because they will become dry and leathery, losing their sweetness as well.

To make the sauce, remove the scallops from the pan, heat some more oil in the pan, and sauté the chopped shallot over low temperature until they have become translucent, about five minutes. Then raise the temperature; add the white wine (which can be replaced with Noilly Prat), the juice and zest of a lemon, and the coarsely chopped capers; and reduce the liquid until you have a densely textured sauce. To finish it, take the pan off the heat, cream the sauce with butter, season once more with salt and pepper, and sprinkle with parsley. It is up to you whether you drape the scallops on top of the sauce on the plate or spoon the sauce over them.

STUFFED ZUCCHINI BLOSSOMS FOR 2

8 zucchini blossoms	8 tbsp. flour
160 g (¾ cup) mozzarella	salt and pepper
6 anchovies	rapeseed oil (canola oil) for frying
1 egg	

Although deep-frying is normally forbidden in my kitchen, the combination of anchovies and mozzarella as a filling is so satisfying that as soon as I see zucchini blossoms on the market, I can never resist the temptation to make this dish. For the filling, cut the mozzarella into fine cubes, and mix these with the finely chopped anchovies in a bowl. To make sure that the cheese cubes are evenly coated with the anchovy bits, it is best to use your hands. Dexterous finger work is then called for while filling the blossoms. You must open the leaves of the blossoms wide enough so that you can push in all the filling they can hold without tearing any of the individual leaves. These are meant to envelop the spicy mozzarella like a thin coat. Seal them on top by twisting the upper ends of the blossoms into a curled knot so that no filling can fall out while they are frying.

Whisk the egg in the dish in which you intend to coat the blossoms, and then divide the flour among two further dishes and season it with salt and pepper. Heat the oil in a pan with rounded edges that are roughly six millimeters high so that while they are deep frying, the blossoms will be covered with the hot oil. For this reason, you will also have to work in batches and only fry as many blossoms at one time as have enough room in the pan to expand freely while exposed to the hot oil. Depending on the size of your pan, this may mean doing no more than one or two at a time. Before deep-frying, however, you will apply three layers of coating to the filled blossoms. Begin with the first dish of flour, then move to the whisked egg, and finish with the second dish of flour, then place each coated blossoms on a cutting board. It is almost impossible not to coat your fingers while doing this, even if you grab the blossoms by the green stem at the bottom. Although it helps to use a fork or kitchen tongs, I have found that I still need to use my fingers to make sure that each individual blossom is evenly covered with the coating. It is best not to begin deep-frying until all the zucchini blossoms are ready. They take about three to five minutes, and while they are swimming in the hot oil, they should be turned over several times so that they crisp evenly. Drain them on paper towels, and serve immediately. If you let them cool off, the mozzarella will lose its oozing deliciousness.

CHOPPED

A Dream Hamburger with Shoestring Potatoes |
Teriyaki Tuna Burger | Russian Chicken Kotletki |
Oriental Lamb Kofta | Parsnip Fritters | Potato Pancakes

If it were up to me, I would turn any ingredients that can be chopped, grated, shredded, or puréed into round or flat burgers. The names alone—hamburger, patties, kofta, fish cakes, fritters—evoke a panoply of aromas in my mind with which to vary and refine the flavor of this dish. For me, burgers assume an intermediary position between ingredients seared in one piece and those sautéed in slices. Foregrounded in this case is neither the exquisite quality of a particular cut of meat nor the freshness of a piece of fish but rather the way in which chopping the main ingredient takes away its unique texture and allows it instead to merge perfectly with the other ingredients complementing it. In combination with eggs, cheese, flour, and diverse spices, meat, cut by hand or minced in a meat grinder, comes together again into a smoothly textured whole. The enchanting effect relies on the contrast between the juicy consistency inside each of these balls and the crispy surface where the flavor is particularly intense. And of course, the sauce you serve with it works a magic of its own, be it the ordinary ketchup, a spicy homemade mayonnaise, an exotic chutney, or a delicate wine reduction, which, spooned over a burger, can turn this simple dish into a festive affair.

A DREAM HAMBURGER WITH SHOESTRING POTATOES FOR 4 BURGERS

600 g (1 pound, 5 ounces) not-too-lean chopped beef, 150 g (5 ounces) per burger	1 tbsp. olive oil
	3 tbsp. parsley, chopped
	1 tbsp. dried thyme
1 medium shallot, chopped	salt and pepper
2 garlic cloves, chopped	1 tbsp. soy sauce
1 tsp. Worcestershire sauce	rapeseed oil (canola oil) for frying
2 tsp. Dijon mustard	4 buns
1 tbsp. sherry	

SHOESTRING POTATOES

1–1½ L (4–6 cups) rapeseed oil for deep-frying	4 big waxy potatoes, about 300 g (11 ounces per person)

I admit to owning several cookbooks that play through in luscious detail all the ingredients that can be turned into a burger along with all the varied toppings with which to garnish them. Nevertheless, I always return to this heavenly beef burger, where everything depends on the perfect balance in the seasoning of the meat. Choosing fattier meat not only produces a juicier burger; it also enhances the flavor of the aromatic spicing.

Begin by mixing the finely chopped shallot (you should have two tablespoons), the chopped garlic, and the minced meat before folding in the remaining ingredients. It is best to use your hands to make sure that they all come together to form one consistent whole. While it is advisable to allow the meat to rest in the refrigerator, as this allows the flavors to become richer, it is not absolutely necessary. While forming the individual patties, the one thing to decide is whether you want four large burgers or eight smaller ones. Heat the pan (preferably cast iron) over medium temperature, cover the bottom with a thin film of oil, and while you are waiting for this to get really hot, season the burgers on both sides with a bit of salt. If you want them to be medium rare, as I prefer mine, fry them on each side for three to five minutes. If you want them well done, you can reduce the heat after turning them over, cover the pan, and allow them to finish in the heat trapped under the lid. Don't ever use a spatula to press on the burgers, hoping that this may hasten the cooking process. The only thing you will achieve is that the meat releases some of its juices, leaving you with a dried-out burger.

Along with the obligatory bun and ketchup, the best accompaniment for a hamburger is, of course, shoestring potatoes. They may not be healthy, but as Mae West used to say, "Too much of a good thing can be wonderful." In this case the excessively good thing is the oil, in which—this is the crucial part—you need to deep-fry the thin potato strips twice. In contrast to thicker French fries, use waxy potatoes to ensure maximum crispiness. To slice the peeled potatoes into shoestring strips, about five millimeters wide, a julienne grate comes in handy. If you don't own one, then use a very sharp chef's knife. It may take a bit longer and also require a bit of skillful finger work, but the result will be just as good. It is, in either case, essential that you dry the potato strips thoroughly with paper towels and, in the process, also make sure that they do not cling to each other.

For deep-frying choose a pan with a high edge and heat the oil to 150°C (300°F). Toss a good handful of potato strips into the pan and allow them to fry five to ten minutes. This may mean adjusting the heat, so it is worth testing it with your thermometer from time to time. To prevent the individual fries from sticking together, you will also need to keep stirring them. They should become soft and turn golden. Remove the fries with a slotted spoon, and drain them on paper towels. You will need to work in batches because otherwise the delicate potato strings will not fry evenly on all sides. You can, however, put the drained fries into a bowl and allow them to rest for up to an hour. This way you can wait just before serving the hamburger to deep-fry them a second time. For this, reheat the oil once more to 170°C (325°F), and fry the potato strings for only a few minutes more. Again, you will need to work in batches if you want to get them to become golden brown and crisp. And as before, drain the shoestring potatoes on paper towels to absorb excess fat before tossing them with salt in a big bowl.

TERIYAKI TUNA BURGER FOR 2 BURGERS

400 g (14 ounces) tuna steak	2½ tbsp. olive oil
1 tsp. garlic clove, chopped	pickled sushi ginger (*gari*)
¼ tsp. cayenne pepper	2 buns
¼ tsp. black pepper	

FOR THE GLAZE

1 tbsp. soy sauce	½ tsp. garlic, chopped
1 tbsp. sake	1 tbsp. honey
1 tbsp. mirin	1 tbsp. Dijon mustard
2 tsp. ginger, chopped	½ tsp. white balsamic vinegar

The inspiration for this burger comes from the *Union Square Cookbook*, and it is best to make the glaze first. Bring all the ingredients to a boil, turn down the heat, and allow them to simmer until you have a dense sauce, about five minutes. Strain the sauce through a sieve, and put it aside. It will keep in the refrigerator, so you can make it several days in advance.

While it would be a pity to use sushi-quality tuna for a burger, because you will be mincing it in a meat grinder, you need to not only wash the fish and thoroughly dry it with paper towels but also remove any skin as well as any of the thick white tendons. If you don't have a meat grinder, chop the tuna very finely by hand with a very sharp knife. In a bowl, mix together the tuna with the chopped garlic and the spices, and make either two big or four small burgers. As in the previous recipe, I suggest using a cast-iron pan for frying these tuna burgers, three to four minutes on each side. You want them to be crisp outside but medium rare inside. Before serving, drizzle each burger with the glaze and garnish with slices of pickled ginger, a fitting replacement for the ketchup and gherkin of the American original. Whether you still want to keep the traditional bun or choose a different bed for your burger is up to you. You may just want to eat it as it is.

RUSSIAN CHICKEN KOTLETKI FOR 8 BURGERS (OR 16 SMALL)

500 g (one pound) turkey escalope or chicken breast, chopped	1 pinch nutmeg
	1 spring onion, finely chopped
1 egg	parsley
1 tbsp. melted butter	salt and pepper
1 bread roll (soaked in milk)	clarified butter for frying

While I was still a doctoral student, I bought myself a small hand-cranked meat grinder simply to be able to reproduce the chicken meatballs I first ate in the home of my Russian teacher, Natasha. Even today it isn't always easy to find a butcher that will grind poultry for you. So if you love the idea of chicken or turkey burgers, it may be a worthwhile investment. But then again you can always chop by hand, although this will require a very sharp chef's knife. Because chopped chicken has less of a distinct flavor, various ways of seasoning these small burgers are possible. If you want a Middle Eastern note, use a combination of mint and cilantro as your aromatics and season with cumin, cayenne pepper, and a pinch of *ras el hanout*. If you prefer a more Southeast Asian touch, you can add garlic, ginger, and scallions to the chopped chicken, replace the parsley with cilantro, and spice with a combination of chili sauce and lime juice. Because of its simplicity, this Russian version, however, has remained my favorite.

Wash the chicken breasts (which could be replaced with turkey), dry them thoroughly with paper towels as you would beef or tuna, grind or mince them by hand, and place them in a large kitchen bowl. Soak the bread roll in milk, melt the butter in a small pan, and then add these to the chopped chicken along with the nutmeg, the finely chopped onions, and a handful of chopped parsley leaves. Season the chicken with salt and pepper, and again, using your hand, mix everything together thoroughly before forming the meatballs. It is, once more, up to you whether you want smaller round ones that are more compact or larger, slightly flatter ones. In a hot pan, melt enough clarified butter to cover the bottom with a thin film and, so as not to crowd the pan, work in batches, frying the burgers on both sides for about four minutes. If you find that they have soaked up the butter too quickly, you can add more, but do so from the edges of the pan so that, as it glides along the bottom of the pan, it will heat up immediately. One important difference to the beef or tuna burger, which I prefer to eat medium rare, is that the chicken must be well done. If you find that your burgers have already developed a golden-brown crust but are still rare inside, turn down the heat, and keep turning them in fifteen-second intervals until they are done. This way you can prevent them from becoming too brown on the outside.

ORIENTAL LAMB KOFTA FOR 2–3

400 g (14 ounces) lamb, chopped	2 garlic cloves, chopped
1 onion, grated	120 g (1 cup) pine nuts

80 g (½ cup) raisins	½ tsp. cumin
2 tbsp. mint	½ tsp. curcuma
2 tbsp. parsley	salt
1 tsp. paprika	olive oil for frying
½ tsp. cinnamon	

FOR THE SAUCE

100 g (¾ cup) pine nuts	2 tbsp. pomegranate molasses
8 tbsp. tahini paste	1 garlic clove, chopped
2 lemons	salt and pepper
2 tsp. soy sauce	

You should prepare the sauce for this Middle Eastern burger first. Begin by frying the pine nuts in a dry pan over medium heat until they are a light golden brown, but be careful not to scorch them. Allow them to cool before coarsely chopping them in a food processor (or a mortar). In the meantime, mix the tahini paste with the lemon juice, season with salt and pepper, and stir vigorously until you have a smooth consistency. Add the pine nuts, and set the sauce aside, turning your attention instead to making the lamb kofta. Chop the garlic, parsley, and mint as well as the pine nuts, grate the onion very finely, and in a big kitchen bowl, mix together all these aromatics with the chopped lamb. Add the spices, and season to taste with a bit of salt. For this dish, roll the meat into small balls, place these on a cutting board, and using your fingers, press them down slightly. You want them to be flat rather than round. Heat the olive oil in a nonstick pan and, as in the previous recipes, work in batches, frying the koftas for four minutes on each side. They are best served with bread or couscous.

PARSNIP FRITTERS FOR 2–3

500 g (one pound) parsnips	vanilla salt
1 fennel	cayenne pepper
4 tbsp. parsley, chopped	2–4 tbsp. goose schmaltz (or clarified
2 eggs	butter) for frying
4 tbsp. flour	

Of course you can also fry chopped or grated vegetables in a pan, the most well-known fritter probably being grated zucchini combined with feta. I have chosen parsnips for my recipe suggestion to showcase this root vegetable that in recent years has begun to gain traction again. For the longest time, I only knew parsnips from the Victorian fiction of Dickens, Eliot, and Hardy, where off and on I would read about characters enjoying a dish of roasted parsnip. Because these roots were rarely to be found in vegetable markets on the European continent, whenever an academic conference brought me to England, I would buy several pounds of parsnips and take them home. Only since the slow-food movement rediscovered old vegetables have parsnips begun to appear regularly on the shelves of many a supermarket, often lying next to the parsley root, so similar in looks and equally worth a second culinary glance. My British friends assure me that the best thing to do with parsnips is to make a soup seasoned with curry or to mash them with butter. But I also find them immensely convincing as a fritter.

Peel the parsnips and coarsely grate them, turning them so as to work around the tough inner core (which is best discarded). Rather than using the onion normally called for in a vegetable fritter, I prefer fennel because its flavor is less sharp. Before coarsely grating the fennel, however, I peel the outer, fibrous skin. In a large kitchen bowl, mix together the grated vegetables with the chopped parsley, the beaten egg, and the flour, then season with vanilla salt and a pinch of cayenne pepper. You want the mixture to be dense in texture but not crumbly. As is always the case when frying in a pan, the fritters need to have enough room. They should form a crust quickly; otherwise, they will fall apart. So once again, it is necessary to work in batches. The pan and the goose schmaltz (or clarified butter) must be quite hot before you drop heaped tablespoons of the parsnip mixture into the pan. What is forbidden when frying beef burgers is good practice here. Use the back of your wooden spoon to press down on each of the fritters to ensure that they become crisp quickly in the sizzling fat while not losing their shape. After two minutes, you can usually turn them over and fry them on the other side for a couple more minutes. You might want to drizzle some lemon juice over them or serve them with chutney. But the combination of vanilla salt with the goose schmaltz and the sweetness of the parsnip is also enchanting enough on its own.

POTATO PANCAKES FOR 2–3

6 waxy potatoes	½ tsp. baking powder
1 big onion	salt and pepper
2 eggs	1 pinch nutmeg
5–6 tbsp. flour	rapeseed oil or goose schmaltz

In Bavaria, where I grew up, they were called *Reiberdatschi*; in the Eastern-European Jewish kitchen of my father, they were called *latkes*. Some eat them with applesauce, others with sour cream and smoked salmon. If you are feeling especially generous, you can eat them with caviar and a pinch of horseradish. One way or another, they belong to what is called comfort food, offering up, as they unequivocally do, a sense of well-being and solace. Because she knows how fond I am of this dish, my sister, Susan, even gave me a grater designed especially for producing the perfect potato slivers.

Wash the potatoes thoroughly in cold water. Whether you then proceed to peel them or not is up to you. Important, however, is that you use a medium grater to produce delicate rather than coarse potato strips. Allow the grated potatoes to drain in a sieve, at least thirty minutes. In the meantime, grate the onions and set them aside as well. After thirty minutes, press the potatoes to extract as much liquid as possible, and in a big bowl, mix them with the onions, the beaten egg, the flour, and the baking powder before seasoning with salt, pepper, and a pinch of nutmeg. When you are ready to fry the pancakes, heat the fat in a nonstick pan, and then add a generous tablespoon each of the potato mixture to the hot pan, pressing down on each mound with the back of a wooden spoon. Fry them until they have become golden brown, about five minutes on each side. Pat each potato pancake with paper towels to remove excess fat, and season with salt before serving.

NOTE: If you want to rethink the traditional potato pancake, add grated carrots, kohlrabi, or parsley root to the potato mixture.

FROM THE FRYING PAN INTO THE OVEN

Beef Fillet | Rack of Lamb with Lavender Crust | Tarte Tatin with Apples | Tarte Tatin with Apricots and Rosemary

As the final example for the choices we are confronted with when pan-frying, which this chapter has explored, I offer a hybrid: the happy conjunction between one-sided heat in the pan and all-encompassing heat in the oven. If you have a thick steak or another piece of meat that you can't quickly fry on both sides, you can first sear it in the pan and then finish it in the preheated oven. Or as in the case of a lamb rack, you can first brown the meat and then cover it with a savory crust before roasting it. Or you can wrap caramelized sugar covered with fruit in dough, as for a tarte Tatin, and bake it. In each case, once the ingredients have been transferred from the stovetop to the oven, a low, even temperature gently envelops them on all sides as they finish cooking. Now the attentive readiness so crucial for pan-frying is no longer necessary. While the dish is roasting or baking in the oven, you must trust in your good fortune. You can no longer intervene. Adroitness doesn't come into play again until the dish is ready to be served.

BEEF FILLET FOR 2

300 g (11 ounces) beef fillet	olive oil
rosemary	salt and pepper

It is, of course, entirely possible to fry a sirloin steak in a cast-iron pan, and if you keep turning it every fifteen seconds, it will also remain juicy because it is thus exposed to continuous short heat impulses. However, to prepare a thicker fillet steak, flavored with aromatic herbs, I prefer to sear it in the hot pan first and then allow it to finish cooking in the oven. Before doing so, however, you must not only make sure that your meat is at room temperature but also dry it thoroughly with paper towels. If it is moist, it won't sear properly in the pan.

Heat the oven to 180°C (350°F). In an ovenproof pan, sear one side of the beef fillet in olive oil, around thirty seconds, and then once you have turned it over, generously season the seared side with salt and pepper. After thirty seconds, flip the beef fillet over, and season the second side with salt and pepper as well. Now drizzle olive oil over the beef, place one or two rosemary twigs on top, and transfer the pan to the oven, where it can finish cooking, around eight minutes. I tend to check every now and then and baste the fillet with the liquid that has formed at the bottom of the pan.

RACK OF LAMB WITH LAVENDER CRUST FOR 2

½ medium fennel	2 tbsp. butter
3 tbsp. parsley, chopped	salt and pepper
1¼ tsp. fresh lavender	1 rack of lamb (3 chops per person)
2 garlic cloves, chopped	olive oil for frying
80 g (2 cups) panko (or bread crumbs)	

An elegant rack of lamb is simple to prepare as long as you bear in mind that in this case as well, your meat should be room temperature. If it is too cold,

Smelling herbs

it won't sear properly. Preheat to oven to 200°C (400°F) in advance so that it will have the proper temperature when you are ready to cook.

In the meantime, you can prepare the mixture for the crust with which you will cover the rack of lamb. In a kitchen bowl, mix the finely grated fennel with the lavender, the chopped garlic, the chopped parsley, and the panko, and then add the melted butter. Using your hands, mix everything thoroughly until the panko has fully absorbed the herbs and the butter. Season the crust mixture with salt and pepper and place it aside while preparing the rack of lamb for roasting. To be on the safe side, you should dry the meat once more with paper towels before seasoning with salt and pepper. Add enough oil to a sauté pan to cover the bottom, and then fry the meat side of your rack of lamb over medium heat without turning it, two to three minutes. Place the rack in an ovenproof pan or casserole dish, with the bones at the bottom and the seared meat on top. Now you want to press the panko-herb mixture into the lamb, for which it is best to use your fingers to make sure that it is actually clinging to the meat and that nothing is about to fall off. Roast the rack of lamb in the oven around twenty-five minutes, or until it reaches 60°C (140°F). Allow the meat to rest for ten minutes before serving. If you find you have made too much panko-herb mixture, you can roll it up in aluminum foil and roast it along with the rack of lamb.

TARTE TATIN WITH APPLES FOR 4–6

80 g (⅓ cup) sugar and 2 tsp. vanilla sugar

4 tbsp. butter

8 golden delicious apples

juice of 1 lemon

270 g (10 ounces) puff pastry (store bought or homemade)

It is worth investing in a tarte Tatin dish. Once you have mastered the preparation of this delicious dessert, I am certain that you will want to experiment with different fruits. And although it is rarely the case that I have leftovers, I adore having cold tarte Tatin for breakfast the next morning.

The type of apple you use is up to you, but they should be tart and crunchy. Heat the oven to 180°C (350°F), peel and core the apples, and cut them into slices, roughly one centimeter (one-half inch) thick. To prevent them from turning brown, place them in a bowl, and as you work your way through your batch of apples, drizzle the slices with lemon juice. Once done slicing the apples, pour away the lemon juice that has collected at the bottom of the bowl so the fruit filling will not be too liquidy. Now comes the tricky bit.

Caramelize the sugar over fairly low heat, making sure that it doesn't scorch. You want to have a thin layer of evenly textured dark-brown liquid, covering the entire bottom of the tarte Tatin pan. For this reason, you must constantly watch what is happening in the pan. If some parts brown more quickly than others, you can gently shake the pan and rotate it on the stovetop, making sure that as it slowly melts, the sugar is evenly distributed. Do not, however, stir the sugar with a wooden spoon.

Once the sugar has caramelized, take the tarte Tatin pan off the heat; add two-thirds of the butter, cut into small bits, into the hot sugar, where it will immediately begin to foam. Now place the apple slices into the pan, forming overlapping circles as you work your way from the edges into the center. You don't need to be all too perfectionist in the arrangement of the apples, since they will be mushed in the process of roasting. Use smaller pieces to fill gaps. Dot the apples with the remaining butter, cut into small bits, and over very low heat, warm the sugar-apple mixture. It is not necessary to stir them. Then cover the apples carefully with the rolled-out puff pastry, folding it along the inner edge of the dish, as though tucking in the apple slices. Place the tarte Tatin pan into the middle of the oven, and bake it for about twenty-five minutes. Although the successful outcome is no longer in your hands, you should check on your tart now and then. Once it has turned golden brown, you can take it out of the oven and let it cool off. If it is not developing an even crust, you will have to open the oven and carefully rotate the pan. Once you have taken the tarte Tatin out of the oven, it should cool for at least ten minutes.

The final step is one I was afraid of for the longest time. You need to cover the tarte Tatin pan with a plate and with an agile movement of both hands, flip it around so that the tart falls onto the plate. To quote Hamlet once more, "Readiness is all." Once you have successfully flipped over the tart, you can use the blade of a knife to lift off the dish and, by uncovering the apple tart, examine what has occurred in the oven. It helps to be alone in the kitchen at this moment. If something goes wrong while flipping the tart around or if something falls out while taking off the dish, you can always correct the appearance of your tarte Tatin without anyone noticing.

TARTE TATIN WITH APRICOTS AND ROSEMARY FOR 4–6

80 g (⅓ cup) sugar and 2 tsp. vanilla sugar
4 tbsp. butter
1 kg (2.2 pounds) apricots

2 tbsp. fruit marmalade
1 tbsp. rosemary, finely chopped
270 g (10 ounces) puff pastry

To conclude this chapter, I have chosen a variation on the classic tarte Tatin because not only do apricots roast brilliantly, but because they are sprinkled with chopped rosemary, they develop an enticing aroma. While the oven is heating up to 180°C (350°F), wash the apricots, cut them in half, and remove the pits. To prepare the filling, follow the previous recipe. First caramelize the sugar, then take the dish off the heat and melt two-thirds of the butter, cut into small pieces, into the hot sugar, where it will immediately begin to sizzle. At no point should you stir the sugar with a wooden spoon; instead, shake the pan and rotate it so as to better conduct the heat. Then place the apricot halves into the dish in a circular pattern, beginning with the outer edge and working your way to the center. So that you end up with the entire bottom of the dish generously covered, you can cut the apricots into smaller pieces and fill any gaps.

For this version, I add a thin layer of marmalade before covering the fruit with the puff pastry. If you want to enhance the tartness of the apricots, you may well choose an orange marmalade, but apricot, peach, or mango will do just as well. Simply make sure you choose one with a fitting color. Only then do I dot the sliced apricots with the remaining butter, cut into small bits, and heat up the pan again, over low heat, for about three minutes. Now is the time to generously sprinkle the rosemary over the apricots. It is worth chopping it very finely so that it blends perfectly with the aroma of the roasted fruit. Then as in the previous recipe, cover the apricots with the puff pastry, tucking it in along the edges before baking the tart for about twenty-five minutes in the oven. Before flipping it onto the serving plate, allow it to cool, about ten minutes. Crème fraîche or vanilla ice cream goes with both versions. But being a purist, I usually enjoy my slice of apricot tarte Tatin all on its own.

❧ 3 ❧

ALL STOCKED UP

Close at Hand | *In the Pantry* | *Prepared and Stored in the Refrigerator* |
Pestos and Hummus | *Leftovers* | *Flavors and Aromas*

As is so often the case in life, when it comes to stocking up your pantry, you want to strike a happy balance. I am prone to a feeling of panic at the sight of an empty refrigerator, as though some protective force had left the kitchen. Yet some of my guests, upon opening the door to mine, bulging with jars, tins, and bags, will shake their head in gentle dismay. It doesn't help to remind them that in former times, every home had not only a larder but also cool cellar rooms in which to store preserved fruits, pickled vegetables, homemade marmalades, sausages, and spirits. I am never able to fully convince my friends that this abundance is, in part, my version of magical thinking, an apotropaic gesture aimed at averting a state of culinary emergency. I must admit, of course, that at issue in this accumulation of delectables is also the thrill of anticipation I feel when, on a shopping spree, I come across an unusual herb mustard or a rare maple cream or when I am finally able to locate the truffle honey I have been longing for. Each item represents a trouvaille, whose discovery evokes ideas about what I might prepare with this treasure. Now I am perfectly aware that hoarding food is unwise, because this means running the risk of not being able to make use of these delicacies before they have passed their shelf life. As we all know, over time, oil will become rancid, flour becomes bitter, and pulses lose their taste. Furthermore, I am so likely to forget what is hidden behind the front row of the supplies in my kitchen cupboard that I am compelled to rearrange them constantly. Looking for the sweet pistachio pesto that I suddenly remember having bought during a trip to Naples can also become tedious it if means clearing out an entire shelf before being able to use it.

In a concerted effort to convince myself of the surplus value of minimalism, I have repeatedly tried to curb my enthusiasm for shopping. Going to one of the smaller grocery stores close by would, indeed, have the charm of an everyday ritual. It would encourage more impromptu cooking. And yet, because Chronos, the god of time, often thwarts such spontaneity, reducing the time I actually have for leisurely shopping, I can't help but stockpile. A particularly good excuse is, furthermore, the widespread fantasy that it must be possible for me to cook a grand meal for guests even if they show up unexpectedly or at the wrong time. A well-stocked pantry also helps keep in check the fear of failure so familiar to any cook. If preparing a dish turns into a fiasco, you can always start over again. Because there usually isn't enough time to go out and buy new ingredients, you can fall back on what you have on hand. And what, of course, makes everyday cooking easier is to not think of shopping and preparing food as one but rather treat them as two separate acts that can occur at different moments in time. While it makes sense to only buy certain ingredients fresh, there are others that will keep or that can even be prepared in advance. And to be honest, some foods actually improve in the refrigerator.

A well-stocked pantry is predicated on asking yourself the following: What ingredients can I buy in bulk because it is perfectly safe to store them for a longer period of time? What ingredients do I really use regularly so that it is worth stocking up on them? When is it wiser to buy something in smaller amounts so as not to compromise the quality? And what do you buy only when a dish asks for this particular ingredient? At the same time, you want to be prepared for all contingencies. To my mind, the perfect image for this is the string bag my Russian teacher, Natasha Nikitina, used to tell me about in the 1980s. In the Soviet Union, it was called *avoska*, or "maybe bag," a gesture toward the fact that given the shortage of consumer goods, procuring certain products was considered a stroke of luck. Because the *avoska* could fit as easily into a handbag or into an attaché case, Soviet women and men would carry this string bag with them all day long on the off chance that they might find something to buy walking along a street. While in Russia today, *avoskas* are a thing of the past, Natasha's stories have inspired me to always carry a foldable nylon bag with me. I would never want to miss out on any lucky opportunity at the farmers' market, be it a particularly scrumptious sausage, an enticing truffle, or simply a loaf of bread whose fragrant smell attracted me as I was walking by the baker's stall. I am, however, particularly happy with my own, far more elegant *avoska* when I travel, because it is then that I have enough leisure to be on a constant lookout for delicacies I might bring home. I like to visit local supermarkets in foreign cities on principle because I am always interested to see what is on offer there. But I am particularly drawn to small specialty stores and tourist gourmet markets. It is almost impossible for

Me between work and dining

me to leave these with an empty bag. I already know in advance the pleasure this booty will afford once I have safely carried it back into my own kitchen.

Indeed, I have come to compare my pantry to the shelf of reference books behind my desk. Like the cherished books that, when writing, I need to have close by just in case I want to consult them, the ingredients I have carefully chosen and arranged in a certain way (even if I might reassemble from time to time) are what I know I can fall back on when I want to experiment; when I need to correct the flavor of a dish; when in the course of cooking, I suddenly feel like changing the recipe; or when I simply didn't have the opportunity to go shopping. An air of promise hovers over this space because a prudently stocked pantry is really a site of available opportunities and possibilities. My pantry allows me to be ready to cook at all times, to prepare something impromptu and in a short period of time, but also to respond serenely to all coincidences, be they chance opportunities or accidents. It calms as well as satisfies me to know that, if necessary, I could cook for an entire week using only the quotidian as well as all the extravagant things I have assembled in my pantry. But my stockpile of supplies is also the source of culinary inspiration for me. While my eyes wander along the kitchen shelves, I start thinking about what I might prepare or about which ingredients I could try to combine. As in any library, the collection is decidedly personal. Not only does my own experience with certain products play into any decision regarding the salts and oils, pulses and pasta types, canned tomatoes and pickled vegetables, spices and herbs I always have at my disposal; the limited space in most kitchens today already dictates that this will always only be a manageable selection. Spring cleaning, an annual ritual I strictly adhere to, has its own beneficial effect. Along with cleaning my clothes closets, I also rigorously clear out my kitchen cupboards. This allows me to take stock and see not only what needs to be used up soon but also what has already expired.

If then, regardless of all judicious deliberation, a love for collecting food products remains, quality is crucial. During my weekly visit to the grocery store, I am more than willing to buy things that are regularly on special offer. For a well-stocked pantry, however, it is worth spending more to assemble the best possible ingredients. The difference between an ordinary tuna pickled in brine and the costly tuna belly preserved in olive oil—for which I may need to drive to a specialty shop clear across town—will determine whether a pasta sauce is merely all right or whether I will dazzle my guests with a truly spectacular dish. I don't have a pantry of my own next to my kitchen, and I envy all my friends who do. But this means that I can store my supplies in different locations—in shelves and in the kitchen cupboard, in the refrigerator and on the balcony. There is an added benefit to this. The reassurance, as well as the anticipation, that I attach to my sundry supplies is disseminated across the entire kitchen. Like the reference shelf in my home library, the arrangement of all the food products I always have in stock is thus conceived in spatial terms—depending on the way certain ingredients are deployed during the cooking process. Below I begin the description of my kitchen with ingredients such as salt, pepper, oil, and vinegar, which, because they must be close at hand at all times, are located near the stovetop. In this interior architecture, other ingredients have been allocated in their place based on the manner in which they are most frequently deployed. Spices and dried herbs stand next to each other on a shelf in the darkest corner of my kitchen where, like paint on a palette, they offer shades of aromatic embellishment. Other ingredients are stored together in the one pullout pantry I have or the refrigerator because they are often used in combination. The arrangement of my kitchen, in other words, mirrors the various steps, choices, and decisions of the cooking process itself.

CLOSE AT HAND

Lavender Salt | Chili Oil

A kitchen without **salt** and **pepper** isn't a kitchen. How wide a selection you want to have at hand is, in turn, a question of your personal preferences. When a recipe asks for pepper, regardless of whether black, white, or red, this always refers to peppercorns, freshly ground in a pepper mill (or in a mortar). While I am particularly fond of the magnificent pepper from Kampot, Cambodia, the range of choices these days is huge. One thing to bear in mind, however, is not to economize when it comes to this spice. A fundamental rule to skillful seasoning applies: better have only one truly outstanding pepper than several of inferior quality. On the kitchen ledge close to my three pepper mills, I also keep jars with two types of chili, **cayenne pepper** and *piment d'Espelette*, which, used in careful dosage, will intensify the poignancy of any dish.

Directly behind my stovetop, I also keep a small saltbox filled with ordinary **sea salt**, used only for water in which I cook pasta, potatoes, or vegetables. The palette of salts that I use to season dishes, in turn, varies, although I try not to be seduced by the extraordinary range of salts now available in fancy gourmet shops. Not least of all because of the variation in color, I will sometimes use a coarse *sel gris*, sometimes smoky **brown salt flakes**, sometimes **black Hawaiian salt**, which brings a delicate egg flavor to any dish. While this assortment may change, there are three aromatic salts that I always fall back on: **vanilla salt**, **chili salt**, and **celery salt**. And also always close to my stovetop is a box of **fleur de sel**. Particularly suitable for making your own herb salts, this also makes a perfect gift for when someone else invites you over for a meal. You can use any mixture of fresh thyme, rosemary, or sage; first grind the herbs with a teaspoon of fleur de sel in a spice mill (or mortar) before stirring in the remaining salt. Allow the salt to dry for several hours on a chopping board before filling it into a jar. If you prefer a citrus taste, you can mix the fleur de sel with finely chopped dried lemon zest, tangerine zest, or orange zest. For a more intense floral taste, use dried rose blossoms, ground in a spice mill (or mortar); for an Asian touch, use finely chopped kaffir lime leaves. Or you can take a tablespoon of Japanese matcha green tea powder. My favorite aromatic flavor, however, is lavender salt.

LAVENDER SALT

225 g (1¾ cups) fleur de sel   1 tbsp. dry lavender, chopped

I find combining lavender with salt so convincing because, while this seasoning gives a fruity note to any marinade or salad dressing, the herb itself doesn't dominate. Rather, you simply sense a touch of lavender. Just make sure that the lavender you buy is meant for edible consumption and that the salt (if not using fleur de sel) is not too fine-grained. Put the salt into a small kitchen bowl, and grind the lavender in a spice mill; if you don't have this nifty kitchen tool, chop it very finely with a sharp knife. Add the ground lavender to the salt, and mix well before pouring it into a jar with a closely fitting lid. I tend to do this in stages, always shaking the container a bit so as to blend the salt and the lavender more thoroughly. The salt will keep for many months.

Vinegar and **oil** are also a fixed staple in the reserve shelf in my kitchen. Although, in a pinch, one could always replace the fruity tartness that vinegar gives to a dish with lemon juice or wine, I always have several **balsamic fruit vinegars** at hand. I not only use these to make marinades or dressings but also fall back on them whenever a soup or a sauce needs a flavor boost. I will use the less costly **white balsamic vinegar**, as well as an **apple balsamic vinegar** when sweetness would improve a sauce or a marinade, while **sherry vinegar** allows me to draw out a touch of acidity. As with pepper, you should not economize when it comes to buying *aceto balsamico di Modena*. You will only need a small spoonful of this dark, lush liquid to give the crowning touch to a sauce or to drizzle over a piece of fish before serving. For salad dressings, I prefer my less costly balsamic vinegar, which, as a variation on the classic French vinaigrette, I will blend with mustard or with olive paste.

When it comes to my selection of oils, I am a bit more generous. I use two different types of **olive oil**: an ordinary one for frying and a more expensive one for salad dressings and marinades. For briefly searing or stir-frying an ingredient, I prefer **rapeseed oil** and for a more supple fat, **coconut oil**. Moreover, there are two less common nut oils—**argan oil** and **pistachio oil**—whose intense taste I like to make use of in salad dressings as well as when adding a drizzling touch to a dish. A further triad of flavored olive oils includes the **lemon oil**, **orange oil**, and **truffle oil** that I also keep close to my stovetop. The latter fits perfectly not only to any ravioli but also surprisingly—and totally unconventionally—to couscous. For my experiments with Asian flavors that, in the spirit of fusion cooking, I like to make use of when cooking traditional European dishes, I also always have **sesame oil** and **chili oil** close at hand.

CHILI OIL

250 ml (1 cup) olive oil
2 tbsp. red chili flakes
zest of 1 lemon
a thumb-size piece of ginger, peeled
and cut into thin longish slices

1 garlic clove, peeled and cut into
thin slices
1 tsp. fennel seeds, crushed
2 rosemary twigs

Like any aromatic salt or spicy sugar and indeed any pickled vegetable or pesto, you can, of course, buy chili oil readymade. And yet not only is making your own very easy, but it also allows you to control the dosage of the spices you use for seasoning. Plus, like herb salts, this also makes for an excellent gift to bring to friends who invite you over for dinner.

In a small pot, heat the olive oil to 120°C (250°F) over medium heat. You will need a digital thermometer to get the temperature just right. Once the oil has reached 120°C (250°F), take the pot off the heat; you don't want it to come to a boil. Now add the chili flakes, the lemon zest, the ginger, the fennel seeds, and the rosemary twigs, and allow the spices and herbs to steep in the warm oil for at least ten minutes. Once the oil has cooled down completely, remove the ginger and the lemon zest, and pour it into a sterilized bottle, but retain the rosemary twig and the other spices. The chili oil will keep for months if stored in a cool, dark spot in the kitchen.

The **spices** and **herbs** on my culinary reserve shelf have been chosen with an eye for the flavors and aromas I concentrate on in my cooking. If a particular dish requires a special spice, I can always buy a small amount of it or replace it with something similar I have in stock. The flavor may be slightly different, but that also means giving a personal signature to the dish. Having said that, it is worth trying out different seasonings with courage and conviction, even if this means embracing the possibility of failure. This will allow you to discover for yourself not only what flavor a particular spice will unleash—such as vanilla with pumpkin—but also what new flavor the interaction of certain spices will yield. To find out what spices absolutely don't work together can be as inspiring and useful as the serendipity of coming upon a flavor combination hitherto unfamiliar. As with pepper, it is best to grind or grate spices just before using them. This way they retain their freshness.

Furthermore, it is also best to store spices in airtight jars in a dark and cool spot in the kitchen. On my spice shelf, I always have **cloves, sticks of cinnamon, caraway seeds, cumin, coriander seeds, black and white sesame seeds, chili flakes**, and **nutmeg**. Only recently have I added **tonka beans** to my permanent stock. Its spicy vanilla aroma enhances any stew or soup, as it does any dessert such as crème brûlée or ice cream. And finally, there is always a jar with precious **saffron threads** (never saffron powder) on my spice shelf, lending vibrant golden color to any couscous or tagine. Although sparsely, I also use these precious threads in pasta sauces and in the filling of quiche.

There are, however, some ground spices on my spice shelf as well, especially those I use for Middle Eastern– and Asian-inspired dishes—first and foremost two types of **curry powder**, one mild, the other spicy. Along with fiery red **paprika** and golden **turmeric** (which readily stains anything it comes into contact with but, because it isn't impermeable to light, will disappear again when brought into contact with direct sunlight), I also always keep ground **cinnamon, coriander, cumin**, and **ginger**. These spices offer important colors on my aroma palette, allowing me to experiment with combinations until the dosage seems just right. Other aromatics that I keep in the same part of the kitchen are more often used to sprinkle over ingredients, such as the Middle Eastern **za'atar** (the mixture from Aleppo is said to be the best), which works for roasted vegetables as well as for a casserole. I will, however, also sprinkle Japanese **furikake rice seasoning** over tofu steaks, poached fish, or a salad. And finally, I always have a jar of **dried tomato flakes** on hand, which not only make a wonderful cold pasta sauce when stirred into olive oil and seasoned with thyme but also lend an intense sweetness to any stew.

As you can often read in cookbooks, **fresh herbs** are preferable to dried ones. If you have no garden of your own, you can keep them for months on the balcony or on a windowsill. Each spring I go to the farmers' market and procure my set of potted herbs, which I then proudly watch grow. I tell myself that the aroma they lend to my cooking is particularly delicious because I take care of them daily. On my balcony, you will find next to the obligatory **basil, thyme, sage**, and **bay leaf** tree a small pot of **tarragon**, a **vervain** plant, and several different **mint** plants, herbs I use for tea as well as for salads or for making a pesto. The jewel in the crown, however, is my **shiso plant**, a Japanese basil that has recently begun to appear on farmers' markets. You can harvest leaves from a pot of shiso for many months, because like my pot of **chives**, this herb is indestructible. Indeed, the husband of my Japanese friend Keiko, who gave me my very first shiso plant, calls it a delicious weed that neither wind

Herbs in a glass jug

nor rain can harm. This is his way of saying that he finds the ubiquitous usage to which his wife puts it slightly unnerving. But I don't agree.

Experience has taught me that **parsley** fares less well on the balcony and is better stored in the refrigerator. It will keep for a week, either together with a damp piece of paper towel in an airtight container or, treated like a flower bouquet, in a small vase with water. In contrast, fresh **cilantro**, which I also use constantly, can only be stored for two to three days in the refrigerator. Like other herbs—above all **chives**, **basil**, **mint**, **tarragon**, and **parsley**—when chopped it will keep in the deep freezer. While all these herbs will take on a darker color when defrosted, their aroma will have been preserved. **Kaffir lime leaves** as well as **lemongrass**, which you usually only find in large amounts in Asian grocery stores, also deep-freeze well. And finally, it is worth reminding oneself that the skin of any citrus fruit can be preserved.

No lemon, lime, or orange goes unzested in my kitchen. I deep-freeze these in small containers. This isn't just because of my obsession with thriftiness but also because I know they will come in handy when I have forgotten to buy fresh fruit.

At the same time, I must confess that I find the demonization of **dried herbs** (a standard in my mother's cooking) to be exaggerated. Once, when I needed to buy tarragon at a market in Nice, the vendor at the vegetable stand assured me that it was perfectly fine to use the dried one she had for sale, in part, of course, an elegant way to excuse the fact that she had sold all of her fresh tarragon. Certain recipes—like my pea soup—actually require a mixture of dried and fresh mint. For this reason I encourage common sense when it comes to dried herbs, which have their own designated spot in my kitchen, right next to my spices. It is important to remember not only that you will need less but that you should buy them in small quantities because the intensity of the flavor of dried herbs diminishes quickly. As a rule of thumb, use a quarter tablespoon of dried herbs for one tablespoon of fresh ones. Another thing to bear in mind is that, in contrast to fresh herbs, you shouldn't wait until the last minute to add dry herbs to a dish; they should be either part of the marinade or part of the *soffritto*, in which case they will cook in the sauce. Here is a list of dried herbs that are well worth having on hand: **dill**, **thyme**, **lavender**, **bay leaves**, *herbes de Provence*, **rosemary**, and **mint**. Like spices, dried herbs can be stored in airtight jars for months, but they are best kept in a cold, dark part of the kitchen.

And finally, **onions**, **garlic**, **lemon**, and fresh **tomatoes**, which I treat as though they were part of my aroma palate, also belong to the stock of fresh ingredients I always have on hand, usually in a bowl on my kitchen table. Other condiments I also draw on regularly include a bottle of **Noilly Prat**. I fall back on this when I don't have an open wine bottle in my refrigerator, and a bottle of **verjus**, which, made from unripe grapes, provides even more acidity. While some condiments essential for Asian flavoring—**soy sauce**, **mirin**, **sake**, and **fish sauce**—can be kept in bottles on a kitchen shelf close to the stovetop, once opened, **oyster sauce** and **chili-bean sauce** should be stored in the refrigerator. There they stand next to small bottles of **ketchup**, **Tabasco sauce**, and **Worcestershire sauce**. And two further condiments must never be missing from my kitchen: **pomegranate molasses**, which endow any sauce or marinade with a sweetly acidic note, and **vanilla paste** (or **vanilla extract**), which I often use to replace the standard **vanilla bean**.

IN THE PANTRY

In my **pullout pantry**, I have arranged my supplies according to common traits. The nuts I use to embellish a salad or to garnish a soup—**pine nuts, roasted pumpkin seeds, pistachios,** and **goji berries**—have their place next to **raisins** and **dried cherries**, which I use not only for desserts but also in couscous. In close proximity, I keep **sun-dried tomatoes, dried porcini mushrooms,** and dried **morels** for a risotto, a pasta sauce, or a stew. When soaked in warm milk, morels are almost more intense in flavor than when bought fresh. On another shelf in my larder, I keep **risotto rice,** which I always have in supply, along with **linguine, penne,** and **small pasta** for soups. I strongly recommend buying *artigianale* pasta, which, made popular by the slow-food movement, can be found in many Italian grocery stores these days. It may be a bit more expensive, but the chewier consistency makes it so much more satisfying. So as to introduce a bit of variety into my pasta supplies, I also have **barley** along with **Moroccan** and **Israeli couscous** on this shelf. Pulses that come in handy when making a soup or a salad also belong to this group of supplies. As a great lover of lentils, I always have **green Puy lentils, black beluga lentils,** and **red lentils** on my pantry shelf. Next to them I keep **chickpeas** and **borlotto beans,** both in tins, to use when I either have no time to soak pulses overnight or when I can't buy them fresh in the grocery store. For sauces, stews, or a curry, I always have several tins of **San Marzano tomatoes** as well as **coconut milk** on hand. And because I only rarely make chicken soup from scratch, even if this is easy to freeze, I have several types of stock cubes—**beef, chicken,** and **vegetable bouillon cubes,** along with those for a **porcini broth.** It is, of course, a commonplace that any well-stocked pantry must contain **flour** and **cornstarch,** but mine also includes **panko, ground almonds,** and **ground pistachios** as well to vary the coating often required in pan-frying. While I use sugar only sparingly in my kitchen, I often replace it with **marmalade, honey,** or **maple syrup.** For certain dishes, like my mother's sweet potatoes roasted in orange juice, **brown sugar,** however, is absolutely essential, while most Asian cuisine will require **palm sugar.**

❦

I think of my **refrigerator** both as a storage space and a treasure trove. When I return home from traveling, I immediately go and buy **butter, milk, eggs,** and **yogurt,** along with some **cream** (or **crème fraîche**). While I tend to buy cheese based on what appeals to me at the market, I always have a piece of **Parmesan** in my fridge. Once it is used up, I keep the rind for my minestrone. In fact, I sometimes make this luscious vegetable soup only in order to use up the Parmesan rind that will otherwise go bad. Perhaps because it was a rarity during my childhood, I adore **ham** and usually keep several varieties in my fridge—both cured and boiled. Cut into slivers, it lends a succulent intensity to any *soffritto*, to the filling in a quiche, or to an egg soufflé. My addiction to what Japanese cooking calls umami also means that I always have a jar of **anchovies** in my fridge, the other aromatic I use most often to embellish a *soffritto*. And because so many sauces, vegetable dishes, and stews are based on some kind of *soffritto*, I always also have **carrots**, **celery**, and **ginger** in the vegetable drawer of my fridge. For sauces and marinades, I keep a variety of condiments in the other lower drawer of the fridge, along with a jar of **mayonnaise**, **Dijon mustard**, the coarser **Pommery mustard**, **olive paste**, **sun-dried tomato paste**, and **tomato purée**. On one of the shelves in the middle of the fridge, in turn, I always store **capers**, **cornichon**, **olives**, and **sun-dried tomatoes preserved in oil**.

⚜

I treat my **freezer**, in turn, as the place in my pantry where I store ingredients that I can keep longer if they are frozen or that will otherwise spoil: **herbs** I haven't used up, the **leftovers** of a soup or a stew (which, when frozen in small portions, come in particularly handy when you are cooking for yourself), or cut into slices, the **bread** that wasn't eaten up. In general, I tend to buy several loaves of my favorite bread and deep-freeze it immediately. For the longest time, I was jealous of my American friends who have space in the cellar of their homes for a huge freezer, which means that they can not only blithely buy produce in bulk but also precook all kinds of dishes. If you only have a few shelves in the deep freezer attached to your fridge, as I do, you have to be more selective and think carefully how to deploy it most efficiently. For this reason, my freezer compartment is the place where, in the spirit of the *avoska*, I keep several types of **ravioli**, separated into different bags, just in case. Along with a bag or two of **small green peas** (which I buy frozen), I also always have raw **tiger prawns** in my freezer. They don't even need to defrost before being put to use. You can simply pour boiling water over them and leave them to steep until they have turned pink before frying them or adding them to a risotto or a stew. In my freezer compartment, I also store the **wrappers for pot stickers** (which are usually only sold frozen in Asian grocery stores), along with **puff pastry** and **short-crust pastry**, just in case I decide to make a quiche on the spur of the moment.

When it comes to a well-stocked freezer compartment, you need to not only ask yourself what you want to have on hand for unexpected occasions like guests appearing on your doorstep unexpectedly, the proverbial blizzard that prevents you from going out to shop, or when you need to prepare something quickly; what you also need to consider is which ingredients freeze well. You can, for example, first freeze flavor-intense **homemade bouillon** in ice cube trays and then transfer the cubes to freezer bags. **Béchamel sauce** as well as **tomato sauce** do equally well in the deep freezer, so it is worth making more than you need. I even find that homemade **pesto** improves when left in the freezer for a while (with or without the Parmesan added). **Bacon** and **ham**—to have on hand for a pasta sauce, a risotto, or a soup—also freeze well. And if you bought too many **sausages**, you can freeze these too. My friend Gesine even suggests freezing individual portions of chopped garlic, ginger, and chili. When making a *soffritto*, you then only need to chop the onion and the celery. Even a piece of **ginger**—which so often tends to spoil in my refrigerator—can be frozen. Just peel and grate as much as you need and return the rest to the freezer. And finally, concerned with food sustainability, before going on a trip, I will freeze anything that might spoil. Even if they are a bit mushy when thawed, vegetables can always be used in a sauce or a stew and fruit or berries for a smoothie or a compote.

PREPARED AND STORED IN THE REFRIGERATOR

Preserved Lemons | Lemon Paste | Marinated Baby Artichokes |
Preserved Tuna | Roasted Red Peppers with Za'atar | Roasted Cherry
Tomatoes with Vanilla and Thyme | Roasted Red Beets

My refrigerator has, above all, become my treasure trove for unexpected occasions and happy experimentation because it is here that I store roasted and preserved ingredients. These come in handy when, during a lunchtime meeting, you don't want to eat yet another one of the sad sandwiches they tend to serve or when, in the evening, you want to prepare a quick supper. These pre-cooked vegetables can be turned into delicious appetizers, add texture to a salad, or enhance a pasta dish. Or they can become—as is the case with preserved lemons—the secret ingredient, making for the very special flavor of a dish.

PRESERVED LEMONS

5–8 lemons	2 small cinnamon sticks
100 g (1¾ cup) salt	9 cloves

| 10 whole coriander seeds | 4 bay leaves |
| 10 black peppercorns | 1 medium jar, about ¾ L (3 cups) |

Preserved lemons are indispensable when preparing a chicken tagine. And yet their use is many and varied—in a salad, a stew, with roasted chicken, in the marinade for a fish ceviche, or as the garnish on a beef carpaccio. The velvety texture of the skin is enticing, while fresh lemon or lime juice can never re-create the intensely tangy acidity of the pickled fruit pulp. It is extremely simple to make preserved lemons. You simply need to tend to them afterward—and therein lies the charm—by giving the glass jar in which they are being pickled a shake a few times a day. You should continue turning it upside down and right-side up for several weeks, which also means that you are taking an active part in the slow transformation occurring inside the jar. The idea of this recipe comes from Paula Wolfert, British doyen of Mediterranean cuisine, who offers the following advice in her book *Couscous and Other Good Food from Morocco*. What is crucial when preserving lemons is that they are completely covered with the salty lemon juice. You can only achieve this, however, if you press the lemons into the sterilized jar very firmly and add some additional lemon juice to cover them on top. For this reason it is wise to buy more lemons than actually fit into the jar. And, of course, buy only organic lemons, whose peel is edible.

Quarter each lemon but only up to one centimeter (one-quarter of an inch) at the bottom so that the four segments are still attached to each other. You want to be able to open each of the lemons, but they should not fall into separate segments. It is best to begin with five lemons and then see, depending on their size, whether you can add a few more. But first cover the bottom of the jar with one tablespoon of salt. Use a cutting board large enough to catch all the excess salt and juice, generously cover the fruit pulp of each of the lemons with salt before closing the lemons again, making sure that the salt remains inside. Then one after the other, cram the lemons into the glass jar so that, when pressed together tightly, they completely fill it. Use a bit of force while pressing each new lemon into the jar, and keep adding a bit more salt each time. After the first three lemons, however, also begin adding the other aromatics—the cinnamon sticks, cloves, cilantro, peppercorns, and bay leaf—distributing them evenly before pressing as many more lemons into the jar as will fit. If you vigorously push down on the lemons, they will release some of their juice, but probably not enough to cover them completely, which is why, before closing the jar, you may well need to add some additional lemon juice.

Room temperature is just right for fermenting the lemons. For a month or so, you should, however, give the jar a shake a few times a day, turning it upside down and then right-side up again so that the salty juice is evenly distributed among the lemon pieces. As long as you don't open the jar, the lemons will continue to ferment, and with time, the skin will perhaps even turn slightly brown. Once you open the jar, you should keep it in the refrigerator, where preserved lemons can be stored indefinitely. Many recipes will tell you to rinse them before using and discard the flesh. I prefer using all my lemons, taking care, however, to chop the peel very finely. Why waste any part of them?

LEMON PASTE

3 lemons   30 g (¼ cup) sugar
30 g (¼ cup) salt

There is a faster way to preserve lemons, which I learned from my friend Daniela. The flavor isn't as multilayered; nevertheless, these chopped lemons endow any soup, stew, and above all risotto with an intense lemon aroma. As in the previous recipe, use only organic lemons, and thoroughly wash and dry the lemon peel before chopping the entire lemon into very fine bits. Then in a small kitchen bowl, mix the chopped peel and pulp with the salt and sugar and pour the lemon paste into a sterilized glass jar. While the jar does not have to be full, it is important that the lemon pieces are completely covered with the salt and sugar mixture. Before using it for the first time, allow the lemon paste to rest in the refrigerator for at least twenty-four hours, where it will slowly transform into a coarse pesto. These preserved lemon bits can be stored for many months in the refrigerator.

MARINATED BABY ARTICHOKES

20 baby artichokes   2 tbsp. salt
500 ml (2 cups) water   5 bay leaves
500 ml (2 cups) white wine vinegar

FOR THE MARINADE

600 ml (2½ cups) olive oil   2 rosemary twigs
4 juniper berries   3 garlic cloves, cut into thin slices
8 peppercorns   200 ml (1 cup) white balsamic
6 sage leaves   vinegar

The baby artichokes that appear in early spring on the farmers' market don't yet have the bothersome downy interior choke, which, in their larger siblings, you have to first scrape out before you can finally indulge in the artichoke heart. For this reason, you only need to generously trim the outer leaves before sautéing them in a marinade. Using a sharp knife, first cut off the upper third of each baby artichoke, and then trim the bottom, cutting off the remaining stem as well. Now pluck off the tough outer leaves until you are left with only the delicate lighter ones. Though it may seem a bit wasteful, it is worth taking off more rather than less. Only a well-trimmed *carciofini* will have the desired velvety texture. Place each peeled artichoke into a bowl with lemon water so that the outer skin doesn't turn brown while you are still preparing the others. This also allows you to wash them once more.

In a second step, blanch the *carciofini*. Bring the water, white wine, vinegar, bay leaves, and salt to a boil, and cook them for about five minutes. You want them to remain firm. Drain them in a sieve, and allow them to cool. In the meantime, you can prepare the marinade. Heat the olive oil in a pot that is large enough to hold all the *carciofini*, and add the juniper berries, the peppercorns, the garlic slices, the sage, and the rosemary. Sauté the herbs only briefly, making sure that they don't brown. Then pour in the white balsamic vinegar, and allow the marinade to simmer for another three minutes before adding the baby artichokes. Allow them to come to a boil very briefly before taking the pot off the heat and letting the *carciofini* cool off in the marinade. Using a slotted spoon, remove the baby artichokes from the pot, and place them into the sterilized glass jars. Pour the marinade through a sieve to remove the garlic and the herbs before adding enough of the seasoned oil to each jar to completely cover the baby artichokes. Closed tightly, they will keep for three months in the refrigerator. If you have some marinade left over, you can reuse it for a salad dressing.

PRESERVED TUNA

2 tuna steaks, each 225 g (8 ounces)	1 tbsp. thyme, chopped
250 ml (1 cup) olive oil	1 bay leaf, crumbled
zest of 1 lemon, chopped	2 tsp. coarse salt
2 garlic cloves, peeled and cut into thin slices	2 tsp. white pepper

Ever since I began cooking for myself, tins of tuna have been a key staple in my pantry, perfect not only for a salad but also for a delicate mousse or a variety of sauces. Since I discovered how to preserve tuna myself, I fall back on these tins only when I am in a hurry or if I was able to buy tins of the exquisite (and far more costly) tuna belly preserved in olive oil. The preparation may be a bit time-consuming—because the fish needs to rest in a marinade for several hours before being cooked in oil—but this extra step produces both a stunningly supple consistency and an enticingly intense flavor.

Begin by brushing the two tuna steaks with a bit of olive oil. In a bowl, blend together the lemon zest, the garlic, and the herbs; season with salt and pepper; and toss the tuna steaks in this flavorful mixture until they are completely coated. Wrap the two fish steaks in plastic wrap, and allow them to rest in the refrigerator for four to six hours. Half an hour before you want to cook them, take them out of the fridge, remove the plastic wrap, and season them once more with salt. For cooking, choose a pot (or a pan with high edges) in which the two steaks will fit snugly, and pour in enough of the remaining oil to cover them—not, however, so much that they are swimming in oil. Allow the tuna to rest for twenty minutes in the oil before heating it, over very low temperature, until it reaches 83°C (181°F). Then remove the pot from the heat, and allow the tuna to cool to room temperature. Using a slotted spoon, remove the tuna, which is allowed to fall apart, into a sterilized jar. Pour the oil through a sieve into the glass as well. Tightly closed, the tuna will keep up to four days in the refrigerator.

ROASTED RED PEPPERS WITH ZA'ATAR

2 red and 2 yellow peppers	salt
4 tbsp. olive oil	balsamic vinegar
1 tbsp. za'atar	

I always keep some roasted peppers in my fridge because they fit so perfectly in a salad or in a pasta sauce. Above all, however, I like serving them with burrata (or buffalo mozzarella) with a touch of costly balsamic vinegar on top.

Heat the oven to 200°C (400°F). Quarter the peppers, remove the stem and the seeds, and cut away the white bits inside. Place the peppers, skin side up, on a baking dish. In a small bowl, blend the olive oil with the za'atar and the salt, pour it over the peppers, and mix thoroughly, using your hands to make sure that their skin is evenly covered. Roast the peppers for about forty-five minutes. The skin should be scorched, the flesh soft and succulent. Remove the baking dish from the oven, and while it is still hot, cover it with plastic wrap. This will begin to curve as the air trapped inside begins to condense. This moisture is precisely what will later make it easier to peel the peppers. Once the peppers have cooled down, remove the plastic wrap, carefully pull off the skin, and put them, along with the marinade collected on the bottom of the baking dish, into an airtight container. These roasted peppers will keep up to a week in the refrigerator.

ROASTED CHERRY TOMATOES WITH VANILLA AND THYME

500 g (1 pound) cherry tomatoes	3 tbsp. olive oil
1 tsp. salt	1½ tbsp. vanilla paste
1 tbsp. brown sugar	1 tbsp. thyme, chopped

Cherry tomatoes, in turn, are best roasted at a fairly low temperature for a long time. Helped along by a flavorful marinade, they can develop their own sweetness to perfection. Heat the oven to 140°C (275°F). Cut the cherry tomatoes lengthwise without cutting through them completely so that the two halves are still attached on one side. Place them on a baking tray, cut side up, and season with salt and brown sugar. In a small kitchen bowl, blend the olive oil, vanilla paste, and thyme; pour this marinade over the tomatoes, and mix thoroughly, using your hands. Then rearrange the tomatoes, making sure the cut side is facing up, before roasting them one and a half to two hours. It is worth checking in on them from time to time though. You want them to caramelize and the fluid they release to evaporate, but they shouldn't dry out. If your tomatoes are larger, then simply extend the roasting time.

Oven-roasted tomatoes fit beautifully with fresh ricotta. They make a good companion for any pasta or couscous, but they are also perfect with poached chicken breasts or pan-fried fish.

ROASTED RED BEETS

3 medium red beets	coarse salt
3 tbsp. olive oil	

Heat the oven to 200°C (400°F). While it is perfectly fine to simply cook red beets, roasting them in the oven endows them a more supple consistency and, owing to the seasoned oil, a more flavorful sweetness. Begin by thoroughly washing the beets and drying them with paper towels. You can simply place them next to each other in a baking dish and cover them with aluminum foil, but I have discovered that they turn out particularly well if I wrap them individually. Before closing each package, I drizzle a bit of olive oil over each of the beets and season generously with salt. Ultimately, the roasting time will depend on the size of the beets, but ninety minutes should do the trick. Allow the beets to cool before peeling them and placing them in an airtight container. They will keep in the refrigerator for a good week.

Argan oil is a perfect fit for dressing oven-roasted beets, to which you can add feta, nuts, or cooked lentils. Fresh horseradish is another perfect accompaniment. Use it in a yogurt dressing, and add a piece of smoked fish to accompany the beets.

PESTOS AND HUMMUS

Master Recipe with Basil | Shiso and Tarragon Pesto | Sun-Dried Tomato Pesto | Oven-Roasted Tomato Pesto | Red Beet Pesto | Curried Hummus

For the longest time, I allowed myself to be seduced by the panoply of pestos—made from green and black olives, tuna, diverse nuts, or vegetables—that have become available on farmers' markets and in gourmet food stores, only to stack them lovingly in the shelves of my kitchen cupboards. Then I discovered how effortlessly one can make a pesto on one's own. If the point is simply to use up all the excess herbs on the balcony before the cold of winter sets in, you can simply mix together what serendipity has left for you. This has led to unusual and unanticipated flavor combinations on my part. More often, however, I experiment with a more specific interaction between herbs and nuts in mind to figure out, for example, what goes best with shiso or tarragon. As is so often the case in home cooking, it is all a question of the quality of your main ingredient, in this case the Parmesan you use. As with the wine you pour into a stew, the flavor and suppleness of a pesto will depend on whether you economized on the cheese or not. And you really shouldn't. You can, in turn, vary the amount of the other ingredients, use somewhat less garlic, and instead increase the nuts or herbs. You can also work with a mixture of Parmesan and pecorino. And even though in the traditional Italian cuisine, a pesto is made in a mortar, I always use my Vitamix blender. You do need to bear in mind, however, that you can never quite tell in advance how much oil you will need; the amount depends on the consistency of the other ingredients. For this reason, it is wise not to add all the oil at once but rather to add it gradually, regulating the amount according to the way the pesto develops.

Sealed in sterilized glass jars, pestos will keep two to three weeks in the refrigerator. Two rules, however, apply. The jar must be properly filled. There should be no empty space for air bubbles to form at the bottom or on the sides, because this is where mold may develop. The jar doesn't, however, need to be filled to the top. Simply cover the pesto with a thin film of olive oil after each use. This coat will protect it against mold.

While classic Italian cuisine deploys pesto primarily as a sauce for dried (never fresh) pasta or for a risotto, you can just as readily fold it into couscous or mashed potatoes. I like to blend it with Greek yogurt and use it as a dip for pan-fried fish, poached chicken breasts, boiled potatoes, or potato pancakes. A layer of pesto will ennoble any sandwich. A spoonful of pesto can be blended into a scrambled egg or an omelet, while it works equally well at the bottom of a quiche or a gratin. You can coat tomatoes, cut in half, with pesto and roast them in the oven, much as a roasted poussin will benefit from being marinated in a pesto first. You can spread pesto over fish or vegetables before roasting them *en papillote*. Mushrooms and other vegetables like zucchini or peppers can be sautéed in a pesto, as you can also fold a pesto into steamed vegetables. I am particularly fond of using a pesto to add flavor to a flattened chicken breast, coated in ground almonds. If you spread the pesto immediately onto the chicken after removing it from the hot pan, it will melt into the crisp surface and give the dish that extra bit of succulence.

MASTER RECIPE WITH BASIL

2 big bunches of basil	2 big garlic cloves
150 g (5 ounces) Parmesan	about 300 ml (1¼ cups) olive oil
100 g (4 ounces) pine nuts	salt and pepper

Wash the basil first and dry it thoroughly with paper towels before plucking off the leaves. Although I make my pesto in a blender, I nevertheless chop the garlic, even though only coarsely, and I break up the Parmesan into coarse bits. Then I first pulse the cheese, but not too long. The Parmesan pieces should be the size of bread crumbs. Next I add the pine nuts and the garlic and pulse these briefly before adding the basil leaves. I only blend these briefly as well before adding the olive oil but do so gradually, preferably while the motor is running. Use only as much as you need so that the pesto has a creamy consistency; it should be liquidy but still a densely textured paste. Season with salt and pepper.

SHISO AND TARRAGON PESTO

60 g (2 cups) shiso leaves

20 g (⅔ cup) tarragon leaves

150 g (5 ounces) Parmesan

100 g (4 ounces) pine nuts

2 garlic cloves

zest and juice of 1 lemon

about 150 ml (⅔ cup) olive oil

1 tsp. white balsamic vinegar

salt and pepper

Once you get the hang of making your own pesto, there are no limits to your creativity. Instead of the classic pine nuts, you can use pistachios, macadamia nuts, or walnuts. Since I have started growing my own shiso, I have become particularly fond of the combination of this Japanese basil and tarragon. If you can't find shiso, you can replace it with a mixture of basil and mint, even though this means forfeiting the specific grassy tartness of the Japanese herb.

Begin by washing both the shiso and the tarragon leaves and drying them thoroughly with paper towels. As with the classic pesto, pulse the Parmesan first, until all the pieces are the size of bread crumbs, then add the pine nuts and the coarsely chopped garlic and blend these briefly with the cheese. Then add the shiso and the tarragon, along with the lemon zest, the lemon juice, and the white balsamic vinegar. Blend these briefly as well before adding the olive oil. Take care not to pour it in all at once (you may not need all of it); instead, drizzle it in gradually, until you have a viscous, coarse paste. Season with salt and pepper.

SUN-DRIED TOMATO PESTO

200 g (1⅓ cups) sun-dried tomatoes

1 garlic clove, peeled

2 tbsp. olives, seeded

20 g (⅔ cup) shiso leaves

20 g (⅔ cup) bunch cilantro

130 g (5 ounces) pistachio

2 tbsp. salted capers

5 tbsp. olive oil

350 ml (1½ cups) hot water

The charm of this pesto stems from the fact that only very little oil is used, as the hot water is what produces a smooth, velvety paste. Cut the sun-dried tomatoes as well as the olives and the garlic into chunks. Pluck the cilantro, and then cut the shiso (which can be replaced with basil and mint) into coarse strips as well. Wash the capers. Then put all these ingredients, along with the nuts, the olive oil, and the hot water into the blender and process them into a viscous, dense paste. Season with salt and pepper.

OVEN-ROASTED TOMATO PESTO

1 pound tomatoes, cut in half and deseeded	140 ml (⅔ cup) olive oil
salt	1 tbsp. salted capers
2 tbsp. fresh thyme	50 g (2 ounces) pine nuts
	salt and pepper

Roasted tomatoes can also be used for a pesto, even if this requires a bit more preparation time. Heat the oven to 125°C (257°F). Place the halved tomatoes, cut side up, into a baking dish, and drizzle them with olive oil. Season them with salt, and sprinkle chopped thyme over them. Allow them to roast for at least three and a half hours, until they have shriveled and dried out. The longer they roast in the oven, the more intense their flavor will become, thus the low heat. When they are done, process the oven-roasted tomatoes along with the pine nuts and the capers, adding the olive oil gradually to the blender, until you have a paste that is dense but runny. As in the previous recipes, wait until the end to season with salt and pepper.

RED BEET PESTO FOR 6–8

1 tbsp. black pepper	1 tbsp. olive oil
6 cloves	2 tsp. whiskey
1 chili pepper, deseeded and finely chopped	3 medium red beets
zest of 1 orange, finely chopped	2 tsp. white balsamic vinegar
2 garlic cloves, finely chopped	1 tbsp. lemon juice
1 tbsp. coarse salt	30 g (1 ounce) Parmesan, grated
2 tsp. strong vinegar	3 tbsp. pumpkin seed oil
	500 g (1 pound) spaghetti

FOR THE CRUNCHY TOPPING

220 g (8 ounces) pumpkin seeds	2 tbsp. olive oil
220 g (8 ounces) pistachios	3 garlic cloves, chopped

The recipe for this unusual pesto comes from an art historian friend of mine named Sebastian, who is particularly taken with the startling image of deep-red spaghetti. The preparation is elaborate and a bit time-consuming because the beets have to be roasted in the oven first, and you also need to make a spice paste in advance. According to Sebastian, this pesto also really needs a certain crispness to bring out the peppery flavor. If you take the time, however, you will be rewarded with a truly astonishing interaction between aroma and texture.

Begin by preparing the spice paste. As everything depends on the pepper, use only the best. Process this together with the cloves, chili pepper, orange zest, garlic, vinegar, olive oil, whiskey, and some salt in a blender (or mortar) until you have a smooth paste. Because the spice paste needs to infuse for a while, you have enough time to roast the beets next. Heat the oven to 200°C (400°F). Wash the beets, and then dry them thoroughly with paper towels. Wrap each beet individually into a piece of aluminum foil. Drizzle each with a bit of olive oil and salt before closing the package. They should roast for one and a half hours. Once the beets are cool enough to handle, peel and grate them, and then, in a blender (or mortar), fold in the spice paste until you have a creamy consistency. To balance the sweetness of the beets, season with lemon juice and white balsamic vinegar before adding the grated Parmesan and the pumpkin seed oil. The pesto should be spicy but not overwhelmingly intense, which is why you may want to correct the flavor by adding more acidity (lemon juice and vinegar). Hold back, however, with the salt, and instead—as Sebastian notes—be generous when cooking the pasta in salt water, of which you want to retain some for creaming the pasta sauce in the end.

For the crunchy topping, dry roast the pumpkin seeds in a small pan, and then grind them in a mortar. Add the pistachios (or walnuts), and grind them as well; they, however, do not need to be roasted in advance. Then over low heat, sauté the chopped nuts in one and a half tablespoons of olive oil, along with the other three garlic cloves, taking care to press the chopped garlic into the nuts. They should caramelize in the oil. To serve, first toss the spaghetti with the beet pesto, adding some of the cooking water to make the sauce creamier. Then top the pasta with the nut crunch rather than folding it into the pasta as well to retain its crispiness.

You can, of course, use this pesto to accompany an escalope, a fish fillet, or meatballs. Mixed with yogurt, it also makes for a perfect dip.

CURRIED HUMMUS

1 jar or tin of chickpeas	juice of 1–2 lemons
2 tbsp. neutral oil (rapeseed oil or grape-seed oil)	1 tbsp. pomegranate molasses
	2 garlic cloves
4 tbsp. tahini paste (or peanut butter)	salt and pepper (or cayenne pepper)
½ tbsp. ground cumin	½ tbsp. curry powder

Traditionally, hummus is made with dried chickpeas, soaked overnight and cooked the next day. You can just as well, however, as my friend Tobias has

taught me, use canned chickpeas. I am indebted to him for the special seasoning in this recipe as well.

Drain the chickpeas, but make sure to retain the water in a bowl. Process
the chickpeas with the olive oil in a blender (or an immersion blender) until
you have a dense paste, then add the tahini, lemon juice, pomegranate molasses, garlic, cumin, and curry powder and season with one tablespoon of salt.
Now use the water you have saved from the jar (or tin) to dilute the paste
until you have a creamy consistency, around five tablespoons. Season with
salt and pepper.

If you want more spice, add more curry powder; if you want a more fruity
flavor, add more lemon juice or molasses. In an airtight jar, hummus will
keep for a week at least in the refrigerator. It tastes best, however, at room
temperature, so don't forget to take it out of the fridge half an hour before
serving. You can drizzle it with olive oil and paprika, but if you want to be a
bit more inventive, try some za'atar and chopped cilantro instead.

LEFTOVERS

*Chicken Gratin with Broccoli | Chicken Salad with Celery and Apple |
Asian Spiced Chicken Salad | Chicken Sandwich | Minced Chicken
on Toast | Chicken Mushroom Pie | Couscous with Chicken, Cherries,
and Preserved Lemons | Chicken Risotto with Mushrooms |
Rigatoni with Vegetables | Meat Ragout Pot Pie*

In one of Barbara Kavka's cookbooks, I found the following comforting
insight: Because the leftovers of today can be transformed effortlessly the next
day into an elegant salad or a tasty stew, they are like having a sous-chef in
one's own kitchen. Someone has already done half the work for you, leaving
you to put the final touches on a new dish. The idea of throwing away food
is anathema to me not least of all because my mother, who could never quite
forget the hardship and deprivations of the Second World War, was a mistress
of culinary sustainability. She was the first person to teach me not only that
almost everything—a soup, a stew, a ragout—can be warmed up again the
next day but that these dishes sometimes even taste better when reheated and
can be further improved with a handful of nuts, chopped herbs, a shot of nut
oil, or some cream. Even without being reheated, roasted meat and poultry,
risotto, or sautéed vegetables can be eaten the next day at room temperature.
In the same spirit, it is always worth making more meatballs than you need

for a particular dish in advance so that you can eat more of them the next day with a pesto dip or as part of a salad. At the same time, figuring out what to do with leftovers can be a true test of your creativity. You are called upon to come up with ways to combine the remainder of a previous meal, left over in your fridge, with fresh ingredients or supplies from your pantry and, by preparing this food again, give it a new touch. Precisely the fortuitousness regarding the ingredients you are compelled to work with can prove to be a lucky chance.

Let's begin our deliberations—which will be followed with some concrete recipe suggestions—with how to use leftovers in a soup or a casserole. Whether sautéed or roasted, the easiest way to reuse what remains of a vegetable dish is to make a soup by warming up the vegetables in some broth and then processing them in a blender (or an emersion blender). However, you can just as easily scatter sautéed vegetables and potatoes in short-crust pastry, pour a cheese-egg-cream mixture over it, and turn it into a quiche. Or you could put the leftover vegetables in a baking dish and, by replacing the egg-cream filling with béchamel sauce or simply grated cheese, make a casserole. In either case, you could enrich the dish by adding a bit of leftover roast or chicken or the pieces of bacon that have been waiting in your refrigerator for exactly such an occasion. Taking a different route, you can turn any vegetable, meat, or chicken leftovers quickly into a stir-fry, a risotto, or a pasta sauce. Leftover pasta itself can be transformed into a gratin by mixing in sautéed vegetables, adding some liquid—be it béchamel sauce, tomato sauce, or broth—sprinkling grated cheese on top, and roasting it in the oven. It helps to have cooked the pasta al dente so that it won't lose too much of its bite in the process of reheating. Excess sauce—from a roulade, a stew, or a fricassee—can be used the next day to sauté strips of chicken, chunks of beefsteak, slices of pork tenderloin, or even pieces of tofu. Only when it comes to reheating fish or seafood would I recommend caution. Shrimp, salmon, or tuna are best used the next day in a salad. You can, however, chop up any leftover fish and seafood, purée it with cream, and use it as a pasta sauce.

The most versatile way of adapting leftovers is, of course, in a salad. Roasted chicken or turkey can serve as a topping for a mixture of green salad, watercress, arugula, or kale, but so can the slices of leftover pork tenderloin or a beefsteak. Roasted, steamed, or sautéed vegetables can make a wonderful salad, especially when combined with precooked couscous or barley. For this reason, it is worth preparing more vegetables than you need so as to always have some on hand in the fridge. Dressed with pesto or a salad sauce and garnished with nuts, dried fruit, and chopped herbs, any leftover vegetables will make for a nutritious and uncomplicated yet satisfying meal—just what you need for a lunch meeting or when, in the evening, you want to throw something together quickly. If you want some protein, you can always add a bit of ham, smoked salmon, tinned tuna, or quickly fried tofu.

However, what is more unexpected perhaps is the advice given to me by my Japanese friend Keiko. She would never throw out a salad just because the dressing has already been added, claiming that it is the perfect basis for a stir-fry the next day. This makes sense, of course, because the combination of oil, acidity, and pungency contained in many salad dressings corresponds to the Asian style of seasoning. Thus you can breathe new culinary life into wilted salad leaves of yesterday when you sauté them along with shredded carrots, mushrooms slices, zucchini rounds, or minced ginger and use condiments such as soy sauce, chili sauce, and sesame oil to enhance the flavor.

And finally, all leftover fruit that needs to be consumed quickly can be turned into a delicious compote by cutting it into coarse bits and simmering it in a mixture of acidity (Noilly Prat or lemon), sweetness (honey, syrup or marmalade), and aromatic seasoning (lavender, rosemary, vanilla). If, then, the charm of cooking with leftovers depends on the power of transformation that produces something new out of what happens to have remained from a previous meal, the following recipes are conceived as a guide to trying out your own combinations and ways of preparation.

EIGHT SUGGESTIONS FOR ROASTED CHICKEN LEFTOVERS

If you have meat left over from an oven-roasted chicken or turkey, remove it from the bone, and cut it into slices, shred it, or cut it into coarse chunks. Be meticulous and use your fingers to pull off any meat you can't get at with a knife because everything can be used. Indeed, the bones themselves make a wonderful soup that, if you aren't going to use right away, you can freeze in an ice-cube tray.

CHICKEN GRATIN WITH BROCCOLI FOR 2

3 tbsp. dry sherry	50 g (2 ounces) Parmesan
150 g (1½ cups) broccoli	(or pecorino), grated
salt and pepper	170 g (6 ounces) roasted chicken
	breasts

BÉCHAMEL SAUCE

3 tbsp. butter

3 tbsp. flour

150 ml (⅔ cup) warm milk

about 300 ml (1¼ cups) chicken broth

salt and pepper

nutmeg

Heat the oven to 190°C (375°F). Make the béchamel sauce first. Melt the butter in a small pot before adding the flour, and whisking constantly for about two minutes, turn it into a roux. This way you eliminate the taste of flour. You will, however, need to keep the temperature low because you don't want the butter to turn brown. Then pour the warm milk and the broth into the roux, alternating between the two, and again whisk vigorously. To thicken the sauce, keep the temperature low, and continue stirring for about ten minutes. Once the consistency is that of a medium dense soup, season the béchamel sauce with sherry, salt, pepper, and a pinch of nutmeg.

Cut the broccoli into small florets, peel the stem, and quarter it. Then steam the vegetables a few minutes before assembling the gratin. Place the broccoli into a gratin dish, and season with salt and pepper. Pour half the béchamel sauce over the broccoli, sprinkle with half the grated Parmesan, and place the roasted chicken slices on top. Season once more with salt and pepper, pour the rest of the béchamel sauce over the gratin, sprinkle with the remaining Parmesan, and bake it in the oven for twenty-five minutes. Finally, place it briefly under the broiler so that the surface forms a sumptuous brown crust.

CHICKEN SALAD WITH CELERY AND APPLE FOR 2

300 g (11 ounces) roast chicken

3 tbsp. olive oil

1 tbsp. white balsamic vinegar

½ tsp. Dijon mustard

salt and pepper

2 celery stalks

1 green apple

1 handful fresh herbs (such as parsley, tarragon, chervil), chopped

3 tbsp. yogurt

3 tbsp. mayonnaise

2 tsp. lemon juice

salt and cayenne pepper

1–2 tsp. curry powder

1 handful nuts

First, cut the roast chicken into bite-size pieces and place them in a salad bowl. For the dressing, blend the olive oil with the balsamic vinegar, mustard, and salt, and pour it over the chicken so that it can steep in it while you prepare the remaining ingredients. Peel the celery and the apple, and cut both into small cubes. Add these, along with the chopped herbs, to the chicken, and mix everything thoroughly. In a small bowl, blend the mayonnaise (preferably homemade) with the yogurt and lemon juice, and season with salt, cayenne pepper, and curry powder before pouring this dressing over the salad as well. Once more, mix thoroughly. To finish the chicken salad, scatter some nuts on top. Walnuts, pistachios, or pumpkin seeds are particularly delicious.

NOTE: You can embellish this salad by adding a ripe avocado, steamed green asparagus, or steamed broccoli.

ASIAN SPICED CHICKEN SALAD FOR 2

120 g (4 ounces) cooked soba noodles
225 g (8 ounces) roast chicken,
   coarsely sliced or diced
2 tbsp. mayonnaise
1 tsp. wasabi paste
2 scallions
8 shitake mushrooms (or button
   mushrooms)

1 small green pepper
1 tsp. mustard
2 tsp. sweet chili sauce (or honey)
4 tsp. soy sauce
2 tsp. sesame oil
4 tsp. apple balsamic vinegar (or
   Japanese rice wine vinegar)
1 bunch cilantro

While the soba noodles are cooking, blend the mayonnaise (preferably homemade) with the wasabi paste, cut the roasted chicken into chunks, and prepare the vegetables. Cut the scallions into thin rings, clean and slice the mushrooms, and peel and slice the pepper. Once the soba noodles are done, drain them in cold water; pour them into a salad bowl, along with the chicken pieces; and then toss both with the wasabi mayonnaise. The noodles and the chicken should infuse while you prepare the second component of the dressing. In a small bowl, blend together the mustard, chili sauce, soy sauce, sesame oil, and apple balsamic vinegar. Then add the mushrooms, scallions, and peppers to the chicken salad; add the sesame oil vinaigrette; and mix everything thoroughly. To finish the salad, sprinkle with chopped cilantro.

CHICKEN SANDWICH FOR 1

1 small baguette
100 g (4 ounces) chicken breast
mayonnaise

tomato chutney
3 shiso leaves (or basil and mint)
3 baby artichokes preserved in oil

The day after Thanksgiving, my mother always made turkey sandwiches for us. The leftovers of the bird would be scattered over a piece of toast, topped with stuffing and maybe even some of the leftover peas, and everything would be doused with gravy. My mother's ritual, of course, picks up on a piece of culinary history. While the warm chicken sandwich was already a favorite dish among the American working class around 1900, since the 1960s, the cold sandwich, with chicken meat placed between two pieces of toast, became a staple in diners as well. It was this deli special she brought into our German kitchen.

For my version of this American standard, I prefer a small baguette, cut in half and coated with homemade mayonnaise on one side and with tomato chutney on the other. You could, however, just as well use tomato or olive paste. Traditionally, iceberg lettuce should serve as the bed for the roast chicken, but since I find this salad both too watery and a bit dull in taste, I prefer to use shiso leaves or other herbs such as basil, mint or even the spicy arugula. Whichever you choose, place the chicken slices generously on the lower half of the baguette and cover it with the artichokes, best cut into slices as well. As further trimmings for your chicken sandwich, use oven-roasted peppers, oven-roasted tomatoes, or pan-grilled zucchini. That said, a slice of ripe avocado, a few slices of kiwi, or even a sliced fig would also provide a nice touch.

MINCED CHICKEN ON TOAST FOR I

2 tsp. butter	salt and pepper
3 button mushrooms, minced	60 ml (¼ cup) cream
1 spring onion, minced	1 piece of toast
1 tbsp. Madeira wine (or sweet sherry)	tarragon to garnish
225 g (8 ounces) roasted chicken, minced	

For a more elegant way of transforming leftover chicken into a sandwich, mince it and fry it once more in a pan. To do so, first melt the butter, and then sauté the spring onion along with the mushrooms, about five minutes. The onions should be translucent, the minced mushrooms soft. Deglaze the pan with Madeira wine, and over low heat, continue simmering the mushrooms until the liquid has been reduced to a syrupy consistency. Then add the minced chicken to the pan, season with salt and pepper, and add enough cream so that the mushrooms and the chicken are perfectly blended together.

Generously cover the toast with this mixture, and sprinkle chopped tarragon on top. Any salad made with green vegetables, such as asparagus, beans, peas, or broccoli, will make for a perfect accompaniment.

CHICKEN MUSHROOM PIE FOR 3–4

225 g (8 ounces) roasted chicken	500 g (1 pound) button mushrooms,
3 tbsp. butter	cut into fine slices
3 tbsp. flour	1 tbsp. verjus (or Noilly Prat)
150 ml (⅔ cup) milk	1 tbsp. tarragon, chopped
150 ml (⅔ cup) chicken broth	1 tbsp. parsley, chopped
2 tsp. Dijon mustard	salt and pepper
juice of 1 lemon	200 g (7 ounces) puff pastry
1 tbsp. olive oil	1 egg
2 leeks, cut into thin slices	

The covered meat pie, so typical of the Anglo-American cuisine, is really a mixture of gratin and sandwich. And as you would for any gratin, you have to prepare the béchamel sauce first. Thoroughly whisk together the butter and the flour in a small pot, then add the warm milk and the chicken broth (alternating between the two), and continue stirring the sauce until it has become velvety and yet, like a paste, retained its density. Season with mustard and lemon juice, and put it to one side. Next, sauté the leeks and the mushrooms in butter until they have become soft, then deglaze the pan with verjus, and season with salt and pepper. You can now add the mushroom-leek mixture to the béchamel sauce and, over low heat, allow the vegetables to simmer. In the meantime, cut the leftover chicken into bite-size pieces, and add them, together with the chopped herbs, to the mushrooms as well. Before filling the pie, allow the chicken-mushroom filling to cool off.

Heat the oven to 200°C (400°F). Pour the chicken-mushroom filling into a round quiche form (about twenty-three centimeters / nine inches), and cut the puff pastry into a circle large enough to cover the top of the pie completely, not only to protect it when exposed to the heat in the oven but also to produce moisture underneath this cover. You can even tuck a bit of the dough into the inside of the quiche form to more thoroughly seal off the filling. With a sharp knife, make five small incisions into the puff pastry, and then coat it with the whisked egg. Bake the pie, around thirty minutes, until the top has become golden brown.

COUSCOUS WITH CHICKEN, CHERRIES, AND PRESERVED LEMONS FOR 2–3

1 tbsp. dried cherries (briefly soaked
   in water)
2 dried apricots
125 g (1¼ cups) couscous
250 ml (1 cup) broth
200 g (7 ounces) roasted chicken, cut
   into coarse slices or cubes
½ preserved lemon (see "Prepared
   and Stored in the Refrigerator")

20 mint leaves
1 tbsp. pumpkin seeds
1 tbsp. pistachios
salt and pepper
1 tbsp. lemon-scented olive oil
1–2 tbsp. pomegranate molasses
Greek yogurt (or labne)

Leftover chicken also lends itself well to the embellishment of a couscous, transforming this into a meal unto itself. Soak the cherries in hot water, and cut the dried apricots into thin slivers. Pour the hot broth over the couscous, cover the bowl with plastic wrap, and allow it to infuse, about twenty minutes. In the meantime, chop the preserved lemon as well as the mint (keeping a bit on the side for garnishing), cut the leftover chicken into bite-size pieces, and place everything, along with the cherries, the apricots, the pumpkin seeds, and the pistachios, into a big bowl. At this point, season only sparingly with salt and pepper. Once the couscous has absorbed the broth completely, add the lemon oil (or olive oil with a bit of lemon juice), and fluff it up with a fork. Fold the chicken, along with the fruit, into the couscous, and then season with more lemon juice, salt, and pepper. Finish the dish by drizzling pomegranate molasses over the chicken couscous and sprinkling it with the remaining chopped mint. Serve the yogurt in a separate dish so that everyone can take to their own liking.

CHICKEN RISOTTO WITH MUSHROOMS FOR 4

2 tbsp. olive oil
1 garlic clove, finely chopped
140 g (4 ounces) button mushrooms
   and shitake
170 g (6 ounces) roast chicken,
   coarsely sliced or cubed
120 ml (½ cup) cream
salt and pepper
1 L (4 cups) chicken broth

320 g (11 ounces) risotto rice
3 tbsp. olive oil
120 ml (½ cup) white wine
2 tbsp. onions, finely chopped
1 tbsp. lemon paste (see "Prepared
   and Stored in the Refrigerator")
100 g (3 ounces) Parmesan, grated
1 tbsp. parsley, chopped

In this recipe, the leftover chicken and the mushrooms serve as the *condimenti* for the risotto. Melt the oil in a pan, and over medium heat, fry the chopped garlic very briefly. Then add the mushrooms, and sauté them until they have become soft, about five minutes. Then add the bite-size chicken pieces; they should brown but not dry out. Deglaze the *condimento* with cream, season with salt and pepper, and allow it to simmer over low heat another five minutes or so, until the cream has thickened, and then take the pan off the heat. In the meantime, warm the broth before turning your attention to the *soffritto*. In the pot in which you will be preparing the risotto, heat three tablespoons of olive oil, and sauté the chopped onions until they are soft and translucent, about five minutes. Add the risotto rice, stir it with a wooden spoon, and then pour in the wine and stir again. As with any risotto, keep ladling in the warm broth over the rice, bit by bit, about eighteen minutes, until it is firm to the bite. Then add the chicken-mushroom *condimento* along with the lemon paste and, if the risotto is too al dente, a bit more broth. Cover the pot, turn off the heat, and allow the risotto to infuse for a few minutes before vigorously folding in the grated Parmesan and sprinkling it with the chopped parsley.

NOTE: If you want to play with the flavor and texture, you can also sauté the leftover chicken with some prosciutto and chopped tomatoes or with garlic, olives, and chopped capers. Or you could garnish the risotto with pan-fried pine nuts.

RIGATONI WITH VEGETABLES FOR 2

250 g (9 ounces) precooked rigatoni (from the day before)
2 tbsp. olive oil
60 g (2 ounces) bacon (or pancetta), cubed
1 big onion
1 garlic clove, minced
1 pinch chili flakes
2 big artichokes
1 big zucchini
300 ml (1¼ cups) vegetable broth
Parmesan (or pecorino), grated

Although any Italian cook would probably let out a scream of outraged horror at the thought of precooking pasta, this can come in handy for the busy home cook. What is crucial, however, is that the first time around, your pasta is cooked a bit less than al dente so that it doesn't become too soft and squishy when it is reheated. Vegetable and herb pestos lend themselves particularly well for a quick preparation of precooked pasta. While reheating, the pasta can fully absorb the flavor of the sauce, especially if you also add some liquid, like broth, cream, or milk.

Pasta precooked a bit less than al dente can, however, also be quickly prepared with sautéed vegetables. Begin by warming up the broth, and over low heat, keep it at a simmering point. Then prepare the artichokes. Trim off the outer leaves, cut off the top and stem, and pare down the inner leaves until you can remove the furry choke itself, leaving you with two artichoke hearts. Cut these into coarse pieces, and steam them (about five minutes). Cut the zucchini into chunks, add them to the pot, and steam these for a few minutes as well. You could also use broccoli, fennel, or carrot; simply adjust the time it takes to steam these. The vegetables should still be quite firm to the bite because, along with the pasta, they will continue to cook in the warm broth. In the meantime, brown the bacon cubes in oil, add the finely chopped onions to the pan, and sauté them for about ten minutes, until they have begun to caramelize. Add the minced garlic and a pinch of chili flakes, and fry the *soffritto* for another minute. Put the vegetables into the pan first, tossing them with the *soffritto*, and then add the precooked rigatoni as well. As though you were making a risotto, pour some of the broth over the pasta and keep adding more, until the vegetable and the pasta are perfectly combined with each other. Grate cheese over the finished dish; it should cream the sauce and give it a velvety, rich consistency.

MEAT RAGOUT REDUX

While any leftover steak, escalope, or roast can be used the next day in a salad, what remains of a stew or ragout can just as readily be reheated the next day. If you change the side dish, replacing mashed potatoes or pasta with bread or another vegetable dish, you have an entirely different meal. As in the recipe for minced chicken on toast, however, you can also use any meat stew for an open sandwich. You simply need to mince the meat and enhance the remaining sauce with some broth or cream to make it more velvety. Combined once more with the restyled sauce, the minced meat makes a perfect topping for sliced baguette or ciabatta. For crispness, fold some lamb's lettuce or arugula into the minced meat or scatter some chopped herbs over the open sandwich. Steamed vegetables would also work well on top.

My friend Wendelin has come up with his own idiosyncratic way of giving a European twist to the pot sticker (see "Dishes Made Quickly"). He suggests mincing the leftovers of a stew and using this to fill the dumpling wrappers.

You then proceed to fry them in a pan before pouring some water over them and covering the pan so that they can finish cooking in the steam. When most of the water has evaporated, the wrappers should be translucent. Take off the lid, and fry them once more until they are perfectly crisp at the bottom. You can serve them like the classic Italian ravioli with either some olive oil and grated Parmesan or a tomato sauce. In either case, the combination of stewed meat with pasta has been transformed into something new. The flavor of the meat has gained intensity while two new textures complement it—the crisp bottom and the thin, chewy coat. The beauty of this hybrid is that you can make use of the leftovers of a ragù Bolognese in exactly the same way rather than freezing it.

The leftovers of a meat stew can also be transformed into a casserole the next day. Regardless of whether you choose pasta or sliced vegetables—such as eggplant, zucchini, or potatoes—you use these as the bottom layer of your casserole. Cover them with a second layer of stew, some béchamel sauce, and grated cheese, and then begin with a second layer of pasta or vegetables, meat, and sauce. Just make sure that the top layer consists of grated cheese, which, exposed to the heat in the oven, will melt and become crisp. If you prefer to make a gratin, perhaps because you don't have enough leftover stew, you can spread out the meat, combined with some sautéed or steamed vegetables, over the bottom of a shallower baking dish. Pour béchamel sauce or a combination of eggs and cream over the stew, sprinkle with grated cheese, and bake the gratin in the oven. And finally, you could also turn the leftovers of any stew into a quiche. Mince the meat, and sauté some vegetables. Cover the bottom of the baking dish with short-crust pastry, and sprinkle it with some grated Parmesan. You may want to bake it blind first before adding the meat and vegetables along with the egg, cream, and cheese mixture that is obligatory for any quiche. The following pie recipe offers a fourth variation. In contrast to a quiche, the dough is not used as the bottom layer of the dish but rather as the coat covering the reimagined stew.

MEAT RAGOUT POT PIE FOR 3–4

500 g (1 pound) meat ragout
1 tbsp. olive oil
1 onion, finely chopped
350 g (3 cups) vegetables
(mushrooms, peppers, green peas)

3 tbsp. flour
300 ml (1¼ cups) meat broth
herbs
320 g (11 ounces) puff pastry

Flowers at the market

Using the leftovers of a chicken stew or a meat ragout, you can make a covered pie effortlessly. Fry the chopped onions in olive oil until they begin to caramelize. In the meantime, cut the vegetables into small cubes or strips. You can either use more of the same vegetables that were in the stew or choose some that complement what you already have. Add the vegetables to the pan, and over medium heat, sauté them for several minutes, and then add the ragout meat as well. Dust both with flour and sauté, about five minutes, before pouring the broth into the pan, but do so gradually. The amount of broth you need will depend on how liquidy the ragout is. If you still have some of the wine you used for cooking it, you could also add some of that as well. The flavor can also be enhanced by adding some chopped herbs. While reducing the sauce, to intensify the flavor further, you may want to add more broth to get the consistency just right. The pie filling shouldn't become as thin as a goulash soup but rather should be dense and creamy.

Heat the oven to 180°C (350°F). To assemble the pie, use a round casserole dish as your template to cut out a round piece from the puff pastry with which you will cover the pie at the end. Use the rest of the dough to line the bottom and the sides of the casserole dish. You want the ragout to be enveloped by the dough as though this were a protective coat. Pour the ragout into the casserole dish, using a spatula to smooth the surface, and then carefully place the cutout piece of dough on top. With a small knife, make three incisions into the top so that air can escape while the pie is exposed to the heat in the oven, and bake it for around forty minutes. A salad composed of steamed green vegetables makes for a perfect contrast to this homey dish.

FLAVORS AND AROMAS

The art of seasoning relies on a combination of the flavor we experience with our tongue and the aroma we detect with our nose, especially as, when eating, the sense of taste and smell always go in tandem. The aroma supports the sense of taste in more ways than one, giving an intense yet nuanced quality to the finished dish. While it is possible to compile thousands of aromas, there are, strictly speaking, only five basic tastes: salt, sweet, sour, bitter, and umami. To season a dish well thus depends on finding a happy balance of flavors; aromatic possibilities should be considered in light of how to exploit the natural taste of the ingredients to a maximum degree, deepening and rounding off their flavor. For this reason, nothing is perhaps as significant in cooking as being able to control the flavor of a dish. It helps, of course, to have a feel for spices at your proverbial fingertips, which you can rely on spontaneously. The art of seasoning is, above all, however, a skill that you acquire through systematic trial and error. When it comes to the question of how best to use spices and herbs in a dish, it is worth not only recalling over and over again the features of the five tastes but also drawing on your memory of successful aromatic combinations.

How, then, do the five tastes work? As the essential component of almost all dishes, salt is probably the most important ingredient in the kitchen. Basically, it serves to accentuate the flavors of the other ingredients that are brought together in a particular dish to enhance them and allow them to shine. When used properly, salt should always remain in the background and never dominate. If you sense it as a flavor on its own, then you have probably used too much. Only if you are lucky can you correct the saltiness of a dish with a shot of milk. It is, furthermore, worth taking one's cue from professional chefs who never wait until the end to season a dish with salt. By repeatedly tasting what you are cooking, you will be able to tell whether the aromatic flavor of your dish is developing in the direction you want. If this is not the case, a pinch of salt will usually do the trick. Salt, however, not only serves to intensify a savory dish but can also be used to underscore sweetness or acidity. For this reason, I season orange slices, tossed in honey and olive oil, with a pinch of salt. At the same time, salt can help balance the pungency of a bitter taste, which is why it goes so well with dark chocolate. Therefore, when a sauce or marinade has become too bitter, don't spontaneously reach for sugar and instead use salt first to correct the flavor.

While everything you do in the kitchen is based on salt, sweetness functions as a source of energy. Our first association with this flavor is, of course, sugar, be it white or brown or coarse, finely ground, or powdered. But we encounter sugar also as molasses or syrup. Sweetness is, moreover, found not only in fruit and honey but also in milk. Sweetness can, in turn, both balance and revive the aroma of a dish. With a shot of balsamic vinegar, dull tomato soup will be invigorated because this calls forth the natural sweetness of the tomato, much as a dollop of ketchup will breathe new life into a boring stew. For this reason, I use a combination of savory soy sauce with sweet mirin in a marinade for salmon steaks or sweet potatoes, season my chopped liver with sweet port, and add a dollop of marmalade to oven-roasted pumpkin. And when onions don't seem to caramelize properly while being sautéed in a pan, a pinch of sugar will almost always accelerate the process.

On the tongue, the taste of sourness, in turn, has the property of contracting the mucous membrane in the mouth and stimulating the flow of saliva. It literally encourages the mouth to ingest more nourishment. For this reason, we declare a particularly delicious dish to be mouthwatering. If, while checking a dish for seasoning, I have the feeling that something is missing, my first intuition is to add a touch of acidity. Usually a shot of lemon or lime juice is enough to round off the flavor of a soup or pan-fried fish. Sherry vinegar, or the less intense white balsamic vinegar, can be used to bring about the aromatic balance of a dressing or a marinade without actually drawing attention to the vinegar as such. As with salt, bitterness should also remain in the background, supporting the meeting of and happy conversation between the other ingredients without drawing attention to itself. While our first association with sourness is vinegar or citrus fruits and apples, this flavor can also be found in the lactic acid used in yogurt and cheese, but it can also be present in sausages.

It comes as no surprise, then, that precisely this flavor can be used as a corrective to balance or contain the rich fat content or intense sweetness of a dish. A shot of bitter will avert the sense of oversaturation; it allows the mouth to water again. This applies not only to a sumptuous cream dessert but also to watermelon, which can so splendidly be seasoned with lime juice and finely chopped herbs. If you serve foie gras with orange slices, they will balance the fatty opulence of this delicacy. Sour tamarind paste in a curry will temper the sweetness of the coconut milk, while in a salad dressing that contains mustard and mayonnaise, vinegar will reduce any sense of over-richness. Only by adding lemon juice does the combination of cream and chopped garlic I am so fond of reach true harmony. For this reason, the red wine in the glass not only complements the food on the plate; added to a stew, the sour effect of the tannins will also stimulate the appetite. You simply mustn't be overgenerous and pour a whole bottle into the coq au vin, because then the wine's acidity will overpower the flavor of all the other ingredients.

The taste of bitter is particularly tricky because it can be perceived not only as quite literally distasteful but often also as a signal that something might be poisonous. For this reason, more than all others, this taste can trigger an inborn defense mechanism. In the magical thinking of the early modern period, we find a bodily correspondence. Bile, produced by the gall bladder, was thought of as a bitter fluid whose overproduction, when inundating the body, called forth emotions like anger, vexation, and weariness. Yet the notion of bitterness also contains a countermeaning. We call something that is very unpleasant but must be accepted "a bitter pill to swallow." And indeed, this flavor is comparable to the *pharmakon* in Plato's dialogue between Phaedrus and Socrates, in which everything depends on the dosage used. If you take too much, it will become a dangerous poison; if you take the proper amount, it will work wonders.

If we think of drinks that operate with a bitter note, the second aspect becomes most pronounced. While coffee stimulates our nervous system, tonic water was part of the standard equipment of the British colonial army because its quinine content was thought to be a protection against malaria. Gin and tonic, the cocktail offspring of the medicinal quinine water, is, however, not the only liquor that showcases the beneficial side of bitterness. A shot of Angostura bitters is obligatory in a Manhattan cocktail, much as a Campari is best mixed with bitter lemon (according to my mother). And then there is beer. We drink such beverages before a meal to stimulate our appetite. Herb liquors—such as Fernet-Branca or Amaro—are, in turn, called cordials and served at the end of a rich and copious meal to aid digestion. Without the inclusion of bitter ingredients, one of the five tastes would be missing from our cookery. Deployed in the right dose, a bitter flavor can (much like acidity) help balance richness and sweetness even while engendering aromatic depth and complexity. In other words, the key is making use of the impact that bitterness has within the spectrum of the five tastes, in exactly the right degree.

We associate this taste primarily with salad ingredients: arugula, radicchio, Belgian endives, or watercress. In the spirit of containing the force of bitterness, you add not only salt to the salad dressing, by way of contrast, but also the sweetness of a balsamic vinegar, honey, or marmalade. When I sauté Belgian endives, I not only sprinkle brown sugar on top to help them caramelize but also add a shot of balsamic vinegar and chopped cilantro at the end, enhancing the marriage between bitter and sweet. For the same reason, I drizzle balsamic vinegar over oven-roasted treviso before serving it. Based on thinking in contrasts, I might garnish a shrimp salad with the bitter zest of an orange or a grapefruit, much as I might embellish a scallop carpaccio with grated horseradish or bring together Belgian endives and walnuts with richly savory blue cheese. In the same vein, salty broth along with the sweetness of roasted pumpkin will balance the bitter flavor of radicchio in a risotto. And like the taste of acidity, bitterness also helps mitigate the opulence of dishes rich in fat. A touch of arugula or watercress will aromatically balance out the lavish splendor of a slice of pan-fried foie gras; dark chocolate or ground coffee will offset a sumptuous cream dessert.

Today, we recognize as the fifth category of taste the savory intensity discovered by the Japanese scientist Ikeda Kikunai at the beginning of the twentieth century. He called it umami, literally meaning "deliciousness." This spicy taste can be found in green tea, meat broth, miso paste, soy sauce, fish sauce, and sake. But anchovies, tuna, mushrooms, olives, tomatoes, truffle oil, and ripe cheeses such as Parmesan also render this savoriness. A casserole made of some (or all) of these ingredients may well be thought of as an umami bomb. Like the tartness of any sour seasoning, this particular taste not only serves to invigorate a dish; umami also gives intensity and depth to a dish, especially when several ingredients engendering its savoriness are combined. You sprinkle Parmesan over spaghetti with tomato sauce or serve a beef burger with ketchup to emphasize the hearty taste of the main ingredient. My particular fondness for this taste has inspired me not only to mix soy sauce with peanut butter or tahini, as we know it from East Asian cooking, but also to add a shot of soy to a tomato sauce. And because umami will balance out the richness of cream, I find the marriage between soy sauce and cream a match made in heaven. While umami offers zest and pungency (think Worcestershire sauce in a beef tartar), it is important to distinguish this taste from ingredients that lend heat to a dish—first and foremost pepper. In contrast to salt, which by penetrating the ingredient dissolves into it, pepper remains on the surface and lends a final, intense bite to a dish. The vitality of this spice can be found in chili, raw garlic, onions, ginger, horseradish, mustard, and wasabi. This is why you combine these ingredients in a marinade for meat, poultry, and fish or in the *soffritto* for a risotto. The piquancy they offer helps develop the flavor of the other ingredients—while pan-frying, braising in a pot, or roasting in the oven.

The art of seasoning entails not only mastering the usage of these five tastes but above all knowing how to play with the immense variety of aromas; these will make up the specific flavor of a dish and endow it with its own special note. Aromatic tastes can range from pungent, spicy, piquant, succulent, and nutty to fruity, flowery, earthy, wooden, and smoky to dark, deep, airy, and velvety. The magic you can achieve with a successful combination of aromas consists of both intensifying the flavor of a dish as well as transforming it. The combination you choose should get the assembled flavors to vibrate. This, then, is where the creativity of the cook, as well as her obsession, comes into play. Of course, a particularly seductive combination of aromas may happen by mere chance. It is, however, better to continually hone this skill. How does one do that? When I, for example, plan a meal and then shop for the ingredients, I already imagine the flavor combinations I am hoping to reproduce. In the same vein, while eating, I can't help analyzing the flavor nuances of the ingredients and think about other combinations for them. It has become a ritual that, when eating at a restaurant with friends, we will analyze the interaction among the aromas of the dishes before us and try to describe the effect these have. When I am invited over to a friend's house, the ritual, in turn, consists of guessing which aromas have been used and discussing how they have mutually influenced each other. At the same time, I also suggest setting up a personal archive of aromas—on paper and in your head—so that, as in chess, you can remember past strategies. I have a black notebook where I write down every new flavor combination I encounter or come up with. This way, while cooking, I can always fall back on this knowledge. However, in this notebook, I also note the experiments that fail because it is equally useful to remember what didn't work.

The point of using aromatic spices and herbs in cooking is, then, to bring into harmony the tastes of the different ingredients as well as to emphasize their particular characteristics. It therefore stands to reason that in your personal archive of aromas, you would note all the flavor combinations in which ingredients have a happy conversation with each other. To me, paradigmatic of such a culinary marriage is vanilla accentuating the fruity sweetness of pumpkin, chopped rosemary complementing the acidity of apricots with an earthy note, or the combination of argan oil and chopped cilantro enhancing the sweet herbal flavor of roasted beets.

More thrilling, of course, is the search for combinations in which the aromas, when married together, produce contrast in taste and in texture. While our tongue senses the flavor of what we eat, our teeth also enjoy the play of consistencies. For that reason, we relish the cheese crust on a gratin and the crisp coating on a veal escalope. That is also why chopped nuts and grated apple work so well as the last ingredient added to a vegetable soup, why a garlic-nut crunch will glory a pasta dish and why grated horseradish on a beet risotto comes as the crowning touch. An appealing contrast of textures can even be achieved with an ordinary green salad—namely, when caraway seeds or sesame seeds are added to the dressing or when the salad is topped with crunchy furikake seasoning. I found a particularly sophisticated example of this in the carrot salad that Jody Williams serves in her West Village restaurant, Buvette. Here, the bitter poignancy of coriander seeds supports the tart sweetness of grated carrots, while chopped pistachios add their tactile charm to the salad.

In addition to aromatic combinations, there are, according to Heston Blumenthal, aromas that intensify the taste of a dish by offering concentrated flavor impulses. For this reason, I will use preserved lemons both in a stew and in a salad. When you bite into one of the pickled bits of lemon skin, an intense citrus taste explodes in your mouth. Or I will fold fish roe into a tuna tartar not only because the crispy pearls offer a perfect contrast to the velvety texture of the chopped fish but also because they disperse additional dashes of saltiness in the mouth when they are bitten into. Grating bottarga over scrambled eggs or pan-fried green asparagus provides not only for an airy contrast but also for a condensed impulse of oceanic brine. And finally, the chopped herbs, added only at the end to garnish a dish, offer up their own aromatic intensity.

For the art of seasoning, the experiences that you, as a cook and a gourmand, have had with the combination of spices, herbs, and ingredients are essential. It is equally important to remember what the best conditions are for herbs to unfold their aroma. Robust ones like bay leaves or rosemary should be cooked along with the other ingredients, while the aroma of more delicate herbs, like basil or tarragon, is more transient so they should only be added at the end. And because the aim is to achieve aromatic balance, the flavoring of a dish must be adjusted to the transformation of the ingredients that occurs in the course of cooking. For this you not only need the supplies on the shelves of your kitchen to draw on to improve or correct the seasoning of a dish; there is also a set of questions you want to ask yourself when seasoning: Would more salt accentuate the flavor? Would some lemon juice or vinegar invigorate the dish? Would the other aromas have more effect if sweetness were added? Would more spice produce the desired bite? Does one flavor dominate to such a degree that it needs tempering? Does the dish have the right dose of umami? Have the desired aromas developed or have they disappeared such that they need a boost? In which case does the aroma need more of the spices already used or an ingredient that would complement the flavor? Does the dish need a dollop of butter to make it more sweet and creamy? Would a dash of herbs or nuts offer an attractive crunch? In the heat of cooking, it is not enough to simply reach for these ingredients. Rather, you want to imagine in advance the effect they will have. And for that you need that personal archive of aromas, safely stored away in your mind.

♣ 4 ♣

THE POT

Flavors Slowly Develop

Soup | Risotto, Penne, Couscous | All in One Pot | In the Tagine |
Stewed and Poached Fruit | From the Pot into the Water Bath in the Oven

There is probably no greater contrast than the one between pan-frying and braising in a pot. Rather than being exposed to a lot of heat for only a brief time, ingredients cook slowly over medium or low heat. Almost nothing happens immediately; instead, a gradual transformation takes place. With the combination of both heat and steam (which is to be avoided at all costs while pan-frying), the dish slowly develops its flavor and consistency. While a meticulous *mise en place* is always an advantage, not everything needs to be ready in advance when you are braising. While the first ingredients are simmering, you can prepare the others bit by bit. Once the ingredients all come together in the process of braising, the eye alone can hardly tell when the desired consistency has been reached. Instead, the delicious smell that begins to permeate every corner of the kitchen allows you to surmise the success of what you are preparing, as does tasting the dish periodically. Patience rather than dexterity is, thus, called for when cooking in a pot, not only because this mode of preparation requires quite a bit of time; usually the ingredients must also be browned individually first. As if building a kind of culinary architecture, you can add one layer of flavor after the other until you have finished constructing your dish. Moreover, in contrast to pan-frying, cooking in a pot does not involve making a series of decisions at each juncture. Whether you are preparing a soup, risotto, ragout, or stew, there is a fixed sequence of steps you must follow, leaving little leeway for alternative routes. When it comes to decision making—and thus to culinary creativity—the issue of choice instead involves the ingredients and spices that are joined together over a longer period of time. Indeed, the possibilities for integrating complexly textured flavors into a harmonious whole are endlessly variable, with hardly any limits to personal improvisation.

One might, in fact, speak of a polyphony of aromas brought to resound among the main ingredient, the vegetables, and the aromatics as well as the braising liquid. What is crucial in this time-consuming mode of cooking, thus, isn't an agile readiness but rather a relaxed tranquility that sets in once you have happily put the lid on the pot. From that moment on, all further developments are literally no longer in your hands. If you have diligently executed all the necessary steps, the pot can now take over. The cook becomes a benevolent witness who, at certain intervals, checks whether the dish is progressing in the desired direction and, if necessary, corrects the liquid, heat, and spicing. In contrast to pan-frying, the amount of time a recipe gives for braising or stewing is, thus, merely an approximate value. It may sometimes be better to give yourself more time.

The serenity that comes over me once I have put the lid on my pot has much to do with the certainty that if I got everything right initially, almost nothing can go wrong. Should the meat not be tender enough after the pre-scribed time, I simply allow it to braise longer. If the aroma isn't quite right, I can experiment with the seasoning until I have seized upon the desired flavor. And if the vegetables have gotten too soft, I declare the dish to be a soup. Although it requires more time, cooking in a pot is actually a soothing activity because it doesn't demand constant attention. The dish can cook on its own while I can turn my attention to other things. I simply mustn't forget to stir what is cooking now and then and keep tasting to adjust the seasoning if necessary.

In the German-American home cooking I grew up with, the pot domi-nated. The recipes often came from cookbooks and women's magazines from the postwar period, which were then reinterpreted by my mother. In the pro-cess, she adapted the traditional German dishes she had learned from her mother not only to the changed tastes of the time but also to what was avail-able in the supermarket. During the week, however, the food preparation was primarily done by our housekeeper, Gerti, who, whether out of protest or because she had little understanding for gourmet cooking, didn't always adhere to my mother's instructions. On the one hand, I remember the way the dinner table was always immaculately set with a white linen cloth, indi-vidual napkin rings for each family member, and silver knife rests (which con-tinue to perplex those of my guests who are uncertain about how to place the cutlery on them correctly). On the other hand, the elegant porcelain bowls in which the food was always served often disclosed a watery stew with chewy and sinewy pieces of beef or crumbly meatballs in a bland white sauce, tasting too much of the roux used to prepare it. Carelessly prepared, the food was sometimes truly quite awful.

And yet, I have retained a deep nostalgia for this type of home cooking that seems almost strange to us today. This has in part to do with the fact that when my mother presided over the kitchen, she could work wonders. As is well known, mothers and daughters don't always have a simple relationship with each other, and I too didn't really take her cooking lessons all too seriously until after I had moved out. It was then that I began to study her hand gestures while preparing food, to write down her recipes, and to pay particular attention to her secret tricks. However, the fastidious diligence with which she performed each step would often trigger an almost unbearable impatience in me. My mother could spend a seemingly endless amount of time in the fresh produce section of the supermarket, carefully turning each piece of fruit or vegetable around in her hand until she had found the perfect specimens. She enjoyed recalling that, as a young girl in Berlin, when sent by her mother to buy meat, she would insist that the butcher turn the piece he was offering her around. She wanted to make sure that he knew that, just because she was young and such a slender girl, she would not let him deceive her into buying an inferior piece of meat. In fact, she always took a lot of time when preparing food. She would always scrape out the very last drop from a bowl, meticulously pluck each parsley leaf from its stalk, chop it in an old-fashioned herb grinder, and then use a fork to retrieve all bits of green that had gotten caught in the blades. As irritating as her deliberateness was at the time, I have since become convinced of one of my mother's basic culinary principles. The difference between a fair and an extraordinary dish depends on the precision with which the ingredients are prepared. Today, I am a bit less rigorous when it comes to cooking regulations, and I often decide spontaneously whether to abide by the instructions to the letter or to improvise.

However, because so much of what I ate at home was prepared in a pot, this type of cooking signifies comfort and well-being for me. Even in fairy tales, the pot on the stove serves as the image par excellence for the comfort of home, which we like to associate with the family. In a wholly elementary manner, cooking in a pot appeals to the magical thinking of our childhood. We imagine that a transformation is taking place that is not altogether removed from sorcery, witchcraft, and spells. Indeed, in the world of fairy tales, the pot has two sides. While the kindhearted mother uses it to prepare her wholesome porridge, the wicked witch stands at her cauldron, stirring an evil brew consisting of all kinds of unidentifiable animal parts and root vegetables. Everything can be tossed into a pot—the familiar and the strange, the felicitous and the disgusting. As for the herbs, which folklore believes are best gathered during a full moon, they can be cooked in a pot to produce either a healing or a poisonous brew. Indeed, concocting something repulsive doesn't need to be in bad intention; it might simply be the unfortunate product of an intense desire for experimentation. I remember how my sister and I were once so taken with an image in a cookbook that we encouraged Gerti, our housekeeper, to braise beef tongue in red wine. What was revealed when she finally uncovered the pot would not have surpassed any sorceress in horridness.

However, when it comes to preparing food in a pot, what is at stake is also the question of working with my own culinary heritage in such a way that favorite family recipes can constantly find themselves enriched by new influences and, as such, can keep developing. While my mother, as the young wife of a returning war veteran, encountered American home cooking for the first time in Washington, DC, at the end of World War II, she was quick to incorporate the German cooking familiar to her. Then once my parents decided to move back to Munich in the early 1950s, she took her American cooking experience with her. If, in turn, my mother's recipes have served as a point of orientation in my own culinary education, I too have sought to include experiences of foreign cuisines, embellishing her family dishes with my own idiosyncratic variations. When I was a pupil in my mother's kitchen, hardly anyone in Germany knew how to prepare a risotto; indeed, buffalo mozzarella, arugula, and sun-dried tomatoes were just being discovered there. Ginger, cilantro, coconut milk, or lemongrass (so familiar to us today) were as uncanny to home cooks then as the roots and bones of the witch's cauldron in my fairy tales. Therefore, one can speak of a magical transformation taking place at the homely stove in yet another sense. By virtue of the amalgamation and metamorphosis that heat and steam accomplish in the cooking pot, ingredients that are initially unfamiliar ultimately become commonplace. Persistent usage not only gradually turns exotic spices into familiar aromas but also renders unexpected correspondences visible. With time, I rediscovered traces of the ordinary European stew in the curries of Southeast Asia and the tagines of North Africa. With all due respect for the excitement of experimenting with novel culinary combinations, it is also important to ensure that family dishes that have been passed on for several generations do not fall into oblivion. They too need to be kept alive.

For me, cooking in a pot is quintessential because the meeting of and happy conversation between the various aromatic layers, which—thanks to the combination of heat and steam—evolves over a longer period of time, culminating in a consistent whole. And yet there is a further reason cooking in a pot strikes me as an embodiment par excellence of the sense of emotional well-being and happiness we connect with the home. I dedicate the longest chapter to this cooking utensil because it is particularly suitable for gathering guests around one's table. Most of the actual preparation is finished before the guests arrive; the dishes may only need some additional seasoning and a bit of final garnishing before they can be served. At the same time, many of the following recipes are also for four to six people because dishes made in a pot often lend themselves particularly well to being reheated the next day. What is, above all, crucial for me is the spectrum of cooking that stewing and braising affords. This ranges from the ordinary to the festive. A stew with select vegetables or a meat ragout cooked for several days can turn any work-related meeting into a special occasion. Repeatedly, I have found that if, on the eve of a conference, I invite the speakers to share a meal at my table (even if all I serve is a minestrone), the discussions the next day will be far more fruitful. Stimulated by the enchanting flavors on the tongue, the conversation grows ever more relaxed as well. In the nurturing warmth that this type of food engenders, everyone comes closer together.

For a long time, my model for these quasi-conspiratorial gatherings at my dinner table has been Mrs. Ramsay, the heroine of my favorite novel by Virginia Woolf, *To the Lighthouse*. In the country house on the coast of England where Mrs. Ramsay—along with her philosopher husband, her children, and sundry invited guests—spends her summer vacations, she turns each evening meal into a work of art. As the emotional custodian of the home, she presides over the dining room with attentive care. The boeuf en daube, which her family and friends share with each other at the candlelit table, brings them all together. Through the window, Mrs. Ramsay perceives the disappearance of the world outside into the nocturnal darkness, making her aware of the ephemerality of this moment. And yet, with—and against—the knowledge of the transience of this meal, she celebrates this fragile togetherness with her family. The cozy, homely scene corresponds to the choice of dish. If, in this French stew, the prime beef unites with the red wine, vegetables, garlic, and *herbes de Provence* to form a harmonious whole, so too the people consuming it connect with each other. And there is one thing of which

Mrs. Ramsay is absolutely certain: her guests will remember this nocturnal scene as an instance of shared culinary sympathy.

☙

The purpose of this chapter is to demonstrate the various ways in which the pot can be deployed to prepare food. While poaching entails cooking ingredients *in* a simmering fluid and steaming means cooking them *above* seething water (which the ingredients do not come in direct contact with), most of the recipes in this chapter make use of a mixture of frying and braising. For a soup, you first brown the vegetables and then add the broth. For a risotto, you first fry the rice before gradually adding the broth. For a stew, you brown each of the ingredients individually first before combining them in the pot and adding the wine in which they will simmer slowly and gently. In all cases, at issue is an exchange between the moisture released by the ingredients themselves and the liquid you add to the pot. The most intense circulation of aromas will, of course, be brought about by covering the pot with a tightly fitting lid. Then the steam of the wine, broth, or marinade in which the ingredients are braising rises up, producing condensation on the underside of the lid, only to drip down again to reunite with the juices released by the ingredients themselves. This mutual enrichment engenders a depth in flavor no other form of cooking can attain—a condensed amalgamation of the flavors of all the ingredients that have gradually come to be fused with each other in the pot.

Perhaps the most basic rule for cooking in the pot is that the ingredients should always be surrounded by gently simmering liquid of some sort or other. Even when making a risotto in an uncovered pot, this principle holds true. Over low temperature, the rice slowly becomes done precisely because each kernel is constantly being moistened by the broth. This is why you must keep stirring the risotto. A further rule is equally vital: once you have combined all the ingredients in the pot, the liquid must simmer very gently. Low temperature is thus as essential as the longer cooking time. Even when preparing a risotto, to which you add the broth gradually, you should avoid any vigorous bubbling in the pot. Instead, patience is called for until the circulation of aromatic moisture has cooked your ingredients to perfection.

Cooking in a pot consists of layering flavors on top of each other—not unlike a pasta sauce. With each step, you underline the aromatic nuance that makes up the unique character of the dish. While culinary creativity can be exercised when it comes to the combination of the ingredients as well as the spices used to season them, the sequence of steps required for cooking in the pot is predetermined, even though there is some room for choice. For a stew, you can either allow the meat to rest for several hours in a spice paste or a marinade or you can wait to season and coat it with flour only just before (or even after) browning. In both cases, however, the first step is to sear the meat, not—as culinary superstition holds—to close the pores but rather to give more depth to the overall flavor of the dish. The floury coating will help make the sauce denser and the aroma more concentrated. If you want to add vegetables, remove the meat from the pot or—as in a risotto—prepare the subsidiary ingredients in a separate pot. In a second step, the main ingredient is supplemented with aromatic ingredients—usually a *soffritto* consisting of onions, garlic, and spices or a roux. The third step concerns the savory liquid with which you first deglaze the pot before using it to braise your main ingredients, regardless of whether it is added all at once, as in a stew, or gradually, as in a risotto. In a final step, depending on your personal desire for improvisation, you can hone the dish by adding a crowning layer of flavor: An egg, some cream, a handful of herbs, or wine all help round off the consistency as well as the overall aromatic tone of the dish.

For cooking soups and stews, I favor pots made of enameled cast iron (such as those made by Le Creuset or Staub). Even if you prefer stainless-steel or copper pots, what is crucial is that the heat is conducted evenly, gently, and slowly. And yet the success of the dish does not depend only on the quality of the pots you use but also on their shape. The lid must fit the pot perfectly so that no steam will escape. In a pinch, you can, of course, cover the pot tightly with aluminum foil. The sides of the pot, in turn, must be high enough so that the braising liquid can, if required, cover the ingredients completely. These ingredients, in turn, should fit snugly into the pot, leaving no empty space. The closer the fit of the pot, the closer the ingredients are to the liquid that will transform into a richly dense sauce. If the pot is too big for the ingredients, the steam will collect on the sides of the pot before coming into close contact with them. The braising liquid in turn will spread out over the bottom of the pot and evaporate far too quickly. If you then add more liquid, you risk diluting the sauce and losing in flavor. For this reason, the ideal pot will correspond to the size and shape of the ingredients that you want to braise in it, which also means, of course, that you may need to invest in several pots. A wide, round casserole is best for braising roulades, chicken drumsticks, or vegetables, because this will give you enough space to spread out your ingredients in one layer. When making a soup or a risotto, choose a pot that is deeper, since you will be cooking with more liquid. For poaching fruit, the pot should only be as wide as is necessary for all the pieces to fit into it snugly. If you are a perfectionist, you may, of course, wish to have an oval-shaped Dutch oven as well, more appropriately shaped for the duck or guinea fowl you may want to braise for a special occasion.

While the width and height of the pot can be decisive, the type of lid is also crucial, as everything depends on whether the steam has the optimal space to produce the condensation on the underside of the lid so that it can then drip back down onto the ingredients below, keeping them moist and succulent. For precisely this reason, I have always been impressed with the conical lid of the cooking vessel in which a tagine is traditionally prepared. This pot, like no other, reminds me of a witch's cottage, making it the perfect cooking utensil for such magic transformations to take place. For this reason, I decided to buy a tagine on one of my visits to New York City. However, I did not want one made of ordinary earthen stoneware; rather, I wanted All-Clad's fancy urban variety, consisting of a stainless-steel bottom and a white enameled top. It was a particularly sultry day in August when my friend Doug, with whom I had just had lunch in a Chinese restaurant in Chelsea, decided to accompany me on my quest. We walked clear across Lower Manhattan, from one store to the next, and although there were many colorful tagines sitting on the shelves, the model my heart was set on was nowhere to be found. In each of the shops we entered, I explained to the bewildered salesperson that I needed this particular style because I wanted to not only make the traditional chicken dish with preserved lemons and olives but also use my tagine to experiment with Asian herbs and spices. As we journeyed from one shop to the next, I kept musing about how the steam circulating in the voluminous conical lid would give an entirely new consistency to the ingredients of a classic stir-fry or curry. And so, walking along the sweltering streets of New York, my thoughts conjured up an imaginary feast while the sticky air around me seemed to be getting muggier and muggier. When Doug finally brought me to a shop in SoHo that actually had my dream tagine pot in stock, I was elated knowing that my thoughts circulating around the dishes I might make with it might soon be realized. Deeply worried about breaking the precious lid, I transported the heavy object in my hand luggage across the ocean back to Switzerland. Since then, my tagine—the jewel of my kitchen shelves—has remained a reliable helper.

My prized tagine

SOUP

❧ BROTH SOUPS
Bouillon Made from Chicken | Bouillon Made from Beef | Bouillon with Garlic and Egg | Avgolemono Soup with Lemon and Egg | Miso Soup with Shitake Mushrooms | Beet Soup

❧ PURÉED VEGETABLE SOUPS
Pumpkin Soup with Vanilla | Pumpkin Soup with Parmesan | Pumpkin Soup with Pears and Cream | Pumpkin Soup with Lime and Cilantro Pesto | Parsnip Soup with Curry | Sauerkraut Cream Soup | Chestnut and Pear Soup | Corn Chowder

❧ VELOUTÉ
Cream of Mushroom Soup | Chervil Soup

❧ A MEAL OF ITS OWN
Barley Soup | Minestrone | Inge Gerstner-Höchberg's Waterzooi

As my friend Martin, a true master of soups, never ceases to assure me—everything you can puree with liquid can be turned into a soup. And because you can pretty much puree anything you have cooked long enough in a flavorful liquid, making a soup allows you to be particularly inventive. Moreover, few utensils are required: You only need a knife to cut the ingredients, a pot to cook them in, a wooden spoon to stir them now and then, a blender of some sort to puree them (either a simple immersion blender or an elaborate Vitamix), and a bowl to serve the soup. The only decision to be made in advance is whether you want to serve the soup as an appetizer (either warm or cold) or whether you want to serve it as the main course.

Because I am more likely to use poultry or meat in a stew, I primarily cook vegetable soups. Once you have mastered the few, simple steps required for making vegetable soups, it is easy to improvise with what you find in your refrigerator or at the market. The first thing to prepare is the aromatic foundation. You do this by browning a mixture of finely chopped onions, carrots, garlic, celery, or ginger, sometimes adding bacon or ham. In Italian cuisine, this is called a *soffritto*, in French cuisine, a *mirepoix*. Over low heat, this foundation should glaze and become soft but not caramelize. In a second step, you add the vegetables that will define the soup and briefly braise them in the *soffritto* or *mirepoix* before adding the broth. Then retaining low heat, you let the soup simmer, usually for about half an hour. Even if you will subsequently puree the soup, the vegetables should be cut into thin slices or small cubes. This allows them to absorb the flavor of the aromatic ingredients and the broth more fully. Unless I am specifically making chicken or beef broth, I often use stock cubes for my cooking fluid. They are so much more convenient (although I realize that purists would see this differently). You can also add herbs, such as thyme, oregano, or bay leaves, to the vegetables; these herbs develop their aroma best while cooking slowly in the broth. Although you can really use any vegetables you want in a soup, you should, however, stick to certain rules regarding the order in which you add them to the pot. The onion family and root vegetables always go first; zucchini, pumpkin, mushrooms, and cabbage go next. You should wait with the tomatoes because they release quite a bit of moisture, and only add them along with the broth. So as to retain their color and texture, spinach, Swiss chard, and peas should only be added to the hot broth in the end.

If you aren't going to puree the soup, make sure you combine different types of vegetables to create a range of aromas and textures. If you puree the soup with an immersion blender—this is a point Martin insists on—you should, in a final step, pass the vegetables through a fine sieve; otherwise, you will not attain the desired creaminess. However, if you are using a professional blender (or a food processor), this additional step is not really necessary. Either way, allow the soup to cool a bit before you puree it because lukewarm vegetables liquefy more easily. If you are using a blender, bear in mind never to overfill it because otherwise—and I speak from experience—you will have an unwanted volcanic eruption in the kitchen. You can adjust the consistency of the soup by adding more broth, coconut milk, yogurt, or cream. Add delicate herbs such as parsley, chives, or dill only at the end, after the soup has been reheated. Before serving it, season with salt, which will accentuate the aroma. If your soup needs more acidity, you can add a splash of lemon juice, balsamic vinegar, or wine vinegar. And to enhance the flavor of your vegetable soup even further, finish with a few drops of nut oil, a dollop of crème fraîche, a touch of pesto, or some grated cheese.

The following recipes are divided according to the complexity of flavors they are built upon. For this reason, I begin with clear broths. Using the pumpkin as my paradigmatic example, I then play through a panoply of aromatic variations for pureed vegetable soup. From there, I move on to further aromatic enhancements, as the soups become meals in themselves. It is worth bearing in mind that not only can a vegetable soup be reheated the next day, but it also tends to improve in the process. However, because eggs curdle when exposed to intense heat, you should never bring any egg-cream mixture to a boil, much as crème fraîche or pesto should only be added just before serving, as both suffer when reheated.

BROTH SOUPS

Hardly any other dish evokes a sense of nostalgia in me as does the thought of a homemade chicken or beef broth. With each spoonful, a soothing warmth infuses the body, and the spirit is made happy by the idea of consuming something wholesome and pure. I admit, however, that more often than not, I will fall back on stock cubes (or stock powder) as the primary liquid in my soups. Not only are there many excellent organic brands available these days, but I also often don't have the time to prepare homemade broth and freeze it. And I don't want to prevent others from exploring new soup variations simply because of certain details that, to a degree, belong to a past world in which one had big kitchens, spacious pantries, and kitchen help. In the same spirit, I have never even attempted to prepare a consommé, which, in a final step, must be passed through a cheesecloth. However, when I long for a clear broth, perhaps with the addition of one or two pure ingredients, I gladly accept the burden of this time-consuming enterprise. Patience, however, is always required. A chicken broth will become perfect only if you reduce it long enough and, if necessary, keep skimming off the ugly gray foam that rises to the surface. Finding the right kind of chicken also helps. Luckily, along with heirloom vegetables, the slow-food movement has also rediscovered the boiling hen, giving back to it the standing it once had in the home cooking of our grandmothers. They knew that the boiling fowl develops a far more intense flavor in the soup pot than any plump chicken can.

BOUILLON MADE FROM CHICKEN FOR 1½ L (5 CUPS)

1.5 kg (3 pounds) boiling hen or chicken (whole or cut into pieces)	2 leeks
	½ celeriac
2 L (8 cups) water	2 celery stalks with leaves
1 glass white wine	1 bunch parsley
2 big onions	10 black peppercorns
4 garlic cloves	salt and ground white pepper
2 medium carrots	

As Claudia Roden writes in her monumental book on Jewish cooking, the chicken broth that was never absent from the dinner table on Sabbath and during the holidays was called "golden soup" because of its amber color and the golden fat globules swimming on the surface. To enhance the color, some add a pinch of saffron. In our home, this chicken broth was called "Jewish penicillin" because, like so many before her, my mother trusted the hearsay of her mother-in-law, who was convinced that because of the anti-inflammatory effect of this dish, it could cure all kinds of ailments (now confirmed by scientific research).

The secret to preparing this delicious medicine is that the chicken should simmer over low heat for at least three hours. To do so, place the chicken, breast side up, into a soup pot, pour water and wine over it, and then bring the liquid to a boil. In the meantime, peel the vegetables—onions, garlic, carrots, leeks, and celeriac—and cut them into fairly large pieces. Once the water begins to boil, add them to the pot, along with the parsley and the leaves from the celery stalks, and season with salt and peppercorns. Add more water if it evaporates too quickly. If you are not using a boiling hen, you can take the chicken out after an hour, remove the meat from the bones, and then return them to the pot again so that they can simmer for another two hours. Refrigerate the chicken meat for use in another dish. Skim off any foam that forms on the surface. When the soup is done, pour it through a sieve into another pot, and allow it to cool down completely—in the refrigerator or (if the weather allows for this) on the balcony. In the process, excess fat will congeal on the surface, making it easy to skim off. But this also means that you will need to prepare the broth at least one day in advance. While you can use the fat for frying, discard the boiled vegetables along with the chicken bones. When reheating the soup, season once more with salt and white pepper.

BOUILLON MADE FROM BEEF FOR 1½ L (5 CUPS)

1 kg (2.2 pounds) fatty beef	1 bunch parsley
6 marrow bones	4 garlic cloves
4 L (16 cups) of water	1 piece of ginger, about 5 cm
1 celeriac	(2 inches)
2 carrots	2 parsley roots (or small parsnips)
2 onions	12 dried juniper berries
2 leeks	salt and pepper

My German grandmother preferred beef broth. From the stories my mother told me, I know that at the end of the 1920s, owing to the stock market crash, her family was in financial trouble, so they turned their spacious apartment in Berlin into a boarding house for young women from good families. For my tremendously convivial grandmother, this proved to be a stroke of good luck because she enjoyed the company of her lodgers, for whom she always had a small pot of beef broth ready on her stove. Whenever one of these nighthawks would come home from her forays into the Berlin cabaret scene, regardless of how late the hour, she would be invited into the kitchen. While sipping beef broth, she was encouraged to recount what she had done that evening. I imagine that this nocturnal nourishment was meant not only as a form of entertainment for my grandmother but also as a means of preventing a hangover the next morning.

The following recipe for beef broth, however, was given to me by my friend Gesine. Once again, nothing can really go wrong with the fairly straightforward preparation she suggests. It simply requires patience. The beauty of this dish, as Gesine maintains, consists of the fact that you can keep adding ingredients to the soup as it simmers quietly on the stovetop, and thus you can adjust the seasoning—be it a piece of butter, a dried lemon, or a branch of lovage. What is vital, however, is simply finding the right balance between the root vegetables and the blend of onions, garlic, and ginger enhancing their aromatic effect.

Cut the meat along with the peeled vegetables into coarse pieces, and then put them into a big soup pot, together with the spices and the cold water. Once the water begins to boil, simmer the soup for three or four hours over low heat. Skim the foam off the surface now and then. If you are preparing another dish in the meantime, you can add any other peeled vegetable bits you would otherwise discard to the soup as well. After three hours, pour the soup through a sieve to remove the vegetable and meat pieces, and then return the liquid to the pot. Continue simmering the broth until it has reduced by half. Culinary purists, whose patience is endless, would pass the broth once more through a cheesecloth-lined sieve. This final step, however, is one that I tend to leave out.

BOUILLON WITH GARLIC AND EGG
FOR 600 ML (2½ CUPS)

600 ml (2½ cups) beef broth	egg yolks (1 per person)
2 heads of garlic	chives
olive oil	

For everyone who attributes a healing effect to garlic, over and beyond its protection against vampires, it makes a perfect additional aromatic ingredient in a beef broth. I discovered this way of embellishing beef broth in a small Austro-Hungarian restaurant in Munich in the heart of the theater district, and it became my dish of choice whenever my mother and I would go there for a light meal after a concert. Although we were in a restaurant (and not in my grandmother's kitchen), our nocturnal conversation was also accompanied by a bowl of invigorating soup.

To roast the garlic, heat the oven to 200°C (400°F). Cut enough of the top off the unpeeled garlic so you can see the individual cloves, and then peel away the outer, paper-like skin with your fingers. Make sure, however, that the individual cloves aren't falling apart. Set the heads of garlic on a piece of aluminum foil, and drizzle the cut side with one to two teaspoons of olive oil, making sure that the oil penetrates into the garlic cloves. Then wrap them in the foil, and roast them in the oven for around forty minutes. The exact time will depend on the size and age of the garlic heads. You can use a small paring knife to test whether the inner part of each clove is soft enough to be mashed into a paste. Once this is the case, allow the garlic to cool off a bit before pressing each individual clove out of its papery skin. Mash all the cloves together into a paste, which will keep for two weeks in the refrigerator in an airtight jar.

A generous teaspoon of roasted garlic is about right for a bowl of soup. Add the amount you want to the soup pot, and allow the beef broth to simmer a bit longer so that it can absorb the flavor of the roasted garlic. When serving the soup, prevent the egg yolk from curdling by placing it into the soup dish first before pouring the beef bouillon over it. Then garnish with snippets of chives.

AVGOLEMONO SOUP WITH LEMON AND EGG FOR 4

2 tsp. olive oil	4 tbsp. lemon juice
2 chicken breasts	salt and pepper
1 L (4 cups) chicken broth	lemon-scented olive oil
90 g (3 ounces) orzo (or rice)	dill to garnish
2 egg whites and 4 egg yolks	

In our home, we often ate a hearty soup with seasonal vegetables, potatoes, and boiled beef on weekdays. Even today, if I want something light yet restorative for dinner, I will warm up some chicken or beef broth, season it with grated Parmesan, and to give more body to the soup, beat in an egg yolk as well. Or in recollection of the alphabet soup my mother used to serve us when we were children, I will add very small pasta to the broth. The following three recipes—one showcasing lemon, the second shitake mushrooms, and the third red beets—are meant as suggestions for honing this minimalist idea of a soothing broth with aromatic supplements. In all three versions, I allow for the usage of chicken and beef stock cubes, which can readily be replaced with vegetable stock cubes for a purely vegetarian dish.

The first recipe, a rich yet refreshing soup, is what I associate with the many years we spent in Greece during our summer holidays. Begin by heating two teaspoons of olive oil in a soup pot. Salt the chicken breasts, and fry them quickly on both sides, without them browning too much. Add the chicken broth, bring it to a boil, and then reduce the heat immediately. Cover the pot, and allow the chicken breasts to poach in the broth for about five minutes. You can turn them over after about two minutes, but make sure to poach them until there is only a touch of pink at the thickest part. Remove the chicken breasts from the soup pot, and allow them to cool, and then add the orzo (or rice) to the broth, and simmer it for about eight minutes. The pasta should be firm to the bite and not yet completely soft because it will continue to cook in the warm broth. In the meantime, cut the chicken breasts into fine strips or cubes. Once the orzo is done, reduce the heat, and wait until the broth is no longer simmering so that the eggs will not curdle. Make sure it is merely lukewarm before proceeding. Prepare the egg mixture in a separate bowl. First, whisk the egg whites until they are foamy; they should be frothy but not stiff. Add the egg yolks, then the lemon juice, and continue whisking the mixture until all the ingredients are perfectly blended. After adding about one ladle of the lukewarm bouillon to the egg mixture, whisk it vigorously once more before pouring everything back into the soup pot. At this point, caution is called for. Over very low temperature, continue stirring the soup so that it can attain a thick, creamy consistency. Under no circumstances should you allow the soup to come to a boil again. If it does, the egg will curdle. After turning off the heat, add the chicken pieces to the soup, season with salt and pepper, drizzle with some lemon-scented olive oil, and sprinkle with dill.

MISO SOUP WITH SHITAKE MUSHROOMS FOR 4

200 g (7 ounces) fresh shitake mushrooms	6 tbsp. light miso paste
	5 tbsp. sake (or dry sherry)
200 g (7 ounces) silken tofu	300 g (1½ cups) spinach
1 tbsp. ginger, grated	1 spring onion
1.5 L (6 cups) chicken broth	furikake rice seasoning

Whenever I feel I am coming down with the flu, I make this soup. Indeed, a bit of magical thinking in the kitchen always helps protect against ailments, even if only because a soup like this one strengthens your spirits as much as it fortifies the body. Because of the additional ingredients, it is best served in deep bowls.

Prepare the mushrooms by trimming them at the bottom, cleaning them with a moist cloth and cutting them into coarse slices. Dry the tofu carefully with paper towels, and cut it into small cubes. Grate the peeled ginger. Then heat the chicken (or vegetable) broth in a soup pot; add the mushrooms, tofu pieces, and the ginger; and allow the soup to come to a boil briefly. Reduce the temperature, and let the soup to simmer, about ten minutes. In the meantime, in a small bowl, mix the miso paste with four to five tablespoons of chicken broth and sake (which you can replace with dry sherry) until you have a smooth paste, which you can then add to the soup pot. Taste the soup, and if necessary, add more miso paste. Wash the spinach, add it to the pot, and let the soup briefly come to a boil one last time. The spinach should wilt but not dissolve. Before serving, sprinkle each soup bowl with slivers of spring onion and furikake rice seasoning.

BEET SOUP FOR 4

2 medium onions, finely chopped	3 tbsp. butter
4 leeks, finely sliced	1¼ L (4½ cups) beef broth
1 celery stalk, finely diced	6 tbsp. white wine vinegar
1 medium kohlrabi, finely diced	salt and white pepper
2 garlic cloves, finely chopped	crème fraîche
1 pound fresh red beets, diced	dill

Begin by peeling and chopping the onions. Then wash the leeks, remove the green leaves, and cut only the white part into fine strips. Peel the remaining vegetables (including the celery stalk), and cut them into fine cubes. The beets can be a bit bigger because they play the main part in this soup. In the soup pot, melt the butter over medium heat, add the vegetables, cover the pot, and sweat the vegetables for twenty minutes, until they become soft. Then pour the beef broth (or vegetable broth) over the vegetables, and simmer over low heat for another ten minutes. The vegetables should be soft but not falling apart. Season with salt, white pepper, and white wine vinegar or, for less acidity and more sweetness, with white balsamic vinegar. Ladle out the soup into individual bowls before adding a dollop of crème fraîche and a sprinkling of chopped dill to each. Black bread is the perfect accompaniment for this soup.

NOTE: As is the case with any vegetable soup, you can also purée this beet soup. Rather than crème fraîche, use a dollop of double cream and some red wine vinegar to embellish the flavor in the end. You can serve this soup either warm or cold.

PURÉED VEGETABLE SOUPS

Each fall, pumpkins in all shapes, sizes, and colors appear at the market, ready to accompany us into early winter. Although this is a perfect vegetable for roasting in the oven, for making a puree, or for combining with other vegetables in a stew, pumpkin soup remains one of my favorite autumn dishes. As the pumpkin has relatively little taste on its own, it makes a perfect carrier for a panoply of different flavors.

The following four recipes are meant to demonstrate both the principle of the pureed vegetable soup and the different aromatic variations that are possible with one vegetable. Once you have grasped the basic idea, you can apply it to other vegetables, even while experimenting with aromatic embellishments—replacing the vanilla bean with a tonka bean, the cream with coconut milk, the Parmesan with Gruyère, or the cilantro pesto with another herb pesto.

PUMPKIN SOUP WITH VANILLA FOR 4–6

2 tbsp. olive oil	1 L (4 cups) chicken broth
1 onion	salt and white pepper
1 kg (2.2 pounds) pumpkin	1 vanilla bean (or 1 tbsp. vanilla paste)

In this simple recipe, a single flavor—vanilla—transforms the ordinary pumpkin soup into something special. As in most vegetable soups, you will need to prepare a *soffritto* first. In the pot you will be using to make the soup, sauté the peeled and finely sliced onions in olive oil over low heat for about seven minutes. In the meantime, peel and deseed the pumpkin, and then cut it into fairly small cubes. The smaller they are, the faster they will cook in the broth and absorb its flavor. Add the pumpkin to the softened onions, season with salt and pepper, and retaining a low temperature, sweat the cubes for about ten minutes. So that the individual pieces don't stick to the bottom of the pot, stir them frequently. Then cover the pumpkin pieces with broth, put the lid on the pot, and continue simmering the soup over low heat. After ten minutes, split the vanilla bean lengthwise, scrape out the seeds, add both the seeds and the bean pod to the soup, and allow it to simmer for another ten minutes. When the soup is done, fish out the vanilla bean pod before blending it (either in a blender or with an immersion blender). Before serving, reheat the pumpkin soup.

PUMPKIN SOUP WITH PARMESAN FOR 4–6

1½ kg (3 pounds) pumpkin	double crème de Gruyère (or heavy
100 g (½ cup) butter	cream)
1½ L (6 cups) chicken broth	salt and black pepper
100 g (1 cup) Parmesan, grated	

If you enhance the flavor and texture of a pumpkin soup with grated cheese, it becomes richer; however, the process is also a bit more time-consuming. In this case, leave out the *soffritto*, and instead, sweat the pumpkin on its own. To do so, peel and deseed the pumpkin, and then cut it into fairly thin slices. In the soup pot, melt the butter until it begins to foam and take on a nut-brown color, then add the pumpkin slices, season with salt and pepper, put the lid on the pot, and over low heat, sweat the pumpkin. To prevent the pumpkin slices from sticking to the bottom of the pan, either use a wooden spoon to stir and turn them or simply shake the pot now and then. Use the time to grate the Parmesan. After fifteen minutes, add the chicken broth (or vegetable broth) to the pot, bring it to a boil, and then add the Parmesan, stirring constantly. Lower the heat, and let the soup simmer another fifteen minutes without putting the lid back on the pot. In order to keep the Parmesan from sticking to the bottom, stir the soup now and then, making sure that the broth is really absorbing the grated cheese. When the pumpkin has become soft and smooth, you are ready to blend the soup (in a blender or with an immersion blender). Before serving, reheat the soup; however, do not let it come to a boil again. Season with salt and pepper, and finish with a dollop of double cream (or mascarpone) in each soup dish.

PUMPKIN SOUP WITH PEARS AND CREAM FOR 4–6

2 tbsp. olive oil	1½ L (6 cups) chicken broth
1 big onion	9 sprigs fresh thyme
2 shallots	salt and white pepper
1 leek	150 ml (⅔ cup) cream
1 kg (2.2 pounds) pumpkin	150 ml (⅔ cup) crème fraîche
2 medium pears	pumpkinseed oil
3 carrots	pumpkin seeds

What is distinctive about this equally rich pumpkin soup is the combination of three different types of onions as well as the pears that give it a deep, sweet note. The preparation called for in this recipe is a bit more elaborate than in the two previous versions because, before you can begin to cook, you will need to have all the vegetables ready. Peel and finely chop the onion and the shallots, clean and cut the leeks into thin slices, peel and cut the carrots into thin slices, peel and deseed the pumpkin and the pears, and cut them into thin slices as well. To save time, however, you can work in stages. Begin by chopping and slicing the onion, shallots, and leeks first, then heat the oil in the soup pot, and sauté them over low heat, about seven minutes, until they are soft. While you are waiting, you can peel and slice the rest of the ingredients. Add the pumpkin, pears, and carrots, and sweat them, about five minutes. Pour the chicken (or vegetable) broth into the pot, add the sprigs of thyme, put the lid on the pot, and over low heat, simmer the soup for about thirty minutes, until the pumpkin has become completely soft. Before blending the soup (in a blender or with an immersion blender) make sure you fish out the sprigs of thyme. Reheat the soup, add the cream, and season with salt and pepper, but don't let it come to a boil again. To give further flavor and texture to the soup, add a dollop of crème fraîche as well as a drizzle of pumpkin seed oil to each plate, and then scatter some chopped pumpkin seeds and a few thyme leaves on top.

PUMPKIN SOUP WITH LIME AND CILANTRO PESTO FOR 4–6

1 kg (2.2 pounds) pumpkin	1 tbsp. brown sugar
5 large garlic cloves	2 tbsp. butter
1 leek	1 onion, peeled and finely chopped
2 tbsp. olive oil	1¼ L (5 cups) vegetable broth
salt and white pepper	1 handful pumpkin seeds, chopped

FOR THE PESTO

2 limes	100 g (⅔ cup) pine nuts
40 g (1⅓ cups) cilantro	1 garlic clove
20 g (⅔ cup) mint leaves	2 tbsp. pumpkin seed oil
20 g (⅔ cup) basil leaves	salt and white pepper

This last variation of pumpkin soup brings the oven into play as well. Rather than sweating the vegetables in oil in a covered pot, you oven roast them first and then bring them to a simmer in the vegetable broth. Roasting brings out a sweetness in the pumpkin.

Heat the oven to 190°C (375°F). In the meantime, peel and deseed the pumpkin, and cut it into medium-size cubes. Clean the leeks, and cut them into thin strips. Peel the garlic cloves, and chop them very finely. In a small bowl, whisk together the oil and the sugar. Then place the cut vegetables in an ovenproof dish, add the sugar-oil mixture, and using your hands, mix thoroughly, making sure that each individual piece is coated with the seasoned oil. Season with salt and pepper before roasting the pumpkin for thirty minutes.

While you are waiting for it to roast, you can turn your attention to preparing the pesto. Blend the juice and zest of the limes with the herbs (in a food processor or with an immersion blender). If you have a shiso plant on your balcony (or in your garden), you can use this herb instead of the traditional basil and mint. Peel and coarsely chop the garlic; add it, along with the pine nuts and the pumpkin seed oil, to the herbs; season with salt and pepper; continue blending until you have a dense, smooth pesto; and set it aside. Just before the pumpkin is finished roasting, melt the butter in the soup pot, and over low heat, sauté the finely chopped onion, about seven minutes. Then add the broth and the roasted pumpkin, stir the soup thoroughly, and over low heat, let it simmer another five minutes or so. Blend the soup (in a blender or with an immersion blender), reheat it, and season with salt and pepper. To serve, add a dollop of pesto to each soup bowl and scatter with chopped pumpkin seeds.

PARSNIP SOUP WITH CURRY FOR 4

2 tbsp. olive oil	1 tsp. ground ginger
2 onions, finely chopped	700 g (1½ pounds) parsnip
2 garlic cloves, finely chopped	1½ L (6 cups) vegetable broth
2 tsp. curry powder	salt and white pepper
1 tsp. turmeric	1 sweet-sour apple (Granny Smith)

My soup repertoire would be incomplete without this classic Victorian dish, not least of all because, owing to their sweet, nutty flavor, parsnips are among my favorite root vegetables. But I have also grown particularly fond of them because there is something entirely literary about them for me. Only with the slow-food movement and the attention it has drawn to locally grown vegetables has the parsnip reappeared in our grocery markets. Before then, I knew about this root vegetable only from reading nineteenth-century British novels, where, under the influence of colonial trading, it was often paired with curry powder.

Melt the butter in the soup pot, add the finely chopped onions, and over low heat, sauté them until they are fairly soft. Add the chopped garlic, and sauté this for a minute or so before adding the curry powder, cumin, and ginger. Stir the *soffritto*, and let it simmer a bit longer. In the meantime, prepare the parsnips. Cut off the top and the bottom, peel them, and cut them into medium-size cubes. It is best to use small parsnips, but if big ones are all you can find, make sure that you also remove the core, which tends to be tough and mealy. Add the parsnip cubes to the soup pot, and stir thoroughly so that they can absorb the oil and the spices. Pour the vegetable broth over the parsnips, season with salt and pepper, and without covering the pot, let the soup simmer, over low heat, for about an hour. Allow the soup to cool a bit before blending it. If you are using an immersion blender, you may want to pass the soup through a sieve to get a smoother texture. Reheat the soup, and season with salt and pepper. As Delia Smith, from whom I have adapted this recipe, suggests, wait until this point to peel the apple, and coarsely grate it directly into the soup. The grated apple should retain its fruity bite, which is why the soup needs to simmer only a few minutes longer, and under no circumstances should it come to a boil again. If you have prepared the soup in advance—or if you know that you will be reheating some of it the next day—wait until just before serving to add the grated apple.

SAUERKRAUT CREAM SOUP FOR 4

250 g (1¼ cup) raw sauerkraut   600 ml (1½ cups) vegetable broth
200 g (7 ounces) potatoes   ½ tbsp. caraway seeds
1 shallot   5 juniper berries
2 tbsp. olive oil   125 ml (½ cup) whipped cream
70 ml (⅓ cup) white wine (Riesling   salt and pepper
    or Gewürztraminer)

Until recently, I thought of sauerkraut primarily in conjunction with hearty sausages and smoked pork loin (or gammon steak) or as the bed for a piece of seared fish fillet. But since my friend Martin served me a delicate sauerkraut soup, I have begun to see this pickled cabbage in a completely new light.

Begin by draining the sauerkraut, firmly pressing it into a sieve, but do so over a bowl, since you want to retain the brine. Peel the potatoes, and cut them into small cubes. Heat the oil in the soup pot, and sauté the finely chopped shallots, about five minutes. Add the drained sauerkraut, the potatoes, the juniper berries, and the caraway seeds; mix this *soffritto* thoroughly; and sweat the vegetables a few minutes before adding the wine and the vegetable broth. Cover the pot, and simmer the soup for about thirty minutes before blending it (in a blender or with an immersion blender). Once the soup is done, whip the cream, and add half of it, along with the brine from the sauerkraut, to the soup. What you want is a frothy consistency, so if the soup is too thick, you can dilute it with butter. Season with salt and pepper, and serve with a dollop of the remaining whipped cream.

CHESTNUT AND PEAR SOUP FOR 4

2 tbsp. butter	1 tbsp. rosemary, chopped
1 onion	1½ L (6 cups) vegetable broth
2 big leeks	450 g (16 ounces) peeled chestnuts,
5 celery stalks, peeled	250 g (9 ounces) if using dry
2 ripe pears, peeled, cored, and diced	chestnuts
1 tbsp. fresh thyme	crème fraîche

You could, of course, use fresh chestnuts, but the peeled ones in a glass (or vacuum packed) are just as good and make for a far quicker and easier preparation of this autumnal dish. If you are using dried chestnuts, you will need to soak them in cold water overnight.

To make the *soffritto*, peel and cut the onions into thin slices, wash the leeks, cut them in half, and slice both the white and the green parts very thinly. Peel the celery stalks, and cut them into thin slices as well. Melt the butter in the soup pot, add the onions and leeks, season with salt and pepper, stir thoroughly, cover the pot, and simmer the *soffritto*, over low heat, for about ten minutes. The onions should be soft, but they should not yet take on a golden-brown hue. In the meantime, peel, deseed, and cube the pears before mixing them with the plucked thyme leaves and the finely chopped rosemary in a kitchen bowl, and then add them to the *soffritto*. Pour the vegetable (or chicken) broth into the pot, add the chestnuts, raise the heat, and bring the soup to a boil. Once it has begun to bubble up, turn the heat back down to very low; cover the pot, leaving a small crack open; and simmer for about one hour. The cooking time depends on the consistency of the chestnuts. They are done when you can mash them with the back of a spoon. Blend the soup until you have a rich, smooth texture. If you are using an immersion blender, pass the soup through a sieve. Reheat the soup, and season with salt and pepper. For a more festive presentation, serve with a dollop of crème fraîche and some pear cubes and chestnut slices as garnish.

CORN CHOWDER FOR 4

1 tbsp. olive oil	2 tbsp. white vermouth
1 tbsp. butter	60 ml (¼ cup) white wine
100 g (4 ounces) bacon (or speck)	1 L (4 cups) chicken broth
3 small shallots	3 fresh corn cobs
salt and white pepper	100 ml (½ cup) cream
2 tbsp. fresh thyme	1 tbsp. butter

My innate suspicion when it comes to bivalve mollusks in a soup has made me prefer a vegetarian alternative to clam chowder. Because this reinterpretation also leaves out potatoes—arguably the other main ingredient of this classic New England dish—some might claim it isn't a chowder at all. But it's still classic home cooking.

In the soup pot, heat the butter and the oil over medium heat, and fry bite-size strips of bacon for about five minutes, turning them now and them because they should be browned on all slices. Then add the shallots, cut into thin slices, season with pepper and just a bit of salt (because of the bacon), and reducing the heat, sauté them until they are soft, about ten minutes. Add the thyme, vermouth (either sweet or dry), and the white wine. Bring the liquid to a boil, turn the heat to medium, and reduce the liquid by half. In the meantime, shuck the corn, and along with the chicken broth (or vegetable broth), add the corn to the pot. Bring the soup to a boil, and then, over medium heat, let it simmer for about thirty minutes. The cooking time depends on the corn, which should be soft but not mushy. To highlight the sweetness of the corn, add the cream and one tablespoon of butter at the end, season once more with salt and pepper, and garnish with thyme leaves.

VELOUTÉ

CREAM OF MUSHROOM SOUP FOR 4

1 tbsp. olive oil	6 tbsp. flour
500 g (18 ounces) button mushrooms	2 egg yolks
1 onion	250 ml (1 cup) cream
1 L (4 cups) chicken broth	juice and zest of 1 lemon
salt and white pepper	2 tbsp. sherry
6 tbsp. butter	

Cream of mushroom soup is another one of the American classics that my mother learned to cook during the postwar years, when she worked in the State Department while my father was attending law school. Today, we associate this soup above all with Andy Warhol's *Campbell's Soup Cans* paintings, and indeed, I suspect that, while she was still living in Washington, DC, my mother used canned soup as the foundation for a reinterpretation based on the classic French velouté. Even after returning to Germany, she would add sherry, cream, and egg yolks to thicken the soup. While I, of course, abstain from using canned soups of all kinds, I have retained my mother's embellishment.

Clean the mushrooms with a moist paper towel, trim the bottom, and then dice them. Peel the onions, and chop them finely. First sauté the onions in oil in the soup pot, about five minutes, before adding the mushrooms and sautéing them another five minutes. Set a few aside to garnish the soup at the end. Then add the broth, season with salt and pepper, and simmer the soup, about twenty minutes, over low heat, before blending it (in a blender or with an immersion blender). To prepare the velouté, you will need another pot that is large enough to hold the soup. To prepare the roux, vigorously stir the flour into the melted butter over fairly low heat, making sure that the butter-flour mixture doesn't take on a brown color but instead turns into a smooth paste. Pour the mushroom soup into the roux in stages, and keep stirring it into the liquid thoroughly to make sure that the soup will not go lumpy when brought to a boil. Then reduce the heat, and bring the soup to a gentle simmer. In a small bowl, whisk together the two egg yolks with three tablespoons of the warm soup. First add the cream, lemon juice, lemon zest, and sherry to the mushroom soup, and then bind it with the egg yolk. You can reheat the soup, but do not let it come to a boil again or the eggs will curdle. Season with salt and pepper, and if necessary, add more lemon juice.

CHERVIL SOUP FOR 4

2 tbsp. butter	salt and pepper
2 tbsp. flour	1 pinch nutmeg
700 ml (3 cups) vegetable broth	lemon juice (or verjus)
100 g–150 g (4–6 ounces) chervil	4 poached eggs
250 ml (1 cup) whipped cream	

It is, of course, entirely possible to enrich this herb soup with an egg-cream mixture as well. My mother, however, always insisted on placing a poached egg into each soup bowl instead and then pouring the soup over it. As a child, I was always intrigued by the play of colors that cutting into my egg with the soup spoon would suddenly call forth. As though it was a paintbrush, I would use my spoon to draw streaks of yellow across the dense green carpet from which it had emerged, until the egg yolk was completely absorbed by the soup. If chervil is not readily available, you can use a mixture of tarragon, watercress, and lovage to replace (or even supplement) it.

Begin by making the roux. In the soup pot, stir the flour into the melted butter until you have a light-yellow paste. Add the broth bit by bit, always stirring it into the roux completely before adding more so that no lumps form. Then let the soup simmer over medium heat for about ten minutes. In the meantime, wash the chervil under cold water, remove any ungainly leaves, shake it dry on a kitchen towel, and coarsely chop it. Add the cream to the soup to bind it first, and then add the chervil. Season with salt, pepper, nutmeg, and some lemon juice (or verjus), and keep the soup warm while you poach the eggs.

A MEAL OF ITS OWN

BARLEY SOUP FOR 4

2 tbsp. olive oil	1 onion, peeled and pricked with
1 onion	2 bay leaves and 4 cloves
175 g (6 ounces) bacon	salt, cayenne pepper, and white
100 g (½ cup) barley	pepper
2 carrots	250 ml (1 cup) cream (or crème
1 celery stalk	fraîche)
1 leek	2 egg yolks
1 small savoy cabbage	chives
1½ L (6 cups) vegetable broth	

Although barley soup with bacon and vegetables is a typically Swiss dish, my mother's recipe includes a cream-egg velouté as the final touch, making it even more rich and creamy but also more elegant. For precisely that reason, it has become the epitome of a homey winter meal for me, to be consumed not only in an Alpine ski resort, where my mother first encountered it in the early 1950s, but in my kitchen as well.

In the soup pot, sauté the finely chopped onions in oil for about five minutes, until they have become translucent. Cut the bacon into fairly thin strips, add it to the onions, and brown it over low heat until it has become crisp before tossing the barley into the pot as well. Increase the heat so that as you glaze the barley, it takes on a golden hue. You need to be careful, however, that the barley doesn't stick to the bottom of the pot and scorch. So with an eye on the pot, peel and chop the carrots and the celery into fine cubes, and clean the leek. Cut both the leek and the cabbage into fairly thin strips. Add the vegetables to the barley, and stirring constantly, braise them for about five minutes. Then deglaze the pot with the vegetable broth (keeping a bit on the side); add the onion (pricked with bay leaves and cloves); season with salt, cayenne pepper, and white pepper; and over low heat, let the soup reduce for one to two hours. The exact time depends on the size of the barley. All you need to do at this point is stir the soup now and then. If the soup boils down too quickly, add some of the reserved vegetable broth. When the soup is done, turn off the heat. Stir the cream and the egg yolks with two tablespoons of the broth, and use this velouté to bind the soup. Sprinkle the barley soup with snippets of chives.

MINESTRONE FOR 4

8 tbsp. olive oil
500 g (5 cups) zucchini
4 medium onions
3 large carrots
4 celery stalks with leaves, peeled
6 tbsp. red lentils
250 g (2½ cups) green beans
400 g (4 cups) savoy cabbage, finely
   sliced
1½ L (6 cups) meat broth

crust from a piece of Parmesan
400 g (14 ounces) net weight canned
   tomatoes
3 tbsp. tomato purée
250 g (1½ cups) canned cannellini
   beans
salt and pepper
cayenne pepper
Parmesan, grated

As familiar as this simple Italian vegetable soup may be to us today, it can become something truly spectacular if you take the time to build up the flavors in stages and then allow it to cook for quite a while. Much like a stew, minestrone requires time to develop the buttery sweetness that makes it so moreish. And because it tastes even better when reheated, the meticulous effort you put into the preparation is particularly worth it when you make enough for the next day (or next days) as well. You can alternate the vegetables for a minestrone according to the seasons, as you can replace the traditional potatoes with barley or farro. If you do so, however, add these pulses toward the end, along with the broth; otherwise, they will dissolve and make the soup too dense. Indispensable, in turn, is the rind of a piece of Parmesan, which you need to scrub thoroughly before using, because it will pretty much dissolve in the soup. So taken am I with the creaminess it provides that I always save the rind after using up a piece of Parmesan, taking this as an excuse to cook minestrone again. Sometimes, I admit, I will buy a piece of Parmesan simply for the rind.

Begin by soaking the zucchini and the green beans in cold water in two separate bowls, and heat the meat (or vegetable) broth in a smaller pot. Then you can turn your attention to making the *soffritto*. Cut the peeled onions into thin slices. In the pot you will be using to make the soup, sauté the onions in olive oil over medium heat for about six minutes. They should become translucent and take on a golden hue but not turn dark brown. Because you will be adding the vegetables to the soup pot one at a time, a *mise en place* is not necessary. You can prepare the next ingredient while its predecessor is already simmering. This calls for a certain degree of concentration. You must not only keep stirring the ingredients, folding each new layer into those that have already begun to cook, but also keep chopping those that are still to be added, making sure that not too much time elapses in the interim. This means, of course, that the slow composition of this dish literally lies in your own hand. What is crucial, however, is the sequence in which the vegetables are added to the soup pot.

While the onions are sautéing, peel the carrots, and cut them into cubes. They should sauté for about three minutes while you peel and cube the celery, and then add it to the pot. Do not discard the leaves, but rather chop them and put them aside to be used at a later stage. Next add the red lentils to the pot for texture, bearing in mind that with each new layer of vegetables added, you must thoroughly stir those that have already browned with a wooden spoon, folding the newcomers into them, so to speak. You must also regulate the temperature so that the soup is simmering at all times.

The next vegetables to add are the green beans. Drain them, cut off the ends, and then cut them into bite-size pieces. They too can brown (for about three minutes) while you cut off the ends of the drained zucchini, quarter and dice them, and then add them to the pot. Next, quarter the cabbage, remove the hard inner core, and then cut it into thin slices. Add the cabbage along with the chopped celery leaves to the pot, stir everything once more, and simmer the soup for another six minutes.

At this point, a delectable vegetable smell has begun to waft around my kitchen, compelling me to focus my attention completely on the final stage of this culinary composition. This is the point at which to add the Parmesan rind, the meat (or vegetable) broth, the tomato purée, and the canned tomatoes with their juices. My thrifty mother taught me to rinse the cans with a bit of the broth so as not to waste a drop of this valuable juice. If you want to use farro or barley rather than potatoes, you can add them to the pot at this point. With my wooden spoon, I mix the vegetables thoroughly one more time, season with salt and pepper, cover the pot with a tightly fitting lid, reduce the heat, and allow the soup to simmer very gently for one and a half hours. If you don't have enough time to do this in one go, it is perfectly fine to interrupt the cooking process. You could, for example, begin the evening before and continue the next day. The consistency of the minestrone should be fairly dense; if it has become too thick, dilute it with some more broth. Don't add the drained cannellini beans until about half an hour before you want to eat the minestrone. When the minestrone is ready, fish out the bits of Parmesan rind that have not dissolved, and season with salt and a pinch of cayenne pepper. Serve with grated Parmesan and dark country bread.

INGE GERSTNER-HÖCHBERG'S WATERZOOI FOR 4–6

4 L (16 cups) chicken broth	500 g (18 ounces) frozen *petits pois*
4 chicken drumsticks and 4 chicken	(or green peas)
breasts	4 tbsp. butter
3 large carrots	5 tbsp. fresh tarragon
1 large celeriac	250 ml (1 cup) cream
2 bunches parsley	2 eggs
8–12 small new potatoes	salt and pepper
500 g (18 ounces) button mushrooms	

This Belgian national dish was completely unknown to me until the day that Inge Gerstner-Höchberg, the mother of my friend Muriel, decided to give me an extravagant gift for my fiftieth birthday. Although she was eighty-three at the time, she prepared a lavish feast for me and some of my closest friends. Some of them were so impressed by this meal that they have repeatedly asked me for the recipe. The ambiance Inge created in her Basel apartment, of course, contributed considerably to the success of the event. The splendidly set table, around which almost thirty people gathered, was reminiscent of the prewar German-Jewish upper class, long since vanished. Together with her parents, the eleven-year-old Inge had not only been fortunate enough to be able to flee from the Nazi terror, moving first from Frankfurt to Brussels in 1936 and then emigrating to Basel in 1940; her clever mother had also succeeded in taking the cabinet holding enough silver cutlery for sizable dinner parties, along with matching porcelain dishes and damask tablecloths, with her to her new home in Switzerland. The sumptuous chicken soup Inge served that day, in itself so appropriate for such an occasion because the ingredients can readily be adjusted should more guests arrive, was a souvenir from her emigration: gift and memory in one, recalling how the fact of losing one home and finding a new one requires—as well as inspires—adapting traditional family recipes to any new situation one is faced with.

Like a minestrone, this chicken soup also tastes better when it is reheated, and since it is quite time-consuming to prepare, it is best to make it the day before. Although the Belgian name indicates that something is to be cooked in water, you actually want to use a particularly rich broth and might even fall back on the old-fashioned boiling hen to do so. Inge, however, was convinced that you could just as well dissolve four tablespoons of chicken broth cubes in four liters of water and, together with the classic German soup *mirepoix* (carrots, leeks, and celeriac), simmer it for an hour to attain an equally savory broth. To make the *mirepoix*, use one of the rinsed parsley bunches (rather than the traditional leeks), one of the peeled carrots, and a part of the peeled celeriac; cut into coarse pieces; and add all three to the chicken broth. While you prepare the other vegetables, allow the broth to simmer. Cut the remaining carrots and celeriac into very thin julienne strips. Clean the mushrooms, trim them at the bottom, and quarter them. Chop the second bunch of parsley.

After the chicken broth has simmered for about an hour, fish out the parsley, the carrot, and the celeriac. Rather than discarding these vegetables, you can mash them and use them for another meal. Now add the chicken drumsticks and the chicken breasts to the broth, along with the carrot and celeriac julienne strips, and over medium heat, continue cooking the soup for another hour. Because you don't want them to get too chewy and dry, it is better to take the chicken breast out after thirty minutes. Cut them into bite-size pieces, and put them aside. In the meantime, in a second pot, cook the potatoes in salt water, and then drain them over cold water before peeling them and setting them aside as well. Melt the butter in a pan, and along with the second bunch of rinsed and chopped parsley, sauté the mushrooms, season with salt and pepper, and set them aside. When the chicken is done and you can turn off the heat, add the frozen *petits pois* (or other small green peas) to the soup. They only need to steep for a few minutes in the hot fluid to cook. At this point, you can also return the chicken breasts to the soup to reheat them without cooking them further. Add the chopped tarragon, the peeled potatoes, and the sautéed mushrooms only at the very end, and then season with pepper and salt. If, however, you have prepared the potatoes and the mushrooms too far in advance and they have cooled completely, you can quickly reheat both in a pan before adding them to the soup.

One final step in the comings and goings of ingredients is to fish out the chicken drumsticks, pull off the skin, and then separate the meat from the bones. Set the meat aside briefly in a bowl before dividing it among the individual soup plates. Inge shared with me the small kitchen trick she developed to bind the sauce while making sure that the egg won't curdle in the hot soup. First mix the eggs with the cream in a small bowl. Divide this mélange among the individual soup bowls (about four tablespoons per person), then place some dark chicken meat and some of the chicken breast pieces, along with the potatoes and the mushrooms, into each bowl, and pour the soup on top. Using their soup spoon, everyone can now blend the egg-cream mélange with the broth on their own, creating a savory sauce for the other cooked ingredients. And there is plenty more for second helpings.

RISOTTO, PENNE, COUSCOUS

Risotto with Mushrooms | *Risotto with Pumpkin and Leeks* | *Risotto with Strawberries* | *Risotto with Beets* | *Risotto with Red Wine* | Pennotto *with Porcini Mushrooms* | Pennotto *with Zucchini and Shrimp* | *Moroccan Couscous* | *Israeli Couscous* (Ptitim)

While I would never make a risotto for myself alone, this is the dish I think of immediately when I invite people over for dinner on short notice. Standing at my stovetop, stirring the rice, I can still partake in the conversation taking place around my kitchen table. At the same time, I can entertain the guests who are eagerly waiting to consume the dish, whose smell slowly begins to permeate the room. As is so often the case, everything depends on the quality of the northern Italian rice used to make risotto, and you should try out different varieties until you have found the one you really like. And as with many of the dishes that cook in a pot, there are only a few basic principles to observe, because in all its many variations, risotto is always prepared in the same way. Once you have internalized these rules, there is no limit to your own experimentation. Accordingly, I understand the following recipes as examples of unusual—and for purists perhaps even unorthodox—flavor combinations. To broaden the room for improvisation even further, I end with a few recipes that illustrate how penne and couscous can be prepared using a similar technique.

Four main elements and one supplement make up a risotto: the Arborio rice (*riso*), the *soffritto* in which you quickly fry the rice, the wine and warm broth (*brodo*) in which you slowly cook it, the *condimenti* you use to season the rice, and the final enhancement that perfects the flavor. In a first step, bring the broth to a boil, and then set it aside over low heat to keep it warm. While you can use homemade stock, it is perfectly acceptable to use a good, organic stock cube. The second step concerns the *condimenti*—be it vegetable, meat, seafood, or simply cheese—which will give the risotto its special flavor and is endlessly variable. These ingredients are prepared in a separate pot and set aside before you actually begin cooking the rice, because you will be adding them to the risotto only toward the end. In a third step, sauté the *soffritto* over low heat in the pot in which you will later be cooking the rice. Traditionally you would use a mixture of olive oil and butter, in which to sauté very finely chopped onions for about five minutes, until they have become soft and translucent but have not yet begun to caramelize. You could, however, decide to use only oil for the *soffritto* (reserving the butter to cream the risotto at the end), as you can augment it with a combination of cubed carrots, celery, garlic, ginger, chopped parsley, and even slivers of bacon.

The fourth step involves the actual cooking of the risotto, for which you begin by briefly frying the rice in the *soffritto*. Once you have added it to the glazed onions, you should immediately begin stirring with a wooden spoon, making certain that each and every kernel is coated with the oil. You can use wine (a dry white wine or Prosecco works well) to deglaze the rice before adding the warm broth, in which it will simmer over low heat, a ladleful at a time. Allow the broth to continue to simmer over very low heat so that it retains the same temperature as the rice you are cooking it with. You should always add only one ladle of broth at a time, and keep stirring the rice so that it can fully absorb the fluid before you add the next ladleful. If you are impatient and add too much broth, the risotto will lose its bite and never achieve the desired creamy consistency. It would be equally wrong to turn up the heat, hoping that this might help the rice cook more quickly. The fluid will simple evaporate too quickly, and the rice will stick to the bottom of the pot. A risotto usually takes about twenty minutes to cook, but it is advisable to start tasting it toward the end, because as with pasta, the cooking time can vary by several minutes. If you find that you didn't make enough broth, you can use hot water at the very end. The risotto is cooked al dente when the kernels are soft but still firm to the bite. You usually wait to add the *condimenti* until this point and, with the last ladle of broth, round off the process with the final, fifth step. Classic Italian cooking calls for cold butter and grated Parmesan to be whisked into the risotto to bring out its creamy consistency. For an even richer main course, you could also use mascarpone. Thomas Keller, from *The French Laundry* in Napa Valley, ups the ante by using whipped cream as the crowning touch.

It is common knowledge that the guest waits for the risotto, and not the other way around. So as a matter of principle, you should always serve risotto immediately. If, however, you have made too much risotto, you can easily fall back on any leftovers the next day. Sometimes, I simply take it out of the refrigerator and eat it once it has reached room temperature. More refined, however, are the fried rice balls that are called *supplì* in northern Italy, from the French word *surpris*. To make these, use two tablespoons of cold risotto to form risotto balls that are more flat than round. Bread them, as you would a schnitzel, with flour; beaten egg; and bread crumbs, panko, or even crushed cornflakes. Then fry them for three minutes on each side in hot oil. This explains why they should be flat. If they are too round, they will form a beautiful crunchy crust outside but remain cold inside.

RISOTTO WITH MUSHROOMS FOR 4

1 L (4 cups) vegetable broth	4 tbsp. soy sauce
30 g (2 cups) dried porcini mushrooms	1 medium onion
	1 tbsp. ginger, grated
3 tbsp. olive oil	50 g (2 ounces) bacon
200 g (2¼ cups) button mushrooms	300 g (1½ cups) risotto
125 ml (½ cup) cognac	1 tbsp. cilantro
125 ml (½ cup) cream	

I understand this recipe as a riff on the classic risotto with dried porcini mushrooms. The cognac adds a note of festivity to the ordinary dish.

As with any risotto, first heat the broth (*brodo*) you will be using to pour over the rice. It is advisable to make a bit more because it is hard to gauge in advance how much you will need. In this case, because of the soy sauce used to flavor the *condimenti*, the broth shouldn't be too salty. For the *condimenti*, soak the dried porcini in a small bowl in two hundred and fifty millimeters (one cup) of hot water for at least thirty minutes, drain them, and then put them on a chopping board. Using a fine sieve to catch all the impurities, pour the porcini soaking water into the broth. Before chopping the porcini, rinse them thoroughly. Clean the button mushrooms as well, and then slice them thinly. In a small pot, sauté first the button mushrooms in one table-spoon of olive oil for about three minutes, until they begin to soften, then add the porcini mushrooms, and sauté these for a few minutes as well. Now increase the heat, add the cognac, bring the fluid to a boil, and lowering the heat again a bit, reduce it to half. In the meantime, mix the cream with the soy sauce. Before adding the cream to the mushrooms, reduce the heat a bit more, and then sauté the mushrooms in the savory sauce until it has become smooth and dense.

Now set the *condimenti* aside, and turn your attention to the *soffritto*. Heat the remaining olive oil in the pot in which you will make the risotto, and then over low heat, sauté the finely chopped onions as well as the chopped ginger for about two minutes before adding the bacon, which has been cut into fine strips. The bacon should be crisp; the onions, however, should not yet be caramelized. Add the rice to the *soffritto*, and stir thoroughly with a wooden spoon to make sure that each kernel is coated with oil. Now begins the meditative part. Over low heat, add one ladle of warm broth to the risotto, stir, and wait until the rice kernels have completely absorbed it before adding the next ladle. Keep stir-ring and turning the rice to make sure it doesn't stick to the bottom of the pot. After about twenty minutes, the rice should be soft but still firm to the bite. Fold the mushroom-soy-cream into the risotto, and stir it again vigorously. Cover the pot, and allow the rice to rest for a few minutes. It will continue to soften, which is why it is important that, when you add the *condimento*, the rice is really al dente. Before serving, sprinkle with chopped cilantro.

RISOTTO WITH PUMPKIN AND LEEKS FOR 4

4 tbsp. olive oil	2 bay leaves
1 handful sage leaves	300 g (1½ cups) risotto
500 g (18 ounces) pumpkin	4 tbsp. soy sauce
1½ L (6 cups) chicken broth	50 g (½ cup) Gruyère, grated
1 vanilla bean	100 g (½ cup) mascarpone
1 leek, washed and finely sliced	salt and pepper

For the *condimento*, heat half of the olive oil in the pot in which the pumpkin (peeled, deseeded, and cut into bite-size pieces) fits snugly. First, however, sauté the sage leaves, which have been torn into bits, over medium heat until they have begun to wilt, and only then add the pumpkin to the pot. Keep stirring with a wooden spoon until all the pumpkin pieces are well coated with oil and sage bits. Scrape the seeds out of the vanilla bean (or use vanilla paste), and add both to the pumpkin pieces. Now increase the heat, pour in two hundred and fifty milliliters (one cup) of chicken broth (or vegetable broth), put the lid on the pot, and allow the pumpkin to cook for about ten minutes (the time will depend on the size of the pumpkin pieces). Once it is soft, mash the pumpkin with a fork, but keep some pieces whole to retain a certain bite, and then set it aside. For the *soffritto*, heat the remaining two tablespoons of olive oil in the pot in which you will be making the risotto. Add the leek, cut into fine slices along with the bay leaves, and sauté until the leek has become soft (about ten minutes). Now add the rice to the pot, stirring thoroughly until it is completely coated with the *soffritto*, and sauté for about a minute before adding the warm broth, one ladle at a time. After twelve minutes, add the pumpkin along with the soy sauce, and cook the risotto for another six minutes. If the rice becomes too dry, pour in more broth. However, wait to add the mascarpone and grated Parmesan until the rice is still firm to the bite. Cover the pot, lower the heat, and allow the risotto to rest for several minutes to fully absorb the flavors and reach its perfect consistency.

RISOTTO WITH STRAWBERRIES FOR 4

1 L (4 cups) vegetable broth	300 g (1½ cups) risotto
300 g (11 ounces) strawberries	400 ml (1¾ cups) dry white wine
2 tbsp. olive oil	250 ml (1 cup) double cream
1 medium onion, finely chopped	salt and white pepper

In this recipe, the *condimento* is composed of coarsely mashed strawberries. Reserve a few on the side to decorate the risotto at the end. For the *soffritto*, heat the olive oil in the pot in which you will be making the risotto, and then sauté the finely chopped onions over low heat until they are soft, about five minutes. Add the rice, stir thoroughly with a wooden spoon to make sure that all the kernels are completely coated with the *soffritto*, deglaze the pot with white wine, and allow it to simmer until it has completely evaporated. Turn the heat to low, and pour the warm vegetable broth over the risotto, one ladle at a time, all the while stirring vigorously. After ten minutes, add the crushed strawberries, and continue cooking (another eight minutes or so) until the risotto is soft and yet firm to the bite. In the final step, add the cream to the pot, season with salt and pepper, turn down the heat to very low, cover the pot, and allow the risotto to rest for several minutes. As it absorbs the flavorful liquid, it will soften to perfection.

RISOTTO WITH BEETS FOR 2

1 L (4 cups) vegetable broth
250 g (9 ounces) raw beets
2 tbsp. olive oil
1 small onion, finely chopped
1 celery stalk, peeled and finely
    chopped
1 garlic clove, finely chopped

200 g (1 cup) risotto
100 ml (½ cup) dry white wine
salt and pepper
250 g (1 cup) soft goat cheese
2 tbsp. butter
chives

In this recipe, the *brodo* and *condimenti* are one entity. Peel and coarsely grate the red beets, and toss the snippets into a pot of warm vegetable broth. As you simmer them, make sure the broth never comes to a boil; otherwise, the beets will turn brown. This won't affect the flavor, but it will give the dish a somewhat grubby appearance. While the beets are simmering, prepare the *soffritto*. Heat the oil in the pot in which you will be making the risotto, and then sauté the onions, garlic, and celery—all finely chopped—until they are soft. Then add the rice; mix thoroughly with the *soffritto*, using a wooden spoon to make sure all the kernels are well coated with it; and then sauté the rice for about a minute before deglazing it with wine. As in the previous recipes, pour the warm broth over the risotto, one ladle at a time, and keep stirring to make sure that moisture travels constantly among all the rice kernels. Make sure to catch the grated beets with each ladleful as well, because you don't want to wait to add them all at once to the risotto in the end, and they may have sunk to the bottom of the pot. After about twenty minutes, when the rice is soft but still firm to the bite, season with salt and pepper, and fold the butter as well as half of the goat cheese into the rice. Turn the heat down very low, cover the pot, and allow the risotto to rest for another three minutes, absorbing the flavor while softening to perfection. Serve with a dollop of goat cheese and snippets of chives on top.

NOTE: If you have too much beet broth, blend it for a soup the next day.

RISOTTO WITH RED WINE FOR 4

1½ L (6 cups) chicken broth
2 tbsp. olive oil
1 medium onion, finely chopped
2 garlic cloves, finely chopped

1 medium-size carrot, finely chopped
6 slices pancetta (or bacon)
300 g (1½ cups) risotto

500 ml (2 cups) full-bodied red wine (preferably Nebbiolo)
salt
2–3 tbsp. butter

250 g (9 ounces) Parmesan
1 tbsp. fresh thyme
chives

In this recipe, the *condimento* is composed of the red wine. In a small pot, bring the wine to a boil, and reduce it by half (about ten minutes). For the *soffritto*, heat two tablespoons of oil in the pot that you will use to cook the risotto, and then sauté the finely chopped onions along with the garlic for about five minutes before adding the pancetta, cut into fine strips, as well as the finely cubed carrots. Sauté the carrots over medium heat until they have begun to soften, about ten minutes, before adding the rice to the pot. Stir while briefly frying the rice in the *soffritto*. Then deglaze the pot with three-fourths of the reduced red wine, turn down the heat, and wait until the wine has almost completely evaporated and taken on a syrupy consistency. Over low heat, pour the chicken (or vegetable) broth over the rice, one ladle at a time, and keep stirring diligently for about twenty minutes. Wait to add the rest of the wine until the risotto is soft but still firm to the bite. Then take the pot off the heat and fold three tablespoons of butter into the risotto, stirring vigorously. Add the thyme, and give the risotto one last stir before sprinkling with grated Parmesan and snippets of chives.

PENNOTTO WITH PORCINI MUSHROOMS FOR 4

70 g (2 ounces) dried porcini mushrooms
1–1½ L (4–6 cups) chicken broth (or porcini broth)
2 pinches saffron
3 tbsp. olive oil
2 small onions, finely chopped
1 garlic clove, finely chopped

1 celery stalk, peeled and finely chopped
500 g (1 pound) penne
100 ml (½ cup) dry white wine
2 tbsp. sherry
1 tbsp. parsley
salt and pepper
Parmesan, grated

This somewhat unfamiliar method of cooking penne originated in bygone times, when Italian seasonal laborers, working in olive groves far away from home, had little or no water to cook their pasta. So they simply cooked it in the sauce. Celina, the wife of my former hairdresser, who first told me about this, calls them *pennotto*. Initially skeptical that pasta would really become soft when braised in hot broth, I was all the more thrilled at the smooth, creamy texture they developed. There is, however, one rule to observe. In contrast to a risotto, *pennotto* not only need to cook in simmering fluid but also require steam to be done to perfection. For this reason, it is best to put the lid back on the pot after stirring in the penne, even if you do so more than once as you check up on them.

Soak the porcini mushrooms in hot water. Drain them, but do not discard the soaking water. Instead, pour it through a fine sieve to remove all the impurities from the porcini. Then under cold water, rinse the porcini thoroughly (to make sure that no grit is still clinging to them), and cut them into fine slices. Warm the chicken broth (or vegetable broth), season with two pinches of saffron, and keep it warm over very low heat. Because you can never gauge exactly how much fluid the pasta will need to be cooked al dente, it is better to have some extra broth on hand, just in case. For the *soffritto*, heat the olive oil in the pot in which you will make the *pennotto*, and then sauté the onions, garlic, and celery, all finely chopped, for about five minutes. As with a risotto, add the penne, and fry them in the *soffritto* for about a minute, stirring with a wooden spoon to make sure they are well coated, and then deglaze with wine. Once the wine has evaporated, add enough broth to cover the penne, give them a vigorous stir, cover the pot, and over medium heat, let the pasta simmer, about twelve minutes (a bit longer than the instructions on the package recommend). You will, however, need to check on what is happening in the pot now and then, stirring the penne to make sure they aren't sticking to the bottom of the pot and, if they have greedily absorbed all the broth, adding some more. They shouldn't, however, be swimming in broth all the time. Instead, after the first five minutes, they should be moist but no longer covered completely with broth.

In the meantime, you can prepare the *condimenti* in a second pot. Heat one tablespoon of olive oil in a second pot, sauté the finely chopped onions (about five minutes) before adding the porcini slices, and then deglaze with sherry. If you want a more liquid consistency, use a bit of the porcini-soaking water. Add the chopped parsley, and season with salt and pepper. After the penne have been cooking for about ten minutes, add the porcini to the pot, and stir thoroughly. If the *pennotto* are too dry, you can use some of the porcini-soaking water here as well. Once the penne are cooked al dente—which you can only know by trying one—season with pepper, take the pot off the heat, and cover it with a lid. Let the penne rest for a few minutes before serving them with grated Parmesan.

PENNOTTO WITH ZUCCHINI AND SHRIMP FOR 4

500 L (2 cups) fish stock	1 tbsp. fresh thyme
120 ml (½ cup) olive oil	500 g (1 pound) penne
2 garlic cloves, finely chopped	100 ml (½ cup) dry white wine
400 g (14 ounces) raw shrimp, peeled	salt and pepper
1 small onion, finely chopped	butter
500 g (1 pound) zucchini	2 tbsp. parsley

For this version, the *soffritto* and the *condimenti* are prepared together. It is perfectly fine to use a stock cube to make the fish stock, which should be kept warm over very low heat once it has been brought to a boil. Peel the shrimp, and then pull away the thin, dark intestine on the inner side. Heat the olive oil in the pot in which you will be making the *pennotto*, and then briefly sauté the finely chopped garlic (only thirty seconds) before adding the shrimp. Sear them on both sides, no longer than three minutes, before removing them from the pot and setting them aside. Next, sauté the finely chopped onions, about five minutes, until they are soft and translucent before adding the zucchini, cut into bite-size cubes, along with the thyme leaves and sautéing them as well. Then add the penne to the zucchini cubes, and fry them for a minute or so, all the while stirring vigorously to make sure they are well coated with the *soffritto* before deglazing with wine and seasoning generously with salt and pepper. Once the wine has evaporated, pour enough broth over the penne to barely cover them, give them another vigorous stir, put the lid on the pot, and then, over medium heat, cook the penne, around twelve minutes (a bit longer than recommended on the package). After five minutes, however, you should stir the *pennotto* to make sure that none of the pasta is clinging to the bottom of the pot. At this point, they should be moist but no longer covered completely with broth, so add some more if they have absorbed the broth too quickly. Once the *pennotto* are cooked al dente, cream them with butter, and then fold in the shrimps. Season with more salt if necessary, turn the heat very low, cover the pot, and allow the *pennotto* to rest a few minutes. Scatter chopped parsley over them before serving.

MOROCCAN COUSCOUS FOR 4–6

300 g (11 ounces) sweet potatoes	300 ml (1¼ cups) vegetable broth
2 tbsp. olive oil	1 pinch saffron
1–2 tbsp. za'atar	¼ tsp. turmeric
2 tbsp. sherry	200 g (2 cups) couscous

2 tbsp. olive oil

zest of 1 lemon

½ preserved lemon (see "Prepared and Stored in the Refrigerator")

mint, tarragon, parsley, chopped, about 2 tbsp. each

150 g (¾ cup) soft goat cheese

While you can find instant couscous in many supermarkets these days, which you simply soak in hot broth, I prefer a slightly more elaborate mode of preparation, not least of all because oven-roasted vegetables and couscous make such a perfect match.

Heat the oven to 190°C (375°F). In the meantime, peel the sweet potatoes, and cut them into bite-size pieces. In a bowl, season with salt, pepper, and za'atar; drizzle with olive oil and sherry; and mix everything thoroughly, using your hands to make sure that each piece is coated with the marinade. Then place the sweet potatoes into an oven-proof dish in which they can lie together snugly in one layer. Roast them for fifteen minutes, then turn over all the pumpkin pieces, and roast them another fifteen minutes or longer if they are not yet firm to the bite. In the meantime, heat the vegetable broth, and season with saffron and cumin so that the broth is immediately flavored with these spices. First, mix the couscous with the olive oil, the lemon zest, and the preserved lemon, and cut into very fine slivers before pouring the seasoned broth over it. Stir everything again thoroughly before covering the bowl tightly with plastic wrap, and then allow the couscous to rest for fifteen minutes. Then fluff it up, season with salt and pepper, add the roasted sweet potatoes and the chopped herbs, toss it again, and then fold chunks of the soft goat cheese (or feta) into the couscous.

NOTE: Sweet potatoes can be replaced with other roasted vegetables such as pumpkin, peppers, or eggplant. Dried apricots, cherries, or raisins, soaked in hot water before using them, can be added for sweetness. Pistachios, pumpkin seeds, or pecan nuts, in turn, give a pleasant crunch to a couscous.

ISRAELI COUSCOUS (*PTITIM*) FOR 4–6

600–700 ml (2½–3 cups) vegetable broth

250 g (1½ cups) Israeli couscous

1 pinch saffron

2 tbsp. olive oil

1 big onion

½ tsp. cumin

½ tsp. turmeric

½ preserved lemon (see "Prepared and Stored in the Refrigerator")

5 sun-dried tomatoes

6 olives without pits

2 tbsp. butter   60 g (½ cup) pistachios

4 tbsp. herbs (parsley, basil, mint),
    chopped

Not only are these pasta pearls larger than North African couscous, but they also have to be cooked in boiling water. In some cookbooks, *ptitim* is also called Ben Gurion rice, because in Israel in the 1950s, this couscous often served as a substitute for ordinary rice. Toasted, these pasta pearls also resemble fregula from Sardinia, but in a pinch, if you can locate neither in your supermarket, you could also use Greek orzo instead.

To give more flavor to my *ptitim*, I use vegetable broth, seasoned with a pinch of saffron, rather than salt water, which I keep warm over low heat while I prepare the *soffritto*. For this, I first heat oil in the pot in which I will cook the *ptitim* and then fry the cumin and turmeric for about a minute before adding the finely chopped onions. These should sauté over low heat until they are soft and translucent, about seven minutes. As with a risotto, I then add the couscous to the pot, mix it thoroughly with a wooden spoon, making sure that all the pasta pearls are coated with the *soffritto*, before I pour five hundred milliliters (two cups) of the warm vegetable broth over them. Once the broth has come to a boil, I turn down the heat and let the couscous simmer for about ten minutes. The pasta pearls should absorb the broth completely, but they may need a bit more broth. Since they like clinging to the bottom of the pot, I also stir them now and then. While the couscous is simmering, I cut the preserved lemon, sun-dried tomatoes, and olives into fine strips and put them, together with the butter, the chopped herbs, and the pistachios, into a salad bowl. Once the couscous is done, I add it to the salad bowl and toss it, until all the ingredients are perfectly blended.

ALL IN ONE POT

❧ VEGETABLE STEW

Fennel with Honey and Wine | Cauliflower with Curry |
Parsnips in Coconut Milk | Artichokes with Oranges and Lemons

❧ MEAT STEW

Ragù alla Bolognese | Three-Day Beef Ragout | Beef Roulade with
Potato Purée | Mashed Potatoes | Veal Goulash with Paprika and Cumin |

Rabbit in a Mustard and Cream Sauce | Drunken Venison Ragout with Mushrooms | Königsberger Meatballs in Caper Sauce | Italian-American Meatballs in Tomato Sauce | Thai Curry Meatballs

❧ POULTRY
Chicken with Tarragon and Cream | Coq au Riesling | Coq au Vin Rouge | Chicken Fricassee

❧ POACHED AND STEAMED
Chicken Breasts Poached in Broth | Salmon Poached in Oil | Steamed Salmon with Orange-Ginger Sauce | Velvet Chocolate Mousse

As with a risotto, there are certain basic principles to follow if you want to produce the complex interplay of flavors that transforms an ordinary stew into a delicious event. Once the ingredients are all safely contained in the pot, there is little else to do than wait patiently for the alchemy that will take place there. Almost nothing can go wrong as long as, every now and then, you check to see how the stew is developing and, if necessary, regulate the heat. From reading experts on braising and stewing, I have learned that the reason for using cheaper, sinewy, and seemingly chewy ragout from the shoulder for a stew instead of premium-quality lean meat is the collagen and fat content, a connective tissue glue of sorts. When the meat is braised very slowly, the collagen produces gelatin, which, in turn, not only allows the meat to become extremely tender and juicy but also binds the braising fluid, rendering its flavor more intense and creating a richer, denser sauce. For this reason, however, the meat must never come to a boil when braising. The size of the pieces of meat, in turn, depends on the desired cooking time. The longer the meat is meant to braise, the larger the chunks should be so that they don't fall apart completely. Using ground meat will allow you to shorten the braising time accordingly.

You need to follow four crucial steps when braising and stewing. Although, with slight variations, these also apply to vegetables, the principle is best explained with meat. To get the delicious cycle going—whereby as the braising liquid simmers, it vaporizes into steam that swirls around the pot and condenses under the lid, only to drip back down and moisten the meat and vegetables, which release their own flavorful juices, further enriching the liquid—you must first brown the meat. This first step produces the initial layer of flavor on which all others can build. I usually use just enough olive oil to barely cover the bottom of the pot and, over medium heat, wait for it to begin sizzling. If you use too little oil, the meat will not brown evenly; if you use too much, it will become greasy. In contrast to pan-frying, the pot does not have to be hot before adding the oil. The pieces of meat, however, should be dry before browning; otherwise, they will not develop the desired crust. And as in pan-frying, you must never crowd the pan with the individual pieces of meat. If they are lying too close to each other, the juices they release can't evaporate, which will produce steam in the pot before you want it to. For this reason, you will most often need to work in batches, and under no circumstances should you leave the stovetop at this point. Instead, you must wait patiently, turning each individual piece of meat over once it has developed a deep-brown outer crust. If you try to turn the meat too early, it may well stick to the bottom of the pot and rip. If the meat needs more fat, let it trickle down along the side of the pot so that, as it moves across the bottom of the pot toward the meat you are browning, it can heat up.

The second step concerns the finely chopped vegetable cubes, herbs, and spices that, together with the browned meat, make up the second layer of a well-flavored braised dish. They contribute to the aromatic density that the meat or poultry can't offer on its own and, in so doing, provide the decisive flavor of the dish. This *soffritto* should be prepared in the same pot in which the meat or poultry has been browned, as it is meant to mingle with the savory, brown bits that have remained on the bottom of the pot. A classic mélange consists of onions, celery, and carrots. However, you can add spring onions, garlic, ginger, chili peppers, or dried spices, such as caraway seeds, cumin, or paprika, depending on your desire for experimentation.

The *soffritto* will dissolve into the braising liquid, with which, in a third step, you cover the meat or poultry after having returned it to the pot. As with a soup or a risotto, this fluid not only serves to moisten the meat (or poultry) and to produce steam; it also conducts the flavors of all the ingredients that have been assembled in the pot and thus keeps the alchemic circulation rolling. The broth supports the hearty, savory note of the stew, and the wine brings a certain acidity into play and balances the other rich aromas. If you are using dried mushrooms, you can use the soaking liquid just as well as tomato juice (or tomato purée), a brandy, or another spirit. What is important, in all cases, is that the braising liquid doesn't cover the meat completely but rather comes up only halfway. Furthermore, the meat should only simmer in the braising liquid; the latter should never come to a boil. If you are using additional vegetables in the stew, either brown this first as well or—if it requires substantially less time to cook—don't add it until halfway through the process.

Delicate herbs, like dill or basil, belong to the last step, called the finish, which serves to round off the flavor and texture of the dish. If, once the meat is finally tender and juicy, the sauce is too watery and needs to be reduced, remove the meat and vegetables from the pot, and set them aside in a covered dish (to keep them warm). This requires your full attention. The braising fluid may bubble merrily, but it mustn't boil vigorously. Once the desired consistency is reached, you must stop the cooking process immediately; otherwise, you may end up with a thick paste. After you have returned the meat and vegetables to the stewpot comes the moment when the dish receives its aromatic signature. How you flavor it—with *double crème de Gruyère*, yogurt, lemon juice, brandy, or simply with freshly chopped herbs—is up to your own creativity.

VEGETABLE STEW

FENNEL WITH HONEY AND WINE FOR 4

2 medium-size fennels	125 ml (½ cup) dry white wine
2–3 tbsp. olive oil	2 tsp. butter
250 ml (1 cup) vegetable broth	salt and pepper
3 tbsp. honey	

The three steps of a vegetable stew can be demonstrated with this recipe (since no aromatic *soffritto* is necessary). Cut the fennel in half, peel the tough outer skin, and with a small knife, remove the stem. Then cut each half in half again, taking care that the fennel slices don't fall apart. Pluck the delicate green fennel fronds, and set them aside to use as garnish at the end. Then heat the olive oil in a pot, and brown—your first step—the fennel pieces on each side, about four minutes each. The fennel should caramelize, which is why if the pieces don't all fit into the pot in one layer, you should work in batches. As the second step, add an aromatic braising liquid—in this case, the mélange of honey, water, and wine. My friend Philip, in whose kitchen I once prepared this dish, has increased the dosage of wine significantly and renamed it "drunken fennel." He also suggests using absinthe instead. Allow the liquid to come to a boil briefly, then reduce the heat to medium, put the lid on the pot, and let the fennel simmer until the water has almost completely evaporated, about thirty to forty-five minutes. If the braising liquid evaporates too quickly, you can add some more water; if the dish is too watery, take the lid off the pan, raise the heat for a few minutes, and boil down the remaining liquid. Finish the braised vegetables as your last, third step by folding in the butter, seasoning with salt and pepper, and sprinkling with the reserved fennel frond.

CAULIFLOWER WITH CURRY FOR 4–6

1 tbsp. rapeseed oil
1 medium onion, finely chopped
3 garlic cloves, finely chopped
1 tbsp. curry powder
1 tsp. turmeric
1 pinch red chili flakes
400 g (14 ounces) canned tomatoes

1 big cauliflower head, about 1 kg
  (2.2 pounds)
500 ml (2 cups) chicken broth
juice of 1 lime
salt and pepper
2–3 tbsp. raisins
2–3 tbsp. goji berries
2–3 tbsp. cilantro

In this recipe, which I have adapted from Alfred Portale's wonderful *Simple Pleasures*, you first prepare the *soffritto*, as if for a risotto, so as to season the broth in which the cauliflower will subsequently be braised. Heat the rapeseed oil in a pot that is large enough to hold the cauliflower and the finely chopped onions, and sauté them for about five minutes until they are translucent before adding the finely chopped garlic. Sauté for another two minutes. Next add the aromatics—the curry powder, turmeric, and chili flakes—along with the canned tomatoes and their juices, and simmer them for about five minutes. Next, cut the cauliflower into rosettes, peel the stem, and cut it into cubes. Then add everything to the *soffritto*, including the chicken (or vegetable) broth. When the braising liquid comes to a boil, lower the heat, cover the pot with a tightly fitting lid, and let the cauliflower simmer for about ten minutes. In the meantime, soak the raisins and goji berries in warm water. Using a slotted spoon, fish out the cauliflower with the exception of two rosettes, and put it aside in a covered bowl so that it will stay warm. Cover the pot again, and cook the remaining cauliflower until it is extremely soft, about ten minutes. Then mash it with a fork into the braising liquid to thicken the sauce. Season with salt, pepper, and lime juice, and pour it over the cauliflower. Scatter the raisins and goji berries on top along with the chopped cilantro.

PARSNIPS IN COCONUT MILK FOR 4

2 tbsp. rapeseed oil

1 large onion, finely chopped

2 garlic cloves, finely chopped

1 thumb-size piece of fresh ginger, peeled and finely chopped

2 small chili peppers (or 1 tsp. dried chili flakes), deseeded and finely sliced

2 stalks lemongrass, peeled and finely chopped

2 kaffir lime leaves, finely chopped

80 g (⅓ cup) tomato purée

½ tonka bean, grated (or vanilla mixed with almond)

400 ml (1¾ cup) coconut milk

1 kg (2.2 pounds) medium-size parsnips

1 L (4 cups) vegetable broth

1 bunch cilantro

1 generous handful unsalted peanuts, crushed

3 tbsp. soy sauce

juice of 1 lime

In this recipe, you also sauté aromatics—onions, garlic, ginger, chili peppers, lemongrass, and kaffir lime leaves—over medium heat about five minutes to produce a *soffritto*. They should begin to caramelize. In the meantime, peel the parsnips, and cut them into bite-size pieces. If you have large ones, remove the hard, inner core. Add the parsnips to the pot (which you can do bit by bit as you cut them), and then brown them briefly before adding the tomato purée. Stir everything thoroughly before adding the coconut milk and enough broth to barely cover the parsnips, about one liter (four cups). Put a tightly fitting lid on the pot, bring the braising liquid to a boil briefly, and then turn the heat down. In the covered pot, let the parsnips braise for about twenty-five minutes until they are soft. In the meantime, wash the cilantro, and if there are some with roots, use them as well. Pluck the leaves off the stems, and set them aside before chopping the stem and the roots very finely and adding them to the pot. To finish the dish, coarsely crush the peanuts in a mortar, and add them to the pot. Season with soy sauce and lime juice, and let the parsnips simmer a few minutes longer before taking off the heat. To serve, sprinkle with chopped cilantro.

ARTICHOKES WITH ORANGES AND LEMONS FOR 4

4 large artichokes

juice of 3 lemons

2 large onions

juice of 4 big oranges

4 tbsp. white balsamic vinegar

8 tbsp. olive oil

salt and pepper

2 tsp. capers

4 anchovies

1½ tsp. brown sugar

Although artichokes have always belonged to my favorite vegetables, for the longest time, I was intimidated by them, unsure how best to remove the hard and thorny outer petals and the fuzzy choke in the center. The advice a biologist friend gave me initially seemed expensive, but it ultimately paid off. He told me to cut them open and analyze them as though I were in a laboratory. So one afternoon, I invested in four artichokes, and I dissected them until I had truly understood their anatomy. And suddenly it all made perfect sense.

Cut the stem off close to the actual heart of the artichoke, and remove the outer petals at the bottom. Next, cut off the upper two-thirds of the artichoke to lay bare its heart. To scrape out the prickly hairs of the choke on top of the heart, I have found that a sharp grapefruit knife works best. Then I immediately drizzle lemon juice on exposed surfaces so that they don't turn brown while I cut off the remaining outer petals. In the end, I am left with only the precious artichoke heart.

Once you have prepared all four artichokes, bring salt water to a boil in a pot large enough to hold them, add the juice of one lemon, and poach them for about three minutes. Carefully remove them with a slotted spoon (you don't want them to break into pieces), and drain them thoroughly. Cut the peeled onion in half, and then slice it into very delicate, moon-shaped slices. Cover the bottom of the pot in which all four artichoke hearts fit snugly with half of the onion slices. Place the artichokes, bottom side up, on top, and then cover them with the remaining onion rings. Pour the orange juice, the remaining lemon juice, as well as the white balsamic vinegar and olive oil over the artichoke hearts, and then add enough water to cover them. Before putting the lid on the pot, season with salt and pepper. Over low heat, braise the artichokes, about thirty minutes. Remove the lid, and let them simmer, uncovered, for another fifteen minutes until they are soft. With a slotted spoon, remove the artichoke hearts, and set them aside in a bowl before adding the finely chopped capers and anchovies as well and the sugar. Stir constantly about fifteen to twenty-five minutes, reducing the braising liquid until you have a thick and syrupy sauce, and then pour it over the artichokes. Because these braised artichokes do not need to be served right away, you can prepare them in advance, keep them in the refrigerator, and serve them the next day at room temperature.

MEAT STEW

RAGÙ ALLA BOLOGNESE FOR 4

4 tbsp. olive oil

2 large onions, finely chopped

4 slices of bacon (or pancetta)

2 celery stalks with leaves (about 4 tbsp.), peeled and finely chopped

2 medium carrots, peeled and finely chopped

2 garlic cloves, crushed

2 tbsp. tomato flakes (optional)

400 g (14 ounces) ground meat (just beef or a mixture of beef and pork)

2 tbsp. parsley

2 tbsp. thyme

2 tbsp. sage

2 tbsp. basil

250 ml (1 cup) full-bodied red wine

3 tbsp. tomato purée

salt and pepper

Parmesan

500 g (1 pound) spaghetti

In our home, ragù Bolognese was synonymous with spaghetti because my mother had only this pasta sauce in her repertoire, yet this ragù is actually far more versatile. Together with a béchamel (or white sauce), it can be used to make a lasagna or finished with cream; it also works with sautéed zucchini or oven-roasted eggplants. You can also stuff tomatoes or peppers with this ragù and roast them in the oven. You can use it as a filling for a ravioli or a pot sticker. Or if you want to be very minimalist, you can simply eat the Bolognese with a piece of warm country bread. And because it is easy to freeze this sauce, I tend to make at least double the amount so that I always have some in reserve.

For the *soffritto*, sauté the finely chopped onions and the finely sliced bacon over medium heat in olive oil for about seven minutes. The onions should be translucent but not yet taken on a brown hue. In the meantime, peel the carrots and the celery, and cut both into fine cubes, add them to the pot, stir the vegetables thoroughly with the onions and bacon, and then sauté for another five minutes. My mother always insisted that the chopped garlic should be added at this point and not earlier, probably so that it wouldn't scorch. Once the vegetables are firm to the bite, add the ground meat, brown it thoroughly, season with salt and pepper, and then fold the finely chopped celery leaves as well as the finely chopped parsley and the dry herbs into the meat. Finish the aroma with a shot of red wine and tomato purée, stir thoroughly, cover the ragù with water or broth, stir once more, and then put the lid on the pot and let the sauce simmer for at least an hour. Check in now and then, however, to see how the ragù is developing, and if necessary, add more salt if it tastes bland and more water if it has become too dry.

THREE-DAY BEEF RAGOUT FOR 4–6

3–6 tbsp. olive

2 celery stalks, peeled and finely chopped

1 medium onion, peeled and finely chopped

1 large carrot, peeled and finely chopped

6 garlic cloves, peeled and crushed

500 ml (2 cups) chicken broth

1½ kg (3 pounds) beef (preferably boneless chuck roast), cut into bite-size cubes

salt and pepper

250 ml (1 cup) full-bodied red wine

300 g (1 cup) tomato purée

zest and juice of 1 orange

2 tbsp. fresh thyme

5 bay leaves

500 g (1 pound) fettuccine

There are no such things as mistakes. As the great modernist author James Joyce claimed, "Mistakes are the portals of discovery." This soothing piece of wisdom is particularly appropriate for my own accidental creation of this dish. In one of his cookbooks, *Simple Pleasures*, Alfred Portale describes using boneless chuck roast rather than ground meat for a ragout with tagliatelle to offer an urban spin on the dish he used to eat in his Italian-American home. One day, I decided this might be the perfect dish for two friends whom I knew were particularly fond of beef. Looking over the recipe, however, I began to worry that the cooking time might not be enough for the meat to become really tender, and so I decided to try it out in advance first. And indeed, after three hours, I wasn't quite happy with the texture of the meat, but more important, I suddenly realized I had absolutely no space in the refrigerator to store it. So there was nothing to do but let the ragout simmer over very low heat for a couple of hours during each of the following three days, until I had made room for it in my refrigerator. The evening Andreas and Franz came for dinner, I simply reheated the sauce, and we were all impressed not only at how tender and juicy the meat was but also at how intense the beef flavor had become.

For the *soffritto*, sauté the finely chopped onions, carrots, celery, and garlic in olive oil in the pot in which you will make the ragout, about eight to ten minutes. The onions are allowed to caramelize before you add half of the broth. Turn up the heat, bring the broth to a boil, and stir vigorously because you want to deglaze the savory brown bits that have formed on the bottom of the pot. The broth may reduce but should not evaporate completely. Pour the *soffritto* into a bowl, and set it aside. Then cut the meat into bite-size pieces, season with salt and pepper, and brown them in the remaining olive oil, about five to six minutes. If the pieces do not all fit into the pot in one layer, you will need to work in batches, making sure that each piece really comes in contact with the hot oil on the bottom of the pot; otherwise, it will not develop the obligatory crust. It is equally important that you turn each piece individually, using tongs or a fork (rather than flipping them over collectively with a slotted spoon) to make sure that each one is browned on all sides. Once the beef is done, add it to the bowl with the *soffritto*.

Then stirring vigorously once more, deglaze the pot with red wine, and then reduce it to a third, about ten minutes. Add the tomato purée and the remaining two hundred and fifty millimeters (one cup) of chicken broth to the pot, as well as the aromatics—the thyme, orange zest, bay leaves, and orange juice. Return the meat and vegetables to the pot, season with salt and pepper, and after putting the lid on the pot, reduce the heat. Check in on it now and then to make sure that the braising liquid is simmering gently. If it is bubbling intensely or completely without movement, you must readjust the heat. After about two hours, you can turn off the heat completely. Over the next two days, keep reheating the beef ragout, letting it simmer over very low heat for an hour or so. On the third day, the vegetables will have transformed into a rich sauce; the meat will be astonishingly tender; and the herbs, tomato, and orange will have been enticingly blended into an aromatic whole. Before serving, simply make sure to fish out the bay leaves. While fettuccine is the obvious choice for accompaniment, I sometimes eat this ragout just as it is.

BEEF ROULADE WITH POTATO PURÉE FOR 4

4 slices of flank steak, each 130 g (5 ounces)	flour for coating
salt and pepper	3 tbsp. schmaltz, or 60 ml (¼ cup) olive oil
2 onions, finely chopped	1 small onion (for the sauce)
1 big carrot, peeled and finely chopped	120 ml (½ cup) full-bodied red wine
80 g (3 ounces) cornichon	125 g (½ cup) tomato purée
4–6 tbsp. Dijon mustard	250 ml (1 cup) beef broth
8 slices of bacon	150 g (1¾ cup) button mushrooms
	100 ml (½ cup) cream

The roulades should not be thicker than six millimeters (one-fourth inch), which is why you may have to pound them yourself to the desired width with the smooth side of a meat tenderizer (or a meat mallet). To protect the meat while pounding it, put the slices into a refrigerator bag or use a piece of plastic wrap. As you flatten the meat, try to get a rectangular shape that will be easy to roll around the filling. Then dry each meat slice thoroughly with paper towels before seasoning with salt and pepper. Next prepare the filling. Cut the onions into very fine slices, and julienne the carrots and cornichon. Lay out the beef slices on a cutting board, and spread a thin layer of mustard on one side. Place two strips of bacon lengthwise in the center of each roulade, and then divide the onion, carrots, and cornichon among them. Leave some room at the bottom and the top, as well as on the sides. Fold in the two longer sides of each roulade, as though to make a seam, and then roll the beef around the filling, and secure them with toothpicks. If you find that you have filled the roulades too generously, remove some of the julienne slivers. You can braise them later with mushrooms when making the sauce. As you would a schnitzel, dredge each roulade lightly in flour. In the stew pot, heat the schmaltz (or olive oil) over medium heat until it begins to shimmer, and then, taking care not to lose any of the filling, add the roulades to the pot. Sear them on all sides, about five minutes, before removing the roulades along with their juices and putting them aside on a plate.

Next, sauté the finely chopped onion in a bit more schmaltz until the diced pieces have become soft and taken on a golden-brown hue. Stir the tomato purée into the chopped onion, and sauté for another minute before pouring in the red wine. Let it come to a boil, and then reduce it by half. Now you can return the roulade and any juice to the pot and pour in enough beef broth to come halfway up the sides of the meat. Add the mushrooms at this point as well, put a lid on the pot, and let the roulades braise over low heat for one and a half hours (or until they are tender). If they become too dry while braising, add some more broth to the pot. Once the roulades are done, remove them from the pot, and set them aside on a plate, moistened slightly with some of the gravy. Cover them so that they stay warm while you reduce the braising fluid until you have a rich sauce, season with salt and pepper, and finish with cream. Dark country bread can serve as an accompaniment, but the side dish typically served in German cuisine would be mashed potatoes.

MASHED POTATOES FOR 4

1 kg (2.2 pounds) starchy potatoes   16 tbsp. butter
200–300 ml (⅔–1¼ cups) milk   salt

This recipe is a variation on the world-famous one created by Joel Robuchon, in which an astonishing amount of butter turns this ordinary dish into something truly extraordinary. Because you want the potatoes to cook evenly, try to use only those that have more or less the same size. However, what is also crucial for this dish to succeed is that you use only the best quality butter you can find. The butter, in turn, must be cold for the mashed potatoes to become really delicate and creamy. And because everything depends on the butter, you must have the courage of your culinary conviction and really use a lot. In a pot, pour salt water—one tablespoon of salt to one liter (four cups) of water—over the washed but not yet peeled potatoes, covering them at least 2.5 millimeters (1 inch), and then cook for thirty minutes over medium heat. Once the potatoes are done, drain them immediately, and then peel them while they are still hot. Pass them through the finest bottom plate of a food mill (or press them with a potato masher). In a second pot, stir the mashed potatoes energetically over very low heat with a flat wooden spoon, about three to four minutes, until they are really dry. This is the moment when you should add the cold butter, one tablespoon at a time, stirring the potatoes with utmost vigor all the time. The butter should blend into the potatoes completely before you add the next dollop. Only this way will the mashed potatoes become fluffy and yet rich in texture. At the very end, add enough hot milk to the mashed potatoes until you have the desired creaminess, and then season with salt. Robuchon recommends that if you want even lighter, finer potatoes, you could pass them through a very fine sieve once more before serving, but that is too much effort for my taste.

VEAL GOULASH WITH PAPRIKA AND CUMIN FOR 3

3 tbsp. olive oil   salt
2 medium onions, finely chopped   8 cornichons
½ tsp. cumin   3 small chili peppers
½ tsp. caraway seeds   250 g (1¾ cups) button mushrooms
1 tbsp. sweet Hungarian paprika   100 ml (½ cup) sour cream
900 g (2 pounds) veal shoulder   100 ml (½ cup) whipping cream
2 veal feet (or bone marrow)

Cut the onions into coarse cubes. In a pot in which the meat will fit snugly, heat the oil, and sauté the onions until they are soft and translucent, about fifteen minutes. Season the onions with paprika, caraway seeds, and cumin. My Hungarian friend Anka, who gave me this recipe, says to use as much of the powdered spice as it takes to really see the red color. Once the *soffritto* is done, brown the veal, cut into bite-size pieces, on all sides, and season with salt. Add the veal feet (or bone marrow), which are essential for binding the sauce and making the flavor even more intense. Because the meat is meant, as Anka explains, to "stew in its own juices," no additional braising liquid is necessary. Instead, put the lid on the pot, and let the meat simmer, over low heat, for about an hour, or until it is tender. In the meantime, cut the cornichons in half, deseed the chili peppers, and clean the mushrooms. Slice everything thinly, and then, after the veal has been stewing for thirty minutes, add them to the pot as well. The chili peppers are necessary because the paprika on its own is too sweet; however, they can be replaced by chili flakes. If the braising liquid evaporates too quickly, you can add some broth. Once the meat is tender, juicy, and soft, remove the veal feet and finish the stew with a mélange of sweet and sour cream. Traditionally, *pörkel*, as this goulash is called in Hungary, is served with spaetzle, but Anka suggests eating it simply with a piece a dark country bread.

RABBIT IN A MUSTARD AND CREAM SAUCE FOR 4

1½ kg (3 pounds) rabbit drumsticks
4 tbsp. olive oil
2 shallots, finely chopped
2 garlic cloves, peeled and finely
   chopped
1 tbsp. *herbes de Provence*
1 tsp. dried thyme
250 ml (1 cup) dry white wine

150 ml (⅔ cup) double crème
   de Gruyère (or heavy cream)
3 tbsp. Dijon mustard
3 tbsp. grainy mustard
250 g (1¾ cups) brown button
   mushrooms
500 g (1 pound) small, waxy potatoes

You could, of course, always buy an entire rabbit and carve it into pieces, but I have discovered that when braised, the legs become particularly juicy and tasty, so I use just them. And because rabbit isn't always available, it makes sense to order it in advance from your butcher, though in a pinch, you could substitute it with chicken drumsticks. While the principle is the same as in the previous recipe for veal goulash, the spices are different, as is the fact that the cream isn't added in the end to round off the flavor but rather is part of the braising process.

Wash the rabbit legs, and pat them dry with paper towels before seasoning them generously with salt. Heat the oil in the stew pot over medium heat; brown the legs, about five minutes on each side; and then set them aside on a plate. For the *soffritto*, sauté the finely chopped shallots, together with the finely chopped garlic, stirring constantly until they have become soft and translucent, about five minutes. Season the *soffritto* with *herbes de Provence* and thyme, and then deglaze with white wine. Mix everything together thoroughly, and then allow the wine to come to a boil before reducing the heat and adding the cream as well as both types of mustard. Allow the sauce to simmer for a few minutes so that the various aromatics can blend together before returning the browned legs to the pot. Season with salt, put the lid on the pot, and let the rabbit stew in the mustard-cream sauce for about thirty minutes. In the meantime, cook the potatoes, peel them, and cut them in half. Clean the mushrooms, and quarter them as well. After twenty minutes, add only the mushrooms to the stew pot. Because the potatoes shouldn't cook any further and instead simply need to be reheated, you shouldn't add them until the very end. If you have enough time, you can, however, turn the heat to very low after thirty minutes and braise the rabbit gently for another hour; this will make it particularly savory and tender. In that case, however, hold back the potatoes, and don't reheat them in the stew until the very end.

DRUNKEN VENISON RAGOUT WITH MUSHROOMS FOR 6

FOR THE MARINADE

6 slices of bacon, cut into fine strips

3 celery stalks, peeled and finely chopped

2 large carrots, peeled and finely chopped

8 shallots, peeled and finely chopped

1 large onion, peeled and finely chopped

7 garlic cloves, peeled and finely chopped

juice and zest of 1 orange

12 basil leaves

1 tbsp. fresh thyme

2 bay leaves

2 tsp. black peppercorns

10 dry juniper berries

4 cloves

1 tsp. cinnamon

2 bottles full-bodied red wine (each 750 ml)

125 ml (½ cup) fruity red port wine

60 ml (¼ cup) red wine vinegar

THE RAGOUT

3 pounds venison (preferably shoulder), cut into large cubes	370 ml (1½ cups) chicken broth
salt and pepper	1 tbsp. olive oil
2 tbsp. butter	100 g (4 ounces) bacon
2–3 tbsp. olive oil	2 handfuls seasonal mushrooms
2 tbsp. flour	crème fraîche
	cranberry compote

This elaborate (and not exactly cheap) dish has a truly drunken note, not least of all because of the marinade, and thus belongs to the category of particularly festive stews. It is also the consummate recipe for braising pieces of bite-size meat, because it combines all the steps that belong to this method of cooking.

Make the marinade for the venison the day before. In a medium-size stewing pot, reduce the two bottles of red wine by half (about thirty minutes). In the meantime, season the venison pieces with salt and pepper. For the marinade, combine the bacon, celery, carrots, shallots, onions, garlic, and the zest and juice of the orange together with the basil, thyme, bay leaves, cloves, ground cinnamon (or a cinnamon stick), and crushed peppercorns and juniper berries in a bowl. Then add the reduced wine along with the port wine and the red wine vinegar. Mix everything thoroughly, and then add the venison pieces. Using your hand, mix everything again, making sure that all the pieces of meat are coated well. Cover the bowl with plastic wrap, and let the meat rest overnight (or at least three hours) in the refrigerator, imbibing all the flavors of the marinade.

Begin making the stew the next day by taking the venison out of the marinade and then pouring it through a sieve. Reserve the liquid in one bowl and the bacon, vegetables, spices, and herbs in a second one (but discard the bay leaf and the cinnamon stick). Both the marinade and the vegetables will be added to the stew. Heat the oil and the butter in the stew pot, sear the pieces of meat on all sides so that they form a light crust, and then set them aside. If you are working in batches, you may need to add a bit more oil. Any juices that the meat releases should be added to the marinade for future use as well. They contain the drunken flavor. Once you have browned all the venison pieces, return the bacon, vegetables, spices, and herbs (which had been part of the marinade) to the pot, put on the lid, and over medium heat, let them simmer for about fifteen minutes. Then dust the vegetables with flour, stir them thoroughly, and allow them to simmer for another minute before deglazing with the broth. Make sure to dissolve all the flavor-intense brown bits that have formed at the bottom. At this point, you can pour the reserved marinade into the stew pot, add the browned pieces of venison as well, stir everything thoroughly once more, and then regulate the heat so that the stew can simmer for about two hours without bubbling too vigorously. Cover the pot with the lid, but leave it open a crack. If the meat is done more quickly, turn off the heat and simply reheat before serving, as you can also prepare it in advance and reheat it the next day.

Just before you are about to serve the venison stew, heat one tablespoon of oil in a pan, and fry the bacon until it is crisp, then add the cleaned mushrooms, and sauté them for several minutes. Then add the mushrooms and bacon to the stew, mix everything thoroughly, and season with salt and pepper. To finish the flavors, add a dollop of cream and some cranberry compote to each individual plate.

KÖNIGSBERGER MEATBALLS IN CAPER SAUCE FOR 4

1 bread roll	1 pinch cayenne pepper
600 g (23 ounces) ground meat (beef and pork)	2 L (8 cups) beef broth
	1 bay leaf
2 big shallots, chopped	1 onion, peeled and pricked with cloves
1 tbsp. butter	8 tbsp. flour
2 eggs	8 tbsp. butter
2 tbsp. parsley, chopped	100 g (4 ounces) capers
juice and zest of 1 lemon	juice of 1 lemon
salt and pepper	8 waxy potatoes

This recipe, another standard of German cuisine, comes from my sister, Susan, who is such a virtuoso at preparing it that several friends of mine have posted rave reviews on Facebook. She always makes double the amount, hoping to freeze the leftovers, but there is usually nothing left to freeze. And I continue to marvel at how an ordinary dish from my childhood, when carefully prepared (although it was often not the case then), can turn into something that evokes pure joy. What is crucial is the fluffiness of the meatballs, which are meant to literally swim on the plate in the lemon-caper sauce. Whether you decide to serve two boiled potatoes each—my sagacious sister doesn't allow more—is up to you.

To make the meatballs, begin by soaking the bread roll in lukewarm water (or a mixture of water and milk) for about ten minutes. In the meantime, sauté the finely chopped onions in butter over medium heat, until they have become soft and translucent but not yet brown. Chop the parsley and the lemon zest. Then squeeze all the liquid out of the bread roll, and in a big bowl, mix it with the eggs first before adding the ground meat, chopped parsley, chopped lemon zest, salt, and cayenne pepper. Knead the ingredients until they are thoroughly blended, and then shape them into meatballs. The size can vary, but Susan recommends they be about four centimeters (one and a half inches) wide.

To poach the meatballs, heat two liters (eight cups) of meat broth, for which I use four stock cubes because it should have an intense umami flavor. Add an onion, pricked with cloves along with the bay leaf. Let the broth come to a boil, then turn down the heat, and poach the meatballs. In order to become fluffy (rather than dry and crumbly), the meatballs should simmer very gently about ten minutes in the broth, which must not come to a boil again, with the lid on the pot. According to Susan, they are ready the minute they rise to the top. Carefully remove them from the broth with a slotted spoon, and set them aside on a plate. For the sauce, pour the poaching liquid through a sieve, because you want a clean broth—without bay leaf, cloves, or little pieces of onions that might have fallen out of the meatballs.

Rinse the stew pot, and dry it thoroughly before preparing the roux for the white sauce. Susan has a piece of advice here as well: make more than you need. It freezes well, so you only need to make the meatballs the next time. Make a thick paste by melting the butter in the pot, to which you add the flour and stir vigorously before adding the broth, one ladle at a time. Make sure the roux has absorbed all the liquid before adding the next ladle of broth. To prevent clumps from forming, you need to stir constantly, especially along the bottom of the pot so that none of the buttery flour can get stuck there, and then wait patiently for the sauce to thicken. If, however, the sauce simply won't condense, you can add more roux. Form a small ball with one teaspoon of flour and one teaspoon of butter, add it to the sauce, and then stir briskly. If, in turn, the sauce is too thick, simply add more broth.

In the meantime, cook the potatoes in salt water. Once the sauce is done, allow it to come to a boil briefly, turn the heat very low, and add the meat-balls, which are only meant to be reheated. Wash the capers, and add them to the sauce, along with the lemon juice. If you want more tartness, you can season with white balsamic vinegar or a mild white wine vinegar. If, however, you used capers preserved in vinegar (rather than those preserved in salt), they will themselves add acidity, so restraint is called for regarding the lemon juice. To finish the dish, allow the dumplings to steep in the sauce over very low heat, with the lid off the pot. Because she was distinctly old school, my mother would have added a velouté, consisting of two egg yolks and two tablespoons of cream, to the sauce at this point. Susan, however, disapproves of such a rich sauce and firmly rejects this final touch.

ITALIAN-AMERICAN MEATBALLS IN TOMATO SAUCE FOR 6

1 bread roll	100 g (1 cup) Pecorino, grated
250 g (9 ounces) ground beef	4 big eggs
250 g (9 ounces) ground pork	salt and pepper
250 g (9 ounces) ground veal	bread crumbs (or panko)
2 garlic cloves, finely chopped	5–6 tbsp. olive oil for frying
3 tbsp. parsley, chopped	Parmesan, grated
8 big sage leaves, chopped	500 g (1 pound) spaghetti
2 medium onions, peeled and finely chopped	

MARINARA SAUCE

120 ml (½ cup) olive oil	800 g (28 ounces) net weight canned tomatoes
1 medium onion, peeled and finely chopped	¼ tsp. chili flakes
1 small fennel, peeled and finely chopped	1 tsp. dried thyme
2 anchovies	2 tsp. brown sugar
5 garlic cloves, peeled and finely chopped	salt and pepper
	fresh basil

In our family, these meatballs were the American equivalent of the "Königsberger meatballs" from the prior recipe. And if the meatballs in lemon caper sauce recipe was part of my mother's Prussian inheritance, by the time she was working for the State Department in Washington, DC, in the late 1940s, this culinary legacy of Italian immigrants had become part of the cooking repertoire of her American friends. The American meatballs were, of course, far bigger than the Italian *polpette*, perhaps to signify the prosperity and abundance achievable in the new world.

Begin by making the marinara sauce (or red sauce), one of the key features of Italian-American cuisine. It can simmer gently on its own, developing its flavor ever further while you move on to making the meatballs. Heat the olive oil in a medium-size pot, and sauté the finely chopped onions, fennel, and anchovies first. After about five minutes, add the finely chopped garlic, and let the *soffritto* simmer, another fifteen minutes. Next, add the canned tomatoes to the pot, and keep mashing them with the wooden spoon as you stir the sauce. Then season with chili flakes, thyme, sugar, salt, and pepper. Allow the tomato sauce to come to a boil briefly, turn down the heat, and let it simmer for about forty minutes. To finish the sauce, scatter fresh basil, finely sliced, over it.

For the meatballs, soak the bread roll in warm water (or warm water and milk). In the meantime, in a big bowl, mix together the ground meat, chopped garlic, onion, parsley, sage, grated pecorino, salt, pepper, and two of the eggs. Knead the meat with your hands to make sure that all the ingredients are blended together thoroughly. Then fold the soaked bread roll into the meat mixture, making sure to spread it evenly before forming small meatballs, about three to four centimeters (one and one-fourth to one and a half) in diameter. For the coating, whisk the remaining two eggs in a shallow bowl with two tablespoons of water. Pour the bread crumbs into a second shallow bowl. Coat the meatballs in the egg mixture first, then in the bread crumbs before frying them in oil (preferably in a nonstick pan) over medium heat. Because they are meant to brown and become crisp all around, you will need to work in batches, around eight minutes each. Wait until all the meatballs are done before adding them to the sauce in one go. Allow the marinara sauce to come to a boil very briefly, then immediately reduce the heat, and let the meatballs simmer in the sauce for the time it takes you to boil the spaghetti in salt water. For this dish, grated Parmesan—and copious amounts of it—is obligatory.

THAI CURRY MEATBALLS FOR 4

500 g (18 ounces) ground beef	2 generous handfuls peanuts, crushed
60 g (½ cup) flour	in a mortar
3 tbsp. rapeseed oil (or more)	1 tbsp. palm sugar
2 tbsp. red curry paste	2 tbsp. lime juice
375 ml (1½ cups) coconut milk	2 tbsp. Thai basil, chopped
1½ tbsp. fish sauce	

As a third example of how versatile my beloved meatballs can turn out to be when cooked in a pot, I have chosen this Thai option, whose special charm resides primarily in the spicy sauce. The ground beef itself is simply formed into small balls, about 2.5 centimeters (1 inch) in diameter and then coated in flour. If you want a more juicy meatball, you could use a mixture of ground veal, beef, and pork. Heat two tablespoons of oil over medium heat in the pot, and fry the meatballs until they are evenly brown and crispy on all sides. Remove the meatballs from the pan, and drain them on paper towels before setting them aside on a plate. Next, fry the red curry paste over low heat in the remaining oil in the pot, or add some more to the pot if necessary. Because it shouldn't stick to the bottom of the pot while you are heating it, keep pressing and stirring it into the hot oil. Add the coconut milk, stir thoroughly with the curry paste, and then add the fish sauce, lime juice, palm sugar (or brown sugar), and crushed peanuts. Taste the sauce, and if necessary, add more fish sauce (for saltiness), more sugar (for sweetness), or more lime juice (for tartness). Once you are satisfied with the flavor, add the meatballs to the sauce, and allow them to simmer for five minutes. To finish the dish, scatter with thin slices of Thai basil, and serve it with rice.

POULTRY

CHICKEN WITH TARRAGON AND CREAM FOR 4

4 chicken breasts (without skin), about 750 g	100 ml (½ cup) Noilly Prat
salt and pepper	200 ml (1 cup) cream
2 tbsp. olive oil	3 tbsp. fresh tarragon, finely chopped
3 tbsp. shallot, finely chopped	2 tsp. lemon juice

For this recipe, it is best to choose a pot that is not too wide and that has a tightly fitting lid. The seared chicken should be completely enveloped by the vermouth cream sauce, in which it will braise only very briefly. If the pot is too big, the sauce will evaporate and the chicken breasts become dry.

Season the chicken breasts on both sides with salt and pepper, and sear them in the heated oil until they are golden brown on both sides but still raw inside, about one minute per side. Set them aside on a plate, lower the heat under the pot, and sauté the finely chopped onions, about five minutes. They should be soft and translucent but not yet brown. Deglaze with the vermouth, and allow it to simmer briefly while you dissolve the brown, savory bits collected at the bottom of the pot, stirring them into the liquid. Add the cream and half of the finely chopped tarragon, and then mix thoroughly before returning the chicken breasts to the pot. Regulate the heat so that the chicken pieces can simmer gently in the vermouth-cream, about four to six minutes. If the sauce thickens too quickly, dilute it with a bit of broth. You can check whether the chicken is done by cutting into the thickest part with a paring knife. To finish the dish, set the chicken breasts aside, and allow the vermouth cream to reduce until you have a smooth, dense consistency. Add the remaining tarragon and the lemon juice, and season with salt and pepper before returning the chicken to the sauce to reheat it briefly.

COQ AU RIESLING FOR 4

2 tbsp. olive oil

3 shallots, peeled and finely chopped

80 g (3 ounces) bacon, cut into fine strips

1 celery stalk, peeled and finely diced

6 chicken drumsticks, deboned

60 ml (¼ cup) cognac

150 g (1⅔ cups) button mushrooms, cut into thick slices

400 ml (1¾ cups) Riesling

salt and pepper

4 thyme stalks (or ½ tbsp. dried thyme)

100 ml (½ cup) cream

Although not all cooks would agree, I prefer deboned drumsticks with the skin still on for my chicken stews. This dark meat is particularly juicy and tasty, and the skin, which I remove just before serving, gives more flavor to the dish.

For the *soffritto*, fry the bacon, which you have cut into strips, in one tablespoon of oil until it is crispy, and then add the finely chopped onions and celery, and sauté over low heat for about ten minutes. In the meantime, clean the mushrooms, slice them finely, and set them aside. Add another tablespoon of oil to the pot, increase the heat a bit, and brown the drumsticks evenly, about five minutes on each side. The skin should not scorch, so you may need a bit more oil. If the drumsticks don't all fit into the pot in one layer without overlapping, work in batches. Once you are done browning the chicken, return all drumsticks to the pot, and then, in a second smaller pot, heat the cognac for about thirty seconds before lighting it with a match, flambéing it before pouring it over the chicken. Shake the stewing pot containing the drumsticks until the flame has extinguished, and then add the mushroom slices, and stir thoroughly before deglazing with the Riesling. Season with salt and pepper, add the thyme, cover the pot, and allow the chicken to braise over low heat for about thirty minutes. When the chicken is done, remove it from the pot, and keep it warm while you reduce the sauce and finish it with cream. Take the pot off the heat, return the chicken drumsticks to the sauce to reheat them, and serve—with buttered noodles or country bread.

COQ AU VIN ROUGE FOR 4

4–6 chicken drumsticks without skin, deboned

2 tbsp. olive oil

100 g (4 ounces) bacon, cubed

salt and pepper

5 pearl onions (or shallots) peeled and cut in half

15 big button mushrooms, cut in half

5 big morels, cut in half

3 tbsp. cognac

400 ml (1¾ cups) full-bodied red wine (same as for the marinade)

FOR THE MARINADE

1 bottle of full-bodied red wine

1 tbsp. dark fruit marmalade

1 small onion, finely chopped

2 celery stalks, peeled and finely chopped

1 carrot, peeled and finely chopped

4 garlic cloves, peeled and finely chopped

4 stalks of thyme (or ½ tbsp. dried thyme)

2 bay leaves

4 cloves

In contrast to the coq au Riesling in the previous recipe, the chicken in this red wine version is marinated in advance, which allows the meat itself to take on a fuller aroma. The advance preparation may seem excessive, but bear in mind, as with many meat or poultry stews, this red wine chicken becomes even more intense when reheated, so the extra work is well worth it. When choosing the wine, it is essential to remember that only good quality will produce a savory sauce, so choose a full-bodied wine that you would serve with the meal itself. It is fundamentally wrong to economize on this score; if the cost seems prohibitive, make a different dish instead. Adding marmalade (which I often substitute for sugar in my cooking) to the marinade gives the necessary sweetness to the dish.

Before beginning to cook the marinade, prepare the *mise en place*. Chop the onion, carrot, celery, garlic, and herbs very finely. Then add the wine and the marmalade to the pot first, stirring thoroughly, and then add all the other ingredients at the same time. Over medium heat, allow the liquid to come to a boil, and then reduce it by half (which will take about twenty minutes). Stay close to the stovetop, and stir the vegetables every now and then, making sure that they don't scorch. You can use the time, however, to wash the drumsticks and pat them dry, and then place them in the dish in which they will rest overnight (or for at least twelve hours) in the refrigerator. Because the marinade is meant to penetrate the meat rather than float around it, a rectangular dish with a flat bottom in which the drumsticks can lie next to each other in one layer is ideal. Once the red wine is sufficiently reduced, pour it over the drumsticks, but use a fine sieve to do so because you want only the liquid as your marinade. The vegetables and spices whose function was to flavor the wine can be stored in a separate bowl in the refrigerator as well (see the following note).

The next day, warm the olive oil in a stew pot in which the chicken fits snugly, and then fry the bacon over medium heat until it is crisp. Remove it from the pan, and set it aside. Season the drumsticks with salt and pepper, and brown them evenly, about three minutes on each side. Remove them from the pot, and set them aside with the bacon. Next, peel and cut the pearl onions in half, and clean and cut the mushrooms into bite-size pieces. Add them to the pot, and sauté them for about ten minutes, and then return the chicken to the pot, increasing the heat. In a small pot, heat the cognac, about thirty seconds, before lighting it with a match and pouring it over the chicken. Shake the pot so that the flambé can move across all the ingredients without the risk of burning your wooden spoon—or hand—were you to stir instead. Once the flame has extinguished, add the red wine, and stir briskly. After making sure that the ingredients are perfectly blended, cover the pot with the lid, and allow the chicken to braise over low heat for about an hour. Once the chicken is done, pull off the skin. If the sauce is too thin, remove the chicken from the pot, and reduce it until you have a smooth, velvety consistency before returning the chicken to the pot to reheat it. You can serve this coq au vin with buttered noodles or simply with country bread.

NOTE: If, like me, you don't like throwing any ingredients away that can be put to further use, you can make a salad with the vegetables from the marinade. Remove the bay leaves and the cloves, and cook the vegetables in broth until they are firm to the bite. Season with a shot of balsamic vinegar and salt and pepper. You can either use them warm or refrigerate them and then reheat them. In a salad bowl, toss the vegetables with lamb's lettuce, using a classic vinaigrette of olive oil, lemon juice, crushed garlic, mustard, salt, and pepper.

CHICKEN FRICASSEE FOR 4

1 L (4 cups) chicken broth

900 g (2 pounds) chicken breasts (1 big breast per person)

300 g (11 ounces) button mushrooms (or a mixture of seasonal mushrooms)

250 g (9 ounces) *petits pois* (frozen)

500 g (1 pound) fresh white asparagus   juice of 1 lemon
  (or preserved asparagus in a jar)   salt and white pepper
3 tbsp. flour   100 ml (½ cup) cream
3 tbsp. butter   1 egg yolk
100 ml (½ cup) white wine

For me, chicken fricassee, which seems to have fallen into oblivion, is the epitome of home cooking. The combination of cream, lemon, and white wine is unsurpassable in its simple perfection. From my mother, I learned how to poach the chicken pieces so that they are always juicy and tender. Because she adapted her culinary expertise to the American cooking conventions of the 1950s, she preferred using canned, or frozen, vegetables. Today, of course, the obvious choice is fresh button mushrooms, or a mixture thereof, given that these are readily available in grocery stores. It is perfectly fine, however, to use frozen *petits pois* (or other small peas). Because white asparagus is essential for this dish, I am ready to compromise on this point. If it isn't in season, use the precooked asparagus now sold in jars, but bear in mind that you only add them to the chicken fricassee once it is done. Because the asparagus are already cooked, they simply need to be heated in the warm sauce. Another option is to use thick, green asparagus. This changes the classic style of the dish, but it adds both color and texture.

Begin by heating the chicken broth. In the meantime, remove the unappetizing tendons from the chicken breast, and cut them into bite-size pieces. Clean the mushrooms, and quarter them. In a sieve, drain the frozen peas in warm water so that there is no more ice clinging to them. If you are using fresh asparagus, trim them at the bottom, peel them, and cut each stalk into three pieces (if using the green variety, trim and simply peel the bottom third before cutting them into three pieces). If you are using precooked asparagus, drain them instead, cut each into three pieces, and put them aside on a plate. Next, poach only the chicken pieces in the simmering broth for about fifteen minutes, remove them, and set them aside in a bowl. Adjust the heat so that the chicken broth stays hot but without coming to a boil again, and then poach the mushrooms along with the fresh asparagus for fifteen minutes, adding the peas to the warm broth for the last five minutes. When the poaching is done, you can turn your attention to preparing the roux.

Melt the butter in a second pot that is large enough to braise the chicken and all the vegetables afterward. Add the flour, and stir briskly until you produce a smooth paste, and then add the broth one ladle at a time. Initially, the velouté will be thin, but with time, it should become viscous and creamy. The sauce can bubble but should not go lumpy, which is why you have to stir with brio. After about twenty minutes, it should be done and you can season the velouté with white wine, lemon juice, salt, and white pepper until you have the right balance between savory and tart. Once the sauce is ready, add the poached chicken and the vegetables. If you are using pre-cooked asparagus, add them at this point. For the aromatic finish to this dish, you must enrich it with cream and egg yolk. Take the pot with the chicken fricassee off the heat. In a small bowl, whisk the egg yolk with the cream. So that the egg yolk doesn't curdle, stir one to two tablespoons of the sauce into the egg mixture, and then quickly stir this into the fricassee. Serve with boiled potatoes or country bread.

POACHED AND STEAMED

CHICKEN BREASTS POACHED IN BROTH FOR 2

1½ L (6 cups) chicken broth   2 whole chicken breasts

The following two recipes are meant to illustrate how a pot can also be used for poaching. The first recipe for preparing a juicy chicken breast is as simple as it is compelling, not least of all because it entails only one step. In a pot in which the chicken breasts fit snugly, bring the broth to a boil, and then take it off the heat. Immediately plunge the chicken breast into the hot (but no longer boiling) broth, making sure that they are completely covered with the liquid. Put the lid on the pot and allow the chicken to poach in the broth for twenty minutes. To check whether they are done, cut into the thickest part with a small paring knife. If the meat is still pink, allow it to poach another three minutes or so over very low heat. Pull off the skin before cutting the lusciously juicy chicken into pieces to be put to use in a couscous or salad or on a sandwich.

SALMON POACHED IN OIL FOR 2

about 1 L (4 cups) olive oil   fleur de sel
500 g (18 ounces) salmon fillet
without skin

This second recipe is meant to illustrate how oil can also be used for poaching. During a conference in Australia, one of the conveners showed me this less common way to poach salmon. Much later I found an explanation for this method of preparation in one of Heston Blumenthal's books. Not only does poaching salmon in hot liquid suit the fragile consistency of the fish, but it also adds a subtle flavor without overpowering the natural taste of the salmon. The salmon becomes juicy and tender, seemingly almost raw inside while falling apart perfectly at the touch of a fork. You could, of course, use water or spicy fish stock as your poaching fluid, but for a truly astonishing result, it is best to poach the salmon in olive oil. The principle is similar to the previous recipe; however, because in this case the oil must be heated to the precise degree prescribed, you will need to work with a digital thermometer. It is also essential that you buy premium quality salmon, since the flavor this dish thrives on is very subtle.

Choose a pot in which the salmon—whether in one piece or cut into several pieces—fits snugly so that, when it is completely submerged in oil, there isn't too much excess space around it. If the pot is too large, you will be wasting oil; if it is too small, the salmon won't be completely enveloped by it. At the same time, you also want to add only as much oil as it takes to cover the salmon (rather than having it swim in a pool of oil). Because you won't be adding the salmon until the oil has reached the prescribed heat yet you want to be absolutely precise, you may want to experiment regarding the right amount by testing with water first. Once you have figured out exactly how much liquid you will need, take out the salmon and pat it dry with paper towels.

Now you are ready to try it with the oil. In the pot, heat the oil over medium heat to exactly 50°C (122°F). You may need to practice a bit until you have understood how quickly the oil heats up. If you miss the right moment, take the oil off the heat and allow it to cool off. Under no circumstances should you let the oil rise above 50°C (122°F). Using a slotted spoon, carefully submerge the salmon in the heated oil, which will now begin to cool off immediately. For this reason, regulate the oil, raising it to precisely 50°C (122°F) again, and try to retain this temperature while the salmon poaches, about twenty minutes. Ultimately, it is a question of instinct and practice. Once the fish has reached 45°C (113°F) on the inside, remove it from the oil with a slotted spoon, drain it on paper towels, and cut it into slices. Sprinkle with fleur de sel or furikake rice seasoning, or drizzle with pistachio oil. Serve with soba noodles or a vegetable salad.

NOTE: Although this method of preparing poached salmon requires a lot of oil, you can, according to Heston Blumenthal, reuse it once you have removed the fish. Simply reheat the oil to 100°C (212°F), pour it through a fine-meshed sieve, and use it again for poaching another piece of salmon.

STEAMED SALMON WITH ORANGE-GINGER SAUCE FOR 4

3 tbsp. soft butter
zest and juice of 1 lemon
1 tbsp. chives, chopped
½ tsp. ginger, peeled and finely
   chopped
180 ml (⅔ cup) white wine
¼ tsp. white pepper
salt

½ orange, peeled and cut into thin
   slices
400 g (5 cups) bok choy (or napa
   cabbage)
4 salmon fillet or salmon steaks, each
   about 110 g (4 ounces) without
   skin
watercress (or chives)

The next two recipes are meant to illustrate the principle of steaming in a pot. In a kitchen bowl, mix the soft butter with the chopped lemon zest, chives, and ginger; wrap it in aluminum foil or plastic wrap, forming a roll; and then leave it in the refrigerator (or deep freezer) to become firm again. In a dish in which the salmon fits snugly, mix the wine, lemon juice, white pepper, and orange, and then place the fish into the marinade. Let it rest at room temperature for about thirty minutes. So that the salmon can really soak up the marinade, turn it over once or twice. Cover the bottom of the insert of your steamer with the washed bok choy leaves, and then place the salmon pieces on them; they should be lying close to each other but not overlapping. Cut the cold lemon-chive butter into four slices, and place on top of each of the salmon pieces before seasoning with salt and white pepper. Pour the marinade into the pot along with enough water to fill it up, and then bring the steaming liquid to a boil. Before placing the steamer insert containing the salmon on top of the pot, turn the heat down again, and then cover the steamer with a tightly fitting lid. The fish should cook over the steam for seven to ten minutes without being sprinkled with splashes from the water boiling beneath it. The salmon is done when it has turned a light-pink color on the outside while the inside is still slightly raw. Allow the salmon to rest a few moments before garnishing with watercress (or chives). Drizzle a spoonful or two of the seasoned water in which it was steamed over each piece, and serve with the steamed bok choy.

VELVET CHOCOLATE MOUSSE FOR 4

150 g (5 ounces) dark chocolate

3 eggs

1 tsp. vanilla extract

3 tsp. pear brandy (or other fruit brandy)

The Ukrainian-American woman from whom I got this recipe calls this chocolate mousse (made without cream or sugar) "velvety" because of the rich, dense consistency. I know of no other chocolate mousse that calls for such a terse list of ingredients, but perhaps no other mousse is as contingent on the superior quality of the dark chocolate used either. Don't go much above 70 percent cacao content, however, because your mousse will become dry and bitter.

First melt the chocolate pieces in a water bath, turn off the heat, and allow the chocolate to cool a bit. In the meantime, separate the egg yolks from the egg whites. Whisk the egg yolk in one bowl, and beat the egg whites in another bowl; the whites should no longer be liquid but also should not be dry. Add the whisked egg yolks to the chocolate, and stir until you have an even, dense paste. Pour in the vanilla extract and the pear brandy, and then blend thoroughly. Then add the egg whites to the chocolate as well. However, so as not to destroy the foamy, velvety consistency, you must not stir the mousse at this point; instead, carefully fold the egg whites into chocolate until they come together perfectly. Allow the mousse—divided among individual dishes or kept in one big dish—to cool for one hour in the refrigerator. You can make it a day in advance. Because of the brandy, it goes well with poached pears in the section on stewed fruit in this chapter, but you can also serve it with cream or eat it all on its own.

IN THE TAGINE

Chicken with Preserved Lemons and Olives | Lamb Meatballs with Sweet Potatoes | Seafood with Asian Aromas

This luscious stew from the Maghreb takes its name from the special pot in which it is cooked: traditionally, the tagine pot consists of an earthenware circular base with low sides and a large conical lid that sits on top while the marinated meat, poultry, fish, or vegetables both simmer in an aromatic fluid and steam in the condensation at the same time. If you don't own a tagine, you can use an ordinary stew pot even if this means that you won't be able to produce the additional steam. What is crucial, however, is that—as in any other stew—the pieces of meat fit snugly in one layer. If they lie on top of each other, some will be drowning in the braising fluid, while others will not be adequately moistened by it. If, in turn, there is excess space in the pot, the ingredients will poach rather than braise slowly.

CHICKEN WITH PRESERVED LEMONS AND OLIVES FOR 4

8 chicken drumsticks, deboned (1–2 per person)

6 tbsp. olive oil

1 preserved lemon (see "Prepared and Stored in the Refrigerator"), finely diced

175 g (1–1¼ cups) black olives, pitted and finely diced

1–2 tsp. dried thyme

1 pinch cayenne pepper

FOR THE MARINADE

1 medium onion, coarsely grated

3 garlic cloves, chopped

1 thumb-size piece of fresh ginger, peeled and grated

1 bunch cilantro, chopped

2 pinches saffron

zest and juice of 1 lemon

3–4 tbsp. olive oil

salt and pepper

The page in the cookbook on tagines by Ghillie Basan, which I use as my guide whenever I make this famous Moroccan dish, is beautifully stained, a visual record of the many times I have already prepared it. My own adaptation, however, calls for deboned chicken drumsticks rather than using whole legs with the bones. This way you have the juicy, dark chicken meat, but you don't have to bother with removing the bones while eating it.

The most time-consuming part is preparing the marinade. Grate the onion coarsely; chop the garlic, ginger, and cilantro; and zest the lemon and chop the peel as well. In a kitchen bowl, mix these aromatics with the lemon juice and the spices. Place the chicken drumsticks in a flat bowl in which they fit snugly, preferably in one layer, and pour the marinade over them. Using your hands, rub the marinade into the skin of the drumsticks, making sure they are well coated. Cover the bowl with plastic wrap, and leave the drumsticks to rest in the refrigerator for at least two hours. This means that you can't make this tagine spontaneously. The actual preparation, however, is a matter of only very few steps. Heat the olive oil in the tagine (or stew pot), and having removed the chicken pieces from the marinade, brown them evenly on all sides before adding the marinade to the tagine as well. Add just enough water so that it comes halfway up the drumsticks. Allow the braising liquid to come to a boil, then turn down the heat, cover the tagine with its elegant conical lid, and let the chicken braise for about forty-five minutes. You should, however, take the lid off now and then to turn the chicken pieces and to release some of the steam. In the meantime, chop the preserved lemon, deseed the olives, and cut them into slivers. Together with the thyme, add them to the chicken, cover the tagine once more, and continue to braise for another twenty minutes. Before serving, season with salt, black pepper, and cayenne pepper. Couscous with oven-roasted vegetables makes for a good side dish, as does country bread.

LAMB MEATBALLS WITH SWEET POTATOES FOR 4

450 g (16 ounces) ground lamb
1 onion, grated
1 bunch parsley, chopped
2 tsp. ground cinnamon
1 tsp. ground cumin
1 tsp. ground cilantro
½ tsp. cayenne pepper
3 tbsp. olive oil
1 onion, finely chopped
8 garlic cloves, peeled and finely
   chopped

1 thumb-size piece of fresh ginger,
   peeled and finely chopped
¼ tsp. chili flakes
900 g (2 pounds) sweet potatoes,
   peeled and cut into bite-size cubes
2 medium carrots, peeled and cut
   into bite-size cubes
1 preserved lemon, finely sliced
1 tbsp. turmeric
1 bunch cilantro, chopped
420 ml (1¾ cups) vegetable broth
salt and pepper

This recipe is, in fact, another spin on the idea of braised meatballs, because they are not browned first but are cooked together with the vegetables in a braising liquid flavored with Middle Eastern spices as well as in the steam produced by the conical dome of the tagine. Begin by making the meatballs. In a kitchen bowl, mix the ground meat with the onions, parsley, cinnamon, cumin, ground cilantro, and cayenne pepper, and then knead it until you have an evenly textured mixture. Season with salt and pepper. As with any other meatballs, make sure the ingredients have come together perfectly before forming little balls, about 3.5 centimeters (1¼ inches) in diameter.

For the sauce, heat oil in the tagine (or a stew pot), and then sauté the onions, garlic, ginger, and chili flakes over medium heat until the onions are soft and translucent, around seven minutes. Add the sweet potatoes together with the carrots and the preserved lemon slices, and then sauté the vegetables for about three minutes. Next, season the vegetables with turmeric, sauté another minute or so, add two-thirds of the chopped cilantro, and pour the broth over the vegetables. With a wooden spoon, mix the vegetables thoroughly to dissolve any brown, savory bits that might be clinging to the bottom of the tagine. Lower the heat, cover the tagine with its elegant dome-like lid, and allow the vegetables to braise, around twenty-five minutes, before adding the meatballs as well. Mix again thoroughly, cover the tagine once more, and braise the meatballs, another ten minutes. Remove the lid, and allow the tagine to simmer over very low heat until the sauce has become smooth and creamy. Sprinkle with the remaining chopped cilantro, and serve with couscous or country bread.

SEAFOOD WITH ASIAN AROMAS FOR 4

900 g (2 pounds) shrimps
12 scallops
juice of 1 lemon
400 ml (1¾ cups) fish stock
2 tbsp. coconut oil
2 corn cobs, shucked
2 fennel, peeled and chopped (keep
    the fennel fronds to garnish)

4 lemongrass stalks, peeled and finely
    chopped
2 tsp. green chili paste
250 ml (1 cup) coconut milk
2 bunches cilantro, chopped
salt and pepper
fish sauce
1 lime

Somewhat more unorthodox is the use of a tagine to prepare seafood flavored with Southeast Asian spices. Clean the shrimp first, remove the peel, and devein them by scraping away the black string on the inner side. Then wash them briefly, and place them in a bowl with the lemon juice. If you are using frozen shrimp, pour boiling water over them, covering them completely. After about three minutes, they will have begun to turn pink. Using a spatula, remove the shrimp, immerse them in ice-cold water to stop the cooking process, and set them aside on a plate. Wash the scallops, pat them dry with paper towels, and add them to the shrimp. Warm up the fish stock. Heat the olive oil in the tagine, and sauté the fennel, corn, and lemongrass over low heat for about ten minutes. Add the chili paste together with the warm fish stock to the pan, allow it to come to a boil for about three minutes, reduce the heat, and add the coconut milk as well as two-thirds of the chopped cilantro. Allow the sauce to simmer over low heat so that all the flavors can evolve before seasoning with fish sauce and salt and pepper to taste. Only at the very end add the shrimp and scallops to the fennel-corn mixture, cover the tagine, and allow the seafood to simmer over low heat for about five minutes. Finish the dish with a shot of lime juice, and scatter the remaining chopped cilantro over it. Sticky rice makes a perfect accompaniment, not least of all because you can roll it together and dunk it into the sauce.

STEWED AND POACHED FRUIT

Apples with Autumnal Spices | *Whole Pears in Red Wine* |
Cherries in Pinot Noir | *Peaches with Lemongrass* |
Figs in Red Wine | *Rhubarb with Oranges*

An immaculate piece of fruit is something I would always eat raw. However, whenever the silver fruit bowl on my kitchen table contains pieces that are almost too ripe, I will make stewed fruit. Pieces of fruit that are not yet completely ripe are excellent candidates for poaching. They will become softer and richer in taste. To prevent them from turning into a soft puree, however, I reduce the richly flavored poaching liquid first and then allow it to come to a boil only very briefly before turning the heat down as low as possible and putting the lid on the pot. Surrounded by the heat trapped inside the pot and enveloped by the warm syrup, the fruit is then gently poached. You could also turn the heat off completely and simply allow the pieces of fruit to infuse the hot syrup as it slowly cools off. Stewed and poached fruit will keep for several days in the refrigerator.

Unlike other ingredients that change both their consistency and shape in the course of braising, poached fruit will keep its form. The fluid in which they simmer, consisting of water, sugar, and often wine, simply glazes their surface while the spices that are cooked along with them produce a beguiling smell. Once again, a magic trick takes place in the pot. In the course of a brief hour, ordinary fruit, often eaten heedlessly between meals, transforms into a spicy delicacy. The aroma emanating from poached or stewed fruit allows our thoughts to wander into a world beyond the everyday, where, as Baudelaire in his poem "Invitation au Voyage" puts it, luxurious leisure and luscious sensuality rules. At the end of the meal, we begin to dream.

APPLES WITH AUTUMNAL SPICES FOR 4

juice of 1 lemon (or 4 tbsp. verjus)	1 cinnamon stick
7 golden delicious apples	1 tbsp. Chinese five-spice powder
3 tbsp. butter	3 tbsp. vanilla sugar

4 tbsp. ground almonds   4 tbsp. crème fraîche

3 tbsp. vanilla paste

Peel and core the apples, cut them into coarse pieces, and pour the juice of a lemon (or verjus) over them. Use your hands to make sure that each piece is completely coated with the juice. This will not only prevent them from turning brown but also draw out their tart flavor. In a pot in which the apple pieces fit snugly, melt the butter; add the cinnamon stick, the Chinese five-spice powder (a mélange of Szechuan pepper, cinnamon, star anise, fennel, and cloves), and the apple pieces; and simmer for eight minutes. Sprinkle with the vanilla sugar and the ground almonds, and then allow the apples to simmer for another ten minutes or so. In the meantime, stir the vanilla paste with the crème fraîche to serve with the warm apple compote.

WHOLE PEARS IN RED WINE FOR 4

500 ml (2¼ cups) fruity red wine   1 tonka bean (or vanilla mixed with

250 ml (1 cup) water   almond)

150 g (1¼ cup) brown sugar   juice and zest of 1 lemon

1 vanilla bean   4 pears

It is better to poach pears whole rather than cut them into separate pieces. Pour the wine, water, and sugar into a pot in which the pears fit snugly when lying on one side; if there is too much space in between them, the poaching liquid will evaporate too quickly. Over medium heat, stir the sugar until it has completely dissolved, and then bring the liquid to a boil. Lower the heat, and allow the syrup to simmer for another five minutes or so. In the meantime, cut open the vanilla bean lengthwise, scrape out the vanilla seeds, and add both to the syrup along with the tonka bean and the zest and juice of the lemon. Then while the syrup continues to gently simmer, peel the pears, but leave the stem on. Place the pears in the pot, and arrange them so that they are lying on one side, close to each other. Let the syrup come to a boil before turning the heat down as low as possible. Cover the pot, and poach the pears for forty-five minutes. However, since the spiced syrup only comes up half-way and you want all the pears to take on its red color evenly, you must turn them after twenty minutes. When they are done, remove the pears with a slotted spoon, and set them aside on a plate. Reduce the syrup to one hundred and fifty millimeters (two-thirds cup) over high heat, which will take between twenty and thirty minutes. Stir now and then so that nothing sticks to the bottom of the pan or scorches. Once you have a dense, velvety consistency, remove the vanilla and the tonka beans, and then drizzle the syrup over the poached pears. You can make them in advance and keep them, covered with plastic wrap, in the refrigerator.

CHERRIES IN PINOT NOIR FOR 4

500 ml (2 cups) Pinot Noir
100 g (½ cup) brown sugar
1 tbsp. vanilla sugar
4 tbsp. crème fraîche
1 tbsp. butter

500 g (1 pound) cherries without pits
(fresh or frozen)
1 vanilla bean (or 1 tbsp. vanilla paste)
1 pinch salt

In a pot, dissolve the sugar in the Pinot Noir, and then bring it to a boil before reducing the heat and allowing the liquid to simmer for twenty to thirty minutes until it is reduced by half. You can make the syrup in advance, keep it in the refrigerator, and reheat it later. In a pot in which the cherries fit snugly, melt the butter, and stir in the vanilla paste before adding the cherries (pits removed). Sauté them briefly before adding the Pinot Noir syrup. If you are using a vanilla bean, cut it open lengthwise, scrape out the seeds, and add both to the pot; otherwise, simply add the vanilla paste. Season with a pinch of salt, and allow the cherries to simmer over low heat for about ten minutes. In the meantime, mix the crème fraîche with one tablespoon of vanilla sugar in a small bowl, and set it aside in the refrigerator for further use. Before serving, remove the vanilla bean, divide the cherries among the individual plates, and serve with a dollop of the sweetened crème fraîche.

PEACHES WITH LEMONGRASS FOR 4

4 peaches
750 ml (3 cups) fruity red wine (such
as a Zinfandel)
100 ml (½ cup) maple syrup
2 tsp. lemongrass, peeled and
chopped
2 tsp. kaffir lime leaves, chopped
½ tsp. nutmeg, freshly grated

2 thin slices of fresh ginger
1 tsp. white peppercorns
3 cloves
2 tbsp. basil, coarsely chopped
2 tbsp. mint, coarsely chopped
fresh vervain leaves, coarsely chopped
to garnish

My answer to the sad fact that one rarely finds truly ripe peaches these days, even at the farmers' market, is to treat them as though they were tomatoes and use them in a salad. Remembering that at home we usually ate canned peaches, which my Jewish grandmother would call "*geslicete* peaches," I have begun to poach them as well. The result is magnificent, even if the syrup I make is far less sticky and sweet than the one I remember from my childhood.

Begin by blanching the peaches in boiling water for about thirty seconds, and using a slotted spoon, remove them, and drop them immediately into a bowl with ice water to stop the cooking process. When they are cold enough to handle, pull the skin off. Cut each peach in half, and take out the stone, using your fingers or a grapefruit spoon. Put the cloves and peppercorns into a spice bag; otherwise, they will penetrate into the flesh of the peaches, and you will have a hard time removing them. Add the wine, maple syrup, and the herbs and spices to a pot in which the peaches fit snugly. Stir thoroughly, bringing the poaching liquid to a boil, and then turn down the heat as far as possible. Add the peaches, cover the pot with a lid, and allow them to simmer until they are soft, about twenty minutes. Using a slotted spoon, remove the peaches, and set them aside in a shallow dish. Increase the heat, bring the flavored wine to a boil, and then reduce it by half, about twenty-five minutes. Pour the syrup through a sieve; discard the ginger, lemongrass, and herbs; and pour it over the peaches. Cover the dish tightly with plastic wrap, and allow the peaches to rest in the refrigerator for two to six hours. Bring them back to room temperature before serving, and sprinkle chopped vervain leaves over them.

FIGS IN RED WINE FOR 4

100 g (½ cup) sugar	1 tsp. cinnamon
250 ml (1 cup) water	1 orange
500 ml (2 cups) full-bodied red wine	500 g (1 pound) black figs
4 basil stalks	crème fraîche (or yogurt)

For this dessert, small, black figs work best. If you can only find big ones, you should cut them in half, especially if they aren't particularly juicy. This way, they can better absorb the syrup, and they won't dry out. Add the water, wine, sugar, basil, cinnamon, and the zest and juice of the orange to the pot in which you will be poaching the figs, and allow the liquid to simmer, about five minutes, until the sugar has completely dissolved. In the meantime, wash the figs, trim them at the bottom and the top, add them to the flavored wine, cover the pot, and, over very low heat, allow them to simmer for about thirty minutes. Remove the figs with a slotted spoon, and set them aside in a shallow bowl so they can cool. Bring the syrup to a boil, and then reduce it by half until it is dense and velvety; this should take about thirty minutes. Pour the syrup over the figs, cover them with plastic wrap, and keep them in the refrigerator for at least an hour before serving them with crème fraîche or yogurt.

RHUBARB WITH ORANGES

900 g (2 pounds) rhubarb (about 6 stalks)
750 ml (3 cups) water
400 ml (1¾ cups) honey (or maple syrup)

2 tbsp. lavender, finely chopped
zest and juice of 2 oranges
1 tsp. lemon juice
pear or apple balsamic vinegar
pistachio nuts

Begin by trimming the rhubarb at the bottom and the top, making sure to remove all the leaves as they contain toxic levels of oxalic acid. To peel the rhubarb, cut a very thin slice at one end of each stalk, just under the skin, and then pull this sliver down to remove the strings. Continue cutting very small slivers until all the strings have been removed. Cut each stalk into six-millimeter pieces; ideally, they should all be the same length so that they will cook evenly. In a pot, bring the water and the honey (or maple syrup) to a boil, lower the heat, and then add the finely chopped lavender, one teaspoon of lemon juice, and the juice and zest of the orange. Allow the poaching liquid to simmer for about ten minutes until you have a dense, viscous syrup. Poach the rhubarb until it is soft, about five minutes, and then remove it with a slotted spoon because you don't want it to cook any further while the syrup cools down. Pour the syrup into a bowl, add the rhubarb, cover it with plastic wrap, and allow the compote to rest in the refrigerator for at least an hour. To serve, drizzle a fruit balsamic vinegar over the rhubarb, and sprinkle with chopped pistachios. You can dilute the remaining syrup with water as a drink or use it to poach some more rhubarb. Because this fruit is in season only very briefly, make the best of it.

FROM THE POT INTO THE WATER BATH IN THE OVEN

Crème Brûlée with Ginger and Tonka Bean |
Crème Brûlée with Orange and Lavender Honey

Preparing something in a water bath means placing a smaller baking form into a bigger one, filled with water so that the dish is cooked not only in the heat, circulating in the oven, but also in the warm water surrounding it. Any potted cream or custard prepared in this way calls for an interaction between simmering and baking. The crème brûlée brings a third element into play. Once the flavored egg-cream mixture is done, sugar is sprinkled on top and brought in contact with an open flame so that, as it melts and burns, it produces a thin layer of caramelized sugar, which will quickly turn into a hard surface. To make sure that the flavored cream, when just set, is perfectly smooth without having dried out (or curdled), it is best to use wide porcelain ramekins that aren't deeper than 2.5 centimeters (1 inch).

When I discovered crème brûlée in France, it was primarily served in restaurants. Upon asking how one might reproduce the crispy caramelized layer on top at home, I was told that I would need a "salamander." Researching this mysterious kitchen utensil, I discovered that it consists of a round cast-iron plate attached to a long iron handle. It was called a salamander after a mythical amphibian that was supposed to be immune to fire. When it was invented in the eighteenth century, the iron plate had two small feet attached to it on which it could rest while being pushed into the hot coals or open flame. This way the cook didn't have to hold the heavy salamander while the plate was being heated. I finally found a salamander from the Victorian age in an antique shop in London, but when I told the owner that I had no gas stove, he explained that it would be of no use to me. Only an open flame would make the plate hot enough to brown the sugar on a crème brûlée. Even the broiler in my oven wouldn't do. My desire to prepare this beloved dish at home seemed almost doomed, but then, as if overnight, crème brûlée came in vogue, and suddenly blowtorches for the home cook were ubiquitous. While a cheap one would probably do just as well, I bought myself a particularly powerful, professional-quality culinary torch. I relish demonstrating it to my friends, bringing a touch of wonder woman to my kitchen, as I allow its strong flame to glide over the dish, making the sugar crystals jump before turning into liquid gold.

CRÈME BRÛLÉE WITH GINGER AND TONKA BEAN FOR 4–6

50 g (2 ounces) ginger, grated	160 ml (⅔ cup) milk
1–2 tonka beans (or vanilla mixed with almond)	1 tbsp. honey
	6 egg yolks from large eggs
360 ml (1½ cups) cream	90 g (3 ounces) sugar

Because the flavored cream must rest for at least an hour before baking, do not heat the oven immediately. For the custard, add the cream, milk, and

The dining room

honey to a small pot; grate both the ginger and the tonka bean into the cream; stir thoroughly; and over low heat, allow the cream to warm up gently without coming to a boil. Take the pot off the heat, and let the aromatics infuse the cream for at least an hour.

Heat the oven to 150°C (300°F), and reheat the flavored cream-milk mixture (but again, don't let it come to a boil). In a kitchen bowl, beat the egg yolks and sixty grams (two ounces) of sugar with a wooden spoon until they are creamy. To prevent the eggs from curdling, add a spoonful or two of the cream-milk to the egg-sugar mixture, bringing it to the same temperature. Then pour the egg-sugar mixture into the pot, and stir into the warm flavored cream thoroughly before pouring it through a sieve, or better into a measuring cup with a spout to pour from. Discard the tonka bean and the ginger, and then pour the flavored cream into the ramekins. Place these into a deep baking dish, large enough for them all to fit without touching each other. Then pour boiling water into the baking dish until it comes halfway up the ramekins. Place it into the oven, taking care that no water spills over into the cream, and bake for forty-five minutes. Remove the ramekins from the oven, and allow the cream to cool for at least fifteen minutes. It should reach room temperature before being put into the refrigerator, where it needs to rest at least six more hours or overnight. The last step involves the somewhat tricky caramelization of the sugar, of which you sprinkle about thirty grams (one ounce) over the set cream. The layer should not be too thick so that the sugar will melt immediately and form a firm crust without scorching when the blowtorch glides across the surface. The crème brûlée must be served immediately; otherwise, the sugar will begin absorbing the fluid from the custard and become soft. How much sugar you should sprinkle onto the cream, whether you should first spread it over the cream by shaking the ramekins, how close the flame of the blowtorch is allowed to come to the sugar, and how strong the flame should be are crucial details that are best tested advance. With experience comes confidence. But there is another advantage to testing as well: This way, you can enjoy this delectable dessert several days in a row.

CRÈME BRÛLÉE WITH ORANGE AND LAVENDER HONEY FOR 4–6

1 tbsp. lavender honey	zest of 2 oranges
360 ml (1½ cups) cream	6 egg yolks from large eggs
160 ml (⅔ cup) milk	1 pinch chili salt
1 vanilla bean (or 1 tbsp. vanilla paste)	90 g (3 ounces) sugar

This recipe also calls for warming the cream and milk with the aromatics—the vanilla bean and its seeds, finely chopped orange zest, lavender, and honey—in a small pot, taking it off the heat just before it comes to a boil, covering the pot, and then allowing the cream-milk mixture to rest for at least an hour so that the flavors can develop. Once the mixture has rested, turn on the oven to 150°C (300°F), and warm up the cream-milk mixture again. In a kitchen bowl, beat the egg yolks and sixty grams (two ounces) of sugar with a wooden spoon until they are creamy. As in the previous recipe, to prevent the eggs from curdling, add a spoonful or two of the warm cream-milk to the egg-sugar mixture, bringing it to the same temperature. Then pour the egg-sugar mixture into the pot. Stir the flavored cream thoroughly before pouring it through a sieve or into a measuring cup with a spout to pour from. Season the cream with a pinch of chili salt before dividing it up among the ramekins. Place these into a baking dish large enough for them to fit without touching each other, and pour in boiling water until it comes halfway up the ramekins. Place the dish into the oven, and bake for about forty-five minutes. When the cream has become firm, take the ramekins out of the water bath, and allow them to cool, at least fifteen minutes, before putting them into the refrigerator, where they should rest for at least six hours (or preferably overnight). Shortly before serving, sprinkle the remaining sugar on top of the set cream, and caramelize the sugar by letting the flame from the blowtorch slowly glide across the surface of each individual ramekin. Serve the crème brûlée immediately.

♣ 5 ♣

THE OVEN

Enveloped by Dry Heat

Roasted | En Papillote | *Under the Broiler* |
Gratins and Casseroles | *Quiches, Pies, and Cakes*

Who can resist a freshly baked loaf of bread, hot out of the oven? Even though I can't really explain why, this immediately evokes a sense of security in me. I sometimes even inhale the spicy fragrance of the dough and touch the warm crispy surface with the tip of my nose before cutting into the loaf. Indeed, far more intensively than with dishes prepared in a pan or a pot, the idea of roasting or baking something in the oven triggers images of homey comfort for me. I remember the Christmas cookies that my siblings and I always helped cut out, which allowed us to nibble at the extra bits of raw dough, even though this was strictly forbidden. I remember the baked apples for which our housekeeper, Gerti, would hollow out the core before filling them with raisins, nuts, cinnamon, and a piece of butter to sweeten the gray autumn days for us. And I remember our German adaptation of the classic mac 'n' cheese, whose threads of warm melted cheese always inspired me to form delicate figures with my fork over my plate before dipping into the baked macaroni themselves. Much like the famous madeleine in Marcel Proust's *In Search of Lost Time*, the patina of the past, which so often clings to food that is prepared in the oven, makes for an imaginary surplus value when eating them.

In essence, roasting or baking simply means that ingredients are exposed uncovered to dry heat in the oven. While roasting something means adding only very little fat or liquid to the dish, baking something may require pouring a sauce over the ingredients or placing them on a bed of dough. Whether roasted or baked, these dishes thrive on the contrast between the scrumptious crispy surface—be this the savory skin of a chicken or the melted cheese on top of a gratin—and the perfectly done juicy inside. Preparing something in the oven, one might say, is a forthright and straightforward way of cooking, because in contrast to stewing and braising in a pot, the specific traits of the ingredients are preserved. The hot air enveloping the ingredients on all sides simply draws out their distinct taste in a particularly favorable way. Given that it takes a certain amount of time for the full flavor as well as the texture of the dish to develop in the oven, this mode of cooking can be seen as a synthesis between quick frying in a pan and slow simmering in a pot. On the one hand, rather than slowly assembling layers of flavors in stages (as you would for a stew), you simply arrange a certain amount of ingredients simultaneously in a baking dish or roasting pan or place them—as is the case with a moussaka—on top of each other. On the other hand, the ingredients must be exposed to the dry heat of the oven for a sustained period of time before they are done.

It is, of course, true that many cooks use the oven to make a stew as well. I, however, prefer to distinguish between food prepared in the oven and dishes braised in a pot to draw attention to the fact that roasting and baking not only require far less elaborate preparation but, in turn, also produce a less varied and also less complex flavor. At the same time, dishes prepared in the oven—and therein lies another aspect of the imaginary surplus value—continue to function as emblems of cheerful conviviality. Nothing is more representative of the cozy gathering of family and friends as the image of a festively set table at whose center sits a roasted chicken, its crispy skin radiantly golden brown, with a variety of side dishes decoratively assembled around it. The generous gesture of inviting guests to share with each other something that has been cooked to perfection in the oven has become as much the epitome of traditional holidays as the standard of an elaborate dinner invitation.

In our home, there were many meat dishes that came out of the oven, ranging from a simple meatloaf or pork roast to the far more spectacular roast beef at Christmas or the glazed Easter ham garnished with pineapple slices and cloves. And yet, while I am not at all opposed to ordering roasted meat in a restaurant, this is something I rarely reproduce in my own kitchen. For this reason, rather than offering variations on the classic roast, in what follows, I turn to the myriad ways of cooking poultry, fish, vegetables, and fruit in the oven. Furthermore, so as to highlight the basic principle behind each of the different ways one can use the oven—roasting, baking, broiling, or *en papillote*—I have decided to treat savory and sweet dishes together.

One of the charms of all these dishes lies in the straightforward course of their preparation. And although many celebrity chefs will claim that innovation shows itself first and foremost in the art of elaborate pastry making (which is to say, even before it manifests itself in the sauté pan or the braiser), for the home cook, roasting or baking your main dish in the oven has a very simple and altogether practical side. It takes only a few simple steps to produce a vegetable quiche or a fruit tart that, with very little effort—especially if you fall back on the pre-prepared dough available in most supermarkets—will elicit a sense of satisfaction in those you have gathered around your table or simply yourself. More often than not, when I come home from work, I will go directly into my kitchen and turn on the oven, even before unpacking my bags. In the time it takes for the oven to reach the desired heat, I can assemble all the ingredients in a baking dish with fairly little effort. Once I have pushed the baking dish into the oven, I can leave them to their fate while I turn my attention to other things.

Precisely because there are only a few rules that need to be followed when it comes to roasting or baking in the oven, this is an excellent option for busy cooks. In a first step, you have to prepare what you ultimately want to bring together in the baking dish, be it the dough for a quiche, the marinade for ingredients that will be cooked in a paper wrapper or grilled under the broiler, or the sauce for a gratin or casserole. The second step concerns the actual roasting or baking, for which you simply need to keep a very close eye on the temperature of your oven, and if it gives off heat unevenly, keep turning the baking dish. Similar to stirring a stew or ragout, you will need to baste the poultry or meat now and then, as you will need to toss the vegetables you are roasting to make sure they turn crisp on all sides. Other than that, there is little else you have to do once you have placed the dish in the oven. However, as a final rule of thumb, allow poultry and meat to rest for at least fifteen minutes before carving or serving them, much as a cake—in contrast to bread—should cool before being served. And yet, even if roasting or baking in the oven entails a less complex mode of preparation than stewing or braising in a pot, there is still enough leeway for innovation when it comes to the composition of the marinade or the sauce as well as the spices and herbs. By amplifying the intrinsic taste of the ingredients used with either familiar or unexpected flavors, you can regulate how they will develop in the dry heat of the oven. Of course, you can also experiment with the selection and variety of ingredients you bring together in your baking dish.

If the idea of preparing something in the oven often recalls to my mind the kitchen of my childhood, this is in part because this thermally insulated chamber resembles a warm cave or underground chamber. While in the pot, ingredients transform, sometimes changing their shape; something is engendered in the oven. If you have a small window in the front, you can even observe the way the dish develops, but even if you don't, the fragrant heat that penetrates through the oven door into the kitchen turns baking and roasting into a corporeally experienced time of waiting and anticipating.

Many German proverbs demonstrate the extent to which this type of cooking is embedded in magical thinking. If the moment is opportune, for example, one says, "The oven is hot." A deep affinity to someone else can be expressed in German by saying, "We were baked in the same oven." And most importantly, in many old German legends, the oven is the site of confession, where the heroine will secretly bemoan sorrow and thus gain inner strength.

While in the world of fairy tales, both the good mother and the wicked witch can be found standing next to the stove, stirring either a wholesome porridge or a poisonous brew, the shape of the old-fashioned oven has tenaciously been associated with the maternal body as such. Baking is conceived as a quotidian ritual of giving birth to something. What the dish will look like has been determined in advance. In contrast to stewing or braising on the stovetop, the oven's cavern, filled with hot air, effects no fundamental transformation. Instead, it provides the protective space in which raw ingredients can transform into their cooked state; their previous shapes simply become more condensed, their original tastes more intense. Thus one might speak of an act of parturition in a culinary sense as well. Once the roasted or baked dish is ready, the cook removes it from this artificial womb and can now proudly present it to all those who have been anxiously awaiting this moment of delivery.

To my mind, however, cooking in the oven has to do with magical thinking for yet another reason. Because it is the mode of preparing food where I can intervene least, I have to blithely relinquish control over how the dish will turn out. Neither the skillful readiness that pan-frying requires nor the patient preparatory work that stewing demands is called for. Instead, serendipity reigns, because a bit of luck is always involved. The moment you close the door to your oven, you can only hope that it will neither let you down nor play tricks on you. In contrast to the stewing pot, what miscarries in the oven can only marginally be corrected. What you need for the oven isn't technical skill but rather an appeal to the force of destiny, which, as in the ancient myths, will decide whether good luck or misfortune is about to strike.

Even if you have prepared everything carefully and adjusted the heat in the oven correctly, you can never be absolutely certain that the dish will turn

A rack of knives over books

out the way you hoped. Indeed, every cook has her own story to tell about a fallen soufflé, a watery vegetable gratin, or a burnt, dried-out chocolate cake. All a crestfallen cook can do in such cases is assure her guests that this had always been the foolproof dish she could rely on. And yet, because nothing is ever certain when cooking in the oven, a clever cook is one who is prepared for all contingencies. Julia Child remains my paragon, regardless of whether she really did pick up that raw Thanksgiving turkey from the floor and put it back on the counter while the camera was rolling. Her legendary remark—remember, you're alone in the kitchen—remains my mantra. I would simply add, don't ask your guests to join you in your kitchen until the dishes you prepared have already been plated or arranged in their respective serving bowls. However, don't exclude them completely either. Cooking in the oven may be a risky business, but it is also worth presenting these dishes to your guests with panache once they are done. In contrast to the stew, whose charm resides less in its appearance than in its smell and taste, dishes that come out of the oven can have a striking effect.

In our cultural image repertoire, no figure commands this kitchen glamour show as masterfully as the elegant 1950s housewife we know from countless Hollywood films. Immaculately coiffed, her lipstick perfectly in place, a cheeky cocktail apron tied around her waist, she deftly extracts her masterpiece from the oven and, smiling radiantly, proudly presents it to the camera. She has, of course, become a cultural memory riddled with ambivalence. While *Mad Men*'s Betty Draper reenacts this cultivated guardian of the domestic hearth for a twenty-first-century audience, Matthew Weiner's television series also articulates the discomfort we have with this figure. With their resolute entrance into the workplace during the 1950s and 1960s, many women wanted to liberate themselves from precisely such a confinement to the home and kitchen. The other two female protagonists of *Mad Men*, Joan and Peggy, who begin as secretaries but advance to partner and copywriter, respectively, are both able to assert themselves in the male-dominated advertisement world of Madison Avenue. At the same time, they repeatedly despair at the double life they are compelled to lead, unable to balance their professional success with domestic bliss. Today, the home kitchen as a creative workplace for women has, once more, garnered prestige, not least of all because of ambitious and successful businesswomen such as Martha Stewart and Nigella Lawson, who celebrate themselves as domestic goddesses on television and in the publishing world. What you accomplish in the oven is once more up for praise. So you can reach for that cocktail apron again, as long as you do so with a grain of self-conscious wit.

For my own self-image as a cook, my mother's signature dish—her roasted turkey—has come to represent a happy synthesis par excellence between glamorously inhabiting my kitchen and enjoying success at work. My mother became acquainted with the cult around Thanksgiving while she was working in the State Department in Washington, DC, in the early 1950s. No holiday is, of course, as sacred as this one. Regardless of how estranged family members may be, they must come together on this day. And those who are strangers in the country or who do not have family must be included because no one is allowed to be alone on Thanksgiving. So deeply impressed was my mother with this tradition that she insisted on strictly adhering to this culinary ritual even after my parents had returned to Munich. Because neither the obligatory turkey nor sweet potatoes or cranberries was available in German supermarkets in the 1960s, my father always had to rely on friends who were stationed with the armed services in Munich to procure these ingredients for us in the Post Exchange store on the military base (which wasn't entirely legal).

The guests my mother invited, however, were almost exclusively German friends of the family for whom this festive meal was not part of a familiar tradition but rather the epitome of the new prosperity after the war. The horn of plenty that my mother always placed in the center of the table was filled with fruit and nuts, attesting to her idiosyncratic interpretation of this holiday. The turkey was served not at lunch on the last Thursday of November but rather in the evening, much as we all gathered around the table not in casual clothes but rather dressed as for the opera. And if, while preparing the dishes, my mother was still wearing her ordinary kitchen apron, just before the guest arrived, she would appear in her finest cocktail dress with sparkling costume jewelry around her neck and on her arms. In addition to the perennial cast of guests, my father would also always film my mother's strictly choreographed festive event with his Super 8 camera. The opening shots were always close-ups of the latest drawings my siblings and I had made at the Munich American Elementary School: a happy turkey with colorful feathers, a horn of plenty filled with fruit and decorated with leaves, and images of the Puritan settlers amicably sharing their first successful harvest with the indigenous population.

Inspired by this history lesson (as quaintly askew as it appears in retrospect), my siblings and I would recite poems and perform songs for the adults gathered around the dining room table. It was the only time in the year that we were indulged so much sympathetic attention. The anticipation of the actual star of the evening—the roasted turkey—meant that the adults would attend to our spectacle patiently. Indeed, it was a kind of theater within theater because in the performance that followed upon ours, the guests were allowed to play a part of their own. Each guest would carry one of the serving dishes from the kitchen into the dining room, where as an expression of collective gratitude, they would then offer this up to my father's camera before the bowls, platters, and bottles could take up their assigned place on the table. Watching our home movies, I can reconstruct the development of this staging. Over the years, the turkey became bigger and bigger, the horn of plenty more copiously filled, the wine more expensive, and the show, which we performed under the direction of my brother, Michael, more sophisticated and elaborate. Once I moved to Zürich, I also turned Thanksgiving into a festive invitation, and once—as an homage to times past—even with only candlelight as illumination.

The point of the festivities, however, was never just gratitude for the harvest of the past year in a figurative sense but also homage to my personal culinary heritage. Like no other celebration, Thanksgiving dinner can turn into the decisive "denaveling" scene between daughter and mother, a culinary cutting of the umbilical cord of sorts. In one of her cooking memoirs, M. K.

Fischer describes how she once struggled with her mother over the carving knife before the astonished eyes of the family gathered around the table. At issue was proving who the real mistress of the turkey was—and as such, also of the kitchen. For my part, I came upon a far less aggressive strategy to declare my sovereignty. My mother, who was prevented from finishing her doctoral studies in economics by the war, had come to harbor certain doubts about the domestic abilities of a daughter who had chosen the path of literature professor and author. To reassure her faith in my abilities as a cook, I decided to demonstrate to her that I not only had learned from her how to master the art of giving big dinner parties but was, in fact, able to excel in her own game. When she accepted my invitation to spend Thanksgiving with me in Zürich, I knew I had to go over the top. I not only decorated the table far more lavishly but also invited far more people than she ever would have. The menu I came up with was, of course, also far more opulent.

In my childhood home, my mother would serve as side dishes her own special stuffing, roasted sweet potatoes glazed with orange juice and brown sugar, mashed potatoes, a simple pea and carrot mélange, and canned cranberry sauce. As dessert we never had traditional pumpkin pie but rather the more idiosyncratic chocolate cream pie. After becoming professor of American studies, I became an addict of Ruth Reichel's *Gourmet* magazine and Martha Stewart's *Living* and studied their November special issues on Thanksgiving with particular care. So it wasn't particularly difficult for me to serve up reinterpretations of the traditional Thanksgiving side dishes that had emerged from the new American cuisine of the 1990s. They were already bookmarked. In addition to my mother's stuffing and sweet potatoes, my buffet included a salad of spinach, pears, and haricots verts with Riesling dressing; red cabbage with apricots in balsamic dressing; broccoli and cauliflower in a lemon, mustard, and chive butter sauce; potato and leek gratin with thyme; mashed potatoes with ginger and orange; and fennel with shallots, rosemary, and goat cheese. And the crowning finish was a pumpkin cheesecake with caramelized nuts sprinkled on top. The first comment my mother made upon entering my home, filled with the aromas of many hours of cooking, did not bode well. She noted with a certain tone of censure that it did not smell quite like a Thanksgiving feast should. Seated at my sumptuously set table, surrounded by my cheerfully expectant guests, she too began tasting the dishes so familiar to her along with my newly interpreted side dishes with a certain relish. With guarded pride, she then declared that, while everything tasted different than at her table, the meal was nevertheless exquisitely prepared. No triumph could have been more satisfying and more beautiful to a doting daughter. Her quiet praise sealed our mutual culinary acknowledgment.

♣

Sometimes preparing dishes in the oven may take more time than other methods of cooking because the hot air that is meant to envelop the ingredients on all sides warms them more slowly than water or oil in a pot or a pan would. As Molly Stevens notes, roasting involves three methods of heat transfer: "radiation, convection, and conduction." First, heat is emitted from the hot oven walls onto the surface of the ingredients that are being directly exposed to it. At the same time, the hot, dry air swirls around within the closed oven and thus transfers further heat to the dish being roasted or baked. A convection oven is particularly suitable for this method of cooking because hot, dry air that is constantly kept in motion produces consistent heat, which, in turn, browns and crisps the ingredients evenly while caramelizing the natural sugar in vegetables to perfection. Once the outer surface of the ingredients has been heated up with the help of radiation and convection, the heat then travels into the inside of the food.

Regarding the cookware, it is worth bearing in mind that the hot, dry air should swirl around the ingredients unimpeded. For this reason, it is best to choose baking dishes with sides that aren't much higher than what you are cooking. If you have little or no liquids, you can also simply place the ingredients on a baking tray lined with parchment paper or a silicone mat. As in other modes of cooking, what is crucial, however, is that the baking form you use is the right size for the way in which you want to prepare your dish. It will depend on whether you want to roast ingredients in one layer, arrange them on top of each other for a gratin, or place them on a bed of lemon slices. Whether you prefer a square or oval dish and whether this is made of cast-iron, ceramic, glass, or copper is, in turn, entirely up to your own predilection. All you do need to remember is that, depending on what your baking dish is made of, heat will be conducted differently so the cooking time may vary as well.

In fact, because everything depends on the heat level, it is important that the oven be preheated, which can take somewhere between fifteen and thirty minutes. At the same time, so as to diminish unpleasant surprises (although they can never fully be precluded), you should familiarize yourself with the way the heat is distributed in your oven, whether it spreads evenly across the entire space or tends to be more intense in certain places. Because both the cookware you use as well as the oven itself brings chance into play when cooking in the oven, the cooking time given for a particular recipe is nothing other than a suggestion: Sometimes, it may need more time, sometimes less. For this reason, it is advisable to start checking early whether a dish is already done. You can do this by inserting a cooking thermometer into the thickest part of the chicken's drumstick, pricking vegetables with a fork, opening the papillote slightly to gently test for doneness with the tip of a knife, or carefully shaking the custard that is baking in a water bath. Only such hands-on testing will allow you to determine the exact moment when you can remove your dish from the oven with utter confidence.

ROASTED

❧ POULTRY
Roasted Chicken | Poussin with Cilantro Pesto | Stuffed Quail |
My Mother's Thanksgiving Turkey

❧ FISH
Sea Bream with Tomatoes and Herbs | Trout Marinated in Miso Paste |
Sea Bass with Fennel and Potatoes

❧ VEGETABLES
Wintery Root Vegetables | Potatoes with Thyme and Truffle Oil |
Sweet Potatoes with Orange Glaze | Brussels Sprouts with Balsamic
Vinegar and Pomegranate Molasses | Asparagus with Sage |
Radicchio | Shitake Mushrooms, Roasted

❧ FRUIT
Roasted Figs as Appetizer | Roasted Figs as Dessert | Plums with
Lemon and Ginger | Apricots with Rosemary | Peaches in Port Wine

Julia Child once laconically noted that, like Gertrude Stein's roses, a roast is a roast is a roast, because each roast is pretty much prepared in the same way as any other. So as with other methods of cooking, if you understand the basic principle, you can improvise to your heart's delight. Usually, you choose a higher temperature to heat the oven and then lower the heat. Poultry—be it chicken, goose, pheasant, guinea fowl, or turkey—is usually slathered in butter or showered with oil, while vegetables are moistened with an oil-based marinade or dotted with butter. A thin layer of fat helps conduct the dry heat in the oven evenly over the surface of the ingredients. The cooking process becomes more efficient, and you get the brown, crispy crust that makes for the irresistible charm of roasted dishes. At the same time, the layer of fat makes the flavor more intense while roasting because, as the butter or oil melts, it glides smoothly over the ingredients as well. There are, of course, purists among cooks who place their bets solely on their oven's heat, but I have a different ground rule: everything that is exposed directly to the dry heat of the oven should be basted with liquid from time to time. For this reason, I add some water or wine immediately to the roasting pan. If you intend to use more broth or wine once the roasting process has begun, you should keep this liquid in a pot on the stove over low heat. This way the temperature in the oven will remain stable after each new basting.

It is also worth noting that, as a rule of thumb, the cooking time is dependent on the oven, so you should always use a meat thermometer to check the temperature of poultry before taking it out of the oven. If you have done your shopping in advance, salt the poultry a day before you roast it. If, in turn, you bought it the same day that you want to cook it, then salt it generously both in the inside cavity and all over the outer surface. By penetrating into the bird, the salt makes the meat tender, juicy and tasty. You can also stuff poultry the day before, filling the inner cavity with a bread stuffing or a mixture of fruit (lemons, oranges, plums), herbs (thyme, rosemary), or a chili pepper. You can, however, also carefully loosen the skin over the breast and the drumsticks and push herbs, garlic cut into ultrathin slivers, or even truffle slices underneath. Prepared in such a way, the bird can rest overnight in the refrigerator. It is imperative, however, that you take it out of the refrigerator at least an hour before you start roasting so that it reaches room temperature before you push it into the oven. If poultry is too cold, it will not roast evenly, and while the skin turns crisp and the outer layer becomes done, the inside will remain uncooked.

Nothing can go wrong when you roast vegetables as long as you are meticulous in your preparation. Not only do you need to wash and sometimes also peel your vegetables thoroughly, but you should also cut them into pieces that are more or less the same size. Only then will they roast evenly and all be done at the same time. You should also take care not to cut the vegetables into all-too-small or thin pieces lest they end up with overly browned wedges or slices that are dry inside. And it is worth tossing the vegetables in oil and chopped herbs and seasoning them with salt in advance. As with poultry, an outer layer of fat will make the flavor of vegetables more intense and foster caramelization, giving sweetness and texture. You should also make sure that the vegetable pieces are lying next to each other in one layer so that they brown evenly. It is always better not to crowd your baking tray so if you have too many vegetables for one baking dish, fill a second one instead and then roast both at the same time. Although, in contrast to poultry, you should not baste vegetables with liquids, it is nevertheless worth checking on them every now and then to loosen them from the bottom of the pan and push pieces from the edges into the center, all the while turning them over. This way you can be sure that they will brown evenly. And because you can't really use a thermometer to check for doneness when it comes to vegetables, all you can do is taste them on occasion.

As with vegetables, the quality of fruit you roast is not important. On the contrary, fruit that is not yet ripe enough to eat raw gains in taste and consistency if it is exposed to the dry heat in the oven. Seasoning with syrup or honey in turn is as vital as adding a few dots of butter to ennoble the dish. During roasting, the butter will melt and soak into the fruit, making the flesh more intensely sweet and concentrated in texture.

POULTRY

ROASTED CHICKEN FOR 4

1 chicken weighing 1½ to 2 kg (3–4 pounds)	about 4 tbsp. butter, at room temperature
salt and pepper	100 ml (½ cup) white wine
2–4 lemons	250 ml (1 cup) chicken broth
1 lime	1½ pounds vegetables (carrots, potatoes, parsnips, celeriac)
fresh thyme stems	1 tbsp. olive oil
3–5 garlic cloves	½ tsp. fresh thyme
1 chili pepper (fresh or dried)	½ tsp. fresh lavender

Heat the oven to 220°C (400°F). Calculate about one pound of chicken per person. So that the chicken will roast evenly, take it out of the refrigerator thirty minutes in advance, and let it rest at room temperature. Wash it on the inside and outside, and then dry it thoroughly with paper towels. You can fill the chicken either with a flavorful bread mixture (similar to the one I use for my roast turkey) or with a combination of aromatic herbs. For this, I use three peeled garlic cloves, a small bunch of fresh thyme, one chili pepper (it can be fresh or dried), and one lime. Rolling the lime across the surface of your counter will help draw out its flavor. If you want additional spice, you can cut two more garlic cloves into thin slices, pluck the thyme off a few more sprigs, and slide both under the skin of the chicken breast. But do so cautiously to make sure that the skin does not rip. In any case, slide some butter under the skin so that the breast meat can become particularly succulent.

While you can simply place the chicken directly on the baking tray, I prefer to use a bed of thick lemon slices (or thick onion slices). This not only prevents the chicken from sticking to the bottom of the pan but also lends additional flavor to both the chicken meat and the roasting juices to be used as gravy. The chicken should sit breast side up on this bed. It is best to tuck the tips of the wings under the chicken so that they don't scorch. Using kitchen twine, tie together the drumsticks over the filled cavity of the chicken. Slather the bird with butter, and don't hesitate to use your hands. Only this way can you be certain that you have spread the butter evenly over the entire outer surface, including the skin under the drumsticks and the wings. Season the chicken with salt and pepper, and then pour the white wine and broth over the bird. This liquid will lend moisture to the chicken while it is exposed to the dry heat in the oven, and you will want to use it for basting the chicken every now and then. If you have extra broth, keep it warm, and use it for basting as well.

While you could, of course, simply roast the chicken on its own, it makes sense to add a few vegetables while you are at it—I prefer a selection of carrots, potatoes, parsnips, and celeriac. Peel the vegetables, and cut them in bite-size pieces, if possible all the same size. Then toss them with olive oil, chopped thyme, rosemary, and lavender in a bowl; season with salt and pepper; and arrange them around the chicken. They can lie snugly together because, while roasting, they will shrink, lending a comforting smell and more intense flavor to the chicken as well.

After fifteen minutes, lower the temperature of the oven to 190°C (375°F), and use this opportunity to baste the chicken for the first time with the cooking juices that have collected at the bottom of the pan. Allow the chicken to roast for another hour, but baste once more after thirty minutes. The chicken is done when it has turned a golden-brown color. Before carving, let the chicken rest for fifteen minutes. This way the juices that rose to the surface during the cooking process can once more be evenly distributed over the entire chicken and stabilize the inner temperature of the bird. The meat will become more succulent but also easier to carve. Because each drop of the cooking juice is precious, take the chicken out of the roasting pan by inserting a big kitchen spoon into the opening of the cavity. This will allow you to catch any excess liquid that has been trapped inside. If the vegetables aren't ready yet, roast them a bit longer while the chicken is resting before removing them from the roasting pan. Pour the pan juices into a small pot, and over low heat, reduce them until you have a thick, rich sauce.

POUSSIN WITH CILANTRO PESTO FOR 2

2 poussin
1 lemon
2 big kaffir lime leaves (or 4 small ones)
1 thumb-size piece of fresh ginger
2 tbsp. cilantro pesto (see "Pumpkin Soup with Lime and Cilantro Pesto") or another herb pesto

2 tbsp. soy sauce
300 g (2½ cups) carrots
300 g (2½ cups) potatoes
300 g (4 cups) eggplant
2 spring onions
salt and pepper
olive oil

You could, of course, simply roast a poussin—the small chicken also called a Cornish hen—as you would any larger bird: by stuffing it with lemon and rosemary springs and moistening it with olive oil. However, these young chickens become particularly succulent if you marinade them in an herb pesto in advance. Wash the two poussins, and dry them thoroughly with paper towels first. Then fill each of them with half a lemon (best cut into quarters), a big kaffir lime leaf, and a small piece of peeled ginger. Dilute the cilantro pesto with soy sauce, and slather each poussin with this mixture. Let the poussins rest for at least three hours in the refrigerator so that they can fully absorb the flavor of the marinade.

Heat the oven to 230°C (450°F). Peel the carrots and potatoes, and cut them into bite-size pieces. Trim the eggplants on the top and the bottom, and cut them into bite-size cubes as well. Trim the spring onions at the bottom and the top as well, and cut each into three pieces. Place the vegetables into the baking dish first, drizzle with olive oil, season with salt and pepper, and roast for fifteen minutes. In the meantime, remove the poussins from the refrigerator so that they are room temperature when you place them on the bed of the slightly roasted vegetables. This not only prevents them from sticking to the bottom of the pan but also allows the flavorful juices of the small chickens to mingle with the vegetables while roasting. Before returning the roasting pan to the oven, drizzle the poussins with a bit of olive oil, and add some water to the bottom of the pan to give additional moisture to the vegetables. Take care, however, not to pour the water over the poussins, as this will wash away the marinade and ruin the crisp skin. After fifteen minutes, turn the heat down to 190°C (375°F), and use the opportunity to baste the poussins with the juice that has formed at the bottom of the pan. Roast for another forty-five minutes, basting every fifteen minutes. Before serving, let the poussins rest for ten minutes; only then will they be really succulent.

STUFFED QUAIL FOR 4–8

10 g (⅔ cup) dried porcini mushrooms	2 tbsp. cognac
	salt and pepper
6 sun-dried tomatoes	110 g (½ cup) soft goat cheese
4 garlic cloves, finely chopped	8 quail
1 medium onion, finely chopped	5 tbsp. olive oil
1 tbsp. fresh thyme	5 tbsp. soy sauce
125 g (1½ cups) button mushrooms, finely sliced	2 tbsp. honey
	white wine to deglaze
5 tbsp. butter	1 bunch cilantro, chopped

It is, of course, perfectly possible to treat quail as though they were simply another version of a small chicken and slather the quail with butter, season them with salt and pepper, and roast them in the oven in a gratin pan. In Thailand, however, I discovered how well they are suited for a far more savory treatment. So I began stuffing these delectable little birds with a somewhat more elaborate mixture, for which Southeast Asian spices and European cooking techniques are fused. If you can't find quail, you can use very small poussin. How many quail you decide to serve each of your guests may primarily be a question of your purse. Your guests will almost certainly want more than one. However, this is a dish that requires you to use your hands for dissecting the little birds, so it is not for the squeamish.

For the filling, soak the porcini and the sun-dried tomatoes in two separate bowls, in three hundred millimeters (one and one-quarter cups) hot water each. After twenty minutes, strain them, but retain the water, and then pour it through a fine-meshed sieve to remove all impurities. Chop the tomatoes and mushrooms into very delicate little cubes. In a bowl, toss them with very finely chopped garlic, finely grated onions, finely sliced mushrooms, and thyme leaves. Over medium heat, melt the butter, and sauté the mushroom-tomato mixture, about six minutes, and then, along with the cognac, pour in the liquid you have retained from soaking the mushrooms and tomatoes. Season with salt and pepper, raise the heat slightly, and continue sautéing the mushroom-tomato mixture until all the liquid has evaporated, between fifteen and thirty minutes. Allow the stuffing to cool before adding the soft goat cheese. It is best to use your hands to make sure that all the ingredients are perfectly combined.

In the meantime, heat the oven to 180°C (350°F). Wash the quail, and dry them thoroughly with kitchen towels before stuffing them with the mushroom-tomatoes-cheese mélange. Using kitchen twine, tie the little legs together over the stuffed cavity, as though to protect it, and place them on a roasting tray. For the savory sauce, which is meant to seep through the skin of the quail, making them crispy and sumptuous, mix the olive oil with soy sauce and honey. Brush each quail with this marinade until you have used it all up. The quail should roast in the oven between forty-five and sixty minutes, but they need to be basted with the marinade every ten minutes or so. They are done when the skin is golden, the flesh still somewhat pink. It is best to prick the thickest part of the breast with a cooking needle (or metal skewer) to see if the meat is firm and the juices run clear. Remove the quail from the oven, and then let them rest while you deglaze the roasting pan with white wine, making sure to dissolve all the flavory bits that have formed on the bottom, and then reduce the liquid until you have a richly dense sauce. Before serving, sprinkle the quail with chopped cilantro.

MY MOTHER'S THANKSGIVING TURKEY FOR 6–10

As I learned from my prudent mother, a successful Thanksgiving meal must be strategically planned down to the smallest detail and then meticulously executed over several days. So in late summer, I already note in my calendar when I will have to order the turkey from the butcher as well as the vegetables from the produce market. I also have a very precise work schedule that I adhere to year in, year out. In it, I count backward from the actual Thanksgiving dinner to determine when I must begin with my preparations and in which sequence they are to be executed. Two days in advance, so as to get in the mood, I will make my cranberry sauce and season the bread for my stuffing. One day in advance, I turn my attention to the turkey, first giving it a bath and then seasoning it generously with salt before letting it rest in the refrigerator. I also make the stuffing in advance so that the flavors can develop. On the day of the feast, I count backward to determine when the turkey must be put into the oven as well as the sequence in which to prepare all the side dishes so that they will all be done at the same time. This meticulous planning primarily pertains to the time it will take to roast the turkey, which, in turn, depends on the size of the bird. If—as was the case in my childhood home—you are also making glazed sweet potatoes (or other roasted vegetable dishes), you can remove the turkey from the oven for an hour or two to make room for the other dishes you want to prepare and then continue roasting the turkey later on. While it rests, you can then reheat the side dishes in the oven. As for roasting the turkey, be fastidious about basting it every half hour, and use this opportunity to rotate the roasting pan, should your oven be erratic (as mine is) when it comes to the way it disperses heat.

I have kept the instructions my mother typed up for me on her Smith-Corona typewriter when, during my undergraduate studies at Radcliffe College, I couldn't fly home across the Atlantic for the Thanksgiving holidays. Typical of the linguistic code-switching that was standard in our home, she not only moved between English and German but also added the corrections to her typos in handwriting. The detailed directions are probably only comprehensible to someone who has already been initiated into her way of preparing a turkey. But what moves me most about this cherished set of papers is her own appeal to the goddess Fortuna. Following upon her description of how to slide the turkey into the oven, she offers the following piece of advice: "Cross yourself and pray that it will turn out well***." For her, roasting a turkey remained a culinary adventure whose outcome she couldn't control, even after all the years she had perfected this dish. On the last page of her instructions, by way of closure, she writes in capital letters, "LOTS OF LOVE AND GOOD LUCK." This salutation, which countless mothers have sent to their children, wishing them success as they embark on their own cooking exploits, has not lost its charm, even while the patina of yellowed paper it was written on attests to the sustainability of her advice.

CRANBERRY SAUCE

250 g (2 cups) shallots
1 tbsp. butter

200 g (1 cup) sugar
125 ml (½ cup) white wine vinegar

250 ml (1 cup) dry white wine
½ tsp. salt
225 g (1½ cups) dried cherries

300 g (1 cup) fresh cranberries
125 ml (½ cup) water

Blanch the shallots in boiling water, about a minute. Drain them in a sieve, and peel and quarter them. Melt the butter in a pot large enough to hold the cranberries, and then, over medium heat, sauté the shallots briefly, about three minutes, before adding the sugar and just one tablespoon of vinegar. Stir the sugar thoroughly with the buttery onions, and simmer until they have taken on a caramel color. Add the remaining vinegar, white wine, and salt to the pot, and bring to a boil, about one minute. Finally, add the dried cherries, and after covering the pot, allow the sauce to simmer over low heat for about forty-five minutes. The shallots should become soft before you add the fresh cranberries along with the water. Don't put the lid back on the pot; the cranberries should simmer very gently, for about ten minutes uncovered. At this point, you should stay close to the stovetop because you want to stir the sauce from time to time. It is done when the cranberries have begun to burst. Let the cranberry sauce cool off before putting it into the refrigerator. It will keep for at least two weeks in an airtight jar, and it goes beautifully with all cold cuts as well as cheese.

THE STUFFING

500 g (1 pound) old toast bread
4–6 tbsp. poultry spice
2 L (8 cups) chicken broth
1 medium carrot
1 medium onion
3 bay leaves
3 parsley roots
1 small celeriac

2 leeks
1 bunch parsley, chopped
2 handfuls celery leaves
240 g (2 cups) onions, finely chopped
230 g (1 cup) butter
3 eggs
salt and pepper

For the stuffing my mother created, you have to work in two stages. The toasted bread should no longer be fresh, so it is best to buy a loaf several days in advance. Two days before the actual Thanksgiving meal, cut the bread into small cubes, and generously season with poultry spice, making sure (by using your hands to toss the bread) that each individual piece is coated. If you can't find this spice blend, you can make your own, using dried sage and marjoram, coriander powder, pepper, allspice, and celery seeds. Cover the bowl of seasoned bread cubes with a kitchen towel, and let them rest in a dry place for two days.

Although you could, in a pinch, make the stuffing the day of the Thanksgiving meal, it is far more relaxing to make it the evening before. Bring the chicken broth to a boil in a big pot. Make more than you need because you can use it to baste the turkey the next day. Peel and coarsely chop all the vegetables, and then add to the hot broth in the following order: the carrots, onions, bay leaves, and parsley root (my mother's secret ingredient). While these ingredients cook, you can peel and chop the celeriac, clean and slice the leeks, and then add them to the pot as well. The vegetables should cook for about forty minutes; however, start removing individual pieces once they are soft enough, and begin chopping them very finely, except for the onions and the bay leaves, which you should discard. As you chop the cooked vegetables, add them to the bread cubes. Use the time it takes for the vegetables to cook to chop the remaining onions, the parsley, and the leaves from the celery stalks, and then add them to the seasoned bread cubes as well. The celery stalks themselves could be served with a dip as an appetizer or kept for another day.

Melt the butter in a small pot, whisk together the eggs in a small bowl, and then add them to the seasoned bread cubes. The order in which the cooked vegetables, butter, and eggs, as well as the finely chopped onions and herbs, are added to the seasoned bread cubes is irrelevant. However, it is crucial that after mixing everything together thoroughly with your own hands, the mixture is both moist and firm. If the stuffing looks dry, add some of the broth. Season with salt and pepper, and allow the stuffing to rest in a bowl covered with a kitchen towel overnight. Taste the next morning, and season with more salt and pepper if necessary. Keep the remaining broth in the refrigerator to use for basting the turkey the next day.

THE TURKEY ITSELF

1 turkey, 500 g (1 pound) per person	white wine
1 chicken drumstick with skin on	broth (as used for the stuffing)
butter, at room temperature	sherry
salt and pepper	lemon juice

My mother always calculated one pound of turkey per person. She also advised me to order a turkey with as much skin from the neck still on, because this made it easier to stuff the cavity. If your butcher, however, doesn't comply with this wish, there is a trick you can fall back on. You will simply need to procure some extra skin to cover the opening of the turkey and stitch this additional piece of skin on to the turkey. This is why I recommend buying an extra drumstick that has a particularly large piece of skin still attached. Having removed the skin, you can always cook the meat and bones with the vegetables to give more flavor to the broth or keep it in the refrigerator for another purpose.

On the evening before Thanksgiving, wash the turkey, and if it still contains innards, remove these. My mother would have cooked them with the vegetables for the stuffing as well, but since I am not fond of the flavor of giblets, I deviate from her instructions on this one point and simply discard them. Using paper towels, first dry the turkey both inside and outside meticulously and then generously salt it, again both inside and outside. Like the stuffing, the turkey should rest overnight, covered with a kitchen towel, but in the fridge.

On the day of the Thanksgiving feast, heat the oven to 230°C (450°F). My mother always calculated thirty minutes of roasting time per pound of turkey. If, however, it was heavier than six kilograms (twelve pounds), she went down to twenty minutes per pound. Before stuffing the turkey, generously season once more with salt, and then add the stuffing both in the large cavity through the neck and in the smaller opening in the back of the bird. Using kitchen twine, sew together both openings. If the turkey you bought has little skin left around the neck, use the extra skin from the drumstick to sew an extra patch over the opening. I like my turkey to be stuffed to the full, and this patch will prevent the stuffing from falling out during roasting. If, however, you have no desire or inclination to busy yourself with needle and thread in the kitchen, you can also simply wrap any excess stuffing you have in aluminum foil and roast it in the oven on one of the other racks. Truss the turkey by sewing the wings (unless these have been removed as well) with some twine onto each side of the breast. Cross the legs together, and tie them with twine as well.

A turkey lifter will, of course, make it easier to remove the turkey from the roasting pan once it is done. If you don't have such a metal rack, simply place the turkey breast side up on the bottom of the pan (or on a bed of lemon slices), and to ensure that it will brown evenly, make sure it is as balanced as possible. Slather the turkey with the soft butter, for which it is best to use your hands to make sure that you have also covered the area beneath the legs and wings. Pour the white wine over the turkey, and don't forget to also add broth to the bottom of the pan so that, from the start, there is liquid to moisten the turkey from below, and then cover it with aluminum foil. You should use large pieces both lengthwise and crosswise so that, when you lift the foil to baste the turkey, it won't rip. Although it may seem a bit extravagant, baste the turkey every thirty minutes, first using the remaining broth (kept warm on the stovetop) and then the liquid that has collected on the bottom of the roasting pan. One hour before the turkey is done, remove the aluminum foil, and lower the heat to 180°C (350°F). As with any other roasted fowl or meat, check the temperature with a thermometer before removing the turkey from the oven; it should be 83°C (181°F). Before carving, allow the turkey to rest thirty minutes. In the meantime, place the roasting pan on the stovetop, and over low heat, dissolve all the savory bits that have formed on the bottom in the liquid until you have a smooth sauce. Season with sherry (or port wine), lemon juice, and maybe even a splash of cream. Because you have been using wine and broth to baste the turkey, the sauce should be salty enough.

FISH

SEA BREAM WITH TOMATOES AND HERBS FOR 2

2 whole sea bream (or Chilean sea bass / black cod)	1 handful cherry tomatoes
	1 tbsp. fresh rosemary, finely chopped
4 fresh thyme stems	1 tbsp. fresh thyme leaves
4 fresh rosemary sprigs	4 tbsp. olive oil
1 lemon, cut into slices	4 tbsp. white wine (or Noilly Prat)
1 chili pepper, halved and deseeded	juice of 1 lemon
1 garlic clove, peeled and cut in half	salt and pepper

Heat the oven to 180°C (350°F). Crucial when roasting a whole fish is that you fill it with aromatics. Before doing so, wash the two fish, and pat each dry with paper towels. Place two sprigs of thyme, two sprigs of rosemary, and two lemon slices into the cavity of each of the sea bream, along with half of the chili pepper and half of the garlic clove. Place both fish into a gratin dish, arrange cherry tomatoes around them, and sprinkle with the chopped thyme and rosemary. Pour the olive oil, white wine, and the juice of the second lemon over the fish, season with salt and pepper, and then place the gratin dish into the oven. The sea bream should roast for thirty minutes or until they are soft. Lentil salad goes beautifully with roasted fish, but so does sauerkraut.

TROUT MARINATED IN MISO PASTE FOR 2

2 trout	8 big fresh mint leaves
2 tbsp. olive oil	16 fresh tarragon leaves
1 tbsp. yellow miso paste	8 big fresh basil leaves
1 tbsp. mirin	salt and pepper
1 tbsp. soy sauce	

Heat the oven to 220°C (425°F). A whole piece of fish, coated with an aromatic marinade, can also be steamed in the oven first, before exposing it directly to the dry, hot air to finish the roasting process. Wash the two trout, pat dry with paper towels, and then place them into a baking dish into which they fit snugly. Whisk together the olive oil with the miso paste, mirin, and soy sauce, and pour the marinade over the fish. Then, using your hands, turn both trout over a couple of times to make sure they are perfectly coated. Cut all the herbs into fine strips, sprinkle them over the two trout, and then seal the baking dish with aluminum foil before roasting the fish for six minutes. Reduce the heat to 190°C (375°F). Using tongs, carefully turn the two trout around, and—without covering the baking dish with the foil again—allow them to roast another ten to twelve minutes in the oven. Spread some of the thickened miso marinade that has collected on the bottom of the baking dish over the trout before serving.

SEA BASS WITH FENNEL AND POTATOES FOR 2

1 medium fennel	salt and pepper
½ pound waxy potatoes	1 small chili pepper
4 tbsp. olive oil	1 small sea bass, about 500 g
1 lemon	(1 pound)
1 tbsp. pomegranate molasses	

Heat the oven to 200°C (400°F). A further way to prepare fish in the oven is to place it on a bed of vegetables. These will, however, require more roasting time and should therefore go into the oven alone first. For the vegetable bed, cut off the stalks and the bottom of the fennel. Pluck the fine green fronds, clean the stalks, and in two separate dishes, place both to one side. Peel the fennel, and cut it into one-centimeter-thick (one-half-inch-thick) slices. Peel the potatoes, and cut them in half. Zest and then juice half a lemon, and put each aside in a separate dish. Cut the other half of the lemon into fine slices, and put aside as well. In a bowl large enough to marinate the vegetables, mix three tablespoons of olive oil with the lemon juice and the pomegranate molasses, and season with salt and pepper. Cut the fennel and the potatoes in half, and toss them with the dressing until they are thoroughly coated.

In a baking dish—ideally an oval one that corresponds to the shape of the sea bass—spread out the marinated vegetables, season with salt and pepper, and roast for thirty minutes. After fifteen minutes, turn the individual pieces so that they can brown on both sides. In the meantime, wash the fish, pat it dry, and then, with a sharp knife, make three incisions on both sides before seasoning inside and out with salt and pepper. Fill the cavity of the sea bass with the fennel fronds, the finely chopped fennel stalks, the chili pepper, and the lemon slices. After thirty minutes, take the baking dish out of the oven, place the sea bass on the bed of roasted fennel and potatoes, drizzle with another tablespoon of olive oil, sprinkle the lemon zest on top, and return the baking dish to the oven. Roast the sea bass for about thirty minutes. When the incisions on the surface of the fish have taken on an opaque white color, or alternatively when the dorsal fin can be pulled off without any resistance, then the fish is done. Remove the filling, fillet the sea bass, and serve with the roasted vegetables.

VEGETABLES

WINTERY ROOT VEGETABLES FOR 4–6

1 turnip	2 tsp. dried thyme
1 celeriac	4 garlic cloves, peeled and finely
3 small parsnips	chopped
2 big carrots	salt and pepper
1 butternut squash	4 tbsp. olive oil
4 rosemary sprigs, finely chopped	1 tbsp. pomegranate molasses
(about 3 tbsp.)	white balsamic vinegar (or lime juice)
1 tsp. fennel seeds, finely chopped	

I think of this as a master recipe because you can pretty much roast any vegetables in this way. As simple as the preparation is, it concentrates the aroma of the root vegetables, drawing out their natural sweetness. The result is an enticing contrast between caramelized skin and soft, succulent inside.

Heat the oven to 200°C (400°F). The preliminary preparation of the vegetables does require a bit of effort, since you need to peel them and remove the seeds from the pumpkin as well. If there isn't enough room for the vegetables in one baking dish, use two rather than have them lying on top of each other. Chop the rosemary and the fennel seeds very finely, add the thyme, and then mix all the herbs together thoroughly. Scatter the herbs over the vegetables evenly, strew the finely chopped garlic over the vegetables as well, and then splash with olive oil and pomegranate molasses. Toss the vegetable pieces to make sure they are well coated, season with salt and pepper, and push the baking dish into the oven. The root vegetables should roast for one and a half hours or until they are soft and have taken on a golden color. The vegetables are done when you can break them up easily with a fork. Season to taste with salt and a shot of white balsamic vinegar to give a touch of acidity to the dish.

POTATOES WITH THYME AND TRUFFLE OIL FOR 2–4

1 kg (2.2 pounds) waxy potatoes

60 ml (¼ cup) olive oil

2 tsp. fresh thyme (or 1 tsp. dried thyme), chopped

truffle oil for drizzling

salt and pepper

Heat the oven to 200°C (400°F). This recipe is a variation on roasted vegetables, reduced to the essence of one ingredient—the potato. Because the charm of this dish thrives on the contrast between a crispy surface and a succulent interior, it is best to use larger potatoes that can be cut into bite-size pieces of roughly the same size. And because they should really be crunchy, the roasting time depends on the way your oven dispenses heat. So you may need to check on them, and if they aren't done yet, roast them a bit longer.

In a kitchen bowl, toss the peeled and cubed potatoes with the olive oil and chopped herbs, using your hands to make sure that all the bite-size pieces are thoroughly coated. Spread the potatoes out on a rectangular baking dish, making sure that they are in one single layer. Drizzle with truffle oil, season once more with salt and pepper, and put the dish into the oven. After thirty minutes, turn each of the potato pieces individually, and then roast for another thirty minutes. The extra bit of effort is worth it, because only then will they really turn crisp on the other side as well. Season with salt and pepper before serving.

SWEET POTATOES WITH ORANGE GLAZE FOR 4

4 medium sweet potatoes	100 g (½ cup) brown sugar
juice and zest of 2 oranges	(or molasses)
3 tbsp. melted butter	½ tsp. salt
	¼ tsp. nutmeg

My mother adapted this recipe from a bilingual cookbook that not only sought to explain American home cooking to the German housewife after the Second World War but at the same time promised to disclose to her American counterpart the secrets of European cuisines. Because in our home this dish was only served at Thanksgiving, for the longest time I associated it exclusively with this festive meal. Only recently have I begun to cook these glazed sweet potatoes without a turkey to accompany them. They are certainly rich and sumptuous enough to hold their own or to be eaten with other more frugal side dishes.

Heat the oven to 190°C (375°F). In the meantime, cook the unpeeled sweet potatoes in salt water until they are soft, around thirty minutes. They are done when the skin begins to crack. Drain the potatoes, peel them, cut them in half, and place them into a buttered baking dish. Use the time while the sweet potatoes are still cooking to prepare the sauce. In a small pot, melt the butter over low heat, add the orange juice and orange zest, stir thoroughly, and then, while the sauce simmers, add the brown sugar, salt, and grated nutmeg. Continue stirring to make sure that the sugar really dissolves into the buttery juice. Allow the sauce to come to a boil, and then, turning down the heat, simmer for another five minutes, until you have a rich, dense glaze. Pour this over the sweet potatoes, cover the baking dish with aluminum foil, and roast for forty-five minutes. Remove the tin foil, and using a big silver spoon, baste the potatoes with the juices once more, Then roast for another fifteen minutes or so uncovered.

NOTE: It is not strictly speaking necessary to cook the sweet potatoes in advance, as I discovered when, running out of time, I once skipped that step. Simply peel the sweet potatoes and trim them at the bottom and top before cutting them in half or into quarters. Then continue as in the recipe above by placing them into a buttered baking dish, pouring the butter, orange juice, and sugar sauce over them and covering the dish with aluminum foil.

BRUSSELS SPROUTS WITH BALSAMIC VINEGAR
AND POMEGRANATE MOLASSES FOR 2–3

500 g (1 pound) Brussels sprouts	1 garlic clove, peeled and finely
1 pear (or apple)	chopped
60 ml (¼ cup) balsamic vinegar	2 tbsp. olive oil
60 ml (¼ cup) pomegranate molasses	½ tsp. chili salt

For the longest time, I either cooked Brussels sprouts in salt water or cut them into thin slices, seared these in a pan, and then simmered the slivers in broth. Then I began to see recipes that suggested roasting Brussels sprouts in the oven. As with other vegetables, you could easily just toss them in olive oil and season with salt and pepper. However, the following recipe showcases the bitter flavor of the Brussels sprouts themselves by contrasting it with the sweetness of the pears and the acidity of the balsamic vinegar.

Heat the oven to 200°C (400°F). Trim the Brussels sprouts at the bottom, and peel away any ugly outer leaves. Depending on their size, either halve or quarter them. Peel the pear (which can be replaced with an apple), deseed it, and grate it coarsely. In a kitchen bowl that is large enough to hold all the sprouts, whisk together the balsamic vinegar, pomegranate molasses, olive oil, garlic, and chili salt (which can be replaced with salt and a pinch of chili flakes), and then add the Brussels sprouts and the pear slivers. Mix thoroughly with the marinade, and then spread the Brussels sprouts in one layer on a baking tray. Roast for forty minutes. Check on them from time to time, however, and turn them over so that they caramelize evenly.

ASPARAGUS WITH SAGE FOR 4

2 pounds green asparagus	1½ tbsp. olive oil
1 tbsp. fresh sage, chopped	salt

AS TOPPING

250 ml (1 cup) oil for deep-frying	30 medium-size fresh sage leaves

VINAIGRETTE

zest and juice of 1 lemon	4 tbsp. olive oil
1 tbsp. fresh sage, chopped	Parmesan, grated
salt and pepper	

In a cookbook by Jerry Traunfeld, whose Herbfarm restaurant specializes in unusual herbal combinations, I discovered to my great surprise that you can oven roast green asparagus, although very thin asparagus is not suitable because it will shrivel. The dry heat in the oven makes the sweet aroma of green asparagus more intense, and at the same time—as with Brussels sprouts—reduces the water content. This way the asparagus can absorb the vinaigrette better. What makes this recipe so irresistible is the unusual combination of green asparagus and pan-fried sage, which one would normally serve with ravioli.

Heat the oven to 230°C (450°F). While you don't need to peel green asparagus (in contrast to white asparagus), you should trim each stem at the bottom. In a kitchen bowl that is large enough to hold the asparagus, whisk together the olive oil and chopped sage, and season with salt. Toss the asparagus, using your hands to make sure that each of the stems is evenly coated, and then place them in one layer on a silicon mat (or a baking tray lined with parchment). Roast for four to eight minutes in the preheated oven until they are soft and have begun to brown. The roasting time will, however, depend on the thickness of the asparagus. Before dressing the asparagus with the vinaigrette, allow them to cool, as this may make them soggy.

To fry the sage leaves, heat the rapeseed oil in a deep pan until it is very hot. Choose large sage leaves because they will shrink while frying. A bit of skill is called for at this point. Fry the sage leaves for only ten seconds on one side, turn them over, and fry them a few seconds longer on the other side. Using small tongs, remove them from the pan, and drain them on paper towels to remove all excess oil. While frying they should not turn brown and definitely not scorch, which is why you may need to work in stages and add only as many sage leaves at a time to the pan as can swim in the hot oil. As they cool, they will become crisp. Place them to one side while you make the dressing. For this, whisk together the chopped sage with the olive oil and the juice and zest of one lemon, and season with salt and pepper. Then you can assemble the dish. Place the asparagus on a serving dish, and then begin by drizzling the vinaigrette over the stems. Grate the Parmesan on top, and finish by scattering with the fried sage bits.

RADICCHIO FOR 2

1 head radicchio rosso di Treviso
   (or Belgian endives)
1 tbsp. olive oil
salt and pepper

thick balsamic vinegar
1 tbsp. roasted pine nuts
75 g (⅓ cup) creamy chèvre

Radicchio, cherished for its tart, bitter flavor, also roasts beautifully. As it wilts, it becomes juicy and the outer leaves caramelize. I find this dish makes a perfect appetizer for when you want something simple but sumptuous.

Heat the oven to 190°C (375°F). Trim the radicchio at the bottom, and cut it in half. Place it, cut side down, into a baking dish, drizzle with olive oil, season with salt and pepper, and then roast for ten minutes. Open the oven door briefly, and pull out the oven rack just far enough so you can turn the radicchio halves. Roast for another ten minutes so that the other side can become crisp as well. In the meantime, fry the pine nuts over medium heat in a dry pan on the stovetop. Once the radicchio is done, drizzle with balsamic vinegar, and scatter the pine nuts as well as the chèvre on top of the hot salad leaves, where it will immediately begin to melt.

SHITAKE MUSHROOMS, ROASTED FOR 2–3

16 big shitake mushrooms
2–3 tbsp. olive oil
salt and pepper

thick balsamic vinegar
1 bunch cilantro

Heat the oven to 220°C (425°F). Fresh shitake mushrooms, which are particularly suited for roasting, can substitute for a meat dish, serve as one of several vegetable dishes, or accompany a cheese platter. Trim the mushrooms at the bottom, and then clean them with a piece of moist paper towel before placing them into a roasting pan. Drizzle with two or three tablespoons of olive oil, season with salt and pepper, and then roast them for ten minutes in the oven. They should have a tart flavor and be soft and slightly browned. Immediately after removing the mushrooms from the oven, drizzle them with balsamic vinegar and sprinkle with finely chopped cilantro.

NOTE: It is worth experimenting with other vegetables as well. You can roast not only pumpkin, cut in halves, slices, or cubed, but also broccoli, cut up into florets. All it takes is some olive oil, salt and pepper, and a handful of chopped herbs. When roasted on a silicon mat (or a parchment-lined baking tray), eggplants, cut in half or into slices, drizzled with olive oil, and dusted with salt, require far less fat than if you were to fry them in a pan.

FRUIT

ROASTED FIGS AS APPETIZER FOR 4

8 ripe figs   40 g (⅓ cup) Parmesan, grated
125 g (¾ cup) mascarpone   balsamic vinegar

Heat the oven to 200°C (400°F). Here are two recipes for roasting figs in the oven, one savory, the other sweet. While the principle is the same, the difference depends on the aromatic spicing added. In both cases you need really ripe, luscious figs, because they will be exposed to the dry heat of the oven only very briefly.

As in many of the previous recipes, you could simply place the figs out on a silicon mat or a baking tray lined with paper. I, however, prefer using a small gratin dish large enough to hold all the figs without them touching each other. Twist off the stem at the top of each fig, cut them in half, and then place them, cut side up, in a gratin form. Mix together the mascarpone and the finely grated Parmesan until you have a smooth cream, and then scoop a teaspoon or so of this mixture onto each fig half. The cut surface of the fruit should be covered. Don't worry if some of the cream overflows, as it will collect at the bottom of the gratin dish. Drizzle each of the fig halves with balsamic vinegar, and roast in the oven for eight minutes. In a perfect world, the Parmesan-mascarpone bonnets will remain intact, crowning the warm figs that are still firm to the bite. However, if the cream begins to run down the sides, rest assured that it has absolutely no effect on the taste.

ROASTED FIGS AS DESSERT FOR 4

8 ripe figs   2 tbsp. funny honey
125 g (¾ cup) mascarpone   zest and juice of 1 orange
1 tsp. ground cinnamon   30 g (¼ cup) pistachios, chopped

Heat the oven to 200°C (400°F). For this recipe you also need figs of excellent quality—neither too ripe nor too dry. Twist the stem off each fig, and then cut a cross into them, without, however, severing them at the bottom. Rather than a quartered fig, you want a fig that opens like a flower blossom because it is still held together at the bottom. In a kitchen bowl, whisk together the mascarpone with the cinnamon, honey, and the zest of the orange. Spoon a bit more than a teaspoon of the spiced mascarpone into each of the figs and then press them around this filling. You will, of course, not be able to close them completely, but that is the point. Place the filled figs, standing next to each other, into a baking dish, sprinkle with the chopped pistachios, and then pour the orange juice over them. Roast the figs for fifteen to twenty-five minutes in the oven until they have become soft and have begun to collapse, projecting like small islands out of a mascarpone-orange sea.

PLUMS WITH LEMON AND GINGER FOR 4

500 g (1 pound) plums
butter, at room temperature
2 tsp. vanilla paste (or seeds from
   1 vanilla bean)
2 tbsp. brown sugar

zest of 1 lemon, finely chopped
1½ tsp. fresh ginger, finely grated
juice of 1 lemon
3–4 tbsp. rum

Nothing is easier than roasting fruit in the oven. All you need is to come up with a creative combination of spices and liquids to add flavor, and under no circumstance should you leave out the butter. Exposed to the dry heat of the oven, the butter will melt into the meat of the fruit and, while combining with it, intensify the aroma. The following three recipes offer variations on this theme.

Heat the oven to 220°C (425°F). Pit the plums, and cut them in half. Spread the plums over the bottom of a gratin dish (or baking dish), cut side up. If you have chosen a round dish, arrange them in a circle, beginning with the outer edge and working your way inward until you have a rosette of plums at the center. Whisk the vanilla paste (or the seeds of a vanilla pod) with the sugar, lemon zest, and grated ginger into a smooth paste. Because you will also be using the ginger juice, it is best to grate rather than chop the ginger. Begin by drizzling the lemon juice and rum (which can be replaced by port wine) over the plums, and then scoop a spoonful of the vanilla-sugar-ginger paste into the center of each plum. Finally, don't forget to dot the plums with bits of butter before pushing the dish into the oven and roasting for fifteen minutes. Halfway through, check up on the plums, and baste them with the juice that has collected at the bottom of the pan.

APRICOTS WITH ROSEMARY FOR 4

500 g (1 pound) apricots
butter, at room temperature
3 dates (preferably the large and
   particularly succulent Medjoul),
   cut into fine strips

1 tbsp. fresh rosemary
2 tbsp. sugar

Heat the oven to 200°C (400°F). Begin by cutting the apricots in half and taking out the pits. Place them, cut side up, in a gratin dish (or baking dish). Pit the dates, and cut them into very fine strips. Chop the rosemary very finely. Fill each apricot half with slivers of dates, then sprinkle sugar and the chopped rosemary over them. Finally, generously dot each apricot with butter, and make sure none is left out. The butter will make them tastier. Roast the apricots for twenty minutes.

NOTE: Rather than filling the apricots with dates, you can also pour orange juice over them before sprinkling them with rosemary and—this is really obligatory—dotting them with butter.

PEACHES IN PORT WINE FOR 4

4 big peaches

2 tbsp. orange marmalade (or another light fruit marmalade)

2 tbsp. sweet port wine

juice and zest of 1 lemon

4 kaffir lime leaves, very finely chopped

sugar

butter, at room temperature

Heat the oven to 200°C (400°F). Peel the peaches, cut them in half, and remove the pit. Place them, cut side up, in a baking dish. In a small bowl, whisk together the orange marmalade, port wine, finely chopped kaffir lime leaves, and the juice and zest of the lemons. Distribute this sauce over the peach halves, sprinkle with sugar, and dot with butter before roasting the fruit for thirty to forty-five minutes in the oven. To make sure that they become soft and succulent, baste the peaches at least once with the juice that has collected at the bottom of the baking dish.

EN PAPILLOTE

Monkfish with Leeks and Noilly Prat | Sea Bass with Asian Flavors | Fresh Porcini Mushrooms with Herbs | Chicken Breasts with Tomatoes | Chicken Breasts with Dried Porcini Mushrooms | Apple, Quince, and Dried Dates

To roast something *en papillote* in the oven means enclosing ingredients in a parchment paper wrapper cut to size. The French expression recalls not only the paper in which one used to wrap candy but also a butterfly. In the dry heat of the oven, the liquid turns to steam, and the butter melts so that you have a mixture of braising, steaming, and roasting. The ingredients attain a fluffy lightness, and when you open the small parcel, the dish appears like an aperçu that has just fluttered onto the kitchen table from the oven. When it comes to presentation, to roast *en papillote* is, thus, a thoroughly dramatic event. As you open the parcel, allowing the steam to escape, your guests will look on in eager expectation as to what is about to unfold. At the same time, roasting *en papillote* is a very practical way for preparing fish, poultry, vegetables, and even fruit, because you can have the little parcels ready in advance. And if you find folding the parchment paper too tedious, you can also use aluminum foil. Either way, the ingredients, moistened with liquid and dotted with butter, must be sealed perfectly so that no steam can escape. Only then will the aromas and juices develop to perfection.

A bit of finger dexterity is merely required when it comes to assembling the parcels themselves. Cut the parchment paper (or the aluminum foil) into squares, roughly twenty-five centimeters (nine and a half inches) on each side. Fold each square in half to produce a seam in the middle, and then reopen the paper. It is up to you whether you prefer working from the top to the bottom or from the right to the left. In either case, place the seasoned ingredients just on top of (or to the right of) the center seam. Don't add the liquid just yet. Fold the lower (or left) part of the paper over the ingredients so that it is now flush with the other side. To close the parcel, take the farthest end of one side (at this point still open), and begin folding it toward the center, twisting and rolling to produce a thick, airtight seam. Do the same from the other side. Either the package can be lying on one side as you work or you can let it stand upright along the center fold so that you are twisting your way up to the top. Don't make the wrapper too tight, however, as you need space for the steam to expand. In the end, you should have a twisted package with a small opening on top. Only then pour the liquid over the ingredients, and dot these with butter. Finally, seal the parcel completely, making sure that there are really no apertures of any kind along its seam. If all else fails, use a stapler or paper clips.

MONKFISH WITH LEEKS AND NOILLY PRAT FOR 4

2 leeks, cut into very fine slices
1 tbsp. olive oil
4 pieces of monkfish, about 200 g
(7 ounces) per person

1 garlic clove, peeled and cut into
very fine slices
butter for brushing onto the papillote
4 tbsp. crème fraîche

8 tbsp. Noilly Prat   salt and pepper
4 tbsp. fresh basil (or tarragon), cut
    into fine strips

To roast monkfish *en papillote* is both simple, because you can prepare every-thing in advance, and a particularly healthy mode of preparing pieces of fish that are fairly firm. In principle, nothing can really go wrong, because you can always seal the parcel again if need be after testing for doneness. You should, however, check in on your parcel earlier rather than later to prevent the fish from becoming too dry. Given that the technique is always the same, you can experiment with the type of fish as well as the herbs and spices you use to add more flavor. Noilly Prat can be replaced with sherry, verjus, or any fruit grappa, the crème fraîche with double cream or sour cream.

    Heat the oven to 200°C (400°F). Sauté the finely sliced leek in olive oil over medium heat, about five minutes. The leek slices should be soft but firm to the bite and not yet brown. In the meantime, peel the garlic clove, and cut it into very fine slivers. Cut the basil into fine strips as well. Cut the parchment paper into four squares, about twenty-five centimeters (nine and a half inches) on each side. Fold each square in half to produce a seam in the middle, and then reopen the paper. Use the butter to grease the wrap-per, primarily along the center fold. Wash the fish, and pat it dry thoroughly with paper towels. Then place each piece just above the center fold onto the upper half of the parchment paper. With a sharp knife, make four or five cuts into the fish, and then tuck a garlic sliver and some basil strips into each of these incisions. Season with salt and pepper, place the sautéed leeks on top, and then close the package from both ends, twisting and turning the parch-ment paper toward the center—as previously described—until you have only a small opening on top. Whisk together the crème fraîche and the Noilly Prat, and pour this creamy sauce over the four pieces of monkfish. Close the parcels carefully, making sure there are no apertures of any kind along the twisted seam; otherwise, the steam can escape, and with it the flavor and juiciness of the fish itself. Roast the parcels on a baking tray for twenty to twenty-five minutes. To serve, carefully remove the fish from the parchment wrapper, and then pour the hot, creamy sauce that has developed inside the parcel over it.

NOTE: If rather than a firm white type of fish, you have chosen salmon, it will require far less time to roast *en papillote*, only some ten minutes.

SEA BASS WITH ASIAN FLAVORS FOR 4

4 spring onions	zest and juice of 1 lemon
1 big bunch cilantro	4 tbsp. butter
4 sea bass fillet, 160 g (6 ounces) per	1 tsp. ginger juice
person	3 tbsp. sesame oil
salt and white pepper	5 tbsp. soy sauce

Heat the oven to 220°C (425°F), and cut the parchment paper into four squares, about twenty-five centimeters (nine and a half inches) on each side. Fold each square in half to produce a seam in the middle, and then reopen the paper. The Asian-inspired marinade in this recipe requires a bit more preparatory effort. Slice the white part of the spring onions very finely, and put them aside in a bowl. Slice the green stem very finely, and put it aside in a second bowl (you will use these to garnish the finished dish). Wash the cilantro, dry it with paper towels, pluck the leaves, and roughly chop them. Retain the cilantro stems because, together with the spring onions, they will serve as the bed for the fish fillet. Wash the sea bass, pat each fillet dry thoroughly with paper towels, and then season both sides with white pepper and salt. Begin assembling the paper wrappers by dividing the cilantro stems and the spring onions among the four parchment squares, placing them along the center fold of each, and then set the sea bass fillet on top. Sprinkle each piece of fish with lemon zest, and dot with butter, and then begin closing the package by twisting and turning the parchment paper toward the center—as described earlier—until you have only a small opening on top.

For the marinade, mix together the lemon juice, ginger juice, sesame oil, and soy sauce. Divide this sauce among the four parcels, and then close them, making sure there are no apertures of any kind along the twisted seam. Set the parcels on a baking tray, and roast for ten to fifteen minutes. It is, however, worth opening one of the parcels after ten minutes to see whether the fish is already done. You don't want it to dry out. And since you don't want a drop of the sumptuous roasting liquid to spill, carefully remove the sea bass fillet from each parcel with a slotted spoon once they are cooked. Discard the cilantro stem and the spring onion rings. To serve, pour the sauce over each of the sea bass fillet, and then scatter the chopped cilantro as well as the green part of the spring onions over them.

FRESH PORCINI MUSHROOMS WITH HERBS FOR 4

400 g (14 ounces) fresh porcini	olive oil
mushrooms	1½ tbsp. fresh mint, chopped

1½ tbsp. fresh basil, chopped

2 garlic cloves, peeled and cut into fine slices

chili salt

salt and pepper

1 lemon, quartered

butter

You can also roast almost any mushrooms *en papillote*. In Japanese cooking, enoki mushrooms are often cooked in a marinade consisting of yellow miso paste, mirin, and soy sauce. The following Italian version is far more modest in flavor, but it can take on an Asian note if you replace the mint and basil with three tablespoons of shiso leaves.

Heat the oven to 220°C (425°F). Clean the mushrooms with a moistened paper towel, and then cut away all dark, rough bits. Slice them lengthwise, about one centimeter (one-half inch) thick. If you end up with uneven pieces, this doesn't matter. Cut the parchment paper into four squares, about twenty-five centimeters (nine and a half inches) on each side. Fold each square in half to produce a seam in the middle, and then reopen the paper. Brush the paper with olive oil, especially along the center fold. Place the porcini slices just above the center fold, divide the finely sliced garlic as well as the chopped herbs among the four parcels, and then season each with pepper and chili salt (or salt and cayenne pepper). Begin closing the package by twisting and turning the parchment paper toward the center—as described earlier—until you have only a small opening on top. Squeeze the juice of a quarter lemon into each parcel, dot with butter, cut the lemon quarters into slices, and divide these among the parcels as well. You can now close the parcels completely, making sure there are no apertures of any kind along the twisted seam. Set the parcels on a baking tray, and roast for fifteen minutes. Before serving, season the mushrooms to taste with a bit more salt.

CHICKEN BREASTS WITH TOMATOES FOR 4

4 chicken breasts without skin

salt and pepper

1 tbsp. fresh rosemary (or thyme)

4 garlic cloves, peeled and cut into very thin slices

2 tbsp. olive oil

400 g (14 ounces) cherry tomatoes

2 tbsp. soy sauce

4 tsp. butter

In one of his cookbooks, Peter Gordon, a true master of fusion cooking, suggests roasting chicken breasts *en papillote* as you would fish fillet. This has become one of my favorite ways of preparing chicken breasts not only because they always become juicy and tender but also because, as they cook inside the sealed wrapper, they absorb the aroma of the tomatoes to perfection.

Heat the oven to 200°C (400°F). Cut the parchment paper into four squares, about twenty-five centimeters (nine and a half inches) on each side. Fold each square in half to produce a seam in the middle, and then reopen the paper. As with any fish fillet, wash the chicken breasts, pat them dry thoroughly with paper towels, season with salt and pepper, and then place each breast along the center fold onto the top part of each of the paper squares. Fold the lower part of the paper over each chicken breasts so that it is now flush with the other side, and then begin closing the package by twisting and turning the parchment paper toward the center—as described earlier—until you have only a small opening on top through which to pour the tomato sauce over the chicken breasts just before roasting them.

To make the tomato sauce, heat the olive oil over medium heat, and then sauté the finely sliced garlic as well as the chopped rosemary (or thyme), about one minute. The garlic may turn golden but should not scorch. Add the cherry tomatoes to the pot, and sauté them until their skin begins to burst. Season with soy sauce and black pepper. Divide the tomato sauce among the four parcels, and add a dollop of butter to each before closing them, making sure there are no apertures of any kind along the twisted seam. Place the parcels on a baking tray, and roast in the oven, about twenty minutes. Just before the time is up, open one of the parcels carefully, and cut into the thickest part of the chicken breast to check for doneness. In contrast to fish made *en papillote*, chicken, like all other meat, should rest a few minutes before serving. Therefore, after removing the parcels from the oven, open them a bit, but wait some five minutes or so before plating the chicken breasts and the tomato sauce.

CHICKEN BREASTS WITH DRIED
PORCINI MUSHROOMS FOR 4

30 g (1 ounce) dried porcini mushrooms	2 garlic cloves, peeled and finely chopped
100 ml (½ cup) hot water	3 tsp. fresh thyme
2 tbsp. butter	4 tbsp. port wine (or sweet sherry)
2 tbsp. olive oil	cayenne pepper
4 chicken breasts without skin	1–2 tbsp. soy sauce
1 onion, peeled and finely chopped	4 tsp. butter

Heat the oven to 200°C (400°F). Once I discovered how fantastically simple and yet deeply satisfying it is to roast chicken breasts *en papillote*, I began experimenting with other sauces. For this version, soak the porcini mushrooms in one hundred milliliters (one-half cup) of hot water, drain them in a sieve, but retain the soaking liquid in a bowl, to be used later for the sauce. This means that you must not only rinse the soaked porcini thoroughly to make sure that no grit is still clinging to them but also pour the soaking liquid through a sieve lined with paper towels to remove all impurities from it. For the sauce, sauté the chopped onions in one and a half tablespoons of butter over medium heat for about seven minutes. Add the finely chopped garlic, and continue sautéing for another minute before adding the chopped porcini along with the thyme. Sauté the mushrooms for another five minutes, then add four tablespoons of the soaking water as well as the port wine to the pan, and continue to sauté until the liquid has evaporated. You want to end up with a creamy mélange in which the individual mushrooms have almost dissolved, so add more of the soaking water if necessary. Finish by seasoning the mushroom sauce with a shot of soy sauce and cayenne pepper.

To assemble the parcels, proceed, as in the previous recipes, by cutting the parchment paper into squares, about twenty-five centimeters (nine and a half inches) on each side, folding each square in half to produce a center seam and then opening them again. Wash the chicken breasts, and pat them dry thoroughly with paper towels. Season with salt and pepper, and place them along the center fold onto the upper part of each paper. Begin closing each parcel by twisting and turning the parchment paper toward the center until you have only a small opening on top. Divide the mushroom mixture among the four parcels, add the obligatory dollop of butter, and then close them completely. Roast them for about twenty minutes. Because the chicken must rest before being served, remove the parcels from the oven, but open them only slightly, and wait at least five minutes before plating the chicken and mushroom sauce.

APPLE, QUINCE, AND DRIED DATES FOR 2–4

2 tbsp. dried cherries	5 dried dates, cut into slices
125 ml (½ cup) port wine	35 g (¼ cup) pecan nuts, broken into
1 apple, peeled, deseeded, and cut	pieces
into slices	2 tbsp. pomegranate molasses
1 quince, peeled, deseeded, and cut	butter
into slices	dried goji berries

Fruit also roasts astonishingly well *en papillote*. The selection of fruit is up to you. You can also replace the port wine with sherry or grappa. It makes sense, however, to combine different textures, which is why, for this recipe, I chose soft cherries, firm quince, smooth figs, and juicy apples.

Heat the oven to 200°C (400°F). In a small pot, warm the port wine, remove it from the heat, stir in the dried cherries, and allow them to soak for thirty minutes. In the meantime, peel the apple and the quince, and cut both into thin slices, around one centimeter (one-half inch). Finely slice the dates as well. Drain the cherries, but retain the port wine in a separate bowl, and mix it with the pomegranate molasses. This will serve as the stewing liquid. To assemble the parcels, proceed, as in the previous recipes, by cutting the parchment paper into squares, about twenty-five centimeters (nine and a half inches) on each side, folding each square in half to produce a center seam and then opening them again. Divide the fruit, nuts, and goji berries among the four parcels, and then begin closing each by twisting and turning the parchment paper toward the center until you have only a small opening on top. Pour some of the port wine and pomegranate molasses dressing into each parcel, add a dollop of butter to each, and then close the parcels completely, making sure that there are no openings along the twisted paper seam. Place the parcels on a baking tray, and roast for twenty-five minutes. You can serve them with sweetened yogurt or vanilla-seasoned crème fraîche as a dessert. These roasted fruits also make a superb accompaniment for soft cheeses. You can keep them in an airtight jar in the refrigerator for at least a week.

UNDER THE BROILER

Teriyaki-Marinated Salmon | *Teriyaki-Marinated Chicken Legs* |
Spicy Sweet Potatoes

If you want a bit more crust on your roasted vegetables, you can briefly expose them to the intense heat of the broiler in the oven. You can also make use of this concentrated heat to prepare fish or chicken drumsticks. If you have marinated them in advance, they will quickly develop an aromatic crust. As is the case with anything you prepare in the oven, it is important that the broiler be really hot before placing your roasting dish on an oven rack, placed on the highest possible position, about six centimeters (two and a half inches) beneath the heating coil. In contrast to roasting, it is worth keeping an eye on how the dish is developing under the broiler, as it is often only a matter of seconds for the ingredients to scorch or dry out.

TERIYAKI-MARINATED SALMON FOR 4

4 salmon fillets (without skin)   chives

MARINADE

4 tbsp. soy sauce   1 tsp. palm sugar
4 tbsp. sake   1 tsp. ginger, grated
4 tbsp. mirin   2 garlic cloves, pressed

It takes amazingly little time to prepare this broiled salmon, which makes it a perfect dish for the time-pressed cook. You simply mustn't forget to marinate the salmon in advance.

In a small bowl, mix together the soy sauce, sake, mirin, sugar, ginger, and garlic. Put the salmon fillet (which could be replaced with cod or tuna) into a flat dish just large enough so that they lie snugly next to each other. Pour the marinade on top, and using your hands, make sure that each of the pieces of fish is thoroughly coated. They should rest for at least two hours in the refrigerator. After one hour, however, turn the fish to ensure that it absorbs the marinade evenly.

Heat the broiler to the highest possible setting for ten minutes, and place not only the oven rack but also the baking dish as close as possible beneath the heating coil (about six centimeters or two and a half inches) so that it can become hot as well. Remove the fish from the refrigerator. After the ten minutes are up, remove the baking dish from the oven, and place it on the stovetop. Shaking off any excess marinade, place the salmon in the hot baking dish. It will begin to sizzle immediately, indicating that the cooking process has already begun. Return the baking dish to the broiler. Delia Smith, from whom I have adopted this recipe, insists that timing is of the essence at this point. The salmon is to be exposed to the intense heat of the broiler for exactly six minutes. That also gives you just enough time to bring the marinade to a boil in a small pot and reduce it to about a third. It should have a syrupy consistency. Once the six minutes are up, remove the salmon from the oven. To serve, pour some of the reduced marinade over each piece, and sprinkle with chive snippets.

TERIYAKI-MARINATED CHICKEN LEGS FOR 4

8 deboned chicken drumsticks   125 ml (½ cup) teriyaki sauce
1 tbsp. sesame seeds

MARINADE

60 ml (¼ cup) soy sauce   2 garlic cloves, chopped or pressed
2 tbsp. palm sugar (or brown sugar)   1 tsp. tarragon, chopped
2 tbsp. dried sherry   1 tsp. ginger, finely grated
2 tbsp. apple balsamic vinegar   ½ tsp. chili flakes

Teriyaki sauce is based on a mixture of equal amounts of soy sauce, sake, and mirin. In this recipe, a few more aromas are added to produce a balance between salty, sour, sweet, spicy, and umami, which is so typical for all Southeast Asian cuisine. In a small pot, bring all the ingredients for the marinade to a boil, turn down the heat, and continue simmering until the sugar has completely dissolved. Because this sauce will keep in the refrigerator in an airtight jar for at least a week, it is worth making extra to use as a salad dressing or as a dressing for roasted vegetables.

The chicken drumsticks—which I prefer with skin on but deboned—are prepared in a similar way to the salmon. In a flat dish just large enough for them to fit snugly, allow them to absorb the marinade, at least thirty minutes (and up to four hours). It is worth taking them out of the refrigerator at least once and turning the drumsticks so that they can absorb the marinade evenly. Heat the broiler to the highest possible setting for ten minutes. In the meantime, remove the drumsticks from the marinade, and then place them, skin side down, in a gratin dish, where they fit snugly without overlapping. Discard the marinade. Place the drumsticks for eight to ten minutes under the broiler, and then flip them over, and broil them for another eight minutes. Remove the gratin dish from the oven, cut into the thickest part of one of the drumsticks to check for doneness, and then sprinkle all four with sesame seeds. Return the gratin dish to the oven, and broil for another one to two minutes. At this point, they should have taken on a golden-brown color. Don't expose them to the intense heat of the broiler much longer or they will scorch.

SPICY SWEET POTATOES FOR 4

900 g (1.1 pounds) large sweet   125 ml (½ cup) soy sauce
  potatoes   60 ml (¼ cup) mirin

60 ml (¼ cup) vegetable broth
1 tbsp. ginger, peeled and finely grated

2 big kaffir lime leaves, very finely chopped
1 pinch chili flakes
white pepper

Because I find the idea of broiling ingredients that have absorbed a spicy marinade so appealing, I looked for a way to cook sweet potatoes in the same way not only to draw out the sweetness of this vegetable but also to pair it with a pungent flavor.

Heat the broiler to the highest possible setting for ten minutes. In the meantime, peel the sweet potatoes, and cut them into thumb-size rounds. If you have fairly small sweet potatoes, it is best to simply cut them in half. If the slices are too small, they will dry up. Cook the sweet potatoes in salt water for eight to ten minutes. They should be soft enough that you can prick them with a fork, but they should not be falling apart. Drain them in a sieve, and allow them to cool.

While the sweet potatoes are cooking, prepare the sauce. In a small pot, bring the soy sauce, mirin, chicken broth, grated ginger, finely chopped kaffir lime leaves, chili flakes, and pepper to a boil, then turn down the heat, and continue simmering the marinade until it is reduced by half. Since this will take about fifteen minutes, the sweet potatoes and the sauce should be ready at the same time. Place the sweet potatoes in one layer into a gratin form so that they are lying snugly next to each other, and then pour the marinade over them. Broil them for six minutes. If you want a more intensely flavored dish, turn off the broiler, but allow the sweet potatoes to cool in the oven. As the heat slowly decreases, they will continue cooking, fully absorbing the marinade. You may simply need to reheat them briefly.

GRATINS AND CASSEROLES

Potato Gratin | *Potato, Celeriac, and Leek Gratin* | *Belgian Endives, Pumpkin, and Bacon Gratin* | *Chard and Fennel Gratin* | *Eastern Promises Moussaka* | *Zucchini and Eggplant Casserole with Ragù alla Bolognese* | *Pear and Apple Crumble with Dried Cherries*

Since the strategic foundation for a gratin is starch, one usually associates this dish with potatoes. However, parsnips can also be used because their high starch content will help thicken the sauce and give a smooth, rich consistency to the gratin. In fact, many root vegetables—such as celeriac, kohlrabi, red turnips—as well as the ordinary carrot and even red beets can be turned into a gratin. You can either place them in one layer in a baking dish and scatter herbs, cheese, spices, and nuts on top or add broth or cream before exposing them to the dry heat in the oven. However, you can also work with contrasts and supplement the starch content of potatoes or parsnips by adding other vegetables. For herbs, it is better to choose more robust varieties such as thyme, sage, rosemary, or lavender. The more delicate basil, tarragon, or parsley is better suited for garnishing the dish in the end.

What distinguishes a casserole from a gratin is whether you use eggs in the sauce or only cheese. If you want a more savory flavor, you can also assemble a casserole dish in several layers and bring ham, bacon, or—as is the case in a moussaka—meat ragout into play. For a more flavorful crust, you can also scatter bread crumbs and butter over a gratin or a casserole, and then put it under the broiler for a few minutes. The success of this otherwise foolproof method of cooking depends solely on choosing a baking dish large enough to fit all the ingredients so that the ragout and sauce do not spill over. It also helps to cut the vegetables into pieces that are roughly the same size so that they cook evenly. However, for a potato gratin—the pièce de résistance of a classic French festive meal—the potato slices must have exactly the same thickness. If this is a dish you want to make often, investing in a mandolin or a potato slicer may be worth your while.

POTATO GRATIN FOR 4–6

1 kg (2.2 pounds) waxy potatoes	salt and white pepper
½ L (2 cups) milk	100 g (1 cup) Gruyère, freshly grated
200 g (1 cup) crème fraîche (or double crème de Gruyère)	nutmeg to grate
2 tbsp. butter	1 garlic clove, peeled and cut in half

In his cookbooks, Joel Robuchon, who offers different variations of this classic French potato dish, calls this one "le gratin des gratin" because it is the most sophisticated of them all.

Heat the oven to 180°C (350°F). In the meantime, peel the potatoes, wash them thoroughly, pat them dry, and cut them into thin slices (three to four millimeters / one-eighth inch). Because they should really all be the same width, it is best to use a slicer of some kind. It is just as crucial that, before you proceed, you once more pat all the sliced potatoes with paper towels

Flowers from the market in my kitchen

so that there is no moisture clinging to them. They must be absolutely dry. In a pot large enough to hold all the potato slices, bring the milk to a boil, and then immediately add one tablespoon of butter, the crème fraîche, and eighty grams (three-fourths cup) of grated Gruyère. Stir vigorously until you have a dense, creamy sauce. Season with salt, pepper, and a pinch of fresh nutmeg. Place the potato slices into the pot, and then using a wooden spoon, fold them into the sauce, and allow them to simmer over low heat for about twenty minutes. You will need to stay close to the stovetop so that you can keep stirring the potatoes, and it is worth tasting the sauce now and then to check for seasoning.

Use this cooking time to prepare the gratin dish. Begin by greasing it with one tablespoon of butter and then seasoning it with garlic. This may seem like a waste of time, but Robuchon is quite insistent on this point. If you rub the bottom of the gratin dish vigorously and thoroughly with a garlic clove, it will dissolve into the butter, and its flavor will be absorbed by the grease and thus impregnate the dish completely. During the baking process, the garlic flavor will permeate the potatoes and the sauce and, in so doing, endow them with precisely the flavor that makes this particular gratin so special. Pour the potato-cream mélange into the gratin dish. Using a spatula, level the surface of the gratin, and then sprinkle with the remaining Gruyère. Dot with butter, and bake for forty-five to sixty minutes, or until the potatoes are soft and the sauce has become richly dense. You may need to lower the heat toward the end of the cooking time. If the gratin browns too quickly, you can also cover it with aluminum foil.

POTATO, CELERIAC, AND LEEK GRATIN FOR 4–6

4 tbsp. olive oil	500 g (4 cups) celeriac
6 big waxy potatoes, about 1 kg	2 leeks
(2.2 pounds)	chili salt and cayenne pepper
200 g (2 cups) feta	300 ml (1¼ cup) vegetable broth
2 handfuls fresh sage leave	butter

Heat the oven to 180°C (350°F). While you are waiting for the oven to get hot, peel the potatoes, wash them, and pat them dry with paper towels before cutting them into five-millimeter (one-fourth-inch) slices. Peel the celeriac, and cut it into five-millimeter slices as well. Because the potatoes and the celeriac should be the same width, it is worth using a slicer with an adjustable blade. Wash the leeks thoroughly, and cut them into thin slices. Once the vegetables are ready, grease the gratin dish with two tablespoons of olive oil, and then cover the bottom with potato slices. They should be in one layer, but they may overlap. Sprinkle half of the crumbled feta over the potato slices as well as half of the sage, cut into fine strips, and season with chili salt (or salt and chili flakes) and pepper. Cover the feta with a layer of celeriac slices, then a layer of leek rings, and then sprinkle the remaining feta and sage over the dish. The remaining potato slices will serve as the top layer of the gratin. Pour the broth (rather than milk, which is ordinarily used in a gratin) over it, season once more with chili salt and pepper, and then cover the dish tightly with aluminum foil. Bake the gratin for one and a half hours in the oven. When it is ready, remove the foil, dot with butter, and then place the gratin dish under the broiler for about ten minutes so that the top layer can brown and become lusciously crispy.

BELGIAN ENDIVES, PUMPKIN, AND BACON GRATIN FOR 2–3

200 ml (1 cup) cream	400 g (14 ounces) pumpkin
1 garlic clove, pressed	600 g (21 ounces) Belgian endives
1 tsp. celery salt	80 g (3 ounces) bacon
1 tbsp. thyme	salt and white pepper
40 g (⅓ cup) Gruyère, grated	30 g (1 cup) panko (or bread crumbs)
30 g (⅓ cup) Parmesan, grated	2 tbsp. butter

Heat the oven to 180°C (350°F). Start by preparing the sauce. In a small pot, heat the cream together with the pressed garlic, salt, and thyme. Over low heat, allow it to simmer for about ten minutes so that the cream can fully absorb the garlic flavor. Although you should stir it now and then to make sure that the cream does not stick to the bottom of the pot, you can use this time to prepare the other ingredients for the gratin. Grate the Gruyère and Parmesan into a bowl, and mix these two cheeses together. Peel the pumpkin, deseed it, and cut it into thick slices, about one centimeter (one-half inch). Trim the Belgian endives at the bottom, and remove any outer leaves that have brown spots on them. If you have small endives, cut them in half; if they are big and plump, quarter them. Put the pumpkin slices in one layer on the bottom of the gratin dish, and then cover them with the Belgian endives. In a small pan, fry the bacon until it is crisp, drain it on paper towels to remove any excess fat, crumble the bacon slices, and sprinkle these savory bits over the vegetables. Once the cream and garlic sauce is ready, season with salt and pepper, and pour it over the vegetables, making sure that they are evenly coated with the liquid. Using a spatula, level the gratin, and then sprinkle enough panko on top to cover the surface completely. Finally, scatter the grated Parmesan and Gruyère over the gratin, making sure that the cheese is evenly distributed over the surface as well. Dot with butter before putting the gratin dish into the oven, and then bake the gratin for forty minutes. The crust should be golden and crisp, the inside soft and juicy.

CHARD AND FENNEL GRATIN FOR 2

butter	2 fennel
250 ml (1 cup) milk	2 tsp. flour
1 bay leaf	2 tsp. butter
1 tonka bean (or vanilla mixed with almond)	100 g (1 cup) Gruyère, grated
	salt and white pepper
6 black peppercorns	1 pinch nutmeg
250 g (9 ounces) Swiss chard	30 g (⅓ cup) Parmesan, grated

Heat the oven to 190°C (375°F). This dish is somewhat more elaborate to prepare because you have to make a béchamel sauce and poach the vegetables in advance. At the same time, it demonstrates how you can experiment with different sauces.

Begin by generously greasing a gratin dish with butter. In a small pot, heat the milk together with the peppercorns, bay leaf, and the tonka bean, making sure that it never actually comes to a boil. Remove the milk from the heat, and allow the spices to infuse the liquid for about ten minutes. In the meantime, prepare the vegetables. Cut the Swiss chard into coarse strips. Trim the base of the fennel, peel the thick outer leaves of the bulb, remove the inside stem, and then cut the fennel into coarse slices. Blanch the fennel for two minutes in boiling water, then add the Swiss chard as well, and continue parboiling both for another five minutes. Place the vegetables into a sieve under cold water to stop the cooking process, and drain them.

To make the béchamel, melt the butter in a small pot, add the flour, and stir vigorously until you have a golden-brown paste: your roux. Because of the spices (which you can discard), pour the warm milk through a sieve, and then add it, one spoonful at a time, to the roux. Over low heat, allow the sauce to simmer about fifteen minutes, and keep stirring until you have a dense, creamy consistency. Fold in the grated Gruyère, and then season with freshly grated nutmeg, salt, and white pepper. Arrange the poached vegetables in the gratin dish first, then pour the béchamel sauce over the vegetables. Mix thoroughly, and finish by sprinkling the grated Parmesan on top. Bake about twenty minutes in the oven until golden brown.

EASTERN PROMISES MOUSSAKA FOR 6–8

2 kg (4 pounds) eggplant
salt

rapeseed oil for frying

THE BATTER

3 eggs
9 tbsp. flour

½ L (2 cups) milk

THE FILLING

300 g (11 ounces) onions
3 garlic cloves, pressed
1 kg (2.2 pounds) ground lamb
1 tbsp. Lebanese seven-spice mixture
   (or ¼ tsp. grated nutmeg, ¼ tbsp.
   paprika, ¼ tbsp. ground

cinnamon, ¼ tbsp. ground cumin,
¼ tbsp. allspice)
1 tbsp. herbes de Provence
salt and pepper
1 bunch parsley, chopped

FOR THE SAUCE

6 eggs
¼ L (1 cup) cream
¼ L (1 cup) milk

1 pinch nutmeg
100 g (1 cup) Parmesan, grated

Heat the oven to 180°C (350°F). Gordana, the mother of my friend Mic, showed me how to make a moussaka without béchamel sauce and feta. We came up with the name because this reinterpretation of the classic Greek dish was designed by her relatives in Belgrade, so it is a fusion of Eastern Europe and the Mediterranean. I find this variation compelling because the coated eggplant slices that replace the bread crumbs in the Greek original make for a much lighter and yet equally rich casserole. In my own version, however, the promise of a touch of the East also refers to the Middle Eastern spices I use to flavor the ground meat.

As is so often the case with casseroles, the size of the baking dish matters. Because there should be three layers of eggplant slices, use a dish that is about twenty-five centimeters (nine and a half inches) long, twenty centimeters (eight inches) wide, and at least six centimeters (two and a half inches) high.

Peel the eggplants, and cut them into slices about one centimeter (one-half inch) thick. Cover them generously with salt on both sides, and then place them into a flat sieve to drain for at least thirty minutes. In the meantime, you can make the dough and the meat filling. In a kitchen bowl, whisk together the eggs, flour, and milk for a runny pancake batter, and then set this aside. In a pan, sauté the finely chopped onions in olive oil over fairly low heat for about twenty minutes until they are soft. This may seem like a long time, but only then will they fully develop their sweet flavor. Add the ground meat, mix it thoroughly with the caramelized onions, and continue stirring until it is nicely browned. To season the meat, add the pressed garlic, Lebanese seven-spice mixture, herbes de Provence, salt, and pepper, and then stir together thoroughly. Sauté the ground beef for another twenty minutes over very low heat until it has a consistently dry texture. Finish by adding the chopped parsley.

Once the salt has drawn out all the bitter liquid from the eggplant, you can continue processing them. Thoroughly squeeze out all remaining liquid from the eggplant slices, and dab them with paper towels until they are completely dry. Then comes the step on which the magic of this moussaka relies. Coat each individual eggplant slice with pancake batter, and then fry in oil, about a minute on each side, until each slice has taken on a light-brown color. It is best to use a neutral oil that heats well, such as rapeseed oil. At first, this may seem like quite a bit of effort, but if you work with a very hot pan, the browning will go quickly. You simply must remember to add new oil from the side of the pan (rather than drizzling it on top) so that as the oil glides across the bottom, it will already gather heat. As you continue frying one slice of coated eggplant after the other, drain the ones that are already browned on paper towels to remove all excess oil. Gordana recommends frying all the eggplant slices first.

To assemble the moussaka, begin by covering the bottom of the casserole dish with the first layer of coated eggplant slices. They should fit snugly, so they are allowed to overlap. Pour the first layer of meat ragout onto the eggplants, cover this with a further layer of eggplant, and then once more with meat ragout. The top of the moussaka will then be a third layer of coated eggplant slices. For the sauce, whisk together the eggs, cream, and milk; season with salt, some more freshly grated nutmeg, and pepper; and then pour the sauce over the moussaka. Finish by sprinkling grated Parmesan over the casserole and baking it on the lowest rack of the oven for about an hour.

ZUCCHINI AND EGGPLANT CASSEROLE
WITH RAGÙ ALLA BOLOGNESE FOR 6

2 medium eggplants

2 big zucchini

400 g (14 ounces) ripe tomatoes

4 garlic cloves

4 tbsp. olive oil

2 tsp. fresh thyme

salt, pepper and cayenne pepper

300 g (11 ounces) buffalo mozzarella, cut into slices

ragù Bolognese (see "Meat Stew")

30 g (⅓ cup) Parmesan

40 g (1 cup) panko (or bread crumbs)

butter

I have such a serious a weakness for classic Italian lasagna that I throw all caution to the wind and ravenously devour it, but every time I do, it sits heavily in my stomach. This is why I have developed a lighter version that replaces the wide pasta strips with vegetable slices.

Heat the oven to 180°C (350°F). Cut the eggplant, zucchini, and tomatoes into slices, each about five millimeters (⅕ inch) thick. In a kitchen bowl, toss the vegetables with pressed garlic, thyme, and olive oil, and then season with salt, pepper, and cayenne pepper. It is best to prepare the vegetables a bit in advance so that they can fully absorb the flavor of the oil and the spicing. And it is perfectly fine for the tomatoes to fall apart. To assemble the casserole, choose a baking dish large enough to hold three layers of vegetables, and then grease the bottom with olive oil. Cover the bottom of the dish with a layer of eggplant slices, and then scatter mozzarella slices on top. Add a layer of tomatoes over the cheese next, and cover this with a generous layer of Bolognese ragout. Use the zucchini slices for the top layer, scatter the grated Parmesan and panko on top, and then cover the casserole dish with aluminum foil. The shiny side should be facing down, as this will more readily conduct the heat into the dish it is covering. Bake the casserole for an hour or so (depending on how crisp you want your vegetables to be). Toward the end of the baking time, however, remove the aluminum foil, dot the casserole with butter, and place it under the broiler for about eight minutes so that the surface can become golden brown and crispy.

PEAR AND APPLE CRUMBLE WITH DRIED CHERRIES FOR 4

2 Granny Smith apples, peeled and cored

500 g (1 pound) rhubarb (or 2 pears), peeled

50 g (⅓ cup) dried cherries (or raisins)

2 tbsp. apple or pear schnapps

2 tbsp. maple syrup

1 pinch nutmeg

200 g (1⅓ cup) flour

100 g (½ cup) butter

200 g (1 cup) light-brown cane sugar

1 tbsp. ground almonds

Heat the oven to 200°C (400°F). Much like parsnips, fruit crumble makes me think of the late Victorian novels by Edith Wharton and immediately evokes a scene from *The Age of Innocence*, in which elegantly dressed women sip tea from delicate porcelain cups.

You can make this dessert either in individual pot de crème dishes or in a larger gratin dish—ten centimeters (four inches) high and about twenty centimeters (eight inches) wide. My friend Richard, professor of philosophy at the University of Bergamo, who gave me this recipe, has explained the principle of this dessert to me in great detail to clear away all heresy he often finds in restaurants that have adopted this dish insouciantly. As Richard explains, in the most fundamental terms, a crumble consists of two parts: the top having a sweet flavor and the bottom a tart flavor. For the crumble, you could vary the flour, as you could replace brown sugar with white sugar, and you could also—as I suggest in the following recipe—add some ground almonds or even grind in some digestive biscuits and add some nutmeg. The one ingredient, however, that must not be tampered with is the butter. To leave that out would, indeed, be heresy.

To make the sweet crumble, chop the butter into small knobs in a large bowl, add the sugar and the ground almonds, and then run the amalgam through your fingers. As Richard puts it, the result will be that "to ever-smaller blobs of butter, clusters of flour and sugar adhere." The result should be a dry but not quite homogeneous crumble. For the lower, tart part of the crumble, the choice of fruit is vital, given that an excess of liquid must be avoided at all costs. For this reason, the core crumble should be a tart apple, which can be paired with pears, bananas, or apricots, and rhubarb—as in the version I propose—when it is in season.

Peel and core the apples, and then cut them into bite-size cubes. Peel the rhubarb, and cut it into bite-size pieces as well. In a second large bowl, mix together the chopped fruit with dried cherries (or raisins), fruit schnapps, maple syrup, and a pinch of nutmeg. To assemble the crumble, place the fruit, which will make up the bottom of this dessert, in the bottom of the baking dish (or the individual pots), and then scatter the sweet, buttery blobs on top. The crumble should bake in the preheated oven for about twenty to thirty minutes, or until the top bit browns nicely. In the dry heat of the oven, the butter—the key agent in this dish—will melt and meld with the flour and the sugar, forming a crispy crust on top, and as it flows down over the bottom bit, the fruit will transform into a delectable goo. To add to the guilty pleasure of the fruit crumble, add—if you like—a dollop of whipped cream, crème fraîche, yogurt, or ice cream before serving.

QUICHES, PIES, AND CAKES

⅔ SAVORY
Broccoli and Gorgonzola Quiche | Fennel, Leek, and Bacon Quiche |
Tomato and Saffron Quiche | Puff Pastry Pie with Zucchini, Mozzarella,
and Dried Tomatoes | Herbed Mushroom Puff Pastry Pie | Za'atar Bits

⅔ SWEET
Plum Cake | Shortbread | Lemon Cake |
Chocolate Cream Pie | Froma's Cheesecake

I like to tell people that I can't bake at all. When my friends then protest, unwilling to believe that this could possibly be the case, I confess my great love for quiches and tarts. Indeed, I have already baked countless quiches for meetings that ended in dinners at my home or buffet parties to celebrate the end of the semester. In fact, during my early cooking years, the French onion tart, seasoned with bacon, caraway, and nutmeg, was a regular feature at the dinners I would cook for guests when I didn't have much time. Other cooks may opt for roasted chicken when they are pressed for time. But for my part, I will immediately start devising different combinations of vegetables and herbs to spread over short-crust or puff pastry. Precisely because I am often pressed for time, I always use the store-bought variety.

I think of a quiche as a casserole baked inside a pastry shell. The leeway for variation is immense when it comes to preparing the filling. You can either sauté or parboil the vegetables first or use them raw, much as you can either make the sauce with cheese and cream alone or add eggs to it. I have even convinced myself that a quiche, served with salad, is a light meal by simply ignoring the "evil" fat content of not only the cream and the cheese of the filling but also the dough itself.

And yet precisely because it is so easy to impress one's guests with a savory quiche or a fruit tart, I soon understood that this can prove to be a double-edged sword for the professional woman who wants to be recognized as much for her academic accomplishments as for her culinary skills. When it comes to baking, I have two spiritual mothers whose attitudes toward this culinary art were diametrically opposed. The first is Froma Zeitlin, who always served as my encouraging model. Holding a chair in classics at Princeton, not only was she one of the first academics in her field to apply gender studies to ancient literature, but she also knew how to bake the perfect cheesecake. While still an undergraduate, I became privy to a scene that deeply impressed me. The kitchen table where she effortlessly prepared her cheesecake was also strewn with piles of papers. As she explained to me blithely, the time it took for the various layers of this cake to bake in the oven was well spent correcting exams or book galleys.

My other spiritual mother is Ina Schabert, professor of English at the University of Munich, with whom I wrote my dissertation. To this day she remains a cautionary figure. She would often note ironically that the homemade cakes she would bring to difficult departmental meetings helped tame the spite and malice of some of her cantankerous older male colleagues. The applause she was sure to garner for this gift, however, also saddened her. Whenever she presented the same colleagues with an offprint of her articles, she would receive only very hesitant and rather tenuous praise. When it comes to baking, it is thus useful to remember the two sides of Plato's *pharmakon*. As with any medicine, whether the result is harmful or healing is a question of dosage. The professional woman should, therefore, always ask herself when it is wise to draw attention to her culinary skills and when she should draw attention to her academic prowess instead.

SAVORY

BROCCOLI AND GORGONZOLA QUICHE FOR 6

270 g (10 ounces) short-crust pastry
500 g (1 pound) broccoli
3 tbsp. olive oil
1 medium onion, cut into very fine slices
1 tbsp. fresh thyme (or ½ tbsp. dried thyme)
4 garlic cloves, peeled and pressed
¼ tsp. chili flakes

½ preserved lemon (see "Prepared and Stored in the Refrigerator")
4 anchovies
1 tsp. capers, washed and chopped
200 g (7 ounces) Gorgonzola cheese
250 ml (1 cup) crème fraîche
black pepper
Parmesan

Heat the oven to 180°C (350°F). Bake the dough blind for ten minutes. For this quiche, you need to parboil the broccoli in salt water first for about seven minutes and then drain it in a sieve over cold water to stop the cooking process. Shake off any excess water, but do so gently so as not to damage the florets. In a pot large enough to hold the broccoli, sauté the finely sliced onions along with the thyme and chili flakes until they become soft, about ten minutes. After seven minutes, add the pressed garlic, and sauté it as well. Chop the broccoli, and add it to the pot. Chop the preserved lemon, anchovies, and capers, and add these to the pot as well. Stir the broccoli with the aromatics, and allow the vegetables to simmer a few minutes more before adding the crumbled Gorgonzola and the crème fraîche. Season with pepper. When the filling is done, allow it to cool before spooning it into the pastry shell. This way the broccoli can absorb the liquid and the filling will be less moist. Begin by lining a tart pan with the short-crust pastry (store bought or homemade is up to you). Sprinkle a thin layer of grated Parmesan on top, and drizzle with olive oil. Pour the broccoli mixture into the pastry shell, and using a spatula, make sure that it is spread out evenly. Bake the quiche for fifteen to twenty-five minutes (it will depend on how the heat in your oven is distributed). If you want a crisp crust, use the lowest rack of the oven. Some five minutes before it is done, grate a thin layer of Parmesan over the top of the quiche, and finish baking.

FENNEL, LEEK, AND BACON QUICHE FOR 6

1 leek	salt and pepper
1 fennel	2 eggs and 2 egg yolks
3 tbsp. olive oil	250 ml (1 cup) crème fraîche
125 ml (½ cup) white wine	250 ml (1 cup) milk
1 tbsp. white balsamic vinegar	2–3 tbsp. mustard
1 tbsp. fennel seeds	110 g (½ cup) soft goat cheese
1 tsp. caraway seeds	270 g (10 ounces) short-crust pastry

Heat the oven to 180°C (350°F). In contrast to the previous recipe, all the ingredients in this recipe are added to the pastry shell at the same time. Trim and clean the leek, and then cut it into fine slices. Peel the outer leaves of the fennel bulb, trim it at the bottom, and then cut it into fine slices as well. Sauté the vegetables in olive oil, over medium heat, about ten minutes or until the fennel has begun to soften. Deglaze the pan with white wine and white balsamic vinegar, add the fennel and caraway seeds, and season with salt and pepper. Continue sautéing the vegetables over low heat for another ten minutes. In the meantime, whisk the eggs with the cream, milk, and mustard until you have a smooth cream, and then season with salt and pepper. To assemble the quiche, line the baking dish with the short-crust pastry (store bought or homemade is up to you). Spread the vegetables on top, dot with the goat cheese, and pour the egg-mustard-cream mixture on top. Bake the quiche for about thirty-five minutes. For a crisp crust, use the lowest rack of the oven.

TOMATO AND SAFFRON QUICHE FOR 4

270 g (10 ounces) short-crust pastry
1 egg yolk for brushing the dough

1 handful Parmesan, grated

TOMATO SAUCE

3 tbsp. olive oil
2 onion
2 celery stalks
6 garlic cloves
1 kg (2.2 pounds) ripe tomatoes, cut into cubes
400 g (14 ounces) net weight canned tomatoes

1 tbsp. tomato purée
3 bay leaves
1 tbsp. brown sugar
2 tbsp. pomegranate molasses
150 ml (⅔ cup) full-bodied red wine
salt and pepper

CREAM FILLING

1 tsp. saffron threads
400 ml (1¾ cup) crème fraîche
2 eggs and 4 egg yolks

12 basil leaves
salt and pepper

Because three separate layers are required for this quiche, the preparation is far more elaborate and time-consuming; however, the effort is worth it, not least of all because of its splendid appearance. The golden saffron custard sits like a royal blanket on top of the fiery red tomatoes, which only manifest themselves once you have cut into the quiche. The combination of sweet buttery short-crust pastry, the dense tomato sauce, and the fluffy herb egg custard adds to the irresistible charm of this dish. Each separate and yet all combined, these three elements make up a flavorful and richly textured whole.

Heat the oven to 200°C (400°F). Line the tart pan with the short-crust pastry, bake the pastry blind for fifteen minutes, and then remove it from the oven. Use ceramic pie weights, dried beans, or chickpeas. However, be meticulous about removing them afterward, making sure that none is stuck inside the dough. It has happened to me that a somewhat astonished and slightly irritated guest suddenly found himself biting on a stray ceramic bean. Luckily, he didn't break his tooth.

Whisk the egg yolk with grated Parmesan, brush the entire surface of the pastry shell with it, and then bake the pastry shell once more for another ten minutes. Allow the pastry to cool, and lower the heat to 160°C (320°F). In the meantime, make the tomato sauce. Since you will not be passing the sauce through a sieve, make sure that the onions and celery are chopped very finely. This way, they will dissolve into the tomatoes rather than draw attention to themselves as they would if they were chopped coarsely. Sauté the onions, celery, and garlic in olive oil over medium heat for about ten minutes; the onions and celery should be soft. Add the chopped fresh tomatoes, canned tomatoes, tomato purée, bay leaves, sugar, and pomegranate molasses, along with the red wine. Season with salt and pepper, and over very low heat, let the sauce simmer for some forty-five minutes. It may take an hour depending on how watery the tomatoes are. As you stir, keep mashing the tomatoes. Do not turn off the heat until the tomato sauce has a dense, syrupy consistency, neither too runny nor too chunky. This means that there should be no noticeable chunks of tomatoes or onions. Remove the bay leaves.

Make use of the time it takes for the tomato sauce to cook to prepare the third component of this quiche: the saffron custard. Begin by soaking the saffron threads in one tablespoon of hot water for at least five minutes, and then heat four tablespoons of crème fraîche along with the saffron and the soaking water in a small pot; however, the liquid should not come to a boil. Instead, take the pot off the heat so that the saffron can steep for another five minutes in the cream, giving it both flavor and color. Whisk together the two eggs and the additional four egg yolks, stir these into the saffron cream, and then season with salt. Cut the basil into very fine strips, and add them to the custard.

Then you can assemble the quiche. Pour enough tomato sauce into the pastry shell to fill it halfway. If you have too much sauce, don't worry. It will keep in the refrigerator for at least a week. Then comes the tricky bit that requires a steady hand. Pour the saffron custard over the tomatoes, but make sure that they do not blend into each other. The custard should cover the sauce completely and, in so doing, conceal it. Bake the quiche for forty to sixty minutes. As the saffron custard sets, it will take on an intense golden color. Allow the quiche to rest for ten minutes before serving.

PUFF PASTRY PIE WITH ZUCCHINI, MOZZARELLA, AND DRIED TOMATOES FOR 4

320 g (11 ounces) puff pastry
200 g (7 ounces) mozzarella
1 tbsp. thyme
3 spring onions
100 g (4 ounces) pancetta (or bacon)
250 g (9 ounces) sun-dried tomatoes
  preserved in oil
1 bunch basil

100 g (1 cup) Parmesan, grated
2 small zucchini
2 eggs
250 ml (1 cup) cream (or
  half-and-half)
1 pinch chili flakes
salt and white pepper

Heat the oven to 200°C (400°F). This pie is also incredibly quick to prepare. All you really have to do is line a tart pan with the puff pastry (store bought is perfectly fine) and fill it in several layers. Begin by spreading the cubed mozzarella over the bottom. Sprinkle the thyme on top, and then add the finely sliced spring onions. Slice the pancetta, the sun-dried tomatoes, and the basil into thin slivers, and use them as the next layer of the pie. Scatter six tablespoons of grated Parmesan on top. Slice the zucchini into thin rounds, and place them in one layer on top of the cheese—imitating the circular shape of the tart pan—by beginning on the outer rim and working inward. For the sauce, whisk the eggs and cream together, and season with salt, white pepper, and a pinch of chili flakes. Pour the sauce over the pie, sprinkle the remaining Parmesan on top, and bake for about thirty-five minutes.

HERBED MUSHROOM PUFF PASTRY PIE FOR 4–6

5 onions
3 tbsp. olive oil
350 g (12 ounces) mushrooms
150 g (5 ounces) boiled ham
2 tbsp. fresh thyme, chopped

2 tbsp. fresh rosemary, chopped
200 g (1 cup) crème fraîche
450 g (16 ounces) puff pastry
1 egg for brushing the dough

Heat the oven to 200°C (400°F). In the early 1990s, I happened to come upon Nigel Slater's *Real Fast Food* in the legendary bookshop Shakespeare and Company in Paris, and I was immediately taken with his witty way of writing about his culinary obsessions. What I have since learned from him is that cooking is really about understanding basic principles rather than stubbornly following the directions of a given recipe. Once you have grasped the idea behind a certain dish, you can tinker with it and reinterpret it as you please, which is why I was so smitten with one of his subsequent books, *Appetite*. In it, he simply lists the ingredients for a dish and the sequence in which one should put them to use. He also suggests other combinations of ingredients and aromatics that might work. This herbed mushroom pie is an improvisation on one such listing.

Sauté the very finely chopped onions in olive oil over low heat for twenty minutes. They really should be soft, sweet, and caramelized. Clean the mushrooms—you can use button mushrooms or an assortment thereof—and cut them into fine slices. Cut the ham into fine slices as well, add both to the pan, and then sauté for another seven minutes. Although the mushrooms will release some liquid, you may need to add a bit more oil at this point if it looks like the pan is too dry and they might scorch. Once the mushrooms are soft, add the chopped herbs and the crème fraîche, season with salt and pepper, and allow the mushroom mixture to simmer a bit longer until it has become really creamy. The filling should be dense, not runny; otherwise, the pastry dough will not become crispy. Take the pot off the heat, and allow the filling to cool.

To assemble the pie, roll out the puff pastry (store bought is fine) to form two rectangles, 35 centimeters (13.7 inches) by 20 centimeters (8 inches) each. Put one of the pie sheets onto a baking tray dusted with flour. Spread the mushroom mixture over the first of the two sheets of dough, which will serve as the bottom of the pie, but make sure that you leave a thumb-size border all around. Whisk the egg, and then brush the border with it. After you have placed the second sheet of puff pastry on top of the mushroom mixture, press the edges onto this border. The egg will help keep the two pieces of puff pastry attached to each other and prevent the mushrooms from spilling out once the pie is in the oven. Use the remaining egg (or milk) to brush the surface of the pie, and then use a fork to make a few incisions as well so that steam can escape during the baking process. It will take about twenty-five minutes for the pie to develop a honey-golden crust.

ZA'ATAR BITS FOR 4–6

5 tbsp. za'atar spice	1 tbsp. Parmesan
5 tbsp. olive oil	320 g (11 ounces) puff pastry

Heat the oven to 220°C (425°F). It is really quite simple to prepare these little savory bits, and I am sure your guests will be as delighted as mine always are when I serve them at the beginning of a meal. Indeed, there are some who not only request this appetizer in advance but will bring a container hoping they can take some home with them. Because they are so simple yet so enticing, they make a great gift to bring when you are invited.

Mix the za'atar spice with the olive oil, season with salt, and then blend in the grated Parmesan. Spread the puff pastry (store bought is fine) onto a chopping board dusted with flour, and using a cookie cutter (or a glass) about five centimeters (two inches) in diameter, cut out as many rounds as you can. Place these on a silicon mat (or a baking tray lined with parchment paper). Make sure there is a space in between them, as they will expand. Dot each round with one-half teaspoon of the za'atar-oil mixture, and with the back of the spoon, spread it across the surface. It may take a bit of practice to see exactly how much you need. The rounds should be covered, but the oil should not drip over the sides. Bake for twelve minutes or so, until the puff pastry has risen and turned a golden brown.

SWEET

PLUM CAKE FOR 6

750 g (1½ pounds) ripe plums	175 g (6 ounces) sugar
320 g (11 ounces) short-crust pastry	1½ tsp. Armagnac
125 g (5 ounces) butter	½ tsp. vanilla extract
juice and zest of 1 lemon	3 tbsp. flour
1 tsp. ground cinnamon	2 tbsp. cream
2 eggs	

Heat the oven to 180°C (350°F). The charm of this simple late summer cake depends entirely on the quality of the plums. If you do not have plums, you can use other fruit like apricots, peaches, or even cherries and simply adjust the brandy. Begin by lining a round baking tin with the short-crust pastry, and bake it blind for fifteen minutes, using ceramic baking beans (if you don't have these, any dried beans or chickpeas will do). Prick the pastry with a fork in several places, and allow it to cool while you prepare the fruit. Cut the plums in half, remove the pits, and cut them in half once more. Arrange the plums on the dough, imitating the circular shape of the baking dish. It is easiest to begin at the outer edge and work inward. The plums should overlap, and you should have a rosette of plums in the middle.

To make the sauce, melt the butter over low heat until it begins to bubble and turn golden brown. Take the pot off the heat, add the juice and finely chopped zest of the lemon as well as the cinnamon, and then allow it to cool. In the meantime, whisk the eggs with the sugar until you have a dense consistency, and then add the melted lemon butter, brandy, vanilla extract, salt, flour, and cream. Mix the sauce thoroughly before pouring it over the plums. Bake the cake in the upper part of the oven, about forty minutes, until the cream has set and taken on a golden-brown color. Allow the cake to rest at least fifteen minutes before serving.

SHORTBREAD FOR 6–8

100 g (4 ounces) confectioner's sugar (icing sugar)
200 g (7 ounces) flour
100 g (4 ounces) cornmeal (maize flour)

200 g (7 ounces) butter, at room temperature
1 vanilla bean (or 1 tbsp. vanilla extract)
granulated sugar for dusting

It is really not difficult to make a shortbread from scratch that is far superior to the oily, overly sweet cookies one can buy in stores. These homemade shortbread fingers turn out fluffy and light, and as you can decide what spices to use, you can also regulate the sweetness along with the flavor.

Heat the oven to 160°C (320°F). Do not, however, heat the tray onto which you will be putting the shortbread dough. Instead, make sure to remove it from the oven; otherwise, the fingers will begin to melt before they have even begun to bake. You can make the dough either in a food processor or with a hand mixer, although if you have one, this is the moment when your KitchenAid will truly come into its own. Using a sieve, sift the flour and the cornmeal into a bowl. Split and seed the vanilla bean, and together with the soft butter (which should be at room temperature but not melted), mix the vanilla together with the flour and cornmeal. After a while, the dough will become a bit crumbly as the butter begins to cling to the other ingredients. Toward the end, use your hands to roll the dough into a ball without, however, spending much more time kneading it.

On the baking tray lined with parchment paper, spread out the dough using your fingers (or a spatula) to form a rectangle, about seven millimeters (one-third inch) in height. In order to get perfectly straight lines, you may need to trim the dough with a sharp knife and use the cutoffs to make the rectangle you want. Use a knife to make incisions into the dough without cutting it all the way through. You want to use these incisions to mark the "fingers": two horizontal lines along the longer side of the dough rectangle and ten from top to bottom along the shorter side of the rectangle. You should have eleven separate fingers marked by these incisions per row, each three centimeters (one and one-fourth inches) by six centimeters (two and a half inches). Using a fork—although this is primarily for decoration—prick each finger three times diagonally. Bake the shortbread in the preheated oven for about twenty-five minutes or so, but don't take it out of the oven until the edge of the dough has taken on a golden-brown color. The fingers should be airy, which is to say neither crispy nor chewy. Before slicing the shortbread fingers, allow them to cool for at least three minutes on the baking tray. Then while the shortbread is still resting on the baking tray, use a sharp knife to cut along the incisions, finally separating the fingers from each other. Place them on a rack, and then put a piece of parchment paper underneath to catch any excess sugar. Allow the fingers to cool for another five minutes before dusting them with the granulated sugar. They must be completely cool before you put them into a cookie jar.

NOTE: My friend Barbara, the queen of shortbread, who has a real knack for coming up with ever new flavors so that these cookies fit the occasion when they are served, suggests the following variations: You can coarsely chop pan-roasted pecan nuts and add these, together with vanilla seeds (or vanilla paste), to the dough. Or you can leave out the vanilla entirely and instead add two teaspoons of finely chopped rosemary as well as the zest of two lemons to the dough. Or you can replace the vanilla with three teaspoons of very finely chopped lavender blossoms. For one of my Thanksgiving dinners, she concocted a somewhat more complex mixture. She replaced the vanilla with one and a half teaspoons of cinnamon, one-half teaspoon of nutmeg, two pinches of allspice, and three to five chopped pumpkin seeds. Before baking the shortbread, she scattered more chopped pumpkin seeds over the individual fingers and pressed them gently into the dough. Barbara also suggests that rather than discarding the vanilla pod after scraping out the seeds, it can be put into a jar with sugar to flavor the sugar for the next time you make shortbread. One final variation: chop some stem ginger very finely, fold it into the dough, and then dust the fingers with vanilla sugar before baking them in the oven.

LEMON CAKE FOR 6

zest of 3 lemons

5 eggs

350 g (1¾ cups) sugar

juice of 1 lemon

150 ml (⅔ cup) double crème
    de Gruyère (or heavy cream)

275 g (2 cups) flour

1 tbsp. baking powder

100 g (½ cup) melted butter

butter and flour for the baking dish

GLAZE

juice of ½ lemon

100 g (4 ounces) confectioner's sugar
    (icing sugar)

3 tbsp. orange marmalade

A proverb I am particularly fond of offers the following advice: "When life gives you lemons, make lemonade." Given that the "lemon" at issue refers to a useless object, the proverb is normally understood to encourage a positive attitude and a sense of what the American philosopher Ralph Waldo Emerson calls self-reliance. However hopeless a situation may seem, you can always turn it around and profit from it in some way or another. However, I once quite literally had too many lemons on hand, because my potted lemon tree was being sent to a nursery for the winter, and it suddenly dawned on me that there was a culinary truth in this pithy saying. If life gives you lemons, the best thing to do is make lemon cake.

Heat the oven to 180°C (350°F). You will need a longish baking dish—about thirty-five centimeters by ten centimeters by eight centimeters (fourteen inches by four inches by three inches)—for this cake. To make the batter, begin by beating the lemon zest, eggs, sugar, and salt in the bowl of the KitchenAid stand mixer at the highest speed for about seven minutes until you have a thick, dense cream. Then add the lemon juice, and beat this briefly as well. Because you will be preparing the remaining ingredients by hand, now place the bowl on a work surface. Using a spatula, fold the double crème de Gruyère into the lemon mixture gently, then sift the flour and the baking powder into the bowl, and then gently fold the melted butter into the batter as well. It is important not to stir the dough too vigorously so that it will remain fluffy. After greasing the baking dish with butter, dust the bottom and the sides with a thin layer of flour, shaking off any excess, before pouring in the dough. The cake should bake for one hour on the middle rack of the hot oven. It is done when the top begins to arch slightly.

As something unexpected can always happen when baking in the oven, especially if the heat is uneven and temperamental, it is best to probe the middle of the cake with a cake tester or a long bamboo skewer. If, after waiting for a few seconds, it comes out clean and dry, then the cake is done and can be removed from the oven. Turn the cake out of the baking dish. It must cool for at least an hour before you can coat it with the lemon-sugar glaze. In the meantime, raise the heat in the oven to 200°C (400°F). In a small pot, melt the confectioner's sugar in the lemon juice over very low heat, until you have an even, smooth paste. In a second pot, heat the marmalade. To apply the glaze, place the lemon cake on a baking sheet lined with parchment paper. Brush the top and the sides with the warm marmalade, allow it to cool for about five minutes, and then brush the top and the sides with the warm lemon-sugar glaze. Then return the cake to the hot oven, and bake it for another five minutes. After removing the cake from the oven, it must cool for at least an hour so that the glaze can solidify. The flavor improves tremendously, however, if it is prepared a day in advance.

CHOCOLATE CREAM PIE FOR 6

PIECRUST

250 g (9 ounces) oat biscuits (or graham crackers)

4 tbsp. sugar
4 tbsp. melted butter

CREAM FILLING

200 g (7 ounces) vanilla sugar
5 tbsp. cornstarch
½ tsp. salt
4 big egg yolks
750 ml (3 cups) milk

200 g (7 ounces) dark chocolate (70 percent)
2 tbsp. butter
1 tsp. vanilla extract

TOPPING

250 g (1½ cups) whipped cream

1 tbsp. vanilla sugar

Though to many this is probably a fairly ordinary dessert pie, I am deeply nostalgic about it. It evokes the many Thanksgiving dinners of my childhood, when it replaced the more traditional pumpkin pie. Because my mother made it only for this occasion, it was always something festive. She always used graham crackers for the crumbly crust and Dr. Oetker chocolate pudding mix for the filling of this pie (the German equivalent of Betty Crocker). You can use any oat or digestive biscuit for the crust, but I strongly recommend making the filling from scratch. While it is hardly more work, the extra effort is definitely worth it. The chocolate flavor will be far more rich and intense.

Heat the oven to 200°C (400°F). For the filling, mix together over very low heat the sugar, cornstarch, and salt in one pot and the milk and egg yolks in another. Raise the heat to medium, and slowly pour the milk-egg mixture into the pot with the sugar-cornstarch mixture, stirring vigorously to dissolve any lumps, and continue to simmer for another eight minutes. The cream should become thick and dense, but it should not set like a scrambled egg, which is why it is necessary to keep stirring. If the cream isn't thick enough, you may have to add a bit more cornstarch. Take the pot off the heat. Break the chocolate into small pieces, and then, in a bain-marie (or a water bath), gently warm it along with the butter and vanilla extract until the chocolate has melted completely. Stir the chocolate mixture into the thickened milk-egg mixture, and then pour this mélange into a bowl. Cover with plastic wrap by pressing it directly onto the chocolate cream so that no skin will form while it is chilling in the refrigerator, about one to two hours.

For the crumbly crust, process the oat biscuits, sugar, and melted butter until you have a moist, dense texture—I always use my KitchenAid stand mixer for this. Press the dough into a round baking dish, and using a spatula, make sure the surface is smooth and even. I prefer to use a tart dish with a removable bottom, because this makes it easier to serve the pie. Bake the crust for ten minutes, remove it from the oven, and allow it to cool. Once the chocolate cream is cold and firm, pour it into the crust, and then, using a spatula, spread it across the baking dish evenly. Cover the pie with plastic wrap, only this time don't press it onto the chocolate cream, because you now want a delicate skin to form on top. The pie must rest in the refrigerator for at least six hours or overnight. Make the topping a few hours before serving. For this final layer, whip the cream until it is very stiff, season with vanilla sugar, and using a spatula, spread it evenly over the chocolate pudding. Return the pie to the refrigerator until you are ready to serve it. If you are very ambitious, you can decorate the pie with grated chocolate and crushed pistachio nuts.

FROMA'S CHEESECAKE FOR 6–10

250 g (9 ounces) butter biscuits	4 tbsp. melted butter
50 g (¼ cup) sugar	1 handful almond splinters

FILLING

700 g (24 ounce packages)	1 tbsp. cornstarch
Philadelphia Cream Cheese	2 tsp. vanilla extract
4 eggs	1 tsp. lemon juice
200 g (1 cup) sugar	2 tbsp. amaretto

GLAZE

560 ml (2½ cups) sour cream	1 tsp. vanilla extract
100 g (½ cup) sugar	2 tsp. lemon juice

For the longest time, this cheesecake was the only cake I would bake because, whenever I served it, my guests always responded with unreserved amazement and enthusiasm. Though not difficult, this cheesecake takes a bit of time to prepare, because the actual baking takes place in three stages. And a brief warning is also called for: this is a very rich cake, so you shouldn't serve large slices of it. It will, however, keep for several days in the refrigerator. It is, therefore, also worth being just a bit stingy so that you have a treat once your guests are gone.

Froma, who gave me this recipe, always used ultrathin Nabisco Famous Chocolate Wafers to make the dough for the crust of this cheesecake. Because this brand is not available in Europe, I would always bring home boxes of chocolate wafers from my trips to the United States. You can, however, also experiment with butter cookies, digestive biscuits, or even graham crackers. It simply needs to be a dry cookie or biscuit that crumbles easily and whose flavor will match the cream cheese filling.

Heat the oven to 180°C (350°F). Grind the dry ingredients, biscuits, sugar, and almond splinters—I use my KitchenAid stand mixer, but a mortar and pestle would do just as well—and then add the melted butter. You are aiming for a moist, kneadable dough that is easy to press into the bottom of a twenty-six-centimeter (ten-inch) springform pan. After baking the crust for ten minutes, allow it to cool. In the meantime, prepare the filling by beating the Philadelphia cream cheese (one package at a time) with the eggs, sugar, cornstarch, vanilla extract, lemon juice, and amaretto until you have a very smooth mixture. It should be thin, and as Froma explained to me, it should drip off the spoon. Pour the mixture on top of the cooled crust, and bake the cake for about thirty-five minutes. To check the cake for doneness, you can insert a metal cake tester or a skinny bamboo skewer to probe the center. If it comes out clean and dry after a few seconds, the cake is ready and can be removed from the oven. Before glazing it, however, allow it to cool for at least five minutes. If you are impatient and don't wait, the glaze will merge with the cream cheese mixture in an ungainly manner, and you will have, as Froma warns, a mess.

Increase the heat in the oven to 220°C (425°F). For the glaze, beat the cream, sugar (or homemade vanilla sugar), and vanilla extract until you have a smooth cream. Using a spatula, very gently spread the glaze on top of the cheesecake, and bake it for another five minutes before removing it from the oven. Allow it to cool completely before refrigerating the cheesecake, ideally for twenty-four hours. This last step is essential, so make sure to prepare the cake one day in advance.

♣ 6 ♣

DELICIOUS DISASTERS

What Can Be Salvaged in the Kitchen

Burnt | Matching Flavors and Ingredients | A Play of Consistencies

Although the story is apocryphal, the invention of the tarte Tatin is supposed to have been the result of a mishap in the hotel kitchen that the two sisters, Stéphanie and Caroline Tatin, ran in Lamotte-Beuvron in the late 1880s. The way the anecdote goes, Stéphanie was in such a frantic hurry that she almost burned the apples that she was simmering in butter and sugar, intending to make a fruit pie. To save the dish, she had to come up with something quickly, so she simply covered the apples with the pastry dough she had wanted to use for the pie's bottom and, rather than using a baking dish, put the entire pan into the oven instead. Upon removing the pie from the oven and flipping it onto a plate, she was surprised how perfectly the apples had caramelized. The upside-down tart quickly became the signature dish of her restaurant.

If a kitchen accident is to be serendipitous, it is crucial that you respond with poise and ingenuity. The first thing to do is soberly assess how bad the situation actually is and then choose between three options: If there is enough time, you could start all over again and either prepare the same dish a second time or create a different one, using the supplies that you have assembled in your pantry for precisely such a situation. You could, however, also try to cover up your mistake by either using different spices or transforming that which is still edible into a new dish. If, however, there is nothing left to salvage or you have neglected to properly stock up your pantry, you always have the option of going to a restaurant. I would chalk it up as a reward for a failed culinary experiment, because nothing is more instructive than the mistakes one makes—that is, if rather than falling into a state of despair, you analyze what went wrong and try to figure out how to prevent this from happening again.

For this reason, the motto I ascribe to is the following: Never lose your composure in the kitchen. Of course, I attribute this self-confidence to Julia

318

Child, a true master—or should one say mistress?—in the art of correcting culinary mistakes. After all, not only did she encourage several generations of home cooks to dedicate themselves to the technique of classic French cuisine in order to become accomplished in preparing a boeuf bourguignon, a coq au vin, or a soufflé, but she is also famous for never trying to cover up any mistake she may have made on set while shooting her television series *The French Chef.* On the contrary, because she saw only one obstacle for the home cook—namely, the fear of failure—she downright celebrated her own slips of the hand. As she enjoyed saying, "Maybe the cat has fallen into the stew, or the lettuce has frozen, or the cake has collapsed—*Eh bien, tant pis!*" What you have cooked is usually not only better than you think; with enough courage to improvise, much can be covered over (if not covered up). If something turned out truly horrible, then so be it. Any composed cook will simply acknowledge her blunder, smiling all the while, and learn from her mistakes. Julia Child has another piece of reassuring advice: remember, you're alone in the kitchen. Only you know how the dish was meant to look and taste. That is why, when it comes to dealing with kitchen disasters, a bit of conning is never a bad idea. What will also be of tremendous help, however, is knowing your ingredients.

BURNT

As a rule of thumb, while a dish that is completely burned or utterly oversalted cannot be remedied, there are, nonetheless, sometimes ways to salvage such disasters. For example, when staying with my friend Michael in Paris, I once tried to roast a capon in a pot on the stovetop, because his brand-new oven wasn't working properly. After first browning the bird on all sides, I placed it on top of a bed of vegetables, and having added some wine to the pot as well, I wanted to braise it slowly and gently at a medium temperature. However, having miscalculated the heat, I discovered to my horror, half an hour before the other guests were to arrive, that I had allowed the dish to scorch. Because Michael and I had pushed precious black truffle slices under the skin of the capon, there was no way we were simply going to throw it away. Instead, realizing that hasty action was called for, I knew I had to immediately interrupt the cooking process completely. I not only removed the pot from the heat right away but also filled the kitchen sink with enough cold water in which to cool down the bottom of the pot. Next, I quickly severed the capon, which luckily had not been hurt by the excess heat, from the scorched

Dishes inside a cupboard

vegetables. Then using a wooden spoon, I also carefully removed all the vegetable pieces that were not stuck to the bottom of the pot (most came loose readily) and transferred them, together with the capon, into a second pot. Making sure that this time I got the temperature right, I continued simmering the dish. I was lucky! Tasting a piece of the capon, I found it didn't have a hint of burnt flavor. But if it had, I would still have had a trick up my sleeve. I would have covered the pot with a damp towel and allowed it to rest for thirty minutes before tasting the capon once more. If it still had a touch of scorched flavor, I would, indeed, have had to give up.

In the same vein, when salvaging a scorched stew, you can always put whatever is not sticking to the bottom of the pan and comes loose readily into another pot. Add some more water or wine and perhaps a few onions to temper the flavor before allowing the stew to continue simmering. If vegetables have scorched only slightly, put them into a different pot, cover the pot with a lid, and place it in the kitchen sink. Let cold water flow over the pot for five minutes. This should remove the burnt flavor. If something burned in a pan or a baking dish, remove whatever isn't stuck to the bottom. You may need to cut the meat or fish into smaller pieces or reassemble the meatloaf or the omelet. Then cover everything with a sauce to disguise the damage.

When dealing with a cake that has been exposed to excess heat, generously cut away the burnt pieces, then cut what remains into cubes and use them as the bottom layer of a fruit salad or a fruit compote. Top it with ice cream, whipped cream, and chopped nuts, and simply give a new name to the dessert. And even the part of a pudding that hasn't burned can be saved. Transfer it to a second pot, and continue simmering it, all the while stirring with tender care. However, taste it first to make sure that you didn't take any scorched cream along.

If kitchen mishaps are to be turned into fortuitous accidents, it is all a question of nerves, invention, and also panache. As Julia Child was also wont to say, never apologize for anything you have prepared in your kitchen, as no one knows what you intended to make. Instead, always rely on the courage of your culinary convictions. After all, the interpretational sovereignty of any dish you serve rests solely with you. If the dish seems not to have succeeded, take it in a different direction, and simply give it a new designation. In a restaurant in Rome, I once ordered a dish called "cannoli deconstructed." The pastry shell had been broken into bits and scattered over far more sweetly flavored ricotta than would have fit into the tube shape of its Sicilian original. With mirth, my friend Franz noted that this was probably the result of a plate having fallen to the ground and a terrified waiter quickly reassembling the remains—and then, recognizing the beauty of the accident, declaring it to have been his intention all along.

MATCHING FLAVORS AND INGREDIENTS

Improving the flavor of a dish, either by offsetting a taste that is too pungent or by adding a different aroma to balance it, is, of course, far more reliable than repairing kitchen accidents.

The most sensitive dish to correct is one that has been spoiled by too much salt. Whether it can be salvaged depends, of course, on how oversalted it is. You can always try increasing the other ingredients, such as rice, barley, or pasta, without adding more salt. Diluting the dish can also help mitigate saltiness. By adding milk, oversalted potatoes can readily be turned into mashed potatoes. Because milk is, in fact, the best counterforce to salt, you can usually balance the flavor of an oversalted sauce by adding a dairy product, such as cream, butter, or yogurt. A pinch of brown sugar or lemon juice can further help dampen the taste of saltiness. Another option is adding raw potatoes, cut into thin slices. Whether you are trying to correct a sauce, a soup, or a vegetable stew, simmer the potato slices (which will absorb a lot of salt while cooking) with the other ingredients until they have become translucent, and then remove them.

In the case of vegetables (such as broccoli, green beans, carrots, or zucchini) that are only slightly oversalted, you can also put them into a sieve and carefully rinse them under hot water. Afterward, a dash of lemon juice will revive them again. As you would in the case of an oversalted sauce, when correcting a soup or a stew, try first to dilute the fluid with milk. If this doesn't succeed, use canned tomatoes, as they too help absorb salt. To further balance the flavor, you can fall back on a pinch of brown sugar or lemon juice. Or as is the case with an oversalted sauce, add potatoes, cut into thin slices, and cook them along with the other ingredients until they have become translucent. The same principle holds true for dishes that have turned out too sweet or too sour. Either dilute them—with water, milk, or cream—or defuse the intensity of the flavor by working with aromatic contrasts and, by way of correction, spicing up the dish.

Conversely, any dish that has turned out bland and lifeless can be corrected with salt. When used in the proper dosage, salt is what brings out the inherent flavor of any ingredients you use in your kitchen. If seasoning with more salt is not sufficient, you can invigorate a dish by adding pungency (pepper, *piment d'espelette*), acidity (vinegar, lemon juice, pomegranate molasses), or sweetness (balsamic vinegar, sugar, ketchup). You can then round off the flavor by adding butter, cream, or nut oil as a final aromatic touch. If the flavor of a soup isn't intense enough, you can add more broth. Herbs (both fresh and dry) will also help build up flavor. Or you can embellish a soup with sherry, Noilly Prat, or crème fraîche. Pumpkin seeds or nuts—sesame, pine nuts, or pistachio—will transform a bland soup by giving it an aromatic crunch. In the same vein, if a sauce has turned out bland, you can enhance the flavor by adding broth or meat extract, as well as sherry, port, Noilly Prat, or sake. Mustard, soy sauce, Tabasco sauce, and Worcestershire sauce offer additional savoriness. But you can also round off the flavor of a sauce by adding marmalade or honey. And if tartness is what you want, why not fold in some very dark chocolate? If fish is lacking in aromatic complexity, the first thing to add is more herbs. Basil, chervil, cilantro, dill, rosemary, and tarragon are particularly suitable. To spice up a fish dish, saffron, curry, fennel, garlic, ginger, and mustard seeds are particularly fitting.

The following list of combinations is meant as a guide for more sophisticated aromatic experiments with fruit and vegetables. It is meant as an inspiration either for giving new life to a dish that has turned out bland or for enhancing the inherent flavor of the main ingredient.

APPLES: brown sugar, cinnamon, cloves, nutmeg, ginger, sage, horseradish, vanilla, lemon, orange, almonds, walnuts, peanuts, hard cheese, soft cheese, bacon

APRICOTS: cinnamon, cumin, rosemary, ginger, vanilla, chocolate, almonds, orange, goat cheese, hard cheese

ASPARAGUS: mint, orange, lemon, sesame, almonds, peanuts, pistachios, dried porcini, mustard, sesame oil, pistachio oil, soy sauce, egg, hard cheese, prosciutto

EGGPLANT: basil, chervil, oregano, sage, thyme, nutmeg, chili, garlic, ginger, walnuts, tomato flakes, soft cheese, prosciutto, bacon

BEETROOT: chervil, dill, cloves, cumin, allspice, watercress, horseradish, wasabi, onions, oranges, apples, walnuts, anchovies, mustard, capers, coconut, egg, goat cheese

BROCCOLI: paprika, mustard seeds, sesame, peanuts, walnuts, lemon, chili, garlic, anchovies, soy sauce, blue cheese, Parmesan, bacon

BRUSSELS SPROUTS: nutmeg, chestnuts, mustard, balsamic vinegar, bacon

CAULIFLOWER: nutmeg, saffron, poppy seeds, almonds, walnuts, chili, cumin, garlic, capers, anchovies, hard cheese

CHARD: basil, chervil, rosemary, savory, poppy seeds, sesame, garlic, lemon, balsamic vinegar, bacon

GREEN BEANS: basil, thyme, dill, rosemary, sage, fennel, sesame, almonds, vanilla

CARROTS: cinnamon, cumin, cloves, thyme, marjoram, parsley, ginger, hazelnuts, peanuts, walnuts, onions, celery, apple, orange, olives, pomegranate molasses, coconut milk

LENTILS: rosemary, mint, oregano, thyme, garlic, onions, tomato flakes, ginger, dried cherries, bacon

MUSHROOMS: marjoram, thyme, dill, rosemary, mint, parsley, tomato flakes, garlic, onions, chestnuts, walnuts, egg, blue cheese, goat cheese, hard cheese, bacon

PAPRIKA PEPPERS: fennel, chili, onions, tomato flakes, mozzarella, soft cheese, olives, prosciutto, bacon

PEAS: basil, mint, marjoram, rosemary, oregano, sage, dill, mint, sesame, poppy seeds, cumin, paprika, cloves, pepper, horseradish, onions, egg, hard cheese, prosciutto, bacon

PLUMS: vanilla, lemon, marmalade

POTATOES: mint, parsley, watercress, rosemary, saffron, dill, cumin, nutmeg, horseradish, chili, capers, garlic, lemon, anchovies, onions

PUMPKIN: basil, marjoram, oregano, sage, thyme, rosemary, dill, cloves, cinnamon, chili, ginger, porcini powder, almonds, chestnuts, apple, lime, orange, orange marmalade, brown sugar, blue cheese, goat cheese, bacon

RHUBARB: rosemary, saffron, almonds, ginger, orange, vanilla

SAVOY CABBAGE: caraway seeds, chili, nutmeg, curry powder, sesame, mustard, garlic, onions, ginger, apple, egg, blue cheese, bacon

SPINACH: basil, chives, chervil, marjoram, rosemary, savory, poppy seeds, sesame, balsamic vinegar, garlic, lemon, bacon

SWEET POTATOES: thyme, almond butter, peanut butter, orange, ginger, marmalade, brown sugar, maple syrup, soy sauce

ZUCCHINI: thyme, nutmeg, tomato flakes

A PLAY OF CONSISTENCIES

Even when the consistency of a dish has gone wrong, there are a few things that can be remedied. Certain fruit will not only become softer after having been harvested but also develop their flavor. There is, therefore, no need to be vexed when all the apricots, avocados, mangos, peaches, kiwis, or pears you find in your grocery store are still hard. To accelerate their ripening, simply tuck them into a paper bag (preferably along with a ripe apple or a banana), and keep them in a warm spot in your kitchen. If, in turn, overripe fruit has become too soft and threatens to spoil, the best thing to do is make a fruit compote or roast the fruit in the oven.

When dealing with liquid-based dishes, you want to ask yourself the following: Have they turned out too thick or to thin? It is, of course, quite simple to dilute a soup, sauce, or stew that has become too dense. One thing, however, needs bearing in mind. If you add more water, you will thin out not only the texture but also the flavor. For this reason, it is better to work with the liquid on which the dish is based—be this milk, broth, tomato sauce, wine, or juice. To build up the aroma once more, season the dish again. If the liquid has become lumpy, pour it into a blender (or use an immersion blender), and whisk it until it is creamy again. You can also press a lumpy sauce through a sieve and then use a wire whisk to whip it back into the desired creaminess. If liquid has curdled, take the pot off the heat immediately, place the pot into a large receptacle containing cold water (or the kitchen sink), and using a wooden spoon, stir vigorously. It may also help to whisk some cream into the liquid. Only if none of these hands-on techniques work to make your sauce creamy again should you fall back on your blender.

If, in turn, the liquid has become too thin, it is relatively easy to thicken it again. The first option for giving more texture to an overly watery sauce is to continue simmering it until enough liquid has evaporated. However, this isn't just a question of time (which you may or may not have): you may not have enough liquid left to reduce the sauce to the desired consistency. In this case, use cornstarch to thicken it—as a rule of thumb, for two hundred and fifty milliliters (1 cup) of liquid ingredient, use one tablespoon of cornstarch. To prevent lumps in your sauce, you must, however, first stir the cornstarch with one tablespoon of cold water before pouring it into the hot sauce, and bring it to a boil again. You can also, however, do what kitchen chefs prefer and thicken a sauce with a roux. For every two hundred and fifty milliliters (one cup) of liquid ingredient, mash one to two tablespoons of butter with the same amount of flour until you have a thick paste. Add this to the hot sauce bit by bit, and then bring the sauce to a boil. If, by contrast, all you want is a more velvety texture, you can always enhance a sauce with a spoonful of cream or an egg yolk. In this case, however, do not bring the sauce to a boil again. To further prevent the egg from curdling, it is worth stirring in a spoonful of the hot sauce first before adding the blended egg to the pot. Following upon this principle, you can correct any soup that has become too thin by stirring the cornstarch with sherry or Noilly Prat instead of water. And for a final touch, you can again blend an egg yolk with a tablespoon of cream and then add a spoonful of hot soup to warm it first before pouring it into the pot of soup.

When the sauce in a stew has become too thin, follow the same principle. Simply take care to remove all the vegetables and meat from the pot with a slotted spoon first. Set them aside before either reducing the liquid further or thickening it. If you decide to do so with a roux, use one tablespoon of butter and flour each for every two hundred and fifty milliliters (one cup) of liquid ingredient; if you want to use cornstarch instead, stir two to three tablespoons with the same amount of cold water. You can correct a cream based pudding that has not become firm enough in a similar manner. For every two hundred and fifty milliliters (one cup) of milk, take three tablespoons of flour, one tablespoon of cornstarch, or one and a half tablespoons of rice flour. Mix these with some cold milk first before pouring them into the pudding and bringing it to a boil once more. If, in turn, the cream-based pudding has curdled, then proceed as you would with a sauce. Remove the pot from the heat immediately, and place it into a larger container with ice-cold water. Using a wire whisk, stir the cream vigorously until it has become smooth again. As you would when salvaging a curdled mayonnaise, you could also whisk together a tablespoon of the curdled cream with a teaspoon of milk or liqueur in a bowl large enough to hold all the pudding and then beat in the rest of the cream a spoonful at a time. If, in turn, a mousse has not firmed up properly, you no longer have a mouse but rather a delicious sauce—for stewed fruit or a cake.

There are, however, those mishaps for which, rather than correcting, it is better to conceal creatively. While you can simply continue to simmer, braise, or roast liquid-based dishes that aren't completely done, you have to use your creativity in those instances when the food you are preparing has become too dry. You can always, for example, try to produce more moisture. To do so, first cut the roast, poultry, or steak into slices. Place these on an ovenproof plate or into a baking dish, pour hot broth over them, cover the container with aluminum foil, and allow it to rest in the oven for ten minutes at 100°C (212°F). If you are lucky, the meat will absorb the liquid. Once a piece of fish, however, has finished cooking, don't add further heat; it will fall apart and dry out even more. Instead, cover it generously with chutney or pesto or serve it with melted butter, using chopped herbs and chopped nuts to add another texture. Indeed, the most elegant—and often also the most versatile—solution to remedy a dish that has become too dry—whether meat, poultry, or fish—is to cut the overdry ingredient into slices and cover it with a delicious sauce. If you have a large freezer (or ice compartment), it is worth freezing leftover sauces for just such an occasion. Otherwise, you can quickly prepare a sauce by mixing a roux with broth and then adjust the aroma by adding suitable spices and herbs. Or you could use just a bit of broth, cream it with butter, and season with lemon juice or wine as well as with suitable spices. Then again, you could also deglaze the pan (or baking dish) with wine and add mustard or cream to the sauce before seasoning with fitting herbs and spices. As with any dish that tastes bland, simply declare the meat, poultry, or fish to be nothing more than the bearer of the delectable, flavorful sauce, which has now, as if by magic, turned into the main ingredient.

If, in turn, you are faced with ingredients that you accidentally overcooked, you will need to redefine the dish completely. While overcooked pasta or rice can hardly be salvaged, vegetables can. Mash them with butter and suitable spices, and serve them as a purée. Use chopped herbs as well as chopped nuts or a nut crunch to further produce a contrast in texture. Overcooked asparagus, broccoli, savoy cabbage, or potatoes lend themselves particularly well for making a soup. Simply puree them with broth. As for overcooked cauliflower or zucchini, simply continue cooking these vegetables while you prepare a béchamel sauce, and season it with sherry. Puree the vegetables, add them to the sauce, and finally, pour in enough broth, milk, or cream until you have the consistency of a viscous soup. You can also make a soup from overcooked lentils. To do so, first sauté finely chopped onions, carrots, and celery, and cook this *soffritto*, along with the lentils, in broth. As a final touch, add some dried apricots, cut in fine slices, and some freshly grated ginger. By cooking them in broth with carrots and potatoes, overcooked beans can be turned into a soup as well. To round off the aroma of this soup, add some chopped basil, thyme, or dill and a shot of cream.

Overcooked vegetables are also perfect for a casserole. For example, carefully drain overcooked Brussels sprouts in a sieve. For the marinade, bring some olive oil, along with balsamic vinegar, sugar, and soy sauce to a boil in a small pot. Then first sprinkle bread crumbs, ground almonds, or panko over the bottom of a baking dish. Place the drained Brussels sprouts on top, pour the marinade over the vegetables, cover with grated Parmesan, and bearing in mind that the Brussels sprouts are already soft enough, bake the casserole in the oven just long enough for the cheese to melt, at 180°C (350°F). You could, however, also simply drizzle overcooked Brussels sprouts with olive oil and pomegranate molasses and roast them in the oven until they are brown and crisp. As for overcooked cauliflower, asparagus, broccoli, or zucchini, simply continue cooking them until they are completely soft, as you would for a cream-based soup, then dilute them with some milk, and adding slices of cooked potatoes, turn them into a gratin. Or you can sauté chopped onions; season them with nutmeg, salt, and pepper; and bring some milk to a boil. Add the milk to the *soffritto*, along with some whisked eggs, grated cheese, and ground almonds, and blend everything until you have a creamy sauce. You can now mash the overcooked vegetables into it. Cover the bottom of a baking dish with bread crumbs or ground almonds, and then fill the dish with the vegetable mash. In this case, it is best to bake the vegetable casserole in a water bath, around forty minutes at 150°C (300°F).

Above all, however, deconstruction is the best means of choice when dishes turn into a disaster while in the oven. You will need to take them apart, reassemble them, and using your culinary wit, redefine them. If the dough of a quiche broke or crumbled while baking, then before serving, simply cut it into pieces of different sizes, and—as though this was precisely what you had intended—arrange them decoratively on a platter. A sprig of parsley, some basil leaves, and a few more scattered nuts will turn this reassemblage into a visual pleasure. If, in turn, the bottom of a quiche or a pie burned in the oven, take out the filling, and serve it in small bowls, or—if you have more dough in your freezer—bake it blind and refill it. If the dough, however, has turned out too moist, follow the lead of the early British settlers in North America, and make a savory cobbler instead. Turn the quiche into a second baking dish, break the dough that is now on top of the filling into pieces, and briefly bake the quiche once more. The dough should now be crisp. To enhance further the visual effect of having cobbled something together, break the dough some more before serving to let the filling shine through. If the dough or a quiche or pie looks like it hasn't baked at all while the filling seems done, take out the filling, and serve it in small bowls or as a side dish. The dough will then be the collateral damage that you need to sacrifice. Following the same principle, any cake disaster—even a cheesecake that has gone wrong—can be

Silverware

cut into pieces, distributed among individual plates, and garnished elegantly with fruit, whipped cream, ice cream, a fruit balsamic vinegar, and chopped nuts. Your creativity, along with the panache you deploy while serving this redefined dessert, will be the test of your reclaimed success.

And even the nightmare of every cook—the collapsed soufflé—is a candidate for deconstruction. Because the more compact consistency actually makes the flavor more intense, it may even taste better. Remove a savory soufflé from the baking dish, put it into an ovenproof pan instead, cover it with cheese, and briefly place it under the broiler. Now you have a frittata. You could also transform it into a sophisticated egg dish by covering the soufflé bits with sautéed vegetables. If a sweet soufflé has collapsed, turn it into a cobbler by reconstructing the dish and, rather than baking fruit with a crust on top, covering the soufflé bits with stewed fruit or melted chocolate.

To reiterate my motto for kitchen disasters, never lose your composure while cooking. In the spirit of self-confidence, the rescue missions I propose aren't meant solely as a reminder that you alone retain the interpretational sovereignty over whatever you prepare in your kitchen. At issue is also the joy of improvisation, which is to say, a willingness to try your luck. It could be that, like Stéphanie Tatin, you find yourself making an absolutely astonishing culinary discovery.

COOKING FOR ONESELF

The Ordinary Egg | Vegetarian Meals | Tomato Sauce |
Pork Tenderloin for More Than One Meal | Festively for One

Although my passion for cooking has much to do with making the friends
I invite over for dinner happy as well as—to be honest—impressing them a
bit, it also has always included cooking for just myself. Even when I am not
expecting guests, I often prepare a time-consuming, elaborate dish if I happen
to crave this particular type of food. For me, especially after an exhausting day
of work, being able to return to my kitchen and prepare a meal almost always
allows me to fall into a contemplative mood—whether this entails peeling
and chopping ingredients for a small casserole or a pasta dish, composing a
spicy sauce for a salad or a stir-fry, or spontaneously throwing together whatever I find in my refrigerator for a soup. As I concentrate fully on what I am
about to concoct for myself, all my quotidian concerns gradually begin to
dissipate. If I am tired, even listless, as soon as I begin to cook, I am reinvigo-
rated. Nothing can distract or disturb me in my culinary sanctuary when my
entire attention is focused on the meticulous preparation of my ingredients.
The aromas that slowly begin to emanate from the pan, the pot, or the oven
trigger a thrill of anticipation. As I contemplate what I am about to savor, an
invigorating sense of calm sets in. Sitting down with a glass of wine in hand at
the table set just for myself, I begin to relish my privacy. I allow my thoughts
to wander as I take pleasure in the tranquility around me. Once I begin to
consume the delicacies I have prepared, I am completely at one with myself.

It goes without saying, of course, that the type of dish you prepare for
yourself is predicated on whether this is meant to be an ordinary dish or a
special meal. Sometimes you simply want to prepare something quickly for
yourself because you need to eat, or your partner or your family isn't there,
or you simply haven't invited anyone over. This may be just the right moment
to fall back on all the leftovers that have accumulated in your refrigerator. Or
perhaps, at some point in the week, you planned a sequence of dishes (with
certain dishes meant explicitly to follow others) to tickle your culinary fancy

Setting the table for one

for several days. Either way, cooking for oneself should also be a pleasure. For those who cook for themselves a lot, a wisely stocked pantry is absolutely essential. At the same time, the mood you are in while shopping for fresh ingredients will also have an impact on how simple or elaborate the meal you intend to cook for yourself will be. You may even find something particularly delectable and fancy at the market, which, precisely because you are alone, allows you to prepare a more complex dish or even try out something new and unfamiliar. After all, cooking for yourself has the advantage that you don't need to impress anyone. You also don't have to worry whether what you are preparing will turn out perfect. If the dish doesn't pan out as tasty as you had hoped (or if, in fact, it actually fails miserably), you can chalk it up as an important cooking experience. If, in turn, it comes out far better than anticipated, you can add a new, impressive dish to your repertoire. And finally there are those costly, lavish dishes with which you are allowed, now and then, to treat yourself to. Enjoying them on your own may well intensify the satisfaction they bring.

THE ORDINARY EGG

Omelet | Scrambled Eggs in a Pan | Scrambled Eggs in a Bain-Marie |
Eggs in a Glass with Ham and Chives | Classic Egg Salad | Egg Salad with
Asian Flavors | Baked Eggs with Vegetables | Baked Asparagus,
Prosciutto, and Eggs with Parmesan Topping | Soufflé

When cooking for myself, the egg is probably the most versatile ingredient I use. With it, a variety of meals can be prepared at lunchtime or at the end of a busy working day. The simplicity of an egg dish delights me even if—as is the case when making scrambled eggs in a bain-marie or baking a soufflé—dexterity may be required. One could, of course, begin the day with an egg, whether fried sunny-side up, poached, or scrambled. However, I prefer to prepare them in the evening, especially when I don't have the energy to make much of an effort. On such days, a chilled glass of white wine is the perfect accompaniment to the versatile egg.

OMELET FOR I

3 large eggs   1 tbsp. butter
salt and pepper

As the British cookery book author Elizabeth Davis suggests, there is only one infallible recipe for making the perfect omelet—namely, your own. Nevertheless, she provides some useful words of advice. The simple perfection of this dish depends on the quality of the eggs themselves. This is absolutely essential, while the filling is secondary. For this reason, use only the freshest eggs you can find for your omelet. The filling is really meant as a small, scrumptious supplement at the center of the fried omelet. It should neither compete with (let alone dominate) the taste of the eggs nor ooze out at the two ends of the omelet. Whether the filling consists of cheese, ham, mushrooms, or herbs, it is there simply to give another texture to the omelet and to enhance the flavor of the eggs with a supporting aroma. In order to achieve this contrast between the fried egg coat and the soft, light filling, Elizabeth David suggests not whisking the eggs too vigorously but rather stirring them gently with a fork. And finally, the size of the pan is also important. For a three-egg omelet, you need a pan with a diameter of about twenty centimeters (eight inches). One of my stainless-steel, nonstick All-Clad frying pans is reserved exclusively for omelets. While there are cooks who will insist that an omelet can only be made in an iron pan, my choice reflects the fact that the perfect pan for your omelet is the one you prefer.

Don't forget to take the eggs out of the refrigerator early enough for them to reach room temperature. If the eggs are too cold, your omelet will not become fluffy. In a bowl, stir the eggs briefly, and season with salt and pepper. Heat the pan over medium temperature, and then melt the butter. Wait until the butter has begun to take on a golden color before pouring the eggs into the pan, and once they have begun to set, pour the filling into the middle, taking care that it is enveloped fully by the egg. The next step is the tricky one, requiring a certain amount of practice. You want to spread the egg mixture evenly across the bottom of the pan while making sure that it does not mix with the filling. The best way to do this is to turn the pan toward you, and then, with the help of a spatula, gently push the eggs away from the edge farthest away from you to produce some space. Then tip the pan in the other direction so that egg mass that has not yet set can glide to the empty place in the pan. Obviously, the omelet should not, at this point, slide out of the pan. Because an omelet should remain moist inside, it is done when only a paper-thin layer of raw egg mixture still rests on its surface. Using the spatula, fold one-third of the omelet inward, then fold the other side inward as well. To close the omelet, press both sides gently on top of each other. Then your omelet is ready to slide onto a plate. All you need now is a piece of warm toast with butter melting on it and a glass of chilled white wine.

For the filling, I propose two suggestions that demonstrate the basic principle. If you want an herb mixture, you will need two tablespoons of chopped herbs such as parsley, tarragon, or chives per omelet, combined at your discretion. Add half of the herbs immediately to the eggs before stirring them in a bowl. Sprinkle the other half over the center of the egg mixture, just after it has begun to set in the pan. If you want a more savory taste, mix together one tablespoon of diced ham and two tablespoons of grated cheese (such as Gruyère) with a good pinch of chives. Don't add this filling before stirring the eggs. Instead, wait until they begin to fry in the pan before placing the filling into the center of the omelet. As the eggs envelop the filling, set, and become firm, the cheese will melt into them. Whichever filling you choose, you can always spread a bit more butter on top of the finished omelet to give it a final sheen before seasoning it with salt and pepper.

SCRAMBLED EGGS IN A PAN FOR I

3 eggs	2 tbsp. Parmesan, grated
salt and pepper	1–2 tbsp. butter
1 tbsp. chives, finely chopped	

I offer two different methods for making scrambled eggs: either frying them in a pan or cooking them in a bain-marie (see "Scrambled Eggs in a Bain-Marie").

Yet again, what is crucial—as I learned from a biography about Marlene Dietrich—is the butter. According to Dietrich's daughter, Maria Riva, this iconic classic Hollywood celebrity was known to judge the prowess of her lovers based on whether they were able to pass her scrambled eggs test the morning after an amorous night. This included half a pound of butter for three eggs (or two and an extra egg yolk). Refusing to eat this dish (or being unable to do so) meant being excluded from Dietrich's circle of intimate friends. These days, of course, we are no longer quite so reckless when it comes to butter. A good scrambled egg does, however, require the courage of your culinary conviction, which is to say using more butter than the health police might find appropriate.

Using a fork, stir together the eggs, the finely chopped chives, and the salt and pepper. If you want particularly fluffy scrambled eggs, add two tablespoons of mineral water to the bowl as well. Add the grated Parmesan and whisk it into the egg mixture. Melt the butter in a nonstick frying pan, and—as with the omelet—wait for it to take on a golden color before pouring in the eggs. Allow them to set for a few minutes, and then turn the heat down very low. For the eggs to remain fluffy, they must be in constant motion while frying. I find scrambled eggs should be just a touch runny; they should not have turned into dry morsels. For this reason, rather than stirring them vigorously, I use a wooden spoon to fold the eggs into each other as they glide across the bottom of the pan, and in the process, I turn the pan itself now and then as well.

SCRAMBLED EGGS IN A BAIN-MARIE FOR I

3 eggs	1–2 tbsp. butter
salt and pepper	bottarga, grated

In classic French cuisine, there is a more time-consuming method that calls for preparing scrambled eggs in a bain-marie. If you don't have this particular kitchen utensil, you will need to work with two pots, making sure that the smaller sits on top of the larger one but not inside it. It should be heated by the steam of the water boiling beneath it without being immersed at all in it. How quickly the eggs set depends, of course, on how quickly the smaller pot conducts the heat produced by the steam from the lower pot. It helps to prewarm the upper pot before pouring in the eggs. However, what you need most for this method of preparing scrambled eggs is patience (as it takes a bit longer than simply frying them) as well as elbow grease, as my friend Michael puts it. You must constantly stir the eggs on the bottom of the pot, making sure to scrape all the tiny bits that collect at the outer rim. This is, after all, where they will begin to set first.

In a small bowl, whisk the eggs with salt and pepper. Then bring the water in the lower container of the bain-marie to a rolling boil, and turn the heat down slightly. The water should not bubble or splash out of the pot but rather produce steam. Pour the eggs into the pot on top, and add the butter in chunks. Even if it will take a few minutes for the eggs to begin to set, start stirring from the very beginning, although initially only very gingerly. Once the eggs begin to become firm, you can stir more vigorously, always moving from the outer rim inward. Only this constant stirring will produce the desired creaminess. After about ten minutes, the eggs should be smooth and fluffy, not runny but also not dry. Given the effort you have put into them, these scrambled eggs are already decadent, so you could serve them with a dollop of caviar or slivers of truffle. A less expensive—though not entirely cheap—alternative that I am particularly fond of is using bottarga. Grate this sumptuous cured fish roe over the eggs as you would a truffle—covering them with a golden mantel.

EGGS IN A GLASS WITH HAM AND CHIVES FOR I

2 eggs	butter
3 slices of raw ham (or prosciutto)	salt and pepper
1–2 tsp. chives	

Eggs in a glass, or *Eier im Glas*, my grandmother's signature dish, was what I enjoyed with particular relish on those Sunday mornings when my sister and I were allowed to spend the weekend with her. The name for this typical old-fashioned German breakfast fare comes from the small glass bowls, big enough to hold two to three soft-boiled eggs, in which my Omi would garnish them with the other ingredients. Her lovely cut glass bowls, with elaborate decorations on the side, were not wide and shallow, as one might use to serve muesli or yogurt with stewed fruit. Because the soft-boiled egg is meant to sit on top of the bed of ham and chives, the sides were rounded and high enough to make it possible to stir butter into the eggs without everything spilling over. You could, of course, use an egg cobbler, or any tall glass, or any other type of bowl really. Today, I am more likely to make eggs in a glass for lunch, along with a salad, or in the evening, if I am too tired to prepare anything more elaborate. But whenever I make them, I think of my grandmother.

Begin by boiling the eggs, about six minutes. They must still be soft; otherwise, you will have an egg salad. In the meantime, finely dice the raw ham, and using a pair of scissors, snip the chives finely. Toss the ham and the chives into the glass bowl, and season with salt and pepper. Black salt is particularly appropriate because it will enhance the egg flavor. Once the eggs are done, drain them in cold water, remove the shells, and put them into the glass bowl as well. With the spoon you will use to eat them, make a few large incisions into both eggs, and then add the obligatory glob of butter. As you continue to chop up the eggs, the butter will melt into the yolk and bind all the other ingredients into a perfect whole.

CLASSIC EGG SALAD FOR I

2 eggs	celery salt
1½ tbsp. mayonnaise	pepper
4 small cornichon	

Although it is entirely possible to make egg salad in advance and keep it in the fridge, I am particularly fond of eating it while it is still a bit warm. The first version belongs to the treasure trove of family recipes my mother handed down to me. For this egg salad, it is definitely worth making the mayonnaise yourself, although in a pinch, you could fall back on a store-bought one, as long as it is high quality. Hard-boil the eggs, about ten minutes. In the meantime, finely dice the cornichon, and put them into the bowl in which you will mix together all the other ingredients as well. Once the eggs are done, drain them under cold water and peel them. To cube them, I use my egg slicer (one of my most cherished kitchen gadgets). If you don't have one, use a very sharp knife to chop the hard-boiled eggs into delicate rather than coarse bits. Toss them into the bowl, and add the mayonnaise. Then taking care not to smash the eggs, blend everything together, and season—this is the special ingredient—with celery salt and pepper.

EGG SALAD WITH ASIAN FLAVORS FOR I

2 eggs

1 tsp. chili oil

½ tbsp. rice wine vinegar (or apple
  balsamic vinegar)

1 tsp. sesame oil

1 tbsp. roasted white sesame seeds

½ tbsp. soy sauce

1 tbsp. chives, sliced

For this salad the eggs should also be hard-boiled, around ten minutes. While the eggs are boiling, prepare the Asian vinaigrette. First, dry roast the sesame seeds in a small pan. Then whisk the seeds with the chili oil, the rice wine vinegar, the sesame oil, and the soy sauce. Once the eggs are done, drain them in cold water, remove the shells, and chop them before folding them into the vinaigrette. Finish by sprinkling the chives over the egg salad.

BAKED EGGS WITH VEGETABLES FOR I

225 g (2–2½ cups) zucchini, grated

2 tsp. butter

3 button mushrooms

1 spring onion

1 pinch chili flakes

4 tsp. crème fraîche

2 eggs

1 tsp. lemon paste (see "Prepared and
  Stored in the Refrigerator")

salt and pepper

Parmesan

I own egg coddlers in various sizes because I like experimenting with different flavorings. While traditionally you would close the lid and partially immerse the coddler in boiling water, in this recipe, I suggest treating it more like a baked dish. For this reason, if you don't have an egg coddler, use a small gratin or soufflé dish, large enough in any case to hold around three hundred and fifty milliliters (one and a half cups) of fluids, around thirteen centimeters (five inches) in diameter. The great thing about this dish is that, because eggs go so well with all kinds of vegetables, you can make use of whatever you have accrued in your refrigerator: spinach, chard, fennel, or broccoli. The only rule is that you cut, dice, or chop the vegetables very finely. You could, of course, also use root vegetables and carrots, in which case, however, you should steam them before chopping them into small bits. If you want a more savory flavor, add anchovies or chopped capers.

Heat the oven to 180°C (350°F). Grate the zucchini, not all too coarsely; put them in a sieve; rub one teaspoon of salt into them; and allow them to drain, about ten minutes. In the meantime, clean and dice the button mushrooms, and chop the spring onion. Begin by warming your pan, and allow the butter to melt. Then sauté the mushrooms along with the spring onions for about five minutes. Squeeze as much water from the drained zucchini as you can, and then add them to the pan as well. Season with chili flakes and lemon paste before adding the crème fraîche. Now sauté the vegetables until they are softish, about five minutes, bearing in mind that they will continue cooking in the oven. Pour the vegetable mixture into a gratin dish (or a large egg coddler), and using a metal spoon, make a hollow in the center. Break open the two eggs, and pour them into the vegetable mixture. Season the gratin with salt and pepper before adding a generous layer of grated Parmesan. Allow it to bake for about twenty minutes.

BAKED ASPARAGUS, PROSCIUTTO, AND EGGS
WITH PARMESAN TOPPING FOR I

225 g (8 ounces) green asparagus	2 eggs
1 tbsp. butter	pepper
2–4 slices prosciutto (or smoked bacon)	2 tbsp. Parmesan, grated

Heat the oven to 230°C (450°F). While for a casserole, you would sauté the vegetables in advance, for this recipe, you need to steam the green asparagus first. Cut off the stems, and if the skin is very hard, peel each asparagus one-third of the way up. Then steam them over boiling salt water, about six minutes. For the asparagus to retain its vivid green color, drain the stems in cold water, taking care that they don't fall apart, then dry them with papers towels. Grease a small gratin dish with butter, and place the asparagus into it, making sure that all the tips face the same direction. Place the prosciutto slices on top, as if this was a blanket to protect them from the heat of the oven while crisping it in the process. Then break the two eggs over the wrapped asparagus so that they, in turn, will become eggs sunny-side up in the oven. Dust the gratin with grated Parmesan, season with black pepper (because of the prosciutto, you need no further salt), and bake it for about eight minutes. The egg white should be firm; the egg yolk a bit runny.

SOUFFLÉ FOR I

½ tsp. white butter	2 tsp. flour
1 tbsp. Parmesan, grated	80 ml (⅓ cup) milk
2 tsp. butter	salt and pepper

1 pinch nutmeg
2 egg yolks
2 egg whites

28 g (¼ cup) hard cheese, grated
(cheddar, Gruyère, mountain
cheese, goat cheese)

Making a soufflé all for yourself retains a charm of its own, not least of all because you know that, if it should fail, you must apologize to no one. At the same time, it allows you to use up all the little pieces of cheese that have accumulated in your refrigerator. You do, however, need the right soufflé dish, which should be just large enough for a single portion, around 10 centimeters (4 inches) wide and 5.5 centimeters (2¼ inches) high.

Heat the oven to 220°C (425°F). Grease the bottom and the sides of the soufflé dish with soft butter, and dust both with grated Parmesan. Break open the two eggs, and dividing egg yolk from egg white, place them in separate dishes. Now prepare the roux in a small pot by first melting the remaining two teaspoons of butter and then adding the flour and whisking it over a very low temperature, about a minute. Remove the pot from the heat so that the roux can cool off a bit before pouring in the milk, mixing it thoroughly with the roux and allowing it to simmer over low heat. You will need to stir for a while, which is to say as long as it takes to form a thick béchamel sauce. Season with salt, pepper, and a pinch of nutmeg. Take the sauce off the heat, and add the egg yolk, whisking it thoroughly into the sauce. In the second bowl, beat the egg white until it is stiff. At first, add only a spoonful of the stiff egg white to the sauce, along with half of the grated cheese. Then carefully fold in the rest of the egg white as well as the remaining cheese. So that the egg mass doesn't lose its fluffiness, take care not to stir the egg-cheese mixture too energetically.

Now turn the oven down to 190°C (375°F), pour the mixture into the prepared gratin dish, and bake the soufflé in the middle of the oven for about eighteen minutes. The crust should be light brown. The soufflé, as the name suggests, should have inflated like a balloon. A piece of baguette and a salad offer a perfect complement to this egg dish, along with what to me is obligatory—a glass of crisp, chilled white wine.

NOTE: If you have made too much soufflé mixture, you can make the sides of your gratin dish higher by lining it with aluminum foil. It isn't, however, a problem if your soufflé spills over the edges a bit. This actually allows you to see exactly when it is done. The minute the excess egg mixture stops flowing over the edge is the precise moment you want to take the soufflé out of the oven.

VEGETARIAN MEALS

Artichokes and Kohlrabi with Pesto | *Watercress and Tomato Salad with Preserved Lemons and Ricotta* | *Vegetable Broth with Carrots and Parmesan* | *Vegetable Stir-Fry* | *Roasted Lemon Quinoa*

While I was a child, roasts, steaks, or meat stews were reserved almost exclusively for weekends, when we all came together at the table to share a family meal. This often provoked a pronounced culinary jealousy among my siblings and myself, with each vying for the juiciest chicken breast or the slice of pork roast with the crispiest skin. During the week, in turn, we ate primarily meatless dishes: vegetable stews, bread dumplings with mushrooms, a sweet semolina bake with fruit compote, or plum dumplings with fried bread crumbs. While I no longer cook these fairly substantial Bavarian dishes, I still harbor a strong preference for vegetable dishes, especially when I want to make something simple for myself quickly. And on my way home from work, I delight in stopping by the vegetable stands at the local market to see what they have on display. The colors and shapes each season has to offer are always a source of inspiration for my salads, soups, or vegetable sautés.

ARTICHOKES AND KOHLRABI WITH PESTO FOR 1

1 small kohlrabi	chicken broth
4 medium artichokes	100 ml (½ cup) water
1 tbsp. coconut oil	juice of ½ lemon
1 pinch chili flakes	1–2 tbsp. pesto (pistachio, shiso)

Given that chefs in elegant restaurants have rediscovered kohlrabi in the past few years, I too have turned my attention to this underrated vegetable, only to discover how wonderful it tastes when pesto is added to enhance the flavor. For this quick vegetable sauté, first peel the kohlrabi, and cut it into coarse dice. Cut the stems off the artichokes as well as one-third from the top of each; pull off all the hard, outer leaves; and quarter each one. This will make it much easier to scrape out the brittle choke and trim each piece further until you have only the actual heart left. Brown the kohlrabi and the artichoke pieces in coconut oil, seasoning with chili flakes. Add the vegetable broth to the pan, along with the lemon juice and the herb pesto, and then mix all the ingredients thoroughly once more. Cover the pan, and braise the vegetables over medium heat for about ten minutes.

WATERCRESS AND TOMATO SALAD WITH PRESERVED LEMONS AND RICOTTA FOR 1

½ tbsp. white balsamic vinegar

½ tbsp. honey

½ tsp. juice of preserved lemons

2 tbsp. olive oil

salt and pepper

100 g (½ cup) artichoke hearts preserved in oil

1 big handful watercress (or arugula) leaves

½ bunch mint, chopped

70 g (2 ounces) cherry tomatoes, halved

1 small chili, deseeded and finely sliced

½ preserved lemon, finely sliced

20 g (⅛ cup) olives, deseeded and sliced

125 g (½ cup) fresh ricotta

1 handful pistachios

What is special about this salad is the ricotta, which melts into the vinaigrette dressing and gives it a sweet creaminess. This is also an example of an opulent *salade composée* that can be prepared effortlessly as a meal in itself, which is both nourishing and splendid. For the vinaigrette dressing, whisk together the olive oil with the balsamic vinegar, the honey, and some juice from the jar of your preserved lemons, and then season with salt and pepper. If you want more acidity, add a shot of sherry vinegar or more lemon juice. Put the quartered artichokes into a salad bowl, pour the vinaigrette dressing over them, and allow them to infuse while you chop and slice the remaining ingredients. Add these—the salad, the mint, the tomatoes, the chili (or chili flakes), the preserved lemon, and the olives—to the artichokes, and mix together thoroughly. Only at the end, fold the ricotta into the salad, but do so one spoonful after another rather than adding the whole amount all at once. This way, it will cream the vinaigrette dressing more evenly. As a finishing touch, sprinkle the salad with pistachios, best left whole.

VEGETABLE BROTH WITH CARROTS AND PARMESAN FOR 1

2 tbsp. butter (or more)

1 small onion, peeled and finely chopped

1 tsp. ginger, grated or chopped

1 small new potato, peeled and cubed

600 ml (2½ cups) vegetable broth

1 big handful spinach or chard (or other leafy greens)

salt and pepper

Parmesan

Hardly a dish is more soothing after an exhausting day of work than a bowl of vegetable soup. The aromas that slowly evolve as the ingredients simmer in the pot already trigger a mood of relaxation, anticipating the enjoyment to come.

Melt the butter in a small pot, and over medium heat, sauté the finely chopped onions along with the finely chopped ginger until both are translucent and soft, about seven minutes. Then add the potato cubes, put the lid on the pot, and allow these to sweat for a few minutes before pouring in the vegetable broth. Allow this to come to boil, and then turn the heat down. The soup should simmer another twenty-five minutes or so. But make sure the lid is slightly askew so that steam can escape and make the aroma of the soup more intense. Just before the potatoes have become completely soft, add the spinach and the ginger juice, season with salt and pepper, and let the soup simmer for a few more minutes. If you decide to use firmer vegetables—green beans, carrots, or zucchinis cut into coarse bits—sauté these together with the potatoes. If, in turn, you choose delicate young fine peas called *petits pois* (which I always have ready at hand in my freezer), they will need only as much time as the spinach and should, therefore, also only be added to the hot broth at the very end.

VEGETABLE STIR-FRY FOR I

4 tbsp. chicken broth	4 tbsp. rapeseed oil
4 tsp. soy sauce	1 garlic clove, chopped
3 tsp. Noilly Prat (or dry sherry)	1 pinch chili flakes
2 tsp. chili-garlic sauce (or five-spice powder)	400 g (14 ounces) green asparagus (or broccoli)
1 tsp. sesame oil	200 g (7 ounces) button mushrooms
1 tsp. cornstarch	1 shot mirin

As with any stir-fry, crucial in this recipe is a meticulous mise en place. The effort is worth it because the dish itself can be prepared in a very short time and is, thus, particularly suited for when you come home from work hungry.

In a small bowl, whisk together the broth, the soy sauce, the Noilly Prat, the chili-garlic sauce, the sesame oil, and the cornstarch. You will be using this sauce to bind the dish at the end. In a second small bowl, mix together one teaspoon of rapeseed oil with the chopped garlic and the chili flakes. This will serve as the *soffritto*. Putting both bowls to one side, turn your attention to the vegetables. Trim the asparagus at the bottom and cut them into strips, about four centimeters long. Clean the button mushrooms, and finely slice them. Then you are ready to combine the three components of your stir-fry. Heat one teaspoon of rapeseed oil in your wok (or a sauté pan as long as it has high sides), but wait until the oil begins to near its smoking point before adding the asparagus and mushrooms along with a shot of mirin (or sweet sherry). Sauté the vegetables for about five minutes, making sure that you do not stop stirring them. The asparagus should be soft but still crunchy. Now add the garlic-oil *soffritto* to the wok, and allow it to fry for about thirty seconds before pouring in the soy-broth seasoning and mixing this thoroughly with the vegetables. While, traditionally, you would serve rice with a stir-fry, I prefer soba noodles.

NOTE: When it comes to seasoning the sauce, you have plenty of room for experimentation. Rather than a combination of soy and chili-garlic sauce, you could also use oyster sauce with a teaspoon of brown sugar. You could replace the Noilly Prat with orange juice, or you could leave out the sesame oil and chili-garlic sauce altogether and replace this with more chili flakes and a bit of grated ginger.

ROASTED LEMON QUINOA FOR I

50 g (1½ cups) quinoa	lavender salt and pepper
150 ml (⅔ cup) water	1½ tbsp. olive oil
¼ preserved lemon, finely chopped	1 small zucchini
1 tsp. goji berries	1 fennel
1 tsp. white balsamic vinegar	1 tbsp. fresh thyme
1 pinch saffron	

Heat the oven to 200°C (400°F). This oven-baked quinoa is my final example for a simple vegetable dish that you can prepare on weekdays. Begin by dry roasting the quinoa in a small pan over medium heat. The individual kernels should burst and brown slightly. Then simmer the roasted quinoa for about fifteen minutes in a small pot of water until the white germ buds have begun to break loose from the kernel. In the meantime, in a bowl, mix together the vegetables—the coarsely diced zucchini, the quartered fennel—with the oil, thyme, lavender, salt, and pepper, and pour them into a small baking dish. You could, of course, also use different root vegetables, carrots, or mushrooms. Once the quinoa has finished cooking, add the preserved lemon, the goji berries, and the white balsamic vinegar to the pot, and season with a pinch of saffron, lavender, salt, and pepper. Mix everything thoroughly, and put the seasoned quinoa into a second small baking dish. To roast properly, the quinoa needs steam, so either use a baking dish with a tightly fitting top or cover the dish with aluminum foil. Because the vegetables will need more time to bake, put these into the oven first, adding the quinoa after about twenty minutes. After another twenty-five minutes, both will be ready, and you can combine them into one dish.

TOMATO SAUCE

Tomato Sauce with Onions and Plenty of Butter | *Tomato Sauce with Soffritto and Basil* | *Tomato Sauce with Bacon and Herbs* | *Oven-Roasted Tomato Sauce with Vanilla* | *Tomato Sauce with Coconut Milk*

With little effort, any vegetables you have accumulated in the refrigerator can be turned into a pasta sauce. Simply cut the vegetables into small pieces, and sauté these in a *soffritto* (consisting of finely chopped onions and any additional seasoning of your choice), about the same amount of time as it takes to boil the pasta in salt water. In the spirit of a specimen recipe whose variations are meant to demonstrate not only the many different aromatic shades a sauce can develop but also the charm of simplicity, I have limited myself to the famous tomato-based *sugo*. But I must admit, there is hardly a recipe that people will argue over with as much passion and conviction as how to prepare the perfect tomato sauce. Of course, it makes little sense to prepare this sauce just for one, so you will have extra, but then again, any tomato *sugo* will keep for up to a week in the refrigerator, which means that you will have something for the next day as well—to serve with broiled chicken, seared tuna fillet, or a pan-fried beef steak or as the sauce for a vegetable gratin. Of course, you can also freeze any tomato sauce to fall back on in moments of culinary distress.

TOMATO SAUCE WITH ONIONS AND PLENTY OF BUTTER

400 g (14 ounces) canned peeled
Italian plum tomatoes in juice
2–3 tbsp. butter
1 onion

salt and pepper
125 g (¼ pound) spaghetti
Parmesan, grated

For the longest time, this dish was only a childhood memory from summer vacations on the Italian Riviera. Then finally, I found a recipe for this simplest of all tomato sauces in one of Marcella Hazan's books on classic Italian cooking. This enticing sauce requires only three things: the best canned peeled tomatoes you can find, really good spaghetti (and I would always recommend looking for those labeled *artigianale*), and excellent butter. The last of the three is what distinguishes the creamy sweetness of this tomato sauce, which, for so many years, had remained with me as an intense culinary memory.

Pour the tomatoes into a small pot, and add the butter and the peeled onion. While Marcella Hazan suggests cutting it in half, I leave mine whole. This makes it easier to extract it in the end. Use a bit of restraint when seasoning with salt, as you can always adjust the flavor in the end. Without a lid on the pot, simmer the sauce over low heat for about forty-five minutes. I suggest staying near the stovetop to stir the sauce now and then, crushing the tomatoes gently so that they slowly dissolve into the buttery juice. A purist would pass the tomato sauce through a food mill, but I actually like a more diversely textured consistency. After fishing out the onion, I season once more with salt and pepper, pour the sauce over a luscious pile of hot spaghetti, and add a sprinkling of grated Parmesan.

TOMATO SAUCE WITH *SOFFRITTO* AND BASIL

2 tbsp. olive oil	400 g (14 ounces) canned peeled
1 onion, finely chopped	Italian plum tomatoes in juice
1 carrot, very finely chopped	3 tbsp. red wine
1 small fennel, finely chopped	basil, cut into strips
1 garlic clove, finely chopped	white balsamic vinegar
1 pinch chili flakes	salt and pepper
1 bay leaf (optional)	125 g (¼ pound) spaghetti
	Parmesan, grated

My Italian-American friend Linda simply calls this tomato sauce "red sauce." It is somewhat more elaborate to prepare and has a more complex flavor density. For the *soffritto*, sauté the onions, carrots, and fennel in olive oil over fairly low heat (around twenty minutes). The vegetables should become soft and caramelize. If you want less pungency, replace the onions with celery, the garlic with ginger. If you are using garlic, however, don't include it in the *soffritto*; rather, add it along with the tomatoes and the bay leaf. Season the sauce with a pinch of chili flakes and a shot of red wine, and allow it to simmer for about thirty minutes over medium heat. If the sauce becomes too dense, dilute it with a bit of water (or broth). When it is done, remove the bay leaf, season with more salt and pepper, and then add the basil strips. To give more flavor intensity to this red sauce, add a shot of white balsamic vinegar.

TOMATO SAUCE WITH BACON AND HERBS

1 small onion, finely chopped
1 celery stalk, finely chopped
1 small carrot, finely chopped
1–2 tbsp. olive oil
60 g (2 ounces) bacon (or pancetta), diced
120 ml (½ cup) red wine
400 g (14 ounces) canned peeled Italian plum tomatoes in juice

1 tbsp. tomato purée
½ tsp. dried thyme (or 1 tsp. fresh thyme)
1 bay leaf
salt and pepper
125 g (¼ pound) penne or rigatoni
Parmesan, grated

While this recipe works with a similar principle as the classic Italian-American red sauce, the fried bacon adds a distinctive bite. For the *soffritto*, sauté the onions, the celery, and the carrots in olive oil (around ten minutes) in a pot large enough to hold the tomatoes as well. The *soffritto* should be soft and begin to caramelize. Then add the bacon, and fry it for several minutes, until it begins to crisp. Add the red wine, and reduce it until it is almost completely evaporated; the wine is there primarily for flavor. Only now add the tomatoes, the tomato purée, and the herbs to the pot; season with salt and pepper; and let the sauce come to a boil. Turn down the heat so that the sauce can simmer for another thirty minutes. Penne or rigatoni suit this sauce, their hollow shape the perfect repository for the savory bits of bacon.

OVEN-ROASTED TOMATO SAUCE WITH VANILLA

500 g (1 pound) cherry tomatoes
salt and sugar
3 tbsp. olive oil
1 tbsp. vanilla paste (or pulp from 1 vanilla bean)

1 onion, finely chopped
1 tbsp. olive oil
125 g (¼ pound) ravioli

You can also use oven-roasted tomatoes for a *sugo*. While it is true that this preparation requires more cooking time, you can start on the tomatoes in the morning (or the previous day for that matter and store them in the fridge).

Heat the oven to 140°C (275°F). Prepare the vanilla oil first so that it can infuse. In a small bowl, blend the olive oil with the vanilla paste (or the seeds of one vanilla bean), and put it to one side. Wash the tomatoes, cut them in half, and place them on a baking dish, cut side up. Season with salt and a pinch of sugar, and then drizzle the vanilla-oil over the tomatoes. Roast them in the oven for at least an hour. When the tomatoes are just about done, sauté the onions in one tablespoon of olive oil over low heat, about ten minutes. Add the tomatoes to the caramelized onions, and retaining the low heat, allow the sauce to simmer for several minutes more, stirring and mashing the tomatoes with a wooden spoon.

I have found that this sauce works particularly well with ricotta ravioli or fresh tagliolini. And so that really nothing interferes with the flavor combination of vanilla and tomato, I recommend leaving out the Parmesan.

TOMATO SAUCE WITH COCONUT MILK

500 g (1 pound) cherry tomatoes (or other ripe tomatoes)	¼ chili, chopped (or 1 pinch chili flakes)
olive oil	120 ml (½ cup) coconut milk
pepper and salt	1 tbsp. Thai fish sauce
1 pinch sugar	½ tbsp. brown sugar
1 small onion, finely chopped	juice of ½ lime
1 garlic clove, finely chopped	1 bunch cilantro, chopped
1 tsp. ginger, grated	125 g (¼ pound) penne

This recipe also makes use of oven-roasted tomatoes, only in this case an Asian seasoning is added.

Heat the oven to 180°C (350°F). Wash the tomatoes, cut them in half, and place them cut side up into a baking dish. Drizzle with olive oil; season with salt, pepper, and a pinch of sugar; and roast them in the oven for forty-five minutes. They are allowed to brown. Just before they are done, prepare the *soffritto* in a pot large enough to hold the tomatoes as well. Over low heat, sauté the onions along with the garlic, ginger, and chili in two tablespoons of olive oil for about seven minutes. Add the tomatoes to the *soffritto*, and allow them to simmer, about ten minutes. Pour in the coconut milk, and then season with fish sauce, brown sugar, and lime juice. While the sauce continues to simmer (around ten minutes more), mash the tomatoes with a wooden spoon. As a final touch, sprinkle the sauce with cilantro. Penne go well with this rich creamy sauce, which will not only coat them but also penetrate their hollow center.

PORK TENDERLOIN FOR MORE THAN ONE MEAL

Pork Tenderloin with Morels | Roasted Pork Tenderloin with Vegetables |
Roasted Pork Tenderloin with Orange and Pomegranate Molasses |
Pork Tenderloin Stir-Fry with Cabbage and Tonkatsu Sauce

As someone cooking for herself for several days in a row, I find it is worth planning a sequence of dishes based on one main ingredient. A whole pork tenderloin (around one pound) is particularly suitable for such an enterprise as I discovered in a book by Judith Jones, the renowned American cookbook editor of culinary personalities like Marcella Hazan and Julia Child. As the following recipes demonstrate, you can make several meals from it. Judith Jones suggests initially cutting four or so escalopes (cutlets) from the thicker end. The larger middle section is then best roasted the next day. Following are two recipes for roasting the middle section. The thin end of the pork tenderloin (as well as any excess meat you may still have at this point) can then be turned into a stir-fry. If you have leftovers from the roast, you can eat them the following days—inside a sandwich or on top of a salad.

PORK TENDERLOIN WITH MORELS FOR 1

30 g (1 ounce) dried morels
150 ml (⅔ cup) milk
6 slices pork tenderloin
salt and pepper
flour for dusting
1 tsp. olive oil

3 tsp. butter
1 small onion, finely chopped
3 tbsp. broth
1 tbsp. lemon juice
1 tbsp. Noilly Prat

Before cooking with dried morels, they must be soaked in lukewarm milk, about forty minutes. Drain them in a sieve; wash them carefully, making sure that no earth is still hiding in the pits between the ridges of their caps; and then dry them thoroughly with paper towels. Place a very sharp knife on top of the pork tenderloin about six centimeters (two and a half inches) from the thicker end. This will allow you to gauge how much meat is at your disposal for cutting three fairly thin slices, slightly on the diagonal. Having cut the first slice, work your way to the end of the piece of meat you have now cut from the rest of the pork tenderloin. To prepare the escalope, place each slice of pork between two pieces of plastic wrap (or inside a refrigerator bag), and pound them to an even thickness, not so thin, however, that they have holes.

Season both sides with salt and pepper, and dredge them in flour. In a pan large enough to hold all three escalopes, heat first the oil, then add two tablespoons of butter. Once it begins to sizzle, add the pork slices as well. It will take about one minute on each side for them to become browned and crispy. Remove the meat from the pan, and put it to one side. For the sauce, sauté the onions until they begin to caramelize (about five minutes), and if necessary, pour a bit more oil into the pan. Then add the drained morels, lemon juice, Noilly Prat, and three tablespoons of broth, and sauté them for another five minutes. If you find you have too much liquid, remove the morels with a slotted spoon. Reduce the sauce, and then return them, along with the pork, to the pan, and turn down the heat. The escalope should simply warm up again in the sauce, not fry once more. Season with salt and pepper, and if you want more fruity acidity, add a bit of lemon juice. As a final touch, cream the sauce with some butter. Serve a crisp baguette or sourdough bread with this pork tenderloin to bring out the rich flavor of the morels.

ROASTED PORK TENDERLOIN WITH VEGETABLES FOR I

300 g (11 ounces) pork tenderloin	1 generous handful vegetables to roast
1 garlic clove	(carrots, parsnips, root vegetables,
1 tbsp. Dijon mustard	sweet potatoes, celeriac or new
2 tsp. fresh ginger, grated	potatoes)
2 tbsp. soy sauce	olive oil
black pepper	salt and pepper

The middle piece of a pork tenderloin is so good when roasted in the oven that I offer two recipes, each making use of a different marinade. Both serve as a contrast to the natural sweetness of the meat while yielding an aromatic crust. Because the pork tenderloin should infuse the marinade for at least an hour, it is well worth already doing this in the morning. Press the garlic into a small bowl, sprinkle with salt, and stir it until you have a thick paste. Add the mustard, the soy sauce, and the freshly grated ginger, and mix thoroughly. Put the pork tenderloin into a dish in which it fits snugly, slather it on all sides with this marinade, and season with black pepper. Cover the dish with plastic wrap (or an airtight lid), and allow the meat to rest in the refrigerator until you are ready to roast it.

Heat the oven to 190°C (375°F). Place the small pork tenderloin into the middle of the dish in which you will be roasting it. Peel the vegetables, and cut them into bite-size chunks. So that they roast evenly, it is worth making sure that they are the same size. You can use potatoes, sweet potatoes, parsnips, carrots, or celeriac. In a large bowl, toss the vegetable chunks with olive oil, salt, and pepper. Then spread them around the pork tenderloin. Now you are ready to put the roasting dish into the oven. Because the meat will be done more quickly, take the pork tenderloin out after thirty minutes, and allow it to rest while the vegetables roast for another fifteen minutes or so. You may want to cover the tenderloin with some aluminum foil to keep it warm.

ROASTED PORK TENDERLOIN WITH ORANGE AND POMEGRANATE MOLASSES FOR I

300 g pork (11 ounces) tenderloin	2 tsp. fresh ginger, grated
1 garlic clove, chopped	1 tbsp. soy sauce
1 tbsp. mustard (preferably coarse Pommery mustard)	1 tbsp. pomegranate molasses
	juice and zest of 1 orange

This version also calls for marinating the middle piece of the pork tenderloin in advance and allowing it to rest in the refrigerator for at least six hours. To prepare the marinade, blend the garlic with the mustard, the grated ginger, the soy sauce, the pomegranate molasses, and the juice and zest of an orange. Put the pork tenderloin into a dish in which it fits snugly, generously slather it with the marinade on all sides, and cover the dish with plastic wrap. It is worth checking on it now and then while it is resting in the refrigerator and turning the meat around in the marinade to make sure it is really infusing all the flavors.

Heat the oven to 190°C (375°F). Put the pork tenderloin into a baking dish, and roast for thirty minutes. In the meantime, prepare a side dish of couscous, topped with steamed vegetables, or a lentil salad to complement the fruity acidity of this dish.

PORK TENDERLOIN STIR-FRY WITH CABBAGE AND TONKATSU SAUCE FOR I

4 tbsp. rapeseed oil	300 g (3 cups) savoy cabbage (white cabbage)
1 garlic clove, chopped	400 ml (1¾ cups) broth
1 tsp. ginger, chopped	salt and pepper
100 g (4 ounces) pork tenderloin, finely sliced	2–3 tbsp. tonkatsu sauce
flour to dust	

You can use the thin end of the pork tenderloin that still remains for a stir-fry. Once again, a meticulous *mise en place* will help produce the best effects. Cut both the meat and the cabbage into fine slices, and put aside in separate bowls. Chop the garlic and the ginger, and put aside as well. Warm the broth. Then heat two tablespoons of rapeseed oil in a wok (or a nonstick pan with high edges) until it begins to smoke, and stirring constantly, fry the garlic and ginger, about fifteen seconds. Dredge the pork strips in flour, add them to the pan, and stirring them constantly as well, fry them for about a minute. They should brown and form a thin crust. Remove the meat from the pan, and put it aside in a bowl. Then add two further tablespoons of rapeseed oil to the wok, wait until this has become very hot, and sauté the cabbage. It is meant to brown. Pour in the broth, season with salt and pepper, and simmer the cabbage until it has become soft (about fifteen minutes). If the liquid evaporates too quickly, add more broth. Finally, fold the tonkatsu sauce—a type of Japanese ketchup—into the cabbage before returning the pork strips to the wok. They are meant only to reheat, not to fry. You can serve soba noodles with this stir-fry or the traditional rice, but this dish can just as well be eaten on its own.

FESTIVELY FOR ONE

Tuna Tartar with Wasabi Mayonnaise | An Artichoke All to Oneself | Tagliolini with Fresh Truffle | Sautéed Dover Sole with Capers | Tuna Steak with Red Beets | Meatloaf for Adults | Quiche with Bottarga

My friend Mic once proudly showed me iPhone images of a festive meal he prepared for himself one Saturday evening, in part because he wanted to open a special bottle of wine. The images showed an elegantly set table, where, illuminated by the golden-red light of the setting sun, the dishes and bowls with the food he had prepared sparkled. He had wanted to try out a particular gratin about which he had heard so much and decided that a very thick piece of beef fillet, fried in butter, would be the appropriate dish to accompany it, along with string beans wrapped in bacon. In his happy recollection of the serenity with which he celebrated this solo feast, I recognized my own enjoyment in taking time out to cook something truly special just for myself, which means giving myself much time as well to enjoy what I have so lovingly done with delectable (and not entirely cheap) ingredients. The fact that this meal is celebrated as something out of the ordinary turns the transience of the pleasure I have given myself into an advantage. Precisely because I know that the delicacies will soon have been consumed, the precious wine drunken, this feast constitutes a scarcity value in time. As Sigmund Freud once commented on the charm of transience value, the limitation in the possibility of an enjoyment raises the value of the enjoyment. Alone with yourself at the dining table, there is no distraction from this fugitive delight.

TUNA TARTAR WITH WASABI MAYONNAISE FOR 1

120 g (4 ounces) tuna, sushi grade
½ tbsp. soy sauce
1½ tbsp. mayonnaise
1 tsp. wasabi paste

½ tsp. yuzu juice (or lime juice)
1½ tbsp. fine-grained orange masago
from capelin roe
1 shiso leaf (or basil)

I fell in love with a tuna tartar served in a small Japanese restaurant in Kips Bay, Manhattan, because of the contrast between the soft raw fish and the crunchy roe that bursts in the mouth with every bite. This recipe is my adaptation of the classic Japanese dish. Chop the tuna into fairly small bits with a very sharp knife. Mix the mayonnaise (homemade is always best) with the wasabi paste, the soy sauce, and the yuzu juice (or lemon juice), and fold it, along with the fish roe, into the chopped tuna. Because the key to this recipe is the crunch and not an intense flavor explosion, use a fine-grained roe, not the bigger trout roe. If you want more poignancy, add more wasabi at the end before arranging the tuna tartar elegantly on a shiso leaf.

AN ARTICHOKE ALL TO ONESELF FOR 1

1 big artichoke

FOR THE DRESSING

3 tbsp. yogurt
1½ tbsp. mayonnaise
½ tbsp. mustard

1 tsp. white balsamic vinegar
1 tsp. Noilly Prat
salt and pepper

It is equally festive to prepare an artichoke just for yourself. As you pluck each individual leaf, you can indulge fully in your own thoughts. And with each new bite, the anticipation of finally reaching the artichoke's heart increases. You could dip the individual leaves into melted butter with lemon juice or a vinaigrette, but I am particularly fond of the following yogurt-mayonnaise dressing.

It does, however, take a bit of time until the feast can begin because the artichoke needs to be steamed rather than cooked. While preparing the artichoke, you can bring the water under your steamer to a rolling boil. Pluck the tough, smaller leaves at the bottom of the artichoke, and cut off the stem. Cut off the top three centimeters (one and one-fourth inches) of the artichoke as well, and if the outer leaves are already a bit dry, trim them with your kitchen scissors. Then steam the artichoke for about forty minutes. The artichoke is ready when it is easy to peel away a leaf; it should be tender and soft at the bottom.

In the meantime, prepare the dressing. Whisk together the yogurt, mayonnaise, mustard, white balsamic vinegar, and Noilly Prat, and season with salt and pepper. Of course, there is no reason not to have a first glass of wine while waiting for the artichoke to transform in the steamer basket.

TAGLIOLINI WITH FRESH TRUFFLE FOR 1

125 g (¼ pound) fresh tagliolini	60 ml (¼ cup) cream
1 small truffle	pepper
2 tbsp. butter	1–2 tbsp. Parmesan

Why shouldn't you buy a small truffle to spoil yourself? And if you do so, there is hardly a better way to eat it than with delicate tagliolini.

While you bring the salt water to a rolling boil in one pot, melt the butter in a smaller pot that is still large enough to hold the cooked pasta. Add the cream, and grate one-third of the truffle into the sauce. Stir it briefly with a wooden spoon, season with a touch of pepper, and remove it from the heat. This way the sauce can infuse the truffle flavor while you cook the tagliolini. After you have drained the pasta, toss it into the truffle cream sauce along with the grated Parmesan, mix thoroughly, and simmer the pasta over very low heat for about a minute more. Once more turn off the heat, cover the pot, and allow the tagliolini to fully absorb the truffle sauce for several minutes before arranging them on a plate and generously grating the remaining truffle over them.

NOTE: You can replace the truffle with bottarga (the Italian delicacy of salted, cured fish roe) or caviar. For a poor woman's variation, you can also add one tablespoon of lemon juice to the butter and cream instead of the grated truffle and, as in the recipe above, take the sauce off the heat and allow it to infuse while cooking the tagliolini. In a second step, add the zest of half a lemon to the sauce along with the Parmesan, and garnish with chopped parsley.

SAUTÉED DOVER SOLE WITH CAPERS FOR 1

2 pieces of Dover sole	½ tsp. capers
2–4 tbsp. butter	salt and pepper
flour for dusting	lemon juice
1 small bunch parsley, chopped	

Whenever I buy a Dover sole, I remember Nigel Slater's comment that this mighty fish comes at a mighty price. Nevertheless, I find that, like the small truffle, you are allowed to treat yourself to this delicacy every now and then. However, the Dover sole does have to be of the finest quality. Otherwise, it is better to choose a different fish and prepare a different dish.

Melt the butter in a nonstick frying pan until it begins to bubble. Just seconds before you are about to fry the sole, dredge it in flour, shake off any excess, and put it in the pan. Fry the fillets for about a minute, until they have begun to brown. Now comes the tricky part. Carefully turn them, and fry the other side; if they still cling to the pan, wait a few seconds more. Season the browned side with salt and pepper, and scatter the parsley into the pan. Once the second side is golden brown as well, remove the sole fillets from the pan.

For the sauce, add one tablespoon of butter together with the lemon juice and the finely chopped capers to the pan, and as you vigorously mix in the parsley that is already there, make sure to scrape all the flavor-intense browned bits from the bottom of the pan into the sauce as well. Arrange the sole on a plate, pour the sauce over it, and sprinkle with a bit more chopped parsley. As a side dish—if you are so inclined—new potatoes or spinach tossed in olive oil and lemon juice is a perfect accompaniment.

TUNA STEAK WITH RED BEETS FOR 1

200 g (7 ounces) tuna steak (or tuna fillet)	60 ml (¼ cup) argan oil
1 tbsp. sesame oil	1 tbsp. apple balsamic vinegar (or another fruit balsamic vinegar)
1 tbsp. soy sauce	1 tsp. lime juice
pepper	2 tsp. Dijon mustard
1 roasted beet (see "Roasted Red Beets")	salt and cayenne pepper
	cilantro, chopped

So that the tuna stays moist and tender while frying, blend the sesame oil and soy sauce, and use this to marinate the fish, making sure it is really enveloped by this flavor-intense coating before seasoning it with pepper on both sides. Wrap the tuna in plastic wrap, and allow it to rest in the refrigerator for one to two hours, absorbing the marinade. Heat a nonstick pan, and once it is really hot, sear the tuna on both sides for about a minute. The tuna should still be pink inside, though warmed, but it should have a crispy crust.

For me, this becomes a festive meal when I add an oven-roasted beet salad as a side dish. For the vinaigrette, I whisk together precious argan oil with white balsamic vinegar and season with lavender salt and pepper. Then I arrange the sliced beets next to the sliced tuna on the plate, pour the vinaigrette over both, and as a final touch, scatter some chopped cilantro on top.

MEATLOAF FOR ADULTS FOR 1

450 g (16 ounces) ground meat (preferably only beef)	60 ml (¼ cup) Noilly Prat
2 garlic cloves	pepper and salt
1 tsp. salt	5 bay leaves
1 small onion, finely chopped	5–8 slices bacon
1 bunch parsley, chopped	2 new potatoes, peeled and cut into bite-size cubes
3 dried porcini, ground in a spice grinder	2 carrots, peeled and cut into bite-size cubes
1 tsp. *herbes de Provence*	

In my childhood memories, meatloaf figures as a dish that could vary between wonderful and terrible. When my mother, the culinary perfectionist, wasn't there to cook for us, our housekeeper, Gerti, would take over in the kitchen. The quality of her cooking depended on her moods. And because she was far less meticulous than my mother, she would sometimes just throw ingredients together without making sure that the aromas were properly balanced or the textures perfectly matched. When she was happy, however, her meatloaf was the perfect example of what you would want for your birthday—moist and yet smooth on the inside, with a caramelized crust on the outside. The flavor of the meat itself was uncomplicated, given that the rich brown cream sauce she would make with the pan drippings was part of the charm of her version of this dish. The seasoning suggested in this recipe, in turn, is as elegant as it is complex and results in what my friend Gesine calls a meatloaf for adults. Thus this is a dish you might well prepare for dinner guests, but I like to make it for myself, not only because it reminds me of home but also because the leftovers can be used for several more meals in the days to come—including open sandwiches.

You will need to prepare the ground meat the evening before so that, resting in the refrigerator for twenty-four hours, it can fully absorb the flavor of the herbs and the spices that make up the special component of this dish. Begin by pressing the garlic and mixing it with salt until you have a paste. Then in a large bowl, mix together the meat, the garlic paste, the chopped onions, the chopped parsley, and the ground porcini mushrooms. Add the *herbes de Provence* along with the Noilly Prat, and season with salt and pepper. Part of the charm of my childhood memory has to do with the fact that I was always allowed to watch while our housekeeper would knead the ingredients together with her hands. At the time, this had much to do with early culinary voyeurism—which is to say, the pleasure I derive from watching others prepare food. I now, however, understand that this last step is absolutely necessary, because only by kneading the meat with your own hands can you be sure that all the ingredients have really come together. Once you are satisfied, cover the bowl with plastic wrap, and allow the meat to rest in the refrigerator.

The next evening, heat the oven to 180°C (350°F). Before roasting, take a small piece of the meat mixture, and fry it in a pan. This will allow you to check the seasoning and, if necessary, add more herbs or spices. If you are satisfied with the aroma, mold the chopped meat into—as the name of the dish suggests—a shape resembling a long, oval loaf of bread. Break the bay leaves into bits, and scatter them over the meatloaf, then place the bacon slices laterally over the meat, each close to the next so that the loaf is completely enveloped in bacon. Now put the meatloaf into the middle of an oven-proof baking dish. In another bowl, toss the vegetable cubes in olive oil, season with a generous pinch of *herbes de Provence*, and salt (using your hands here makes sense as well), and place these around the meatloaf like a wreath. While the roasting time is about fifty minutes, open the oven after twenty-five minutes to turn the vegetables around to ensure that they cook evenly. Allow the meatloaf to rest for five minutes before slicing it. As a sauce, use the savory juices that have formed while roasting in the baking dish.

QUICHE WITH BOTTARGA FOR 1

60 g (2 ounces) puff pastry
1 egg
90 ml (⅓ cup) cream

about 30 g (¼ cup) Gruyère (or other hard cheese), grated
1 pinch nutmeg, grated
salt and pepper

1 handful Parmesan, grated   bottarga, grated or cut in slivers
1 tbsp. chives, chopped

This is a dish to make when you have some leftover puff pastry in your refrigerator (or deep freezer). But I love this little quiche so much that I don't mind if the result is a surplus of pastry instead. Excess pastry gives me a good reason to make it again (with a slight variation in filling) the next day. You will also need a small gratin dish (or baking dish) about twelve centimeters (around four and three-fourths inches) wide.

Heat the oven to 200°C (400°F). Roll out the puff pastry into a circular shape, and then press it into a small gratin dish, covering the bottom and the sides. Make small incisions across the bottom, and bake the pastry dough blind for ten minutes. In the meantime, in a small bowl, whisk together the egg, the cream, and the grated cheese, and season with salt, pepper, and a pinch of nutmeg. After you have once again removed the pastry dough from the oven, turn the heat down to 190°C (375°F). Be sure you have removed all the baking beans before first scattering grated Parmesan and chopped chives over the pastry dough and then adding a layer of bottarga slivers (which could be replaced by prosciutto). Now pour the egg-cream mixture onto the dough, filling the dish all the way to the top. If you find you have too much, you can store it in the fridge and reuse it, adding another egg to make scrambled eggs the next day. Bake the quiche in the lower part of the oven, about twenty-five minutes. For a festive touch, take it out of the oven after twenty minutes, generously scatter more bottarga slivers on top, and finish baking it with this additional adornment. Allow the quiche to rest for five minutes before eating it.

ACKNOWLEDGMENTS

As with all my other books, many inspiring conversations were part of writing these cooking memoirs. Some lead me to rethink my project in general, others helped me when it came to details. And precisely because writing, as well as developing individual recipes, is such a solitary practice, I was endlessly grateful for the constant encouragement I was given while undertaking this culinary journey. My thanks go to Daniela Janser, who not only read the entire manuscript with sympathetic rigor but also offered constructive comments on many of the dishes. I am equally indebted to Gesine Krüger, whose joyful reactions as a reader, as well as a willing guest, quickly helped disperse any doubts I had about the flow of the text. My sister, Susan Bronfen, patiently helped me reconstruct my mother's recipes, often giving them an idiosyncratic finishing touch. Alexandra Felts and Muriel Gerstner, each of whom shares with me a long history of culinary conversations, assisted me with relish in my search for dishes of times passed. Johannes Binotto, Myriam Zumbühl, Alexander Markin, Doug Kremer, and Thomas Julier also helped me think through—and improve—both the writing and the cooking. Jamie Kulhanek, Alys George, and Katharina Vester encouraged me in transforming the original into an English-language book. Much thanks goes to Frances Ilmberger for her inspired eye while copyediting this translation. Recipes, in turn, were given to me by Alessandra Violi and Richard Davis, Philip Ursprung, Michael Walsh, Linda Nicholas, Martin Jaeggi, Barbara Straumann, Francesca Broggi-Wüthrich, Anka Sasek, Gordana Milic-Trpin, Celina Staub, Sebastian Egenhofer, Froma Zeitlin, Pia Rykert, and Leiko Brand. I hope that they can recognize themselves in my transcription—and slight modifications—of their cooking instructions. Equally important were all those friends who sat in my kitchen and tested all the dishes I wanted to include in this book. Their pleasure was as important as their critical assessment: Mic Milic Frederickx and Sarah Frederickx, Andreas Maerker and Franz Carl Diegelmann, Gabor Fujer, Benno Wirz, Jennifer Khakhshuri, Bettina Dennerlein and Susanne Lanwerd, Therese Steffen, Hannah Schoch, Franz and Elizabeth Kollman, Sylvia Sasse, and Sandro Zanetti. At Echtzeit Verlag, thanks are owed to Matylda Walczak, who has been tireless in promoting the book, and to Wendelin Hess for his confidence. From the onset he understood what it was that I was trying to achieve, sometimes even better than I did. An equal debt is owed to Leslie Mitchner, who showed immense interest from the start in an English translation of my book and made the publication possible. Along with her, my thanks go to Jasper Chang and Nicole Solano at Rutgers University Press.

BIBLIOGRAPHY

While doing the research for these cooking memoirs, I often consulted the books of others, taking seriously the words of advice they offered and profiting from the experiences they shared. This is a selection of those that were most important to me.

Ferran Adria. *The Family Meal*. London: Phaidon, 2011.

Ghillie Basan. *Tagine: Spicy Stews from Morocco*. London: Ryland Peters & Small, 2007.

Heston Blumenthal. *Heston Blumenthal at Home*. London: Bloomsbury, 2011.

Julia Child. *Mastering the Art of French Cooking*. New York: Alfred A. Knopf, 1983.

Elizabeth David. *Classics: Mediterranean Food, French Country Cooking, Summer Cooking*. New York: Alfred A. Knopf, 1980.

Tamasin Day-Lewis. *The Art of the Tart*. London: Cassell, 2000.

Fuchsia Dunlop. *Land of Plenty: A Treasury of Authentic Sichuan Cooking*. New York: W. W. Norton, 2001.

M. F. K. Fischer. *The Art of Eating*. New York: Macmillan, 1990.

Peter Gordon. *Everyday*. London: Jacquai, 2012.

Eric Gower. *The Breakaway Cook*. New York: William Morrow, 2007.

Rose Gray and Ruth Rogers. *The River Café Cook Book*. London: Ebury, 1995.

Gabrielle Hamilton. *Prune*. New York: Random House, 2014.

Marcella Hazan. *Essentials of Classic Italian Cooking*. New York: Alfred A. Knopf, 1994.

Diana Henry. *A Change of Appetite: Where Healthy Meets Delicious*. London: Mitchell Beazley, 2014.

Simon Hopkins. *Roast Chicken and Other Stories*. London: Ebury, 1994.

Judith Jones. *The Pleasures of Cooking for One*. New York: Alfred A. Knopf, 2009.

Sybil Kapoor. *Taste: A New Way to Cook*. London: Mitchell Beazley, 2003.

Gray Kunz and Peter Kaminsky. *The Elements of Taste*. Boston: Little, Brown, 2001.

Nigella Lawson. *How to Eat: The Pleasures and Principles of Good Food*. London: Chatto and Windus, 1998.

Giorgio Locatelli. *Made in Italy: Food and Stories*. London: Fourth Estate, 2008.

Harold McGee. *Keys to Good Cooking: A Guide to Making the Best of Foods and Recipes*. New York: Penguin, 2010.

Danny Meyer and Michael Romano. *The Union Square Café Cookbook*. New York: Harper Collins, 1994.

Richard Olney. *Simple French Food*. New York: Collier Books, 1992.

Yotam Ottolenghi and Sami Tamimi. *The Ottolenghi Cookbook*. London: Ebury, 2008.

Jacques Pépin. *Essential Pépin*. Boston: Houghton Mifflin Harcourt, 2011.

Alfred Portale. *Simple Pleasures*. New York: William Morrow, 2004.

Sarah Raven. *Garden Cookbook*. London: Bloomsbury, 2007.

Claudia Roden. *The Book of Jewish Food: An Odyssey from Smarkand to New York*. New York: Alfred A. Knopf, 1996.

Niki Segnit. *The Flavor Thesaurus: Pairings, Recipes and Ideas for the Creative Cook*. London: Bloomsbury, 2010.

Nigel Slater. *Appetite*. London: Fourth Estate, 2000.

Delia Smith. *Complete Cookery Course*. London: BBC Books, 2002.

Molly Stevens. *All about Braising: The Art of Uncomplicated Cooking*. New York: W. W. Norton, 2004.

Martha Stewart. *The Martha Stewart Cookbook: Collected Recipes for Every Day*. New York: Clarkson Potter, 1995.

Jerry Traunfeld. *The Herbfarm Cookbook*. New York: Scribner, 2000.

Jean-Georges Vongerichten and Mark Bittman. *Simple to Spectacular*. New York: Broadway Books, 2000.

Marcus Wareing. *How to Cook the Perfect . . .* London: Dorling Kindersley, 2010.

Alice Waters. *The Art of Simple Food*. New York: Clarkson Potter, 2007.

Patricia Wells. *Trattoria*. London: Kyle Cathie, 1993.

Jody Williams. *Buvette: The Pleasure of Good Food*. New York: Grand Central Life & Style, 2014.

Paula Wolfert. *Couscous and Other Good Food from Morocco*. New York: Harper & Row, 1971.

INDEX

ABOUT THE AUTHOR

ELISABETH BRONFEN is a professor of American studies at the University of Zurich in Switzerland and Global Distinguished Professor at New York University. She is the author of many books, including *Specters of War: Hollywood's Engagement with Military Conflict* (Rutgers University Press).